Life-Span Developmental Psychology

DIALECTICAL PERSPECTIVES ON EXPERIMENTAL RESEARCH

CONTRIBUTORS

RALPH A. ALEXANDER

PAUL B. BALTES

JOAN H. CANTOR

STANLEY H. COHEN

STEVEN W. CORNELIUS

NANCY DATAN

ROY FREEDLE

KENNETH J. GERGEN

JOHN W. HAGEN

JAMES G. HOLLAND

HERBERT KAYE

JON E. KRAPFL

STEINAR KVALE

JOHN A. MEACHAM

HAYNE W. REESE

KLAUS F. RIEGEL

ALEXANDER W. SIEGEL

CHARLES C. SPIKER

HARVEY L. STERNS

SHELDON H. WHITE

LIFE-SPAN DEVELOPMENTAL PSYCHOLOGY

DIALECTICAL PERSPECTIVES ON EXPERIMENTAL RESEARCH

Edited by

NANCY DATAN and HAYNE W. REESE

Department of Psychology
West Virginia University
Morgantown, West Virginia

 1977

ACADEMIC PRESS   New York   San Francisco   London
A Subsidiary of Harcourt Brace Jovanovich, Publishers

ACADEMIC PRESS, INC.
111 Fifth Avenue, New York, New York 10003

United Kingdom Edition published by
ACADEMIC PRESS, INC. (LONDON) LTD.
24/28 Oval Road, London NW1

Library of Congress Cataloging in Publication Data

Life-Span Developmental Psychology Conference, 5th, West
        Virginia University, 1976.
        Life-span developmental psychology, dialectical per-
spectives on experimental research.

        Includes bibliographies and index.
        1.   Developmental psychology—Congresses.   I.   Datan,
Nancy.   II.   Reese, Hayne Waring,   Date   III.   Title.
BF712.L537   1976   155   76-52726
ISBN 0–12–203560–7

Contents

THEORETICAL ISSUES

1. The Dialectics of Time

Klaus F. Riegel

2. After the Apple:
Post-Newtonian Metatheory for Jaded Psychologists

Nancy Datan

3. Social Proof Structures: The Dialectic of Method and Theory in the Work of Psychology

Sheldon H. White

4. Behaviorism, Cognitive Psychology, and the Active Organism

Charles C. Spiker

5. Cohort, Age, and Time of Measurement: Biomorphic Considerations

Harvey L. Sterns and Ralph A. Alexander

6. The Status of Dialectics in Developmental Psychology: Theoretical Orientation versus Scientific Method

Paul B. Baltes and Steven W. Cornelius

7. Stability, Change, and Chance in Understanding Human Development

Kenneth J. Gergen

8. Another Look at the Issue of Continuity versus Change in Models of Human Development

Stanley H. Cohen

RESEARCH APPLICATIONS

9. Dialectics and Research on Remembering

Steinar Kvale

10. "Remembering" Is Alive and Well (and Even Thriving) in Empiricism

Alexander W. Siegel

11. Discriminative Learning and Transfer: Dialectical Perspectives

Hayne W. Reese

12. Behavioristic Perspectives on a Dialectical Model of Discriminative Learning and Transfer

Joan H. Cantor

13. A Transactional Model of Remembering

John A. Meacham

18. Early Experience as the Basis for Unity and Cooperation of "Differences"

Herbert Kaye

List of Contributors

Numbers in parentheses indicate the pages on which the authors' contributions begin.

RALPH A. ALEXANDER (105), Department of Psychology, University of Akron, Akron, Ohio

PAUL B. BALTES (121), College of Human Development, Pennsylvania State University, University Park, Pennsylvania

JOAN H. CANTOR (253), Department of Psychology, University of Iowa, Iowa City, Iowa

STANLEY H. COHEN (159), Department of Psychology, West Virginia University, Morgantown, West Virginia

STEVEN W. CORNELIUS (121), College of Human Development, Pennsylvania State University, University Park, Pennsylvania

NANCY DATAN (47), Department of Psychology, West Virginia University, Morgantown, West Virginia

ROY FREEDLE (317), Educational Testing Service, Princeton, New Jersey

KENNETH J. GERGEN (135), Department of Psychology, Swarthmore College, Swarthmore, Pennsylvania

JOHN W. HAGEN (285), Department of Psychology, University of Michigan, Ann Arbor, Michigan

JAMES G. HOLLAND (311), Learning Research and Development Center, University of Pittsburgh, Pittsburgh, Pennsylvania

HERBERT KAYE (343), Department of Psychology, State University of New York at Stony Brook, Stony Brook, New York

JON E. KRAPFL (295), Department of Psychology, West Virginia University, Morgantown, West Virginia

STEINAR KVALE (165), Institute of Psychology, University of Aarhus, Aarhus, Denmark

JOHN A. MEACHAM (261), Department of Psychology, State University of New York at Buffalo, Buffalo, New York

HAYNE W. REESE (205), Department of Psychology, West Virginia University, Morgantown, West Virginia

KLAUS F. RIEGEL (3), Department of Psychology, University of Michigan, Ann Arbor, Michigan

ALEXANDER W. SIEGEL (191), Department of Psychology, University of Pittsburgh, Pittsburgh, Pennsylvania

CHARLES C. SPIKER (93), Department of Psychology, University of Iowa, Iowa City, Iowa

HARVEY L. STERNS (105), Department of Psychology, University of Akron, Akron, Ohio

SHELDON H. WHITE (59), Department of Psychology, Harvard University, Cambridge, Massachusetts

Preface

The theme of the Fifth West Virginia University Life-Span Developmental Psychology Conference, dialectical perspectives on experimental research, reflects a convergence of concerns. Life-span developmental psychology deals with the interaction of the individual with his social and historical context; each of the four preceding life-span conferences has dealt with theoretical, methodological, and substantive issues reflecting the current state of the field.

The dialectical perspective, offering the promise of fresh theoretical insight into the developmental process and the interaction of the individual with his environment, has attracted increasing attention recently. One purpose of the Fifth Life-Span Developmental Psychology Conference has been to explore this new perspective and to assess its applicability to the field of developmental psychology. In addition, the application of the dialectical perspective to experimental research involves issues in the philosophy of science. These concerns, in turn, are an outcome of the increased maturity of the field of developmental psychology. The problem of the relationship between the scientist and his subject of study is of special concern in the social sciences; the several applications of the dialectical perspective to experimental research seen in this volume bring us nearer to an understanding of this problem.

The sequence of the chapters in the present volume reflects the format of the conference and its rationale. The rationale was based on our observation that psychological theorists who take perspectives other than that of the behaviorist seem sometimes to begin articulating their point of view by attacking the behavioristic position. They then throw out the behavioristic research literature, invent new research tasks, and finally interpret the outcomes of research with the new tasks. For example, Piaget has not dealt with the traditional tasks in the area of verbal learning and memory, or with the traditional research on intelligence. However, the data from the traditional research do not disappear by virtue of being ignored, and however artificial and ecologically invalid the traditional tasks may be, they yield facts about psychological functioning which must eventually be incorporated into or explained by any psychological theory of wide scope. Kaplan has argued that for the concatenated type of theory, the ultimate truth criterion is the ability to incorporate all facts. This notion is also explicit in the Absolute Truth of dialectical idealism.

There have been a few attempts to extend nonbehavioristic theories, such as Piaget's, into traditional experimental research areas without modifying the tasks. The purpose of this conference was to push analyses such as these to the forefront, not only by explicating how dialectical methods and interpretations can be applied in traditional experimental areas, but also by providing rebuttals from traditionalists and debate between the adherents of opposing perspectives. We come, then, to the sequence of chapters: Each odd-numbered chapter reflects a dialectical thesis, and each following even-numbered chapter reflects a nondialectical antithesis.

Finally, among the hopes if not the goals of the participants in the Fifth Life-Span Developmental Psychology Conference was that at last they would learn exactly what is meant by dialectics. This hope must go unfulfilled, for a while, at least, for the conference generated an aggressive plurality of perspectives, but no single definition of dialectics. Nevertheless, the conference may have served to help locate the position of the dialectical perspective in life-span developmental psychology. If it is true, as Bernice Neugarten remarked in 1968, that we do not yet have a psychology of the life cycle, then it is certainly true that we do not yet have a philosophy of the life cycle. But as we move slowly toward a philosophy of the social sciences, it is safe to predict that the dialectical perspective will be part of its conceptual foundation.

Acknowledgments

The Fifth Life-Span Developmental Psychology Conference was catalyzed by the interest and activities of Klaus Riegel. Special thanks are due him as our Socratic daimon, present and omnipresent, as contributor, critic, participant, and inspiration.

We are once again grateful to Ray Koppelman, West Virginia University Provost for Research and Graduate Studies, for his continuing support of the Life-Span Conferences; his encouraging readiness to marshall University funds made the Fifth Life-Span Conference possible.

The West Virginia University Life-Span Conferences are intended to provide a forum for lively debate among participants. Considerable effort behind the scenes is necessary in order to achieve this goal; for their successful efforts at making the difficult look easy, we thank Ford Pearse of the West Virginia University Conference Office, and our graduate student hosts, Jeffrey Hyde, Vincent Morello, Sandra Reeves Roth, and Richard Stone. For her assistance in the final preparation of the manuscript, we thank Robin DeVault.

For Klaus Riegel

THEORETICAL ISSUES

CHAPTER 1

The Dialectics of Time[1]

KLAUS F. RIEGEL

UNIVERSITY OF MICHIGAN
ANN ARBOR, MICHIGAN

This chapter presents the very simple idea that time always involves at least two interacting event sequences, for example, the handling of the stopwatch by the observer and the succession of the events observed. Although this proposition seems evident enough, it has been overshadowed by the notion originating in classical natural sciences of an absolute, external dimension of time that exists from eternity to eternity without our participatory efforts. In disagreeing with this viewpoint, my attempt is to rediscover a simple concept of time, a concept that, surprisingly, is congruent with what modern natural scientists have been studying during the past few decades.

In the Western world, science has been written in spatial or, as linguists would say, in synchronic terms. Even when temporal processes are analyzed—and this is, of course, a dominant task for sciences—their description consists of comparisons of several timeless slates, for example, cross sections of the fall of a body at various instances. Time has never been a primary and independent mode of thinking; it has always received secondary consideration only.

The major reason for this treatment is that the logic underlying classical natural

[1] An earlier version of this chapter was presented at the conference "The Personal Experience of Time," held at the Graduate Center of the City University of New York on May 30, 1975, and organized by Bernard S. Gorman and Alden E. Wesman. The author is grateful for the opportunity to develop his ideas at the occasion of the conference and is grateful, in particular, to the two organizers. He also appreciates the supportive help and editorial assistance that he has received from numerous friends, especially from Mary Arnold, Donna Cohen, Raymond Harris, Jack Meacham, and Ruth Riegel.

science is a logic of spatial structures or distributions rather than of temporal orders or changes. As a consequence, science has been built upon abstract and stable entities, such as features, traits, and competencies, rather than upon concrete events. Science has given one-sided preference to stability, balance, and equilibrium, rather than to their opposites, broadly defined as contradictions, conflicts, and crises.

A science of development and change is possible but requires a radical reversal in our basic conceptions. Such a science would have to be founded upon the notion of contradictions between concrete events for which identity, balance, and abstract competencies are merely special and momentary states that immediately converge into the flux of new changes. The foundation for such a science of development and change has been laid in dialectical logic. One of its most important and intriguing concepts is the concept of time.

The organization of this chapter is based on the distinction between the temporal progression along four interdependent planes: inner-biological, individual-psychological, cultural-sociological, and outer-physical. After an overview of the history of the concepts of space and time in Section I, the dialectical interdependence of temporal progressions along the biological and physical dimensions is discussed in Section II under the topic "Time as Energy." Section III, under the topic "Time as Transformation," focuses on individual-psychological progression and its dependence on the changing historical conditions, whereas in Section IV, under the topic "Time as Construction," the cultural-sociological progression is emphasized with due consideration for the individual's development. In Section V, finally, an interpretation of temporal structures is presented by relying on an analysis of narratives, dialogues, and musical compositions.

I. On the History of the Concepts of Space and Time

Our concept of time, as much as our concept of space, has been guided by the notion of universal, external dimensions within which we believe ourselves to exist and that, in our search for knowledge, we believe we must recognize. While, undoubtedly, the notion of external time and space has attained extraordinary historical significance, it burdens our investigations of behavioral and social processes rather than assists in their understanding. In this first section, I will briefly review stages in the history of the concepts of space and time. The excellent treatises by Jammer (1954), Whitrow (1961), Fraser (1966, 1975), and H. Reichenbach (1928) will be relied on, as well as several publications by Piaget on the concepts of space, time, and movement in the child (Piaget, 1970a, 1970b; Piaget & Inhelder, 1956).

A. The Concepts of Space

Simplifying the issues to a considerable extent, we can distinguish four stages in the history of the concept of space that correspond in principle, though not in some details of their developmental order, to the periods of cognitive development proposed by Piaget, that is, sensorimotor, preoperational, concrete operational, and formal operational. A fifth or final stage leads to the developmental synthesis of dialectical operations (Riegel, 1973b).

1. The first stage represents the Greek concept of space. Here the primary focus was on substances or objects. Space was regarded as filling the gaps between these substances; space was regarded negatively, that is, as a void. This orientation is diametrically opposed to modern views, which give priority and independence to space. Subsequently, objects are considered to be located in space and can be defined and measured within it. The distinction between these two orientations is pointedly explicated in Cassirer's work (1910) on the concepts of substance and function. Similarly, Piaget regards the young child's concept of space as categorical. Children see or grasp objects here and there without being able to derive a generalized notion of space. Insofar as they stretch their arms toward objects or move from object to object, their space concept has become relational. This represents the second stage of spatial representation.

2. In one of his major confrontations with Newton and Locke, Leibniz (1646–1716) developed the relational concept of space. He was supported by his English correspondent Clarke (1675–1729) and by the Dutch physicist Huygens (1629–1695). But much earlier a relational concept of space had been proposed in Arabic philosophy, most notably by Al-Ghazālī (Algazel, 1927). According to Jammer (1954), "Leibniz rejected Newton's theory of an absolute space on the ground that space is nothing but a network of relations among coexisting things. In his correspondence with Clarke, Leibniz likens space to a system of genealogical lines, a 'tree of genealogy' or pedigree, in which a place is assigned to every person [p. 48]."

Piaget explored the relational space concept of the child, which supercedes and elaborates the infant's concept of substance, object, or categorical space. As children look at objects and then move their sight from one object to the next, a relational space concept is explicated. Eventually, the relations connecting the observing child with object A and B or his movement from A to B will yield three connected points that form the basis for a primitive plane. Any further movements and fixations by the child define additional planes and more complex relational structures. Expressed in a different form, the relational space consists of concentric spheres whose radii are defined by the child's own movements, for example, by an object held in his hand and moved around in front of him. When generalized at a later stage, this onion-layer model of space becomes the Cartesian system of coordinates. Most notably, the observer remains a part of such a relational space, indeed its most important part, its central anchor point.

3. The third stage in the development of the space concept results from two operations Piaget has called "decentration" and "seriation." These operations lead to an extrapolation of the relation connecting, for example, the observer and the object. Thus, the vector is extended both forward and/or backward into an infinite line. Such an operation implies the notion of transitivity of a series, such as $A < B$

$< C < D$.... The geometry corresponding to the resulting space, projective geometry, is historically much younger than the geometry appropriate for the next stage, that is, Euclidean geometry. In the history of painting and design, however, the techniques of representing space projectively were already developed many centuries ago. For example, the history of Renaissance painting can be regarded as the history of the development of projective techniques (Boring, 1957).

Piaget has shown that increasingly with age concrete operational children will be able to decenter by moving conceptually from their own position to that of another observer, for example, at either side of or opposite to them. As demonstrated by the "three mountain problem," the older child might judge correctly whether the mountains cover each other when seen from the positions of several different observers. Thus, the self-centered space concept of the young child becomes flexible and is no longer bound to the particular location of the observer.

By being able to conceive a projection line defined by the observer and an object, or as defined by two different objects, a constructive representation of space emerges that is not bound to the conditions here and now but attains a generality similar to the representation of the three-dimensional space on the two-dimensional canvas of the Renaissance painters. In painting, the two (and occasionally three) projection points (vanishing points) are externally given; commonly they lie on the horizon. The projection lines of the psychological observer, however, diverge like rays from his pupils. Thus, in painting, a decisive step in the abstraction from the human observer is achieved.

4. The projective space of the child remains concrete, that is, observer centered. But the observer can now take various positions, even imaginary ones. The important further shift toward the concept of classical, absolute, Euclidean, or Newtonian space consists of nothing less than providing an ideal position for an ideal observer, that is, to move him infinitely far away from the observed objects and onto God's lap. Thereby the crucial eighth axiom of Euclidean geometry is met, namely, that there is one line through a point on a plane that does not intersect with another line on the same plane, not even in infinity. By moving the observer infinitely far away, the projection lines that either converged upon the vanishing points on the canvas or diverged from the eyes of the observer have become parallel. Thus, a purely conceptual (*reine Anschauung*) space, in terms of Kant's philosophy, or a formal operational space in terms of Piaget's stages has been acquired that relies on classical mathematics, especially on analytical geometry. The space implied can never be perceived (except by the observer on God's lap); it can only be thought about. But the purely imaginary character of this space also guarantees that it remains immutable, that is, ideal.

5. The concept of an absolute, formal operational space has dominated our thinking to such an extent that modern natural scientists and philosophers faced considerable difficulties when they were trying to overcome the restrictions of this orientation. Traditionally, philosophers have either regarded this type of space as an externally given container in which all objects and events were located (Locke's primary qualities) or as a property of the mind that induces law and order upon

nature (Kant's a priori form). In contrast to ancient Greek notions, the concept of substance became less important than the concept of space. Rather than focusing on the distribution of substances, these substances were reduced to their microscopic particles (atoms or points), and their varying locations in space were explored in the laws of classical natural sciences.

The concept of time played an important role in these explorations, yet it was merely regarded as a "spatial metaphor" (Clark, 1973) or as a mysterious "fourth dimension" (Wallis, 1967). Toward the end of the 19th century, modern natural scientists either tried to reduce time to space (as in thermodynamics) or to fuse time, space, and/or substances (as in relativity and quantum theory). Behavioral and social scientists have failed to keep up with these important developments. They remained fixated upon the 19th-century notion of science.

B. The Concepts of Time

As much as Greek philosophy subordinated both the concepts of space and time to that of substance, so has Western philosophy and science subordinated the concept of time to that of space.

Since the history of the concepts of time is not as well explored as that of space, the following discussion emphasizes the psychological rather than the historical basis of time concepts. I will begin with the categorical system, the simplest and proceed, as in the theory of numbers and measurements (Hölder, 1901; Stevens, 1951), to more complex realizations, to ordinal, interval, and absolute systems. Each of these relies on some additional requirements that presuppose and embed all the preceding ones.

1. What objects are in space, events are in time. During the early stages of human development, there is no separation of stable objects and changing events. A child will attend to an object only if the object is in motion or if, through the child's own motions, the impression of such a change is created. For the mature person also, the separation of stable objects and changing events remains arbitrary and artificial. Events involve objects, and objects change. Indeed, only through the conceptual separation of space and time has it become possible to regard objects (being in space) as independent from events (being in time).

Simultaneity is the basic property of temporal descriptions. It corresponds to the notion of equivalence or—most important—to that of identity in formal logic and therefore creates the greatest difficulties in temporal descriptions. Simultaneity or coexistence in space is relatively easy to comprehend. Space itself can be characterized—as we have seen—by the simultaneous existence or distribution of objects. It is difficult to determine, however, under what conditions two events can be regarded as simultaneous in time. This is not only a problem of measurement, that is, of the determination as to when two durations of performance are exactly alike, or as to when two children are exactly of the same age; it implies conceptual difficulties. The recording of two events as simultaneous requires the attending to two events by one person or, in the case of interrupted activities, for example, of a sleeper, two observers and not only one observer.

In spite of these difficulties, simultaneity provides the most important basis for the measurement of time, that is, points of coincidence or "time knots" at which different types of movements intersect. But if temporal statements were to imply nothing but judgments of simultaneity, they would reveal little about time. Directional or relational properties have to be considered.

2. When we recollect past events, we rarely reconstruct them with the aid of a temporal yardstick such as the clock or the calendar. Various events will appear in our memory and provide some spontaneous markings. These events are not haphazard collection, merely organized in terms of their simultaneity; they often appear in their temporal order and movements. Moreover, such a sequential organization does not occur along one single time series but within a set of different temporal orders, illustrated, for instance, when we alternately reflect on our career in school, our vocation, our family, our friends, the political or economic situation, and so on. The selection of critical markings differs between these sequences.

As immediate as the notion of temporal direction and order seems to be in our understanding of time, this notion has been as difficult to tackle in science. Its exploration is related to attempts in thermodynamics to depict time as a sequence of spatial conditions. Typically, this argument is based on the example of two different gases (substances) enclosed in two containers (space). If both containers are joined, the gases would slowly reach a mixed state. The distribution of their particles in space would allow us to conclude that the mixed state is temporally later than the state in which the two gases were less completely mixed or were separated altogether.[2]

3. The notion of different event sequences crisscrossing each other but converging upon the momentary state of the reflecting observer is comparable to that of projective space during the concrete operational period of late childhood. This notion will be substituted by the concept of absolute time during the period of formal operations. As a prerequisite for this transition, the operation of "decentering," introduced by Piaget, attains significance again. If the child succeeds in looking at the past (as well as into the future) from various "angles" or points of view, this transition will have been achieved. Already the notion that different time sequences might be partially independent of each other and interact at only a few event points, or "knots," prepares the child for this transition. The transition is achieved if children succeed in seeing the past (or the future) from the perspectives of others, if they recognize, for example, that what appears to be an intense period with many temporal markings to them is but an insignificant set of events to their parents or that what appears well timed to them might appear belated to others.

[2] Historically, the attempts to reduce time to a sequence of spatial conditions in the distribution of substances signaled the departure from the concept of absolute time in classical natural sciences and opened the way for the time concept in modern natural sciences, that is, in quantum physics and relativity theory.

4. In addition to an increased degree of decentering, and thereby of viewing the past (or the future) from various "perspectives," the transition to the period of an absolute time concept depends on the proposition of an ideal observer who is infinitely far removed from the present, either into the past or into the future or, most likely, into both. This proposition provides a concept of time that is unidimensional, uniform, and stretches positively and negatively into infinity. From this perspective the temporal experience of the individual counts for little and fills but an infinitesimal stretch of the universal time dimension. Now the individual has ceased to take any active part in the construction of time but is subordinated to an impersonal and alienated concept. In exchange, time has become quantifiable, even if the procedures employed for attaining this goal remain somewhat arbitrary, that is, rely on selected periodic systems, such as the solar year, the lunar month, or the swing of a pendulum.

5. As the concept of absolute space has given way to a dialectical interpretation in which not only space is reunited with time but in which also the human being has regained an appropriate place, the concept of absolute time will have to be subordinated within a dialectical interpretation. In such a reevaluation, the concept of time will, first of all, converge upon the concept of space, but a new and integrative perspective will also emerge. As relational time is comparable to a single intrinsic event sequence, represented, for example, by a monophonic melody, absolute time is comparable to the extrinsic standard of such music, that is, the meter and the bar lines. Dialectical time is like polyphonic music in which various monophonic sequences are interwoven and in which temporal markings are generated by the harmonies and disharmonies of such a composition. Also absolute time plays a role in such an arrangement, namely, as one of several monophonic sequences that enter into the arrangement. In particular, it may serve as an extrinsic yardstick and may be useful for the synchronization of the different voices or instruments in their temporal progression, which, nevertheless, is internally generated. As a consequence, dialectical time is both intrinsic and extrinsic and not one or the other.

C. Conclusions

The history of the concept of space has revealed four major orientations coinciding with Piaget's periods of the development of the space concept in the child. The history of the concept of time is less clear, but on the basis of the general properties ascribed to time, that is, simultaneity, direction, duration, and zero point, it is possible to construct a developmental sequence resembling the four major periods in Piaget's theory of children's cognitive development.

Although space and time are not yet clearly separated during Stage 1, the coexistence of objects in space and the simultaneity of events in time are apprehended. The notion of direction and order at Stage 2 leads to an understanding of time as movement. Movements affect objects and create events. Although objects and events can never be distinctly separated—for events always occur with objects and objects are the carriers of events—even a crude differentiation leads to the separate apprehension of space (through coexistent objects) and of time (through shifting events). At Stage 2 different event sequences are conceived as independent. At Stage 3 the child apprehends the relations between these sequences and succeeds, as in projective geometry, in viewing them from an increasing number of different perspectives. As the degree of decentering increases, the resulting concepts of space and time become more sophisticated and, according to Piaget, provide a transition to the next stage of the absolute space and time concepts of classical natural science and philosophy. At Stage 4 both concepts become ideal abstractions. The individual observers have been removed from consideration; indeed, they have become subordinated to the uniform and universal systems, which—I hasten to add—they themselves have created during the course of history. Although now space and time have become conceptually differentiated, they remain interdependent because they rely on the same mathematics and formalizations, namely, on the mathematics and formalizations of space. Consequently, time did not attain a higher status than that of a mysterious fourth dimension derived by analogy from the concept of space. Not surprisingly, therefore, a reduction of the concept of time to that of space was promoted in thermodynamic theory. This attempt, in turn, signaled a more radical break with the concepts of absolute space and time promoted in classical natural sciences and philosophy.

Whereas Newton postulated particle substance, space, and time as independent and necessary properties of nature, modern science has reduced time to the probable order of different spatial conditions of particles. In particular, Maxwell described electromagnetic fields in terms of space—time instances. Here, as in thermodynamics, the particle substance lost its place. In his attempt to harmonize electromagnetic field theory with Newtonian mechanics, Einstein introduced the notion of a space—time compound measured in terms that referred to the observer as well as to the observed object. In a further extension, Planck consolidated the notion of particle substance with its counterpart, the notion of wave, which, as for Einstein, is depicted in a compounded space—time system. Thus in all these modern theories the three basic entities of classical natural sciences, particle substance, space, and time, are compounded or reduced to one another.

The compounding of the three entities revives interpretations prevailing in the early developmental stages of the individual and society in which the concepts of space and time are not yet clearly differentiated and in which a rudimentary concept of time relies on the notion of coexistent motions and simultaneous events. In the following pages I will discuss some recent scientific and philosophical interpretations (Bachelard, 1972; Fraser, 1967; Günther & von Foerster, 1967; Whitrow, 1967; M. Wundt, 1949) that are akin to these views and seem much more appropriate for the problems studied in the behavioral and social sciences than those derived through formal abstractions in classical natural science and philosophy. These interpretations will lead toward an explication of a dialectical concept of time.

II. The Multiple Bases of Time: Time as Energy[3]

Time can be defined in several different ways: on the cosmic level by the expansion of the universe, on the thermodynamic level by entrophy increases, on the microscopic level by radiation changes. Whatever the level of analysis, describing time as a linear flow of events along any single dimension represents a vestige from Newtonian mechanics. Modern natural science has proposed new constructs that consider the relations between events on different levels or world lines. Such a concept necessitates the introduction of higher dimensional systems in which time is represented as transformation across two or more event sequences either in the horizontal, in the vertical, or in any other direction. Such a transformation results from a conflict or constrast and indicates a change in the distribution of energy.

A. Time in Modern Physics

Most applications of the time concept in behavioral and social sciences have neglected the relation between the time of the organism and that of its inner and outer environment. In seeking to describe this relation, H. Reichenbach (1928) and M. Reichenbach and Mathern (1959) adopted a definition from relativity theory. The age of an organism is characterized by its location on the world lines of different subsystems. Healthy development represents the synchronized movement along these world lines; pathological development represents a lack of synchronization. Chronological time is one particular functional unit of analysis for the world lines. Since it is an external descriptor and arbitrarily measured by the clock on a linear scale, it is not necessarily a meaningful index of developmental processes.

If we consider living systems as composites of various subsystems, that is, cells, cell clusters, organs, organ systems, or some other functional groupings, their analyses will depend on their quantum, atomic, molecular, cellular, organismic, individual, cultural, or cosmic states. Development consists of a series of processes along several of these dimensions, with time marked by their transformations. For example, Figure 1 represents liver cells posited on their respective world lines. Each cell is dependent on others for the healthy functioning of the organ system. Similar to these cullular changes, whole organ systems may develop at different rates, determined, for example, by their metabolic conditions. The liver and lungs may be changing rather fast, while the heart may be changing in a negative direction relative to the lungs or neuronal tissues. Birren (1959) has suggested that there may be as many processes of development as there are cells, cell clusters, organs, and so on. The dotted lines in Figure 1 suggest alternative directions for the world lines.

---

[3] This section has been influenced and much inspired by an unpublished manuscript by Donna Cohen, "Time as Energy: On the Application of Modern Concepts of Time to Developmental Sciences." The author is very grateful to his friend and teacher.

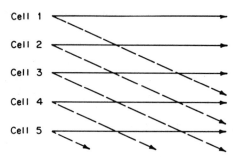

Fig. 1. Alternative world lines of liver cells.

Time is intimately connected with observation; each observation is an irreversible process. Observers derive a sense of time from the recognition that the total number of events increases from moment to moment. Occasionally the observed events may combine into new configurations. Such an outcome represents a vertical transformation of events across different levels.

World lines at any level are irreversible, but their rates of accumulation may vary. If we imagine an observer within a developing cell (as proposed with Leibniz's monads), the duration of physical processes in Cell 1 may appear to be lengthened when seen from Cell 2. But an observer in Cell 1 would say the same about Cell 2. The apparent time dilation is the result of the velocity perspectives. Relativity theory is concerned with the recordings of different clocks in different coordinate systems. In an analysis of the organism, likewise, we have to identify different clocking mechanisms and their interactions.

If we observe sequences of events on several different world lines, we can study how they relate to one another. Sidereal time measurements permit us to order the events in the form of a series, $E_1, E_2, E_3, \ldots E_n$. But the nature of the event order would remain insufficiently explored if, by using a clock, we merely imposed such a horizontal order on the events in any subsystem. In Popper's (1958) terms, the observer would have become the causal center in this analysis. If we reject this time concept and consider some vertical E_{1j}-to-E_{mj} axes in Figure 2 rather than single points in the series of events E_{11} to E_{mn} then a two-dimensional time model has been derived.

In Figure 2 an instant of "now" is represented by the intersection of the time axes at some event E. Various E_{ij} may form different "now lines." With an added dimension of time, an infinite number of alternative new event points can be realized, a possibility not permitted in a one-dimensional model. A change in velocity of the event accumulation could provide the result of curvilinear now lines also illustrated in Figure 2. The vertical axis can assume many functional forms. Consider, for example, a leaky faucet with drops of water falling rhythmically from the opening. The time rhythms result from the interaction of two processes involving weight and surface tension.

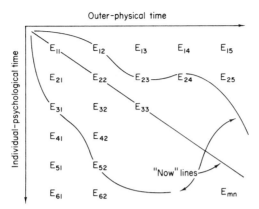

Fig. 2. Two-dimensional time matrix with world lines of events accumulating along several levels of analysis and with alternative "now" lines.

B. Interaction between Biological and Psychological Event Sequences

Energy transformations in metabolic processes provide a possible definition of time-dependent changes in the organism. According to Hoagland (1933, 1936), time judgments are dependent on the velocity of oxidative metabolism in parts of the brain, that is, they are determined by the chemical velocities of biological reactions. Raising the internal body temperature increases the speed of reaction such that the chemical clock runs faster than a laboratory clock; about 2 minutes of performance time equals 1 minute of clock time. Lowering the body temperature makes clock time seem faster; about 1 minute of performance time equals 2 minutes of clock time. Supportive data were collected from an individual tapping and counting seconds at different induced body temperatures.

Time seems also to pass more slowly for the child than for the adult. Kety (1956) has reported positive correlations between cerebral blood flow, oxygen consumption, and age. Slowing of oxygen consumption observed in aging organisms would be congruent with the observation that time passes more quickly with increasing age. If the temperature of an organism were lowered, metabolism would slow down. Time, defined by the reciprocal of metabolism, should pass more quickly for the organism. Therefore energy transformation in metabolic processes provides a reasonable definition of time-dependent changes in the organism. "We find that whenever there is an interaction involving an energy change, there is also a relativistic time transformation and vice versa [Fraser, 1967, p. 836]."

The examples describe inner-biological and individual-psychological observations within an interphenomenal transformation system. An instructive demonstration of the interdependence between phenomena within a single domain of changes, that is, at the individual-psychological level, has been provided by Schaltenbrand (1967). He argues that all our perception is brought about by the experience of incongruity or contradiction. For example, three-dimensional spatial impressions are created "by the fusion of two pictures of the world which are not completely congruent, since both eyes see the objects at a different angle. We attain the conception of movement in a similar way. Here, too, pictures with a particular contradictory content are integrated into something new. The conception of movement is therefore similar in performance to the conception of three-dimensionality [p. 632]." Since our perceptual system can handle only a limited number of frames per time unit, a presentation at a slow rate, that is, at a rate below the "critical flicker fusion," will lead to the discrete experience of these contradictions in the form of jerky movements, comparable to quantum jumps in modern physical analysis. If the rate of presentation is high, our perceptual system succeeds in resolving the contradictory states into smooth movements.

Whereas the contradictory states in time are serially experienced, those of three-dimensionality in binocular vision are simultaneously given by the incongruencies between the retinal images of the left eye and the right eye. These differences between objects in space and events in time should not overshadow the close interdependence between both conditions. Objects are best perceived if we either move ourselves or if we move the objects; indeed, even if we are not intentionally doing this, the rapid movements of our lenses guarantee that the retinal image is never stable but always in contrastive flux. Events, however, are best perceived if the observer remains at apparent rest. Simultaneous movements of the observer and the observed events would overburden the perceiver and would be comparable to the concurrent movements of two systems analyzed in relativity theory.

In extending the comparison between perception and quantum physics, Schaltenbrand (1967) remarks that

> physicists consider atoms of matter as standing waves, similar to electric clouds rotating around the atomic nucleus. There is no way of localizing or identifying the single particle as long as there is no interaction—a quantum jump. Between the quantum jumps we are dealing with a closed box system. Its influence on the world is a steady state, or "a present". Only the quantum jumps change one present into another and allow a recording of an event in time . . . [Similar for perception,] only when a disturbance or a change appears do we experience a progress of time [p. 638].

Such a disturbance may either be induced by outer-physical conditions or by actions at the inner-biological and individual-psychological levels.

C. Interaction between Psychological and Sociological Event Sequences

Although experimental psychology of the late 19th century regarded the conditions of the mind as timeless structures, these viewpoints nevertheless represented a substantial advance compared to earlier conceptions. The discovery of the reflex arc, the physiological evidence for reflex actions provided by Marshall Hall, and the measurement of the speed of nerve transmission by Fritsch and Hitzig all provided the basis for revolutionizing viewpoints and for casting them into the language of experimental physiology and psychology. Nevertheless, from a dialectical perspective the changes provided were but a small step toward an understanding of the changing individual in a changing world.

Perceptual and cognitive processes consist of a transformation of the ever-changing flux of experience and thought into momentary stable structures which we communicate to others by means of linguistic expressions or which we exchange in the form of physical and mental products. Cognitive analysis, guided by formal logic, tells us little about the way in which these products are generated; dialectical logic, by focusing upon disequilibrium and contradiction, analyzes the processes that lead to their creation. The study of time contraction, especially as carried out by Fischer (1967), explores the simultaneity of contradictory experiences and provides some insight into these processes. Thus, it contrasts with serial contradiction in the perception of those events discussed in Section I.

Time contraction occurs in states of mystical fusion, in creative moments, in syncretic integrations, in pathological conditions (especially in epileptic fits), in dreams, in sudden fear of death, and so on. It can also be induced by drugs. All of these states lead to a fusion of subject and object by creating a sense of extended simultaneity in which a manifold of events, which, under normal conditions, would require a considerable amount of time for their exploration, are experienced at once. Numerous examples of such experience have been reported in the literature. They range from the art historian, who comprehends the extended simultaneity of patterns that he calls the "style" of an historical period, to "Mozart's ability to perceive a complete musical work as a single event, . . . [in] his own words, 'Nor do I hear in my imagination the parts successively; I hear them . . . all at once.' . . . Similar in the realm of pictorial art, Giotto intuitively guessed almost all principles of representation [perspective] which required nearly two centuries of enthusiastic research to establish scientifically [Fischer, 1967, pp. 452–453]." Art and creativity are dependent upon the simultaneous apprehension of what appears as separated both in space and, especially, in time. "Aesthetics is the study of those intuitive and rational rules and of those natural phenomena that in the creator or in the beholder enhance a feeling of timelessness [Fraser, 1967, p. 840]."

Depicting creativity in this manner also indicates that in every act of performance the flux of changing condition will have to be brought to a halt, as represented in the timeless documentation of the book, the statue, or the painting. Only in the spoken arts of plays and in musical performances is the temporal character fully retained. These art forms, therefore, lend themselves most readily to interpretation of the time concept (Zuckerkandl, 1956, 1973). Similar arguments can be made for human experience in the cultural-historical context.

Man generates culture and history, which, in turn, transforms man and all future generations of man. For example, human beings have created supportive tools, communicative language, and social order. These products, in turn, have transformed their activities. When we are talking about historical time, we are commonly considering the sequence of "objectified" products that mark these stages of transformations. Congruent with the proposal to characterize time by energy exchanges, historical transformations, rather than these objectified markings, constitute historical time.

In developmental studies, likewise, the processes, activities, or transformations should be regarded as the essence of development; they change the object as much as they are changed by the object. Intellectual development, for example, has been depicted in the past as a process of abstraction culminating in the formal logic required by Newton's science and implied in Locke's philosophy. Concrete thinking lies at the point of departure for such development; creative thinking has to overcome the alienation of abstraction; mature thinking has to return to the dialectical, contradictory basis of thought (Riegel, 1973b). Scientific thinking likewise—as argued by M. Wundt (1949), Kosok (1976), and the present author (Riegel, 1976a)—has to realize its dialectical character. The proposal to study the multiplicity of time, to study time as transformation and energy, represents such a dialectical reformulation, which as yet has not been applied in the behavioral and social sciences.

D. Conclusions

An analysis of time has to consider an array of world lines: quantum, atomic, molecular, cellular, organismic, individual, cultural, and cosmic. Traditionally the organism has been described in structural terms (Carnap, 1928) and development as a change of structures. Consequently, development was thought to occur only at the higher levels; atoms were regarded as "lifeless" and nondeveloping. The implied distinction between living and nonliving substances failed to take account of transformations between levels or interactions across world lines.

The concept of time as energy was derived from quantum physics and relativity theory. The energetic property of time is documented for behavioral and social sciences by the temperature (energy) exchanges and age dependence of temporal judgments. In extension, the concepts of individual-psychological and cultural-sociological time were suggested. Through their activities individuals change the cultural-historical conditions which at the same time change the individuals. Historical time, as traditionally conceived, has been restricted to sequences of rigidified products; historical time as energy represents activities of transformations. Such an interpretation does not support a sharp cut between inanimate and animate substances; time represents interactions between both. The same holds for specific transactions across different levels of analyses represented by different world lines; time as energy presupposes these event sequences as distinct but synthesizes them in a dialectical manner.

III. The Interactive Determination of Time: Time as Transformation

The lives of well-known scientists demonstrate the interdetermination of individual and cultural changes. The individual's impact upon the scientific community and the scientific community's impact upon the individual can be fairly well assessed. In a simplified manner we might select, for example, the major publications of a well-known scientist and list them as major markings of his academic career. In addition, we can consider his appointments at various institutions and the ranks attained, realizing, thereby, that these events are the products of temporal interactions of the individual with his cultural, in this case, scientific community. On the basis of such information, I have previously presented a synopsis of the academic life of two well-known behavioral scientists, Wilhelm Wundt and Jean Piaget (Riegel, 1975a). In the following, brief references to this study will be made.

A. Interaction of Individual and Cultural Event Sequences

Figure 3 shows the changing interactions between the individual-psychological and cultural-sociological developments presented orthogonally to each other. The vertical arrows indicate Wundt's adult life span subdivided into six distinct periods. Inasmuch as these vertical arrows remain beneath the zero point along the individual-psychological time line, they represent the scientist's life still to be lived at

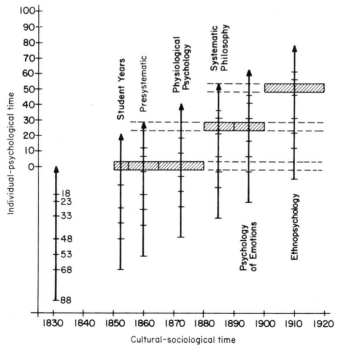

Fig. 3. The changing roles of one eminent scientist, Wilhelm Wundt, participating in three paradigmatic orientations at different historical times. The vertical vectors represent world lines for the individual at different historical times; the horizontal bars represent world lines for society at different individual times. The vectors and bars are marked in terms of the developmental level in the individual's career. [Adapted from Riegel, 1975a, p. 117.]

particular historical dates. The horizontal bar across Figure 3 at the zero point shows periods of Wundt's scientific career as seen from the historical perspective. The growing conflict between his own activities and the degree to which they became accepted by the scientific community is indicated by the elevated portions of the bar in the right part of the figure. Here his contributions to systematic philosophy and the psychology of emotions are depicted as if the latter were made during his major life period of 33 to 48 years, whereas in fact they were made between 1890 and 1900, that is, at a time when Wundt was already between 58 and 68 years old. The discrepancy becomes even larger if one performs a similar shift for his contributions to ethnopsychology, which were made between 1900 and 1920, that is, when Wundt was between 68 and 88 years old.

In particular, the first period (1851–1856) of the historical event sequence finds Wundt among other students under the influence of their teachers. During the second period (1856–1865) he has gained more independence but has remained under the shadow of his superior, Helmholtz. Wundt revealed his first paradigmatic orientation, that of introspective elementism, during the third period, from 1865 to 1880. Throughout his career he was never able to remove the image that he had created during this period, which can best be denoted as that of "mechanistic psychology" (Riegel, 1972a). He also became an influential teacher and writer. Being preoccupied with the administration of his laboratory, with academic duties, and with the publication of several philosophical works, Wundt underwent a change in his teaching role during the fourth period (1880–1890). Instead of interacting face to face with his students, he was more likely to have been hidden behind his assistants, doctorants, and visitors. Although he addressed his collaborators in small seminars, he reached his students only through large lectures and publications. The fourth period has been regarded as a preparation for Wundt's second paradigmatic orientation, one represented by the research and theory of emotions that he developed fully during the fifth period (1890–1900). Because of the discontinuity in his interaction with the successive generations of students and despite the intensive debate among his followers and opponents, his theory of emotions never became an accepted part of psychological inquiry. This period can be described best as representing his "mentalistic psychology." His extensive efforts to develop a third paradigmatic orientation, representing ethnopsychology, suffered the same fate. This third orientation can be regarded as an incomplete attempt to develop a dialectical integration with his two-pronged approach. Although heatedly debated in areas other than psychology during his last period (1900–1920), this work did not receive serious attention from even Wundt's associates and former students. (See, however, the little known work by his last student and successor at Leipzig, Felix Krüger, 1915.) By now, Wundt exerted little direct influence upon the new generation of potential converts. He was retired from academic duties but remained committed to his scientific activities and extensive writings.

Wundt's career shows rather distinctly the changing interactions between the individual and the cultural group. The temporal markings of the individual's life cannot be understood unless the cultural conditions are considered. The same interaction also holds in the opposite direction; thus, the temporal markings in the changing status of the cultural group cannot be understood unless they are seen in light of continuing efforts by the individuals who create these conditions.

The temporal markings of events, such as publication of books, attain significance only if there is an interpenetration between individual progression and that of the cultural group. Only if these books are read, interpreted, and criticized do they become significant happenings in the course of the author's life. Conversely they might also become significant events in the life of the social group. These knots ("*Knotenpunkte*," Hegel, 1969, p. 435) are officially signified by historical dates, but these markings lie neither on the cultural-sociological nor on the individual-psychological dimension alone, they represent the events in which both intersect. Man creates history as much as he is created by history. The particular moments of effective interpenetration will be recorded in the history of the society and in the life review of the individual.

B. *Interaction of Two Individual Event Sequences*

What holds for the relations between individuals and cultural groups holds also for the relations between any two individuals. Detailed analysis might potentially dissolve the history of the cultural group into a multitude of dyadic interaction sequences. While the example of Wundt's life reconfirms the significance of historical studies for the behavioral and social sciences, the following case of a dyadic relation, that is, the changing interactions in the career development of husband and wife, provides some suggestions for the psychological study of temporal markings in the individual's life span.

After leaving school or college, a man and a woman will each enter their first occupational career, he may be drafted, and they may get married. While the attainment of an occupational role is primarily dependent on social conditions that, in turn, are the reflection of the standards at a particular historical time, service in the army applies to males only and therefore, is in part inner-biologically determined. The marital role requires sexual maturity of both partners. But in all these instances a clear separation of biological from psychological and sociological determinants is impossible to achieve.

A determining event at the first developmental level might be the birth of the first child followed by the loss of a wife's job, a change in the job, or the promotion of the husband. The child cannot be born unless a social, or, at least, biological marriage has taken place; a job cannot be changed or lost unless it has been held before. As obvious as these conclusions are, they represent the very temporal markings that structure the progression of the adult's life. They are important for both the recollection of minor events at a later date, such as an accident, the purchase of a household item, a birthday or a party, as well as for the temporal markings of what individuals might perceive as crises in their lives.

Events at the second developmental level include the birth of other children coupled with the execution of specific parental roles during the children's preschool years, changes in job, promotion, the move to a larger house, to a different location, and so on. The delineation of a developmental level determined by the children's preschool years is possible only for families with single or few children, narrowly spaced by birth over a short time period. This limitation indicates the cultural-sociological determination of distinct periods in the adult life. The levels described can be identified only for small nuclear families in industrialized settings. Agricultural societies composed of large kinship groups experience closely spaced arrivals of children which do not allow for the sectioning of life span through generational shifts or career alternations.

In contrast with the events marking the first two levels in the adult life, the following are spread over longer and more variable periods. During the third level, the children attend elementary and high school, and, thus, the mother may enter her second career. Few changes except those of promotion or shift in assignments may be experienced by her husband. This holds also for the fourth level, characterized by the departure of the children from home in search of their own development and career. Undoubtedly, these events profoundly affect their parents. If these departures are accompanied by—what is becoming increasingly likely—the death of one or both members of the older generation, the status of the parents is even more drastically altered. Both husband and wife may now attain the top position among the living members of the extended family, with their own children ready to marry and grandchildren to be expected.

At the fifth developmental level the individual becomes increasingly vulnerable to dismissal, unemployment, and disease. Not only the death of the parents, but of the partner, friends, and relatives may create personal crises and thus temporal markings in the later part of the life span. While most of these events are brought about by uncontrollable outer-physical circumstances or inner-biological changes, one of the most decisive and final affronts, retirement, is caused by conventional regulations. Mandatory retirement provides the last insult to adult persons and initiates their progressive social deterioration.

The grouping of various events into temporal clusters or periods is congruent with and in part determined by social sanctions and institutions. A simple listing of events in their serial order would be an approach more desirable and less dependent on the biases of traditional Western psychology. The distinction of levels or periods may disregard or distort the particular conflicts and coordinations within or between event sequence that lend them their temporal markings and that retrospectively might be recognized as "objective" dates. For example, if on some later occasion one of the partners were to recollect some episodes of the past, he or she would most likely focus upon events that have been brought about by their interactive implications, such as the birth of a child, the move to a different house, the loss of a job, and so on. As these interactions are recognized, a more detailed temporal order of the events can become apparent. Only as a very last step will an external, objective date be associated with the sequence of interactive events.

C. Multiplicity of Interactions Constituting Event Sequences

The two preceding examples have given descriptive evidence for a concept of time that emphasizes event sequences whose temporal markings are generated by interactions of single individuals with their social groups or between two single individuals. The two examples also redirected our attention to both the study of individual life histories and to the study of cultural-historical changes through biographical and retrospective analyses. In neither case does the separate exploration of the individual or of the social group provide insightful answers; only the study of interactive changes in which points of conflict or conflict resolution mark the temporal order will lead to an understanding of time and development.

The analysis proposed coincides with the recent analyses of family history and the sociology of the life course as most cogently developed by Elder (1974, 1975, 1977). Being in full agreement with these interpretations, I have proposed four dimensions of simultaneous progression: inner-biological, individual-psychological, cultural-sociological, and outer-physical (see Riegel, 1975c). If we consider the interactions of any one dimension with any other, we obtain a 4 X 4 matrix, shown in Table 1. Here, the tentative labels attached to the 16 cells either denote interactive markings with a negative (upper word) or positive (lower word) outcome. Events representing conflicts or conflict resolutions within any particular dimension, that is, for the cells along the main diagonal of the matrix, require special elaborations. For example, in the cell denoting interactions within the event sequences along the inner-biological dimension, we might list the cooperation or conflict between two organisms, for example, an attacking and an attacked animal, mother and child, sexual partners, and so on. At more specific levels we might think of the coordination (or lack of it) between different body organs, cell clusters, single cells, cell membranes and nuclei, and so on.

Similar arguments can be made for the interactions within any of the other three dimensions. Individual-psychological interactions include those between two people, for example, husband and wife, parent and child, or employer and employee. At more specific levels they involve subsystems within a single individual, for example, between the sensory and motor system, thought and speech, anxiety and motivation, or whatever categories psychologists are ready to propose. At still more specific levels, we consider the interaction between particular ideas and behaviors, and perceptions and expressions.

While the matrix of comparisons thus becomes exceedingly wide, there are no compelling reasons that all dimensions have to be considered at one and the same time and for one and the same purpose. Quite to the contrary, a selective restriction is necessary for any concrete analysis. But whatever the choice of restriction, event sequences are always generated by interactions of at least two and often of many series of activities. The consideration of separate, single event sequences is an abstraction that prevents any meaningful interpretation of temporal order and time. This is, of course, precisely what is being done when absolute time measurements

Table 1

Crises with Negative[a] and Positive[b] Outcomes Generated by Asynchronies Along Four Planes of Developmental Progressions

	Inner-biological	Individual-psychological	Cultural-sociological	Outer-physical
Inner-biological	Infection Fertilization	Illness Maturation	Epidemic Cultivation	Deterioration Vitalization
Individual-psychological	Disorder Control	Discordance Concordance	Dissidence Organization	Destruction Creation
Cultural-sociological	Distortion Adaptation	Exploitation Acculturation	Conflict Cooperation	Devastation Conservation
Outer-physical	Annihilation Nutrition	Castastrophe Welfare	Disaster Enrichment	Chaos Harmony

[a]Negative outcome is indicated by the upper word.
[b]Positive outcome is indicated by the lower word.

are taken. Absolute time measurements do not generate by themselves any meaningful interaction with the events measured. Even here, however, as modern physicists insist, the measurement creates a conflict or contradiction with the events observed.

Further extensions are necessary in regard to cultural-sociological and, finally, outer-physical dimensions. The constitutive groupings of the former include the family, tribe, nation, or civilization; the peer group, union, party, or religious order; the neighborhood, community, or city; the age and sex group, generation, and many others (see Elder, 1974, 1975, 1977). Equally wide is the distribution of outer-physical conditions. On the one hand, we need to consider large-scale external interventions, such as earthquakes, floods, and droughts; on the other hand, we need to list all those processes within organisms that constitute events on the organismic, cellular, molecular, atomic, and quantum levels (see Cohen, 1972).

D. Conclusions

The life spans of common men and women often represent deficient forms of temporal structures. The major events affecting individuals are arbitrarily induced upon them by social and legal regulations, for example, their departure from school, recruitment into military service, job appointments and dismissals, and, ultimately, retirement. Other changes are brought about by events that are even further removed from the individual, such as depressions, inflations, revolutions, and wars, or droughts, floods, fires, and earthquakes. Only the inner-biological determinants seem to follow a predictable order, revealing first individuals' maturation, later the birth of children, and eventually increasing proneness to incapacitation, illness, and death.

Among the few favored individuals, the life spans of academic scientists allow for structural variations and for some sensible transformations. In the development of their careers, scientists tentatively explicate their paradigmatic orientations through their teaching and affiliation with a few like-minded colleagues and students. As they advance, they establish their own "scientific commune" and disseminate their ideas through reports and papers until these ideas become crystallized in research routines and textbooks. The small team with which they affiliate represents the nucleus of their activities and successes. But the further they advance, the more they will find recognition from other groups that, though geographically remote, become attached to one another by their shared technology and knowledge. Eventually these groups represent a distinct paradigmatic orientation which, through their achievements, has created a new interpretation of a scientific theme.

As one cohort succeeds, others are forced into opposition and rejection of earlier orientations. The resulting condition creates temporal markings through conflicts with coexisting or preceding viewpoints. For a limited period, representatives of the former paradigm will find some like-minded colleagues to lean on, but these persons might adjust more successfully to the changing scientific conditions either by moving forward in their individual careers or by withdrawing from the laboratory into administrative duties. These events thus generate temporal markings which are experienced as crises. Crises can be resolved by structural transformations of the individual's life in concordance with social progression. Ideally we should design structural sequences of events and implement them through proper assignments of people and allocations of resources. Such a design can only be prepared by careful observations of the temporal order of events within both the individual and the social system. The study of cultural history has to be linked with the analysis of individual development.

IV. The Analyses of Event Sequences: Time as Construction

By considering time in reference to the four dimensions described, one can draw the following comparisons: At the inner-biological level, temporal markings appear as developmental changes in activity and passivity, excitement and satisfaction, growth and decay. At the individual-psychological level, they are experienced as conflicts and resolutions, doubts and decisions, movements and rests. At the cultural-sociological level, they are objectified by incentives and restrictions, conquests and defeats, expansions and retreats. At the outer-physical level, they appear as night and day, summer and winter, floods and droughts.

By comparing all of these dimensions with one another, we are made aware of temporal markings through the individual-psychological dimension; the cultural-sociological dimension records events so that they can be transmitted to other people and to other generations. Because of their exceptional status, therefore, these two aspects of temporal order have received the most attention. Their interdependence can be analyzed either in a formal systematic manner or by emphasizing their experiential-individual and normative-cultural bases. The first form of analysis has been explored in the study of developmental research designs.

A. Systematic Analysis of Changes in the Individual and Society

As shown by Schaie (1965) and Baltes (1968), certain variables, such as the amount of mobility and communication, may yield development gradients which increase in magnitude from generation to generation. If these increases are linearly related to age and if, furthermore, we assess age differences by the traditional cross-sectional method, that is, by testing at one time samples from different age groups (which thus represent different generations or cohorts), the results might indicate a curvilinear increase in scores with age and a decline thereafter. Curves like these are all too familiar to developmental psychologists, yet they represent mere artifacts because neither the generation nor the time of testing effects have been controlled as contributing factors.

The proper analysis can best be explained with reference to Table 2, which lists the age of three cohorts (born around 1850, 1900, and 1950) over two times of

Table 2

Years of Birth of Four Cohorts in a Demonstration of Developmental-Historical Research Designs[a]

	Age	
Time of testing	20	70
1920	1900	1850
1970	1950	1900

[a]Adapted from Baltes (1968) and Schaie (1965).

measurements (1920 and 1970). Comparisons within the rows of the table represent cross-sectional designs; those along the main diagonal represent longitudinal designs; a third basic design embedded in the data, the time-lag design, has never been discussed by developmental psychologists. It compares cohort differences at various times of testing within specific age groups, that is, within the two columns of the table.

None of these three basic developmental designs measures in an unconfounded manner either age, cohort, or historical time (time of testing) differences. An inspection of Table 2 shows that results from cross-sectional designs (CSD) confound age (AD) and cohort differences (CD); those from longitudinal designs (LOD) confound age (AD) and historical time differences (TD); those from time-lag designs (TLD) confound historical time (TD) and cohort differences (CD).

These conditions can be summarized in the following equations (Baltes, 1968, p. 156):

$$CSD = AD + CD$$
$$LOD = AD + TD$$
$$TLD = TD + CD$$

If we solve these equations for any one of the three right-hand terms, we obtain the following results:

$$AD = 1/2(CSD - TLD + LOD)$$
$$CD = 1/2(TLD - LOD + CSD)$$
$$TD = 1/2(LOD - CSD + TLD)$$

Thus, in principle it is possible to obtain estimates of the "pure" effects of age, cohort, or historical time differences, but such attempts will always have to rely on the joint utilization of all three basic designs. This conclusion has far-reaching implications for the scientific disciplines involved. Psychology may now justifiably describe developmental differences or changes, sociology may describe cohort or generational differences, and history may describe changes with chronological time.

But these disciplines should not remain in their isolation. An understanding of time and change can be achieved only if their contributions are recognized in their complementary determination. Each alone produces abstract results and fictitious interpretations.

B. Experiential Analysis of Changes in the Individual and Society

The solution proposed by modern research designs does not alter the procedures of psychological inquiries in any other significant way. It merely refines their analysis by considering the individual as changing in a changing world. Otherwise the same measurements and tests can be employed that have been used before and have degraded the human being to an object in the experimenter's hands. A farther reaching modification is necessary, one that reconstitutes the psychological subject's individuality and dignity.

Recently Kvale (1974) provided an insightful comparison of the concepts of time and change as explored by James, Husserl, and Merleau-Ponty. In opposition to the time atomism of British empiricism and the time universalism of French rationalism, James emphasized the stream of experience, which knows almost no boundaries and markings. Husserl, however, gave detailed attention to the momentary synchronic states as well as to their temporal blending in retrospection and prospection. The schema advocated by Kvale relies on an interpretation by Merleau-Ponty (1962) of Husserl's views and is graphically represented in Figure 4.

The horizontal line indicates the world line of a "retentionalizing" individual with three event markings, A, B, and C. The vertical lines at A and B represent some other world lines depicting the changing state of the memorized events. The process of recollection at the time of Events B and C is indicated by obliqued "now" lines. Thus, at the time of Event C, the previous B appears in retention as B', and the previous A appears as A''. From C, A is now seen through the intervening B'. As stated by Husserl (1964): "Retention itself is not an 'act' but a momentary consciousness of the phase which has expired and, at the same time, a foundation for the retentional consciousness of the next phase. Since each phase is retentionally cognizant of the preceding one, it encloses in itself, in a chain of mediate intentions, the entire series of retentions which have expired [p. 161−162]."

Figure 4 utilizes a two-dimensional time plot. Both dimensions represent changes in the individual, whereas in Figure 3 one coordinate designates the individual's

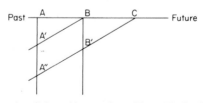

Fig. 4. Retentionalizing of impressions. [From Kvale, 1974, p. 16.]

development, the other the development of the cultural group. The horizontal dimension in Figure 4 represents the remembering individual who, in interaction with other individuals and social conditions, generates the occasions A, B, and C about which he or she may retrospect at this and later occasions. The vertical dimension represents the experienced events as they are changed in interaction with other events experienced either prior to or after they have occurred. The slanted now lines represent cross sections through the memory at particular moments in time. Underlying the representation of Figure 4 is the idea that memory, as well as the human being and society, is in a constant state of change (Kvale, 1975; Meacham, 1972, 1975, in press; Reese, 1976), and because of these changes earlier states can never be attained again. Any new experience alters the structure of the memory, every new event added onto the horizontal dimension extends the slanted now lines over a wider and wider range of past events.

The activities of an individual are determined not only by the interactions with co-occurring events and by the retentional interactions with events of the past, but also by the actor's intention.

> The unity of the present with the past is thus constituted by retentions, and at the forward end of the perceptual arc the protentions join the present to the future. When listening to an enduring tone I more or less implicitly expect it to continue, to change, or to stop, this expecting consciousness is an integral part of the consciousness of the tone. In its most basic form, a protention is an empty intention with an open indeterminateness, constituting the formal basis for eventual more explicit contextual expectations of what is coming [Kvale, 1974, p. 16].

The approach advocated by Kvale is diametrically opposed to the efforts by experimental psychologists and to the goals of developmental psychologists. Experimental psychologists have studied abstract performances or behaviors outside of their developmental and historical contexts. Developmental psychologists have attended to developmental differences and changes but have rarely explored the retrospective memories and the prospective intention of individuals. They have failed to recognize that most of these objectified expressions or products are experientially empty for the individual unless they are understood within the context of the individual's experienced past and anticipated future.

Historians, however, have always relied on recollections of past events. Thereby they have utilized whatever means are available, such as books, treatises, documents in archives or libraries, and advice from other experts, in order to reconstruct the past as accurately and comprehensively as possible. But their efforts are always hampered because the events to be reconstructed are rarely experienced by the historians themselves. They are made known to them through the mediation of other historians and, most important, through the intervention of other historical events. The source material has often been transmitted over long chains, which modify the sense of the reports to the same extent that the abstractness of psychological variables distorts the meaningfulness of developmental interpretations.

Having thus sharply constrasted the approach used by historians and by developmental psychologists, we ought to recognize that combinations have been sought. On the one hand, historians have encouraged the use of objective and quantitative data as collected by archivists and actuaries; on the other hand, historical methodology has been applied in clinical psychological studies and treatments. In particular, psychoanalytical explorations attempt to reconstruct a person's life in order to detect major choice points at which fateful turns were taken and thereby to enable the patients to reprocess their lives in a new and more successful manner (Erikson, 1968; Riegel, 1973a; Wyatt, 1962, 1963). Yet, by restricting these analyses to the personal lives of single individuals, these explorations lack interactive emphasis, just as they lack interindividual and intercultural systematizations. Our inquiries into the past of individuals and of society focus upon the interactive foundation of event sequences and attempt to reach higher levels of individual-psychological and cultural-sociological generality.

C. Reconstruction of Event Sequences

The method by which most of the following results were obtained (see Riegel, 1972b, 1973c) consists of asking persons to write down the names of all persons (relatives, friends, and acquaintances) they can remember within a time period of 10 minutes. At the end of this task, individuals are instructed to go through their lists once more and to indicate after each name the approximate year in which they met that person for the first time.

The data allow us to plot the number of persons recalled as a function of the individual's age. Thus we are studying the developing interaction of memory for persons and the recollecting individual's age status. As shown in Figure 5, individ-

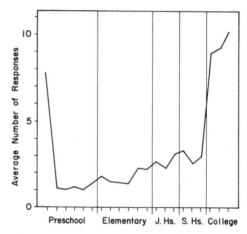

Fig. 5. Average number of persons (relatives, friends, acquaintances) named by 26 college juniors and seniors during a 10-minute period.

uals produce a great many names of persons whom they have met only during their most recent years. Persons who entered early into their lives are also listed frequently. A more detailed inquiry reveals, of course, that the latter are the members and friends of their own families.

The results of Figure 5 raise questions on how the individuals came to recollect the particular names they listed while rarely recalling those connected with intermediate periods of their lives. In order to provide such explanations, the psychologist has to compare the recall data with changes in the individual's cultural-sociological and outer-physical environment. Through means other than the individual's recollections, we would need to learn the names of persons who entered into his social and physical environments. This information could be obtained by asking his friends and relatives, for example; we could look into former school records or listings of tenants and home owners in the neighborhood; we could study census statistics about class sizes for various age groups and school sizes in various locations of the country. In other words, we could search for changes in the sociophysical environment of the developing individuals (Elder, 1974, 1977).

In contrast to psychology, reliable documentation in history is available on a selective basis only and, in most cases, has passed through the hands of many generations of intervening participants. If the methods of developmental psychology could be employed to explore the transformation of historical information, important inferences about the temporal organization of these cultural-sociological event sequences can be drawn (Meacham, 1972; Riegel, 1973c, 1976b). The following study demonstrates some of the issues implied.

I asked three groups of American college students (freshmen, seniors, and graduates) to write down the names of all historical figures influential in political, military, or governmental affairs which they could recall during a period of 10 minutes. The results of Figure 6 reveal, first, a strong recency effect. Many names

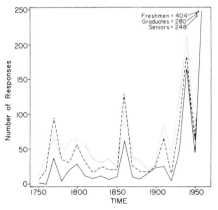

Fig. 6. Number of persons influential in political, military, and governmental affairs named by three groups of 30 students each during 10-minute periods: (———) freshmen; (———) seniors; (....) graduates. (From Riegel, 1976b, p. 240.)

of political figures were listed who entered history less than a few months prior to the study. Second, the earliest accumulation of names occurred for the time of the American Revolution, most notably because of the frequent listing of George Washington. The absence of a steep early accumulation indicates that history lacks an initiation or zero point comparable to the birth of the recalling individual, that is, to an event determined by the interaction of inner-biological and cultural-sociological progressions. American students compensated for this lack by considering the appearance of George Washington as the beginning of history. Thus, the "birth of a nation" is determined by an intracultural-sociological conflict between the British colonists and the American rebels. Third, Figure 6 shows the occurrence of sharp spikes, the first representing the time of the American Revolution, the others coinciding regularly with other major catastrophes, mainly the outbreak of wars. Thus, students seemed to view history as a progression of catastrophes. Of course, we may question the "validity" of their historical constructions, but I would rather propose to accept these lists at their face value, not because they described history as it "really" was, but because they reflected the students' interactions with their own cultural-sociological past. There may very well be other aspects to history that eventually need to be explored, but as long as these are not revealed through historical interpretations by the individual-psychological perceivers, they are of no value for any inquiry.

In further explorations of this issue, I compared the records produced by students with different degrees of education and, presumably, different degrees of historical knowledge. I expected that the more advanced students would show the spiking effect less strongly and would fill the gaps between the spikes more evenly with the names of historical figures not engaged in warfare and uprisings. However, this expectation was not clearly confirmed and, therefore, after two other attempts provided some suggestions but no definite conclusions about selective biases in historical recollection, I analyzed the most likely source of these biases, namely, the professional writing of political history. The results of Figure 7 were obtained from an analysis of an advanced high school book, *A History of the United States,* by Alden and Magenis (1962). They show the number of lines given to each of the decades after 1750 in a summary of historical events as well as the number of pages greater than two on which the names of historical figures appeared according to the index of the book. These results show more clearly than the listing of names by the students that the dominant emphasis given by the writers of this book, and presumably by the teachers who are using it, relates to military interventions and wars rather than to contributions in arts, sciences, education, and social welfare. Very marked spikes are observed for the time of the American Revolution, the Civil War, and World Wars I and II.

D. Dialectical Construction of History and Development

My comparisons demonstrate that history is always perceived and interpreted history. Let us consider the famous example of Caesar crossing the Rubicon during

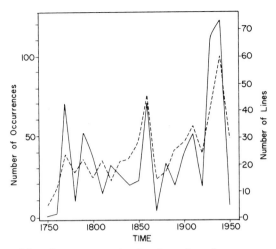

Fig. 7. Number of lines in a summary (--) and number of names appearing in a book on American history (——). (From Riegel, 1976b, p. 242.)

his march on Rome in the year 49 B.C. This event must have been quite accurately reported. After all, if a few days earlier Caesar was found to the north of the river and a few days later to the south, he could not have avoided the crossing. But regardless of how accurately these outer-physical "facts" were recorded, their description does not give them the status of a historical event. Only the interpretation of these steps by the historical perceiver who interprets them in view of the cultural-sociological consequences, that is, as leading to civil war and to the downfall of the earlier form of Roman government, assigns historical status to them.

Our inability to learn "how it really was in history" (von Ranke, 1885) should disturb us as little as our failure, according to Kant, to recognize "the thing as such." As shown in Figure 8, history as it really was is hidden behind a series of interpretive filters at the cultural-sociological level, filters that are formed through the selective preservation of information by archivists, the insufficient scrutiny of scholars, the driving brevity of teachers, and the unchallengeable apathy of students. But even if we were able to look behind all these filters, we would not find what we were hoping for, because the outer-physical events in their infinity and details—such as those involved in the crossing of the Rubicon—are irrelevant and uninteresting to the observer. They are without historical meaning.

Denoting these interpretations as selective filters is misleading, however. A filter presupposes something behind it, "the historical thing as such," which—it is insisted—makes historical interpretations possible at all. A filter selects essential issues from unessential details but presupposes something that is being filtered and recognized in some of its grosser features. Such an approach searches for the facts behind historical interpretations and claims to be objective. Although few would

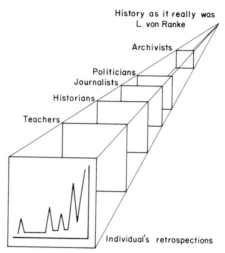

Fig. 8. Representation of historical schemata of interpretations. (From Riegel, 1976b, p. 244.)

question that there exist outer-physical events, a historian only can find behind a historical filter another filter and another filter.

As a solution for the historian's dilemma, we need to think of such a selective filter as a sudarium, similar to the holy veil of Saint Veronica which, when laid upon the face of the dying Christ, is said to have preserved his image forever. Every interpretation derived from looking at or through the sudarium thereafter imposed the image of Christ upon the events studied. Unlike a history derived from the notion of historical filters, the concept of the sudarium proposes a "constructive" interpretation of history that is predominantly concerned with the relationships of the interpreting sudaria to one another. The systematic study of their cultural-sociological transformations and of the invariant properties sustaining these transformations represents the most profound inquiry into history (Riegel, 1976b).

With recognition of the constructive viewpoint, we apprehend both the normative character and the future dimensionality of history. As a person's development is directed by and based upon wishes, expectations, and hope at the individual-psychological level, so are historical changes determined by standards, values, and goals at the cultural-sociological level. If we recognize that our interpretations of history are dominated by apocalyptic views, emphasizing warfares and catastrophes at the expense of welfare, arts, and sciences, we have also gained insights and access to alternative conceptualizations. By exploring these options in discussions, lectures, and writings, we generate a new sudarium, a new interpretation of history, a new conception of man and his development. As emphatically claimed by Lynd (1968), the recognition of new interpretations and the awareness of former fallacies should lead us to the implementation or enactment of history. The historian participates in creating history.

It is perhaps not surprising that psychologists have shown little appreciation for the forward-directedness of knowledge. Like objective historians, developmental psychologists have continued, for example, to screen the individual's behavior through their filters in order to detect "development as it really is." Endless and mostly futile efforts have been invested in refining the methodologies and increasing the abstract quality of theoretical constructs. Little do developmental psychologists apprehend that the most important topic of their inquiry ought to be the changes in experienced and lived development both from an individual-psychological and a cultural-sociological point of view.

As much as the acquisition of advanced historical awareness begins to change history itself, so does an awareness of development change the course of this development. Rather than apprehending our societal origin and cultural history by the products generated, we need to appreciate history by the activities that force it into new directions. Development of the individual, likewise, should no longer be apprehended by the products left behind, such as achievements and test scores, but by the critical awareness of past experiences that remain with the individual and direct him toward his future. What we desire is neither a history of past relics and documents, most often demonstrating our failures and insufficiencies, nor a developmental psychology of petrified performances and test records, but a science of the interactive development of the individual and society based upon lived experiences and directed actions.

E. Conclusions

Some theoretical issues in the study of individual-psychological and cultural-sociological event sequences have been discussed and methodological suggestions for their analysis have been made. The methodologies are based upon traditional historical explorations applied to the study of the individual in the form of biographical inquiries or controlled recall experiments. Both approaches need to be supplemented by sociological and anthropological investigations.

This section introduced additional material for a dialectical analysis of time. This material consists of long-term retrospective individual-psychological and cultural-sociological data but not of information about short-term time perception and cognition. Also information on the inner-biological bases of temporal orders was disregarded. As regrettable as these limitations must appear, such restrictions serve best to introduce some theoretical conclusions about the dialectical concept of time.

V. The Structure of Event Sequences

In searching for a systematic interpretation of temporal structures, we will briefly consider some properties of the structure of musical compositions, and of narratives and dialogues. We will conclude our discussion with a comparison of the three major time concepts, that is, relational, absolute, and dialectical time, and with a general comparison of formal and dialectical logic.

A. Temporal Structure of Music[4]

When two pure sound waves are simultaneously produced, the combination is occasionally pleasing to the ear, that is, is experienced as consonance. More often, however, the impression is one of unpleasant roughness, that is, as dissonance. Helmholtz systematically combined sound waves of different frequency (pitch) with one another by having one violinist hold the lowest C' constant while another, starting in unison, increased the pitch over two octaves to C'''. The values on the ordinate of Figure 9 indicate the judged roughness of the corresponding pitch intervals. The unison, the fifth, and the octave seem to be completely free from dissonance, and "the more perfect the consonance of an interval the more sharply it is bounded by dissonance, so that a mistuned minor third is much less dissonant than a mistuned octave or a mistuned fifth—or, of course, a mistuned unison [Wood, 1965, p. 158]."

An explanation of dissonance relies on variations in loudness of superimposed tones. If two waves are in perfect agreement, compressions and rarefactions arrive together and are perceived as louder than either one of the two sounds alone. If the frequency of one wave is slightly increased, its sounds arrive faster at the ear than those of the other wave. In the course of this process, both will be at times in perfect opposition. As the compression of one arrives at the same time as the rarefaction from the other, the two sound waves will cancel each other out. This creates the impression of a beat whose frequency is equal to the difference in frequency between the two sound waves. When the difference is small (5 or 6 per second) the result is pleasing to the ear; when the difference is larger, the experience is less pleasant.

As this example demonstrates, the organization of time is brought about by the interdependence of at least two event sequences. If these event sequences are pure sound waves, their particular interactions create the experience of beats and, thereby, of temporal order. Without this order there would merely be the sensation of a continuous sound, which, after a while, would cease to register with a perceiver. Only when the sound is interrupted do we suddenly recognize it again. Music is made up of tones that in their interactions either create these interruptions or are interrupted, according to the choice of the composer, by accent, rhythm, and pauses.

Since preceding sounds always reverberate, and are in "holding" patterns, they blend into following ones (and vice versa), and thus, temporal impressions of

---

[4]When this chapter was finalized, I became aware of the work by Zuckerkandl (1956, 1973), which very much supports the viewpoints presented here.

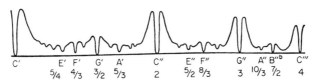

Fig. 9. Roughness of intervals on violin. The lowest C on the violin is held steady on one instrument while the other, starting from unison, glides slowly up through two octaves. The distance of the curve from the axis indicates the roughness of the corresponding interval.

consonance or dissonance are created even in the monophonic arrangements of simple songs. However, modern music achieved its impressive development only when, during the course of its more recent history, complex arrangements were introduced by interlacing different voices or instruments and thereby having them perform either in unison, harmony, or deviation from one another. In polyphonic compositions different sequences, by interacting with one another, create temporal markings and structure.

We can look at polyphonic compositions in two ways, in a cross-sectional or perpendicular manner and in a longitudinal or horizontal manner. In the former, we recognize a multitude of chords which are the elements of harmony. In the latter way, we recognize

a series of layers or strata of tone, i.e., . . . several melodies superimposed.. A choral conductor, if handed a new part-song and told he would have to begin to train his choir in it five minutes hence, would be likely to . . . mentally run through the music, noting how the voice-parts weave in and out, one ceasing for a moment and another entering, one holding a long note while others are engaged with a number of shorter notes, and so forth. On the other hand, the pianist who was to accompany the choir would be likely to look at the music as a series of successive handfuls of notes, observing the nature of the groups of notes to be simultaneously sounded, the way in which these carried the music into new keys. . . , and so forth. In other words, whilst the conductor was engaged in *contrapuntal* exploration the pianist would be engaged very largely in harmonic exploration [Scholes, 1970, p. 441].

In polyphonic compositions various instruments create musical "event sequences" which, by elaborating or supporting a melody, might occasionally be in unison, frequently in harmony, but most often in tension. Such a composition is comparable to the network of event sequences that characterize both the single individual's development and that of various individuals or groups in their temporal interactions. It is comparable, for example, to the individual's attempt to synchronize his wishes with his duties, his affects with his skills, his movements with his thoughts. It is comparable to the attempts by different individuals to synchronize their interests and tasks, for example, in the family, in school, at the job, in a club, and so on.

B. Temporal Structure of Narratives and Dialogues

According to W. Wundt (1911–1912), the most fundamental problem of language consists of the transformation of sets of coexisting ideas into the sequential order of linguistic expressions. This problem is not narrowly restricted to language and to the common contrast between semantic and syntactic organization, but is of much greater generality. It touches upon the simultaneity and sequential order of thought, upon the harmonic and contrapuntal structure of music, upon the synchronic logical and the developmental dialectical analysis in sciences, and, basically, upon the distinction between the concepts of space and time.

The problem encountered is a familiar one to the writer and historian. In particular, Carlyle is credited with handling these difficulties in an eloquent manner, as stated by Clive (1969):

> In ordinary narrative history, "A" occurs; then "B" occurs (possibly, but not necessarily, caused by "A"); then "C" happens, etc. This, of course, is a false rendering of actuality, since not only do many other events transpire simultaneously, along with "A", "B", and "C"; but it is also true that "A", "B", and "C", like all historical events, are anchored in the past and have repercussions in the future. The historian's usual means of dealing with this basic problem is to make use of phrases such as "meanwhile", "at the same time", "while this was happening here, that was happening there"; and to spell out, in so many words, both the background and the aftermath of the events he is narrating.
>
> The trouble with these stylistic devices is that they completely fail to capture the historical *process,* in which nothing is stationary, and everything is constantly in motion and in flux, in which growth and decay proceed at the same time; in which events do not occur in isolation, but are related to each other in a constantly shifting network of interconnections. What Carlyle does is not to evade this problem, but to face it head on, by using linguistic and literary devices to create the equivalent of living reality [p. xxxvi. Reprinted from *Thomas Carlyle: History of Frederick the Great,* J. Clive, editor. By permission of The University of Chicago Press. © 1969 by University of Chicago.]

The temporal structure of narratives has recently been analyzed by Labov and Waletzky (1967). Like Wundt, these authors consider the task of narration as one of transforming a set of simultaneous states of objects into a structure sequentially ordered within itself as well as transformationally related to the external conditions it aims to describe. Thus a narrative coordinates a set of nonlinguistic event states with a sequence of linguistic expressions. The latter imposes temporal order upon the former, which by themselves might be, in their temporal organization, unintelligible to an outside observer. In trying to maximize these transformational aspects in controlled tasks, Linde and Labov (1975) asked individuals to describe, for example, the layout of their apartments (coexisting spatial conditions) in narrative form (sequential description of spatial conditions).

Narratives are produced only if there are listeners to listen or readers to read. These listeners and readers remain relatively passive and rarely interact with the producer of the story. This restriction is eliminated if both the narrator and the listener shift into an exchange of dialogue. In this case either one of the two might tell the other about a different series of events that he has experienced or both might refer to the same series, and their dialogue will elaborate these events in the form of alternative interpretations. Thus the dialogue does not only represent a sequential coordination of a series of event states with the narration of the speaker, but also deals with the coordination of the two speakers' performances with one another.

A dialogue has sequential structure because the speakers alternate in their presentations and because each successive statement has to reflect at least one immediately preceding it. Restricting the range of statements to this degree represents a minimum requirement for a dialogue. The maximum requirement would be attained if every utterance were to reflect all the earlier statements. Every statement would have to be consistent with the proponent's own previously expressed views and must also represent an equally consistent or systematically modified reaction to all statements made by the other participant in the dialogue.

Thus, the simplest form of a dialogue is one in which each of the two speakers always relates his new statement to both the last statement made by his opponent and to that made by the speaker himself. In such a *simple dialogue,* every statement is connected with the last two preceding ones:

$$A_1 \longrightarrow A_2 \longrightarrow A_3 \longrightarrow A_4$$
$$B_1 \longrightarrow B_2 \longrightarrow B_3$$

In successful dialogues each speaker assimilates the other person's statements and accommodates his own productions so that they elaborate and extend the preceding viewpoints. If this were not the case, dialogues would either degenerate into what Piaget (1926) has called collective monologues or would converge into a repetitive cycle in which each speaker merely reaffirms what has been said before. Like the triangular subsection in the truss of a bridge, and the recurrence of a theme, a melody, or a rhythm in musical compositions, repetitive or recursive operations are necessary because they provide stability and a transitory thread to a narrative or dialogue. But neither of these performances can subsist on recursive production alone. The melody has to be varied and the cycle has to be broken by contrastive operations (Riegel, 1974) through which the topic is either moved into new divergent directions or converges upon (is integrated with) previously made presentations.

The development of dialogues during infancy depends on shared knowledge about extralingual objects and events and personal states and wishes. Its beginnings can be traced through the changing relationship between mother and child. Prior to birth the two are firmly coupled with one another by their joint physiology. After birth this relationship, though disrupted, continues to function in unison for a while like the two clocks in Leibniz's demonstration of *preestablished harmony.* But increasingly with age, coordination will depend upon the mother's and the child's experiences and actions through which the child's and the mother's operations become finely tuned to one another. The child begins to look at the mother's face. When she moves, the child follows her with his eyes. When she speaks, the child might look at her mouth. When she stops, the child might vocalize and switch his attention from her mouth to her eyes (Lewis & Freedle, 1972). The development of dialogues thereby leads to interactive temporal coordination of activities and represents an important step in the development of the time concept.

The communication system shared by mother and child is at first private to both of them. As development advances, the signs become congruent with the general linguistic system of the society. In this developmental task, the mother functions as an intermediary between her child and society. Thus, the developmental dialogue is more than an exchange between two individuals; society and history, through the mother, participate in it.

Similar arguments can be made for the more remote interactions between authors and their readers (Riegel, 1976a). The author's task consists of transmitting to the reader the knowledge and values that have been generated in the society throughout its history. Thus, the author, like the mother, functions as an intermediary between the knowledge- and direction-seeking individual and the ideas and values of the society; he transforms the information at the cultural-sociological level in order to make it understandable and useful for the individual.

Most important to the author's and mother's task is the synchronization of their efforts with those of the reader and the child, respectively. Information has to be given at the right moment, in the right amount, and of the right kind. The author may become too abstract and remote; he may progress too fast or lag behind. The mother, in a more concrete sense, has to speak as she influences her child, but she also has to listen and change her own activities in accordance with the development of her child. The development of the child and of the mother are constituted by the synchronization of their activities. Synchronization produces temporal structure.

C. Relational, Absolute, and Dialectical Time

At the beginning of this chapter, I compared the concepts of time with different concepts of space. According to one of the earliest philosophical viewpoints, space was negatively defined as that domain which was not filled with substances (objects); space was regarded as a void. Comparable to this concept, time could be regarded as that stretch which is not filled with events; thus, time would be negatively defined by events. However, events imply action and therefore reflect a higher degree of organization than do substances in space (provided that only their distribution and not their internal structures are considered). A concept of time based on a series of events has been called relational.

Like a musical theme or a passage in a narrative, relational time arises as a consequence of serial interactions between events. In a simple monophonic melody, for example, it is produced by the contrast between preceding and following sounds and sound groupings. The temporal structures of individual experiences and cultural representations, likewise, are based upon variations of event sequences. Since these event sequences usually involve the movement of objects (or substances) in space, relational time compounds the three basic concepts of classical natural sciences and philosophy: substance, space, and time. It relies on the notion of activity as the most basic property of nature.

While relational time is intrinsically defined (not necessarily in the experience of the observer only but by the overt order of the events), absolute time is "regarded as constitutive of nature . . . it regulates the rates of processes . . . [and] is physically prior to events [Fraser, 1967, p. 835]." Thus, absolute time is extrinsically defined. It represents the most abstract form of conceptualization. In music, for example, it is superimposed by means of the clicks of the metronome during rehearsal and by the meter and the bar lines on the score sheets.

Dialectical time, finally, is both intrinsically and extrinsically determined. It is comparable to polyphonic compositions and therefore incorporates a diversity of monophonic or relational sequences. It also incorporates absolute time because polyphonic music too may rely upon an extrinsic yardstick which assists in the synchronization of the different instruments or voices. (This yardstick represents—we should note—one particular monophonic structure which has been elevated to serve as a uniform standard.) The dialectical concept indicates that common or scientific experience of time involves the interaction of at least two event sequences, for example, the phenomena observed and the measurement taken.

Aside from multiple interactions, the dialectical concept of time emphasizes concrete experiences and events. As these lead to the formation of conflicts and resolutions, questions and answers, disharmonies and harmonies, temporal markings, produced by the synchronization of these sequences, are generated. These temporal markings, knots, or points of coincidence represent transitions in the sequence of qualitative changes. Harmonies and disharmonies represent momentary states in a flux of changes. They resemble simultaneous structures that lack temporal extension and are similar to semantic fields in distinction from syntactic orders. These harmonies and disharmonies merge into the temporal organization of melodies. The contrastive comparison between simultaneous spatial conditions and developmental temporal changes elucidates the basic properties of the dialectical concept of time.

Several other conditions demonstrate the contrast between relational and absolute time, on the one hand, and dialectical time, on the other. For example, a dialectical interpretation confounds the concepts of relational and absolute substance (matter) and space with that of time. Such an integration has been promoted in electromagnetic field theory, quantum theory, and relativity theory. Similar conclusions have been reached for the concept of "inertia." As analyzed by Fraser (1967), inertia, in classical physics, has an absolute character intrinsic to matter. Matter is thought to be identifiable without regard to the rest of the world. Like space and time it therefore constitutes a prerequisite for the structure of the physical world. Consistent with what is called Mach's Principle, inertia may also be regarded as a relational entity if the interaction of local matter with all matter of the universe is taken into consideration. A dialectical interpretation would integrate both concepts.

This analysis of inertia, moreover, parallels the comparison between endogenous and exogenous biological clocks.

> The existence of a purely endogenous clock could only be proved in an empty universe without history, the existence of a purely exogenous clock could be proved only if it had no potentially rhythmic internal structure. In practice, the temporal nature of the biological clock must be conceived of as a relationship between its physical self and the world. For convenience, this relationship may be imagined as the fusion of two abstract clocks, an endogenous and an exogenous one. . . . [Thus] absolute and relational inertia, on the one hand, and endogenous and exogenous clocks, on the other hand, are conceptually similar pairs of abstraction. The inertial properties of real matter and the time-keeping properties of real biological clocks are neither of relational nor of absolute nature. . . . They may be better described as being both [Fraser, 1967, p. 835].

Because we cannot resolve such a contradiction in our two-valued Aristotelian logic, this conclusion creates some rather serious problems. All that we can do is to contemplate about the "nature outside of us *or* about our own nature. The glorified formulation to discriminate between subject-object, true-false, body-mind, real-illusion, etc. compels us to perceive-conceive a dual and contradictory character of experience [Fischer, 1967, p. 457]." In our two-valued Aristotelian logic we cannot apprehend that something is both subject and object, true and false, body and mind, real and illusion at one and the same time. In order to develop such notions we have to adopt a multivalued logic, such as dialectical logic.

D. Formal and Dialectical Logic

Traditional logic, as well as traditional philosophy and science, have been exclusively concerned with nontemporal, static conditions. The concept of a nonchanging state of being, as originated within Eleatic philosophy, was thought to reflect the universal order of the cosmos. Traditional logic and mathematics are the remnants of the adevelopmental and ahistorical thinking of Eleatic philosophers.

In his studies of music, Pythagoras began to explore temporal relations. However, being restricted to monophonic music and the simultaneous occurrence of single sounds, but not of chords, his studies were limited and culminated once more in the "detecting" some universal atemporal acoustic lawfulness. Only when the complex temporal structures of polyphonic orchestration began to dominate musical compositions did a new sense of temporal organization emerge.

Still, today, our concept of time is limited. Our sciences, founded as they are upon formal logic, deal exclusively with spatial structures. Even when Galileo investigated the laws of gravity and Newton the laws of motion, the procedure was to measure the spatial conditions at some time slices and then to infer the temporal relations afterward in a second step. But, as cogently argued by Günther (1967),

... the scientific development leading from Archimedes to Einstein was accompanied by a parallel trend—the history of dialectic logic. And dialectic logic poses an entirely different question. Its first concern is not the relation of Time to Being, but the relation of Time to Logic itself. It can be shown that the discussion of Time on the basis of natural science remained incomplete and insufficient because it ignored the dialectic aspect [p. 397].

Dialectical logic, comparable to polyphonic musical compositions, is more than a counterpart to formal logic. Just as the movements in music are built upon simultaneous slices in the sequence of changes, so does dialectical thinking presuppose formal logical structures. Dialectical logic recognizes that it cannot exist without formal logic. This recognition provides a more general basis to dialectical logic than is available to formal logic. Formal logic fails to recognize such mutuality and is bound to consider itself immutable. Dialectical logic represents an open system of thinking that can always be extended to incorporate more restricted systems. Formal logic aims at a single universal analysis. As a consequence it is inflexible and primarily concerned with static conditions. Formal logic cannot apprehend itself. In particular, it cannot apprehend itself in the developmental and historical process.[5]

The development of dialectical logic, especially by Hegel, has not been commonly accepted in the natural sciences (at least not in classical natural sciences), and most suprisingly, it has received even lesser attention in the behavioral and social sciences. Since—as it has been convincingly demonstrated by Kosok (1976)—dialectical logic can be cast into a systematic language that makes it applicable to sciences, and since dialectical logic is the mode of thinking that alone can deal appropriately with change, development, and history, its disregard or neglect is regrettable indeed. Nevertheless, both its rapidly growing appreciation in the natural sciences and the similar, if belated, recognition of its significance among behavioral and social scientists (Buck-Morss, 1975; Buss, 1975; Freedle, in press;

---

[5] Similar limitations hold for existentialism and phenomenology. These philosophies too (with some notable exceptions, e.g., Gadamer, 1960, and Merleau-Ponty, 1963) regard "being" as primary and "becoming" (which the individual completes) as secondary. While there is a shared concern for the concrete experience of the individual, dialectics emphasize human activities (rather than contemplations) in their interactional determination during developmental and historical processes. Thus, dialectics goes only part of the way with Schaltenbrands, (1967) conclusion, that modern man "instead of seeing his living existence . . . sees himself as a kind of albumleaf in a herbarium, dried and pinned onto the abstract scheme of the flow of time. . . . Because he considers time as a stretch, the present as zero, and events ordered by deterministic laws, he has no time to exist. Consequently, he can see himself and the world only from a historical point of view. He is, so to speak, already dead and his future is, also, already dead [p. 643]." While dialectics would agree with the notion that time, as conceived in classical natural sciences, "evolves from the codification of events interfering with living presence, or is created by acts of the present [p. 641]," it does not subscribe to the view that living presence is itself timeless. Quite to the contrary, dialecticians maintain that the living presence is experienced as movement and action, which create and within which is reflected the living past and the anticipated future both of the individual and of society.

Harris, 1977; Lawler, 1975; Meacham & Riegel, in press; Mitroff & Betz, 1972; Riegel, 1975b, 1976a, 1976b; Rychlak, 1976; Wozniak, 1975a, 1975b) indicate that a decisive change is in the making. In pursuit of this goal, the present chapter has attempted to explore a dialectical concept of time and its potential application to the behavioral and social sciences.

REFERENCES

Alden, J. R., & Magenis, A. *A history of the United States.* New York: American Book Co., 1962.

Algazel. *Tahafot Al-Falasifat* (M. Bouygens, Ed.). Beirut: S.J., 1927.

Bachelard, G. *La dialectique de la duree.* Paris: Presses Universitaires de France, 1972.

Baltes, P. B. Longitudinal and cross-sectional sequences in the study of age and generation effects. *Human Development,* 1968, **11,** 145–171.

Birren, J. E. Principles of research on aging. In J. E. Birren (Ed.), *Handbook of aging and the individual.* Chicago: University of Chicago Press, 1959. Pp. 3–42.

Boring, E. G. *A history of experimental psychology* (2nd ed.). New York: Appleton, 1957.

Buck-Morss, S. Socio-economic bias in Piaget's theory and its implications for the cross-cultural controversy. *Human Development,* 1975, **18,** 35–49.

Buss, A. R. The emerging field of the sociology of psychological knowledge. *American Psychologist,* 1975, **30,** 988–1002.

Carnap, R. *Der logische Aufbau der Welt.* Hamburg: Meiner, 1928. (*Logical structure of the world.* Berkeley: University of California Press, 1967.)

Cassirer, E. *Substanzbegriff and Funktionsbegriff.* Berlin: B. Cassirer, 1910. (*Substance and function and Einstein's theory of relativity.* Chicago: Open Court Publ. 1923.)

Clark, H. H. Space, time, semantics, and the child. In T. E. Moore (Ed.), *Cognitive development and the acquisition of language.* New York: Academic Press, 1973. Pp. 27–63.

Clive, J. (Ed.). *Thomas Carlyle: History of Frederick the Great.* Chicago: University of Chicago Press, 1969.

Cohen, D. *Time as energy: On the application of modern concepts of time to developmental sciences.* Unpublished manuscript, University of Southern California, Gerontology Center, 1972.

Elder, G. H., Jr. *Children of the great depression.* Chicago: University of Chicago Press, 1974.

Elder, G. H., Jr. Adolescence in the life course. In S. Dragastin & G. H. Elder, Jr. (Eds.), *Adolescence in the life cycle.* Washington, D.C.: Hemisphere Halstead, 1975.

Elder, G. H., Jr. Family history and the life course. *Journal of Family History,* 1977, **1,**

Erikson, E. H. *Identity, youth and crises.* New York: Norton, 1968.

Fischer, R. The biological fabric of time. *Annals of the New York Academy of Sciences,* 1967, **138,** 440–488.

Fraser, J. T. *The voices of time.* New York: Braziller, 1966.

Fraser, J. T. The interdisciplinary study of time. *Annals of the New York Academy of Sciences,* 1967, **138,** 822–847.

Fraser, J. T. *Of time, passion, and knowledge.* New York: Braziller, 1975.

Freedle, R. Human development, the new logical systems, and general systems theory: Preliminaries to developing a psycho-social linguistics. In G. Steiner (Ed.), *The psychology of the 20th century* (Vol. 7), *Piaget's developmental and cognitive psychology within an extended context.* Zurich: Kindler, in press.

Gadamer, H. G. *Wahrheit und Methode.* Tübingen: Mohr, 1960. (*Truth and method.* New York: Seabury Press, 1975.)

Günther, G. Time, timeless logic, and self-referential systems. *Annals of the New York Academy of Sciences,* 1967, **138**, 396–406.

Günther, G. & von Foerster, H. The logical structure of evolution and emanation. *Annals of the New York Academy of Sciences,* 1967, **138**, 874–891.

Harris, A. E. *Dialectics: A paradigm for social sciences.* Book in preparation, 1977.

Hegel, G. W. F. *Wissenschaft der Logik.* Frankfurt a.M.: Suhrkamp, 1969. (*Science of logic.* London: Allen & Unwin, 1929.)

Hoagland, H. The physiological control of judgments of duration: Evidence for a chemical clock. *Journal of General Psychology,* 1933, **9**, 267–287.

Hoagland, H. The pacemaker of human brain waves in normals and in general paretics. *American Journal of Physiology,* 1936, **116**, 604–615.

Hölder, O. Die Axiome der Quantität und die Lehre vom Mass. *Berichte der Sächsischen Gesellschaft der Wissenschaften, Leipzig, Mathematische-Physikalische Klasse.* 1901, **53**, 1–64.

Husserl, E. *The phenomenology of internal time consciousness.* The Hague: Nijhoff, 1964.

Jammer, M. *The concepts of space.* New York: Harper, 1954.

Kety, S. s. Human cerebral blood flow and oxygen consumption as related to aging. *Journal of Chronic Diseases,* 1956, **3**, 478–486.

Kosok, M. The systematization of dialectical logic for the study of development and change. *Human Development,* 1976, **19**, 325–350.

Krüger, F. E. *Uber Entwicklungspsychologie, ihre sachliche und geschichtliche Notwendigkeit.* Leipzig: Engelmann, 1915.

Kvale, S. The temporality of memory. *Journal of Phenomenological Research,* 1974, **5**, 7–31.

Kvale, S. Memory and dialectics: Some reflections on Ebbinghaus and Mao Tse-Tung. *Human Development,* 1975, **18**, 205–222.

Labov, W., & Waletzky, J. Narrative analysis: Oral versions of personal experience. In J. P. Helm (Ed.), *Essays on verbal and visual arts.* Seattle: University of Washington Press, 1967. Pp. 12–44.

Lawler, J. Dialectic philosophy and developmental psychology: Hegel and Piaget on contradiction. *Human Development,* 1975, **18**, 1–17.

Lewis, M., & Freedle, R. *Mother-infant dyad: The cradle of meaning* (Research Bulletin 72-22). Princeton: Educational Testing Service, 1972.

Linde, C., & Labov, W. Spatial networks as a site for the study of language and thought. *Language,* 1975, **51**, 924–939.

Lynd, S. Historical past and existential present. In T. Roszak (Ed.), *The dissenting academy.* New York: Pantheon Books, 1968. Pp. 101–109.

Meacham, J. A. The development of memory abilities in the individual and society. *Human Development,* 1972, **15**, 205–228.

Meacham, J. A. Patterns of memory abilities in two cultures. *Developmental Psychology,* 1975, **11**, 50–53.

Meacham, J. A. Soviet investigations of memory development. In R. V. Kail & J. W. Hagen (Eds.), *Perspectives on the development of memory and cognition.* Hillsdale, N.J.: Lawrence Erlbaum Associates, in press.

Meacham, J. A., & Riegel, K. F. The final period of cognitive development: Dialectic operations. In G. Steiner (Ed.), *The Psychology of the 20th century* (Vol. 7), *Piaget's developmental and cognitive psychology within an extended context.* Zurich: Kindler, in press.

Merleau-Ponty, M. *The phenomenology of perception.* London: Routledge & Kegan Paul, 1962.

Merleau-Ponty, M. *The structure of behavior.* Boston: Beacon Press, 1963.

Mitroff, I. I., & Betz, F. Dialectic decision theory: A metatheory of decision making. *Management Science,* 1972, **19**, 11–24.

Piaget, J. *The language and thought of the child.* New York: Harcourt, 1926.

Piaget, J. *The child's conception of movement and speed.* New York: Ballantine, 1970. (a)

Piaget, J. *The child's conception of time.* New York: Ballantine, 1970. (b)

Piaget, J., & Inhelder, B. *The child's conception of space.* London: Routledge & Kegan Paul, 1956.

Popper, K. Letter to the editors: Irreversible processes in physical theory. *Nature,* 1958, **181,** 402–403.

Reese, H. W. Models of memory development. *Human Development,* 1976, **19,** 291–303.

Reichenbach, H. *Philosophie der Raum-Zeit-Lehre.* Berlin: Gruyter, 1928. (*The philosophy of space and time.* New York: Dover, 1958.)

Reichenbach, M., & Mathern, A. The place of time and aging in the natural sciences and scientific philosophy. In J. E. Birren (Ed.), *Handbook of aging and the individual.* Chicago: Chicago University Press, 1959. Pp. 43–80.

Riegel, K. F. The influence of economic and political ideologies upon the development of developmental psychology. *Psychological Bulletin,* 1972, **78,** 129–141. (a)

Riegel, K. F. Time and change in the development of the individual and society. In H. Reese (Ed.), *Advances in child development and behavior* (Vol. 7). New York: Academic Press, 1972. Pp. 81–113. (b)

Riegel, K. F. Developmental psychology and society: Some historical and ethical considerations. In J. R. Nesselroade & H. W. Reese (Eds.), *Life-span developmental psychology: Methodological issues.* New York: Academic Press, 1973. Pp. 1–23. (a)

Riegel, K. F. Dialectic operations: The final period of cognitive development. *Human Development,* 1973, **16,** 346–370. (b)

Riegel, K. F. The recall of historical events. *Behavioral Science,* 1973, **18,** 354–363. (c)

Riegel, K. F. *Contrastive and recursive relations* (Research Memorandum RM-74-23). Princeton: Educational Testing Service, 1974.

Riegel, K. F. Adult life crises: Toward a dialectic theory of development. In N. Datan & L. H. Ginsberg (Eds.), *Life-span developmental psychology: Normative life crises.* New York: Academic Press, 1975, Pp. 99–128. (a)

Riegel, K. F. (Ed.). *The development of dialectical operations.* Basel: Karger, 1975. (b)

Riegel, K. F. Toward a dialectical theory of development. *Human Development,* 1975, **18,** 50–64. (c)

Riegel, K. F. From traits and equilibrium toward developmental dialectics. In W. J. Arnold & J. K. Cole (Eds.), *Nebraska Symposium on Motivation.* Lincoln: University of Nebraska Press, 1976. Pp. 349–407. (a)

Riegel, K. F. *The psychology of development and history.* New York: Plenum Press, 1976. (b)

Rychlak, J. F. (Ed.). *Dialectic: Humanistic rationale for behavior and development.* Basel: Karger, 1976.

Schaie, K. W. A general model for the study of developmental problems. *Psychological Bulletin,* 1965, **64,** 92–107.

Schaltenbrand, G. Consciousness and time. *Annals of the New York Academy of Sciences,* 1967, **138,** 632–645.

Scholes, P. A. *The Oxford compendium to music* (10th ed.). London & New York: Oxford University Press, 1970.

Stevens, S. S. Mathematics, measurement, and psychophysics. In S. S. Stevens (Ed.), *Handbook of experimental psychology.* New York: Wiley, 1951, Pp. 1–49.

von Ranke, L. *Geschichte der romanischen und germanischen Völker von 1494 bis 1514* (3. Aufl.). Leipzig: Duncker & Humblot, 1885.

Wallis, R. Time—Fourth dimension of the mind. *Annals of the New York Academy of Sciences,* 1967 **138,** 784–797.

Whitrow, G. J. Some reflections on the problem of memory. *Annals of the New York Academy of Sciences,* 1967, **138,** 856–861.

Wood, A. *The physics of music.* London: Methuen, 1965.

Wozniak, R. H. A dialectic paradigm for psychological research: Implications drawn from the history of psychology in the Soviet Union. *Human Development,* 1975, **18,** 18–34. (a)

Wozniak, R. H. Dialecticism and structuralism: The philosophical foundation of Soviety psychology and Piagetian cognitive developmental theory. In K. F. Riegel & G. C. Rosenwald (Eds.), *Structure and transformations: Developmental and historical aspects.* New York: Wiley, 1975. Pp. 25–47. (b)

Wundt, M. *Hegel's Logik und die moderne Physik.* Köln: Westdeutscher Verlag, 1949.

Wundt, W. *Völkerpsychologie* (Bd. 1 & 2), *Die Sprache.* Leipzig: Engelmann, 1911–1912.

Wyatt, F. A psychologist looks at history. *Journal of Social Issues,* 1962, 18, 65–77.

Wyatt, F. The reconstruction of the individual and collective past. In R. W. White (Ed.), *The study of lives: Essays on personality in honor of Henry A. Murray.* New York: Atherton Press, 1963. Pp. 305–320.

Zuckerkandl, V. *Sound and symbol.* Princeton: Princeton University Press, 1956.

Zuckerkandl, V. *Man the musician.* Princeton: Princeton University Press, 1973.

CHAPTER 2

After the Apple:
Post-Newtonian Metatheory for Jaded Psychologists

NANCY DATAN

WEST VIRGINIA UNIVERSITY
MORGANTOWN, WEST VIRGINIA

> What a friend we have in time,
> Gives us children, gives us wine.
> Folk Song

I. Quantum Mechanics: The Temptation and the Fall

There is a world as real as poetry to us which has no color, is not warm or cold, and is quite silent. This is the world of atomic physics, which is known to us through our prosthetic sense organs, which have indeed, as Freud suggested in 1930, made us like unto gods, with power of life and death Zeus himself might envy. And ever since the intoxicating equations of Bohr's Copenhagen circle of theoretical physicists proved to have not only the intrinsic magic of mathematics but the might now calculated in megadeaths, many students of atomic physics have considered the implications of their science against a broader philosophical perspective.

While physicists—particularly just after World War II—addressed themselves to the social consequences of their astonishing new capacity for destruction (Heisenberg, 1959, 1971), philosophers of the social sciences have recently begun to explore the implications for developmental psychology of the arbitrary and multiple definitions of time, space, matter, and energy (Eddington, 1950; Weyl, 1922, 1952) which interact in the equations employed by theoretical physicists to coordinate their observations of the physical world.

This new intoxication has led philosophers of the social sciences down some peculiar and potentially misleading paths, which, paradoxically, cross the paths taken by philosophers of the natural sciences just a generation ago. Heisenberg's uncertainty principle, a quantified declaration of the limit of our capacity to locate a single electron in time and space, stimulated a generation of physicists into wondering whether electrons could be said to have free will—and whether it could therefore be argued on the basis of atomic physics that atomic physicists, and with them the rest of humanity, had free will also: because of, and perhaps even notwithstanding (Polanyi, 1958; Schrodinger, 1955), quantum indeterminacy. Unfortunately for those of us who have viewed the question of free will as a major issue in psychology, including, among others, William James (1961), Sigmund Freud (1930, 1933), B. F. Skinner (1971), and Carl Rogers (1974), the physicists have failed to solve this problem for us and indeed have abandoned it as an insoluble question of individual consciousness (Schrodinger, 1955). They have, however, left the field wide open for us to explore the implications of their strange syntheses of space, time, and matter.

My central thesis is that current efforts to employ the natural sciences to generate new perspectives on the nature of time in the developmental psychology of the life cycle reflect an unfortunate choice: In selecting the delightful abstractions of atomic physics, we have embraced that which is most alien to our own discipline and therefore most often likely to be irrelevant, trivial, or misleading. Before I offer my own alternative perspective, which has its origin in biology, I should like to show by example how easily physicists and their abstractions can lead us astray.

The example I have selected is a pivotal concept in physics; I have chosen it because I am certain it is well known to all of us, although theoretical physics has better examples, which employ more of the multiple coordinates Klaus Riegel has discussed (Chapter 1, this volume). Among these, for instance, is the statistical measure of entropy, $k \log D$, where k = the Boltzmann constant, 3.2983×10^{-24} cal / $^{\circ}C$, and D is a quantitative measure of atomistic disorder: in other words, an equation expressing a quantified measure of order and disorder, a measure of interest to those of us concerned with the assumptions underlying the stochastic techniques of psychology.

While it bears less directly on issues in developmental psychology, the example I have chosen to discuss at greater length is one familiar to all of us: Einstein's equation expressing the relationship between matter and energy,

$$E = mc^2,$$

where

$$m = \frac{m_{\text{not}}}{\sqrt{[1 - (v^2/c^2)]}}$$

that is, any quantity of matter yields a quantity of energy equal to its mass multiplied by the square of the speed of light. This astounding equation can be shown to have some measure of applicability to life-span developmental psychology—no less and no more than those equations that express multiple meanings of time. The conversion of matter into energy was once theory and then deed: The historical context in which our own generation came to its maturity is one in which the destructive force expressed by that little equation was first shown to be more than mathematics.

It is not, however, the mathematical or physical relationship between matter and energy that concerns the life-span developmental psychologist; rather, our concerns are on a broader scale. Atomic bombs go off, have destroyed cities, and are now stockpiled in sufficient quantities to destroy our earth several times over—and thus serve to create what Mannheim (1952) has called generational consciousness and what we often term cohort effects. This, then, is the nuclear age; but there is little to be found in nuclear physics which will help us to understand the developmental psychology of the generation of the atomic bomb.

II. The Seasons of Man: Toward an Organic Model of Time

It has been suggested that early steps toward civilization were taken when men first learned to defy the rhythm of the seasons, combating the succession of abundance and scarcity, when agriculture began in the Jordan River valley around the oasis that irrigates the city of Jericho. Thus the seasonally paced alternation of food and famine gave way before organized human efforts at cultivation and storage of food.

This primitive agriculture, so distant from our own time, is worth a moment's reflection. Here we see the invariant sequence of the seasons subordinated to the rhythms of the needs of men. To put it somewhat differently, around the oasis of Jericho the cycle of the seasons no longer governed the appetites of men, but instead men imposed their own appetites upon the seasons. Perhaps this can be seen as one of the very first moments in the history of civilization when men restructured time to suit themselves. And if that is so, it gives us further pause, for it may be that one of the most recent harvests of the agricultural and urban revolution that took place in the oasis of Jericho is the garbagemen's strike, not long ago, in New York City. If we have attained independence from the rhythm of the seasons that once governed our hungers, we are now vulnerable to abundance and its attendant waste. We have conquered famine, only to be conquered in turn by vegetable peelings in the middle of winter in a northern climate.

Certainly this is a dimension of human history and part of the paradoxical consequences of centuries of effort to transcend the limits of time and space. Indeed, the concept of time as arbitrary and abstract, as men's invention, can be illustrated simply by the shelves of a supermarket laden with fresh produce in snowy January.

Thus the farmers of ancient Jericho are the forerunners of the physicists whose manipulations of time contribute to the dialectical model of time which Klaus Riegel has described. The history of technology records our progress from the threat of death by starvation to the threat of death by indulgence; the history of science moves from primitive men learning to count to 20th-century men whose equations scribbled on tablecloths brought blood upon their heads.

The abstract and multiple bases of time, therefore, reflect the most recent of humanity's long succession of battles with nature, battles that have often been victorious. It is my own position, however, that from the perspective of life-span developmental psychology the battle with time is lost by every generation, that time is unidirectional, univariate, nondialectical; neither abstract nor arbitrary; but on the contrary, concrete and imperative. Where Klaus Riegel speaks of our successes in transcending the boundaries of time, I speak of our failures.

My point of departure is not atomic physics but animal physiology, and I think it is useful to illustrate the distance between these perspectives. Consider briefly a protozoan and a collection of hydrogen atoms of equal mass. If each is left to its own devices, the hydrogen atoms will diffuse into the atmosphere, and the protozoan will become fruitful and multiply, producing as many copies of itself as the environment will permit. The first process reflects the natural tendency of matter toward disorder or entropy; the second process might be characterized as order from order (Schrodinger, 1955). Furthermore, if a match is brought to each, the hydrogen explodes into a cloud of water vapor; but the protozoan dies, less sensationally but more completely, since chemists can reduce water vapor to its original constituents. Time, then, moves in two directions for hydrogen atoms—but physiologists cannot revitalize the protozoan, for whom time is unidirectional, just as it is for us.

Living organisms such as our protozoan, the atomic physicists, and the life-span developmental psychologists have been characterized by a biologist as points in space at which physical and chemical reactions are occurring at slower rates than in the surrounding environment (Hardin, 1956). Physicists have dealt with organic life even more respectfully: Schrodinger (1955) has said that life is a unique contradiction of the second law of thermodynamics, which states that entropy in the universe is constantly increasing, due to a statistical tendency in matter to be transformed from order to disorder (Bent, 1965).

Living matter evades the decay to equilibrium, as Schrodinger says, by consuming negative entropy. To put it less mysteriously, we eat food, and sustain ourselves by metabolizing our food, a process by which relatively complex and therefore relatively ordered matter is broken down into simpler—and for the physicist more disordered—components.

Thus as living organisms it is clear that we violate the laws of physics in two ways: first, the physical and chemical reactions that sustain organic life are considerably slower than those characteristic of the inorganic world; next, we contradict the second law of thermodynamics, the tendency of matter to decay toward disorder. These two violations of the laws of physics indicate the need for caution in employing physical abstractions of time in the service of developmental psychology. Human life, as a physicist might conceptualize it on temporal dimensions, is not only moving along more slowly than usual but is indeed moving against the temporal mainstream of the universe.

There are additional constraints that govern organic life and cause me to question the facility with which the temporal abstractions of physics have been invoked. The first of these constraints on organic life is biological: While we consume, as Schrodinger puts it, negative entropy in the form of food, as organisms we are highly selective. We consume organic matter and metabolize it into simpler components—some of them the ordinary components of the physical world, carbon dioxide and water vapor—but we are only able to consume organic matter of specific kinds. We can survive by eating apples, but not by eating the wood of the apple tree; although wood will burn in a fireplace, it will not burn in our bodies with the slow, controlled fire that sustains life. One species of mushroom enhances filet mignon; another may kill us. The limitations are species-specific; to put it another way, one organism's nutrient is another's toxin. These physiological constraints can often be explained by known physical and chemical laws, but are not built into the physical and chemical model of the world.

The second of the constraints on organic life is existential. We break the second law of thermodynamics, but only for a brief while: in the end it breaks us. The slow fire of metabolism is extinguished, and the complex organism is broken down—perhaps by other, living, hungry complex organisms—into its component parts. I should like to propose that life-span developmental psychology deals with the interlude between conception and death and with the efforts of the individual to reconcile himself to these two poles of existence.

In summary, my objections to the dialectical model of time, insofar as it rests on the abstractions of atomic physics, are four: (1) we violate the temporal laws of physics by a slower than usual pace of physical and chemical reactions; (2) our physics and our chemistry are not only slow but, in the service of organic life, may even be said to be going in the wrong direction; (3) highly specific physiological constraints govern organic life, and while these constraints often admit of explanation through known physical and chemical laws, they are not incorporated into a physical scientist's world view; (4) it is our nature and our fate to disobey the general laws of physics only briefly, and yet this very brevity generates poetry to capture it, medicine to defy it, physics to transcend it, and life-span developmental psychology to explain it.

III. Epigenesis Reconsidered: Biological Imperatives and Cultural Alternatives

It has become increasingly common to hear developmental psychologists refer to chronological age as a meaningless variable—a forerunner, perhaps, of Riegel's stress on the arbitrary nature of time and its multiple bases. It is not difficult to support this disdain. For example, a 6-year-old boy might better be described by the ratio of his mental age to his chronological age; a 14-year-old girl may be expected to be a junior high school student in one culture, a mother of two children in another; a 45-year-old man might be at the peak of a business career, still moving up in a political career, or retired from a career in major league baseball—or dead and worshiped as an ancestor in a primitive tribe. Clearly the life cycle is shaped by the cultural context into which the individual is born.

However, studies of the aged in our own culture as well as in others indicate that distance from death, which seems to be a function of genetic programming, when this can be differentiated from pathology, is measurably related to cognitive changes (Gutmann, 1969; Lieberman, 1965; Riegel & Riegel, 1972). While chronological age is a poor indicator of these changes, the cultural context is still less useful as a predictor; we discover across the life cycle that internally paced maturational changes set certain outer bounds on behavioral potentials.

We ought not, therefore, to forget that chronological age is a measure of time since birth, and therefore a general guide—far from infallible, but certainly not meaningless—to internal events that do bear on the developmental psychology of the life cycle. To put it more strongly, if I investigate an issue in developmental psychology and am permitted only one independent variable in my sample section, I shall choose chronological age, just as so many of us, myself included, have already done. Whatever its imperfections, chronological age helps the developmental psychologist to know what to expect of his subjects: teething toddlers, sexually mature young adults, older adults with signs of biological decline. If he chooses an age sufficiently advanced—perhaps 175 years—the investigator can safely predict that his subjects will be dead. I cannot subscribe to the current claim that a variable as informative as chronological age is meaningless for developmental psychology.

Indeed, I take chronological age as my own point of departure, since it marks off not only important but irreversible age changes. I am very fond of Klaus Riegel's dialectical model of development (1973), which permits the developmental psychologist—or the atomic physicist—formal operations at the conference table by day and the celebration of sensorimotor processes by night; with him—and with those who argue for regression in the service of the ego (cf. Hartmann, 1958)—I agree that the happy adult has ready access to the more primitive layers of personality and with them the cognitive modes of early life.

Riegel and I part company, however, on the degree of fluidity we permit in our conceptions of time. However he may employ the sensorimotor processes by night, the 35-year-old developmental psychologist is not transformed into a 15-month-old infant: nor, I surmise, would he want to be. Time's arrow, as the physicists call it (Eddington, 1950), travels in only one direction for living creatures. When we are small, we number our birthdays with delight; and then, somewhere in the middle of the life cycle (Neugarten, 1968), we discover that the number of birthdays is finite and indeed not very great—but we cannot escape the count, nor the seasons of our own life cycle, through the dialectical perspective. For a living organism, time is neither abstraction nor arbitrary variable; nor can we by argument become the arbiters of time.

I should like to offer an alternative concept of time, derived from the epigenetic principle employed by Erikson (1963) to support his model of the stages of the life cycle. This is a principle as old as Ecclesiastes (3:1–8), which tells us that for every thing there is a season, and a time to every puipose under heaven. Erikson's slightly less poetic statements are based on the process of embryological development, which is characterized by a finely orchestrated sequence of events with irrevocable consequences. At some point early in embryonic development the fate of cells becomes irreversible; the growth and differentiation of tissues into organ systems follows a precise, prescribed timetable; and deviations from this timetable gives rise to defective organ systems that impair and may even threaten the life of the organism (Arey, 1958). There is no dialectical reprieve for developmental deviations in the life of an embryo.

Postpartum life admits of greater flexibility in developmental stages, but the biological timetable continues to govern development. Perhaps it is simplistic to remind ourselves that we begin life small and helpless and come only slowly to our biological maturity—and still more slowly to the social maturity defined for us by our historical context (Neugarten & Datan, 1973). Yet all of child psychology, from explorations of the Oedipus complex to implementation of operant techniques in the nursery school, reflects implicit or explicit awareness of the difference in size between the child and his adult caretaker, a difference mandated by the biological timetable.

This timetable continues to be reflected in the psychology of adolescent development, a period of potential unease when biological maturity comes without one's asking for it, but social maturity is arbitrarily defined and conferred in accordance with cultural norms. Middle adulthood is perhaps the period of greatest freedom from the biological clock, for there are a plurality of socially acceptable routes through this portion of the life cycle, ranging from the early maturity of the professional athlete to the prolonged youth of the graduate student preparing for an academic career.

At the end, however, the biological clock reclaims us as it runs out. Where Klaus Riegel has chosen to describe the multiple bases of the concept of time and its abstract and arbitrary character, I am reluctantly arguing for our mortality and for the finitude and finality of biological time.

IV. Dialectical Psychology:
A Problem in the Sociology of Knowledge

Over 2000 years ago, Herodotus (*The Persian Wars*) observed with some surprise that the Ethiopians painted their gods black, while the men of Thrace, to the north, painted theirs red-headed. Whether or not this is the first recorded suggestion that men make gods in their own images, it is certainly not the last: I might suggest that our most recent effort is the making of dialectical man.

The concept of dialectical discourse, as distinguished from rhetorical persuasion, is as old as Plato (*Gorgias*); other efforts to understand the physical universe are of comparable antiquity (Aristotle: *Physics;* Lucretius: *On the Nature of the Universe*). Descriptions of human nature begin still earlier. The Mosaic code for the most part targets behavior as Skinner might; and the price, if not the process, of cognition was named by Ecclesiastes (1:18): "In wisdom lies grief, and he who increases knowledge increases sorrow." I am certain that we have all known something of the pain of discovery, though this has not deterred any inquiry from that generation to this.

Today we are embarked on the pursuit of knowledge in a very broad context. Klaus Riegel has shown how we may move from the microlaws governing subatomic particles to the "macrolaws"—a term I have conjured up for its pejorative value, for I do not think there is a comparable regularity to the processes at the subatomic and the social level (Gergen, 1973)—that reflect the social and historical context. He seeks the dialectic at the interface between organism and psyche, person and society, social context and history.

I have intervened with vigor where I see an irrelevant transition from physical laws—which no physicist would apply to a biological organism. I am, however, as guilty as anyone else of employing the dialectical perspective in the service of the study of human development (cf. Datan, 1975a, 1975b, 1975c, 1975d), and I am therefore obliged to go beyond a critical response to Klaus Riegel's conceptual framework and address the more general issue: Why has the dialectical perspective suddenly come to life with such force, manifesting itself in developmental psychology, social psychology, and now experimental psychology? The answer to this question is only in small part epistemological; the broader context we require is that of the sociology of knowledge (Mannheim, 1952).

The epistemological issues raised by Riegel and by me are beyond any possible final resolution. It can be asked, however, where the current revitalized interest in the dialectical approach originated. The impulse to explore across disciplinary boundaries was first seen in this century among the atomic physicists (e.g., Heisenberg, 1959; Polanyi, 1958; Schrodinger, 1955) and shortly afterward among those concerned with issues in evolutionary biology (cf. Tax, 1960; Waddington, 1960). If we have been slow to succumb to the interdisciplinary infection, we are also the newest of the sciences—and are unique in that subject and scientist not only belong to the same species (for the same can be said of medicine) but may also be adversaries of equal intellect. The patient who deceives his doctor harms himself, but the subject who deceives his experimenter harms only the results of the study. Thus psychology is plagued by problems of observation which render Heisenberg's principle of uncertainty, by comparison, an enviably simple declaration.

Faced with the ambiguities of his task and the perversity of his subject of study, the life-span developmental psychologist may well take comfort from the definitive elegance of quantum mechanics and the hope of a resolution of contradictions implicit in the dialectical perspective. As the discipline of psychology matures, as psychologists grow more self-conscious and their breadth of perspective increases, so too does the hope of synthesis grow.

We are the most recent of the sciences to have attempted to address a broader philosophical context. Our predecessors in physics and biology have for the most part concluded that their sciences offer no obvious answers to the questions we ask about the meaning of human existence: Quantum indeterminacy cannot be used to establish free will (Schrodinger, 1955), and genetic determinism cannot be used in the service of social organization (Mayr, 1970; some psychologists concur, cf. Kamin, 1974; but see also Jensen, 1969).

I am afraid that psychologists will not find it possible to draw disciplinary boundaries with equal facility. Indeed, I believe we have inherited many of the philosophical and ethical dilemmas that once belonged to the domain of philosophers, philosophers of the natural sciences, and theologians. We, too, have something of the Faustian power over life, and with it no doubt a measure of Faust's doom. We shall have to continue to ask, no matter how we despair of the answers; and, as Kierkegaard (1954) forewarned us, "Whatever the one generation may learn from the other, that which is genuinely human no generation learns from the foregoing. In this respect every generation begins primitively . . . nor does it get further. . . . Thus . . . no generation begins at any other point than at the beginning [p. 130]."

V. Conclusion: The Fruits of Antithesis

Some have argued that a revolution is incomplete until the counterrevolutionaries have begun to be heard. If that is so, then history will transform my antidialectical battle cry into ·a rearguard action for the dialectical revolution in developmental psychology. But in my own judgment, it is not necessary to wait for history to have its way. It seems to me that Klaus Riegel and I are representing the two poles of a tension much older than contemporary issues in developmental psychology: the bounds of biological morality and the desire to transcend the limits of the human life span. If *dialectical* is taken to mean "that which does not admit of resolution," then it is even possible that together we represent an uncomfortable synthesis. But we have not answered the questions we have asked, not for developmental psychology and perhaps not even for ourselves. We can only say with certainty that no future research will resolve these issues, but rather that they will forever trouble the generations of men.

REFERENCES

Arey, L. B. *Developmental anatomy.* Philadelphia: Saunders, 1958.

Bent, H. A. *The second law: An introduction to classical and statistical thermodynamics.* London & New York: Oxford University Press, 1965.

Datan, N. Astarte, Moses and Mary: Perspectives on the sexual dialectic in Canaanite, Judaic, and Christian tradition. In K. F. Riegel & J. Meacham (Eds.), *The developing individual in a changing world* (Vol. 1), *Historical and cultural issues.* The Hague: Mouton, 1975. (a)

Datan, N. Male and female: The search for synthesis. In J. F. Rychlak (Ed), *Dialectic: Humanistic rationale for behavior and development.* Basel: Karger, 1975. (b)

Datan, N. The narcissism of the life cycle: the dialectics of fairy tales. In N. Datan (Chair), *The life cycle, aging, and death: Multidisciplinary perspectives.* Symposium presented at the meeting of the Gerontological Society, Louisville, 1975. (c)

Datan, N. We get too soon old and too late smart: Dialectical dilemmas in life-span developmental theory. In R. Wozniak (Chair), *Applications of dialectics to developmental psychology.* Symposium presented at the meeting of the American Psychological Association, Chicago, 1975. (d)

Eddington, A. S. *Space, time and gravitation.* London & New York: Cambridge University Press, 1950.

Erikson, E. H. *Childhood and society* (2nd ed). New York: Norton, 1963.

Freud, S. *Civilization and its discontents.* New York: Norton, 1930.

Freud, S. *New introductory lectures on psychoanalysis.* New York: Norton, 1933.

Gergen, K. J. Social psychology as History. *Journal of Personality and Social Psychology,* 1973, **26**,(2), 309–320.

Gutmann, D. *The country of old men: Cross-cultural studies in the psychology of later life* (Occasional Papers in Gerontology, No. 5). University of Michigan-Wayne State University, Institute of Gerontology: 1969.

Hardin, G. *Scientific Monthly,* 1956, **82**, 112.

Hartmann, H. *Ego psychology and the problem of adaptation.* New York: International Universities Press, 1958.

Heisenberg, W. *Physics and philosophy.* New York: Harper, 1959.

Heisenberg, W. *Physics and metaphysics.* New York: Harper, 1971.

James, W. *The varieties of religious experience.* New York: Collier-Macmillan, 1961.

Jensen, A. R. How much can we boost IQ and scholastic achievement? *Harvard Educational Review,* 1969, **31**, 1–123.

Kamin, L. J. *The science and politics of IQ.* Hillsdale, N.J.:Lawrence Erlbaum Associates, 1974.

Kierkegaard, S. *Fear and trembling.* Princeton: Princeton University Press, 1954.

Lieberman, M. A. Psychological correlates of impending death: Some preliminary observations. *Journal of Gerontology,* 1965, **20**(2).

Mannheim, K. *Essay on the sociology of knowledge.* London: Rutledge and Kegan Paul, 1952.

Mayr, E. *Populations, species, and evolution.* Cambridge, Mass.: Harvard University Press, 1970.

Neugarten, B. L. The awareness of middle age. In B. L. Neugarten (Ed.), *Middle age and aging.* Chicago: University of Chicago Press, 1968.

Neugarten, B. L., & Datan, N. Sociological perspectives on the life cycle. In P. B. Baltes & K. W. Schaie (Eds.), *Life-span developmental psychology: Personality and socialization.* New York: Academic Press, 1973.

Polanyi, M. *Personal knowledge: Towards a post-critical philosophy.* Chicago: University of Chicago Press, 1958.

Riegel, K. F. Dialectical operations: The final period of cognitive development. *Human Development,* 1973, **16**, 346–370.

Riegel, K. F., & Riegel, R. M. Development, drop, and death. *Developmental Psychology,* 1972, **6**,

Rogers, C. R. In retrospect: Forty-six years. *American Psychologist,* 1974, **29**(2).
Schrodinger, E. *What is life?* London & New York: Cambridge University Press, 1955.
Skinner, B. F. *Beyond freedom and dignity.* New York: Knopf, 1971.
Tax, S. (Ed.). *Evolution after Darwin* (Vol. 2). Chicago: University of Chicago Press, 1960.
Waddington, C. H. *The ethical animal.* London: Allen & Unwin, 1960.
Weyl, H. *Space, time, matter.* New York: Dover, 1922.
Weyl, H. *Symmetry.* Princeton: Princeton University Press, 1952.

CHAPTER 3

Social Proof Structures:
The Dialectic of Method and Theory
in the Work of Psychology

SHELDON H. WHITE

HARVARD UNIVERSITY
CAMBRIDGE, MASSACHUSETTS

"The great crucial books of human thought—outside what are called the exact sciences, and perhaps something of the sort is true even here—always render articulate the results of fundamental new experiences to which human beings have had to adjust themselves.

Edmund Wilson
To the Finland Station [1972, p. 371]

Our action exerts itself conveniently only on fixed points; fixity is therefore what our intelligence seeks; it asks itself where the mobile is to be found, where it will be, where it will *pass*. Even if it takes note of the moment of passing, even it it seems then to be concerned with duration, it restricts itself in that direction to verifying the simultaneity of two virtual halts; the halt of the mobility it is considering and the halt of another mobile whose course is presumed to be that of time. But it is always with immobilities, real or possible, that it seeks to deal.

Henri Bergson
The Creative Mind [1946, p. 14]

I. Introduction

The intent of this discussion is to consider those historical processes in psychology that arise when systems of action confront systems of thought. About 100 years ago, an organized empiricism began to be directed toward psychological questions. The work was conceived of as an adjunct to philosophical analysis of epistemology. There were then grand theories, broad schematizations of human knowing and understanding developed by the systematic philosophers of the 18th and 19th centuries. Attached to the philosophical enterprise there came to be small laboratories. The small laboratories have grown, and the theories have evolved to meet them, so that today we can speak about the psychology of cognition, genetic epistemology, or information processing as matters of theory and research. How has this reconciliation been brought about?

The business of studying human thought and behavior seems to have originated in miscellaneous small ventures that cropped up in European scientific laboratories in the last century. In laboratories of physics, medicine, and astronomy, procedures were invented by which investigators could observe, count, or categorize features of human sensation, reaction time, memory, and word association. Boring's *History of Experimental Psychology* locates the several origins of such procedures and shows how the procedures were collected together to form the working basis of Wundt's Laboratory of Psychology at Leipzig in 1879.

From an analysis of 109 papers in Wundt's journal, the *Philosophische Studien,* Boring (1950, pp. 339–343) outlines the work of the Leipzig laboratory. There were studies of absolute and difference limens in the several sensory modalities; studies of sensory phenomena such as color contrast, illusions, auditory beats, taste categories, and so on; studies of simple and complex reaction time; studies of word association and rote memory; and a miscellany of introspective procedures directed toward attentional and emotional factors in thought.

The procedures of the Wundtian laboratory were to assist epistemological analysis. One may be impressed by how quickly and diligently the early philosopher-scientists went to work, but at the same time one must recognize that these fragments of inquiry entered into a world where Locke, Spencer, Bain, Husserl, Hegel, Kant, and Hume were under debate. There was a dramatic difference in level of analysis. David versus Goliath: the Weber–Fechner fraction versus Emmanuel Kant.

The instigation of empirical epistemology was in the German laboratories, but it was restrained. One can question the completeness of Wundt's own commitment to his laboratory. Wundt had stated that psychology could be experimental, arguing against the views expressed by some previous German philosophers, but he was not sure that all psychological questions could be approached by experimentation. Many psychological questions might have to be approached by anthropological methods, he thought, and he wrote a 10-volume treatise on "folk psychology" to stand beside his physiological psychology (Haeberlin, 1916). American students who went to work in his laboratory had somewhat mixed memories of his participation in laboratory work. G. Stanley Hall, who was the first, reported that "Wundt was rarely seen in his laboratory, and impressed me as rather inept in the use of his hands"; George M. Stratton reported that he made a daily round of his laboratory; another student reported that he would make a tour of the working rooms "once in a great while [G. S. Hall *et al.*, 1921]." In 1892, W. O. Krohn reported to American audiences on facilities for experimental psychology in 11 German universities, and then later a 12th (Krohn, 1892). There were few good laboratories beyond the Leipzig laboratory, and in at least one German university Krohn found a distinct skepticism that there could be an experimental psychology.[1]

The full transplantation of philosophical questions into the psychology laboratory really took place in American hands. As Geraldine Joncich (1968) put it in her biography of Thorndike:

> Despite its alien origins, however, the new psychology appears really to grow, and perhaps to grow up, in America. It is in the United States that the colleges and universities tumble over one another in their zeal to establish psychological laboratories and graduate programs, both evident even before 1900. Although the charter members of the American Psychological Association, founded in 1892, contain a goodly number of philosophers, nowhere else is psychology's future as a science, empirical and experimental rather than rational, made so much an article of faith. In America alone will psychology rapidly and broadly be judged applicable to education, industrial management, medicine, child rearing, domestic relations, the military. As a result, numerous of its interests and findings will enter the popular idiom, the arts, the marketplace. Where many of the first generation of American psychologists found it necessary to take German doctorates, after about 1895 this migration becomes rare and unnecessary; already it is no longer true, as it had been for James Mark Baldwin in 1886, that German study is a decided advantage in securing a position in the American professoriate. The leadership of experimental and quantitative psychology, of the new psychology, has crossed the Atlantic westward with the earlier generation of psychologists and may well be retained by their students, the products of American departments of psychology and research institutes [pp. 69–70].

---

[1] In Heidelberg, Krohn encountered Fischer who "is openly opposed to all experimental research in psychology. He regards it as a fad, a side issue, an illegitimate method, lying wholly outside the mainstream in the development of psychology as a science" (Krohn, 1892a, p. 585). How could Fischer regard psychology as a science and yet be opposed to laboratories and experimentation? It must be remembered that Wundt established his laboratory at the time of a very active philosophical debate about the methods appropriate to the *Naturwissenschaften* versus the *Geisteswissenschaften,* natural studies versus human studies. Wundt's approach arose from the belief that psychology could be approached in part from the study of nature and in part from human studies; this was also the belief of Wilhelm Dilthey, whom many regard as the "philosopher of science" for human studies. But even Wundt himself did not believe that psychology could be fully experimental. In a book published some 30 years after the founding of the Leipzig laboratory, Wundt argued that he had never meant to create a fully experimental psychology (Wundt, 1913). Such a psychology would be trivial, he argued (A. Blumenthal, personal communication). In fact, Wundt saw psychological phenomena as subordinated to and conditioned by social and cultural phenomena; from language, religion, and custom in the "folk spirit" there arose the corresponding terms of ideas, emotions, and volitions in individual psychology. Adopting an "organicist" view of history, he saw different cultures as arranged along a line of cultural evolution in a manner similar to Hegel's historical view or to Heinz Werner in his contemporary writings (Haeberlin, 1916; White, 1976c).

During the 1890s, the journals of the American philosopher–psychologists showed that they were very much in earnest about establishing laboratories. The *American Journal of Psychology* and the *Psychological Review* offered empirical and theoretical papers about psychology under individual authors' names, just as current journals do, but there were also authored notes describing the work of several investigators in one laboratory, and there were also blocks of authored papers printed under headings such as "From the Harvard Laboratory" or "Minor Communications from the Cornell Laboratory." Scanning these two journals from 1894 to 1898, one finds identified laboratories at Harvard, Clark, Yale, Columbia, Princeton, Wellesley, Chicago, Iowa, Wisconsin, and Stanford–some of them coming through with groups of papers as often as twice a year. The procedures represented in these early American laboratories are pretty much the Wundtian procedures; they fall within the Boring categories described earlier.[2]

The laboratories were fairly modest affairs. Wundt's Leipzig laboratory occupied six rooms, the size of a very modest research empire as things go in American universities nowadays. In 1893, E. C. Sanford offered some practical suggestions on the equipment of a psychology laboratory. He said that a proper laboratory should take $5000 to equip, although he hastened to add that much could be done for much less (Sanford, 1893). This is quite an optimistic figure, apparently, for one later finds J. M. Cattell (1898) waxing sarcastic about an argument by Titchener that a psychology laboratory should take $2000 to establish and $600 per year to run. Cattell pointed out that university trustees, unfortunately, did not read psychological journals and would be unlikely to be sympathetic to so high a spending level.

It seems apparent that up until about 1900, American psychologists undertook the development of empiricism building around the conception that there should be *a* psychology laboratory with a definite range of procedures and empirical issues. Not all of the charter members of psychology remained enthusiastic as this kind of laboratory crystallized. William James and John Dewey moved off, James quite overtly disillusioned; G. Stanley Hall was both pushed and pulled outside the

---

[2] Although in this paper these American laboratories will be referred to as the Wundt laboratories or the Wundt–Titchener laboratories, this is a kind of conventional designation in American terms. It is not at all clear that the American students who went to Wundt's laboratory brought back much more than the procedures, not is it clear that the usual American understanding of his theoretical position is accurate. The American representation of Wundtian structuralism may be a portrayal of Wundt as interpreted by Titchener (Blumenthal, 1975, 1976). The historical situation may be analogous to that prevailing in our own time, when it seems reasonably clear that Piaget's procedures have crossed the Atlantic much more quickly and easily than has his theory. Indeed, it is because procedures seem to move among individuals much more rapidly and faithfully than do ideas that I later take the position here that the bedrock of scientific communication is the sharing of common procedures. But this may be an American perception, I will admit, and perhaps some would care to argue that Americans prefer to traffic in procedures, while Europeans tend to traffic in ideas.

movement; others, like James Mark Baldwin, developed a body of psychological writings that were relatively unconstrained by this kind of laboratory. For all these men, for one reason or another, the laboratory failed to be an interesting vehicle for the development of their epistemological thinking. But many remained, apparently intrigued with the idea that this kind of laboratory, or *some* kind of laboratory, might be a useful vehicle for psychology.

A masterful description of the handling of the Wundtian laboratory is extant, contained in the series of four laboratory manuals that E. B. Titchener produced from 1901 to 1923. There are four volumes, a student's manual and an instructor's manual in qualitative methods (Titchener, 1901, 1909) and a student's manual and an instructor's manual in quantitative methods (Titchener, 1905, 1923). The two instructor's manuals, in particular, are well worth looking at because very little like them has ever been produced in psychology. Twice as thick as the student manuals, they are remarkable for the care and detail with which they set forth both the practical issues involved in implementing the Wundtian procedures and the pattern of findings that one can expect through use of the methods. It is clear that the small body of philosopher–psychologists have learned something using these procedures. That something is not epistemological analysis nor could one reasonably call it psychological theory. What did they learn? We will consider that question in a moment.

Viewed from the perspective of the present, one can regard these elaborately worked out Titchener volumes with feelings of sadness about the transience of human striving. Everyone knows, or thinks he knows, that the Wundtian laboratory died in the first two decades of the 20th century, killed by findings of the Wurtzburg laboratory that went against introspection, killed by functionalism, killed by behaviorism. In a sense, these feelings are justified. The Wundtian laboratory viewed as *the* laboratory for psychological inquiry did die rapidly in the early 20th century. Earnest attempts to fund and instrument this particular pattern of procedures did die away, to be replaced by attempts to fund and instrument other patterns of procedures. When, at last, a modestly theoretical offering did arise out of the Wundt–Titchener tradition, Boring's *The Physical Dimensions of Consciousness,* it was too little and too late to save the tradition.

Boring's book, first published in 1933, was reprinted in a second paperback edition in 1963, and in the preface to the second edition Boring (1963) looked back over 30 years to review the reason he wrote the book and to examine its fate: "The book was an effort to save the factual material of introspectionism . . . through a physicalism formulated, whenever possible, in physiological terms. Did the book accomplish its mission? No—at least psychology did not come to conform to its admonitions" [p. v].

Although Boring's theoretical work was not a strong organizing force for the psychologists of its time, it is nevertheless worthwhile to consider the book in its relation to the Wundt–Titchener laboratory.

II. Research versus Theory in the Wundt–Titchener Laboratory

In the beginning of the Wundtian tradition, one of the striking features of the enterprise was the gross misalignment of theory and action that prevailed in the enterprise. The debate among large and systematic theories of knowledge was aligned with observations arising from a small and rather haphazardly put together laboratory. Philosophers who were eager to get on with the systematic debate did not tarry long amid this puny empiricism. Yet the laboratories had a life of their own. They rapidly became functionally autonomous, so much so that we find Titchener and other psychologists in the early 1900s repeatedly arguing that the problems of psychology be separated from the problem of philosophy. The psychologists had established *their* business independent of philosophical business.

Knowledge came out of their procedures. It was publicly reported in the journal communications flowing back and forth among the laboratories, and this kind of knowledge is collected and organized in the Titchener handbooks. It is interesting to look at the Titchener handbooks and to ask what kind of knowledge they contain. Clearly, they are books informed by the empiricism that had preceded them; they would not have been possible without it. Just as clearly, they are not theory in any of the several senses in which one might take that word. What kind of knowledge do they contain? They appear to offer the following:

1. Specifications for how to act in a laboratory, descriptions of apparatus and procedures, as well as advice and cautions about the management of one's actions.

We may summarize the results of these investigations as follows: (1) The Koenig forks are accurate. The Appunn forks are worthless for the purposes for which they are intended. (2) The Koenig cylinders require correction; but the error is important only in the upper portion of the series, and the set can be employed, as it stands, after redetermination of pitch by the Kundt method. (3) The Appunn pipes are no more reliable than the forks. . . . (4) All the older forms of the Galton whistle (Cambr. Instr. Co., Hawksley, Koenig, Edelmann) must be retested by the Kundt method [1923, p. 35].

The standardising of the hair [on an aesthesiometer], at the different lengths furnished by the experimental series, may be entrusted to an enthusiastic student, but is (in the author's experience) better performed by the Instructor or the mechanician. It is not difficult; but it is slow and tiresome, and demands undivided attention [1923, p. 50].

The following are the rules for the use of the olfactometer. (a) the inhaling tube should be thrust into the forward half of the nostril to the depth of 5 mm . . . (b) The observer must discover for himself, by practice, the best rate and manner of breathing. Sniffing must be avoided . . . [1909, p. 81].

Some laboratories will, doubtless, possess a stand, which can be raised or lowered without noise. Where this is the case, the lamella should be clamped to the stand, and its height varied as the experiment demands. But the money required to build such a stand may be more profitably invested in a set of wire forks [1923, p. 2].

When alternating current motors are employed, they should be carefully safeguarded by high-resistance fuse plugs, and it should be observed that they start at once when the current is applied [1905, p. 40].

2. Terms of reference for patterns of experience to be encountered in commerce with the procedures, with either rough or careful rules for the identification of a pattern to be categorized by a term of reference. More simply put, significant phenomena to be encountered are identified and named.

We may term the extreme limit of red and the extreme limit of violet both alike TR [the terminal stimulus or upper limit of sensation], since the RL for colour is ordinarily interpreted to mean the least amount of objective colour necessary to tinge a grey, i.e., the lower limit of colour saturation [1923, p. 39].

Suppose that the note *a* is sounded on piano, harmonium and violin. We know that the same *a* is given in each case; but we have no difficulty whatever in distinguishing the three 'same *a*'s', and in referring each of them to its own musical instrument. The fundamental tone is identical throughout, but the total impression of the clang varies. Such differences are termed differences of *clang-tint* [1909, p. 46].

Every patch of brightness or colour in the field of vision is affected by the simultaneous presence of all the other patches, and affects them in its turn, in certain quite definite ways. This reciprocal induction of brightness and colours is termed *contrast* [1909, p. 15].

Pressure spots . . . It is well to familiarize the student beforehand with the pressure quality. Let him close his eyes; then let the point be set down several times in the back of his hand, in the near neighbourhood of an isolated hair. If the point is set down at all intensively, there will probably be a dull, diffuse, contentless pressure sensed at every application; this is due to the extension of the deformation of the hair to neighbouring pressure spots, and their consequent weak stimulation. At one place, to windward of the root of the hair, however, the true pressure quality will be obtained: a distinct, sharply localised sensation, of the kind that one might imagine to be set up by the resistance of a hard seed embedded in the cutis and now forced inward by the pressure point [1901, p. 92].

3. Information about the factual and the artifactual. Substantive and methodological conclusions are arrived at, essentially through interpretations of patterns of action in relation to patterns of experience. Certain patterns of experience seem to be derived by or explained by patterns of action. These seem to be artifactual in the sense that they do not reflect the "out there," the psychological makeup of the subject, but rather primarily reflect an influence of the experimenter's pattern of action upon the subject. Other patterns of experience in the laboratory do not seem easily explainable by the experimenter's activities and are attributed to the psychology of the subject.

E must be very careful always to release the disc by the same movement. Otherwise the sound of the pluck may be made the criterion of judgment [1923, p. 3].

Fig. 101 shows H. Griesbach's dynamometrical aesthesiometer. . . . The points are of metal. This is a disadvantage, as it introduces the temperature error [1901, p. 382].

Shall we discard, in the same way, the results of experiments which *O* declares by introspection to be worthless? No! We must keep a record of O's introspections, when he gives them; but we must not throw out any of his results. The object of the experiment is to determine in quantitative terms, O's mode of behavior under certain fixed conditions. O is, for the time being, a psychophysical machine, a reacting machine; and it is a fact of our purpose to discover the variations to which such a human machine is liable. . . . We are in search of O's reaction *time,* and of the manner and limits of its variability. The fact that O occasionally makes mistakes, disobeys instructions, gives extremely high or extremely low time values, is a feature of his reacting behavior which we must record [1905, p. 177].

No attempt must be made, during a single sitting, to verify the spots once found; fatigue is inevitable, and confusion and self-distrust result. Errors are apt to be made in localisations, by the fact that *approach* to a cold or warm spot will set up a weakly cold or warm sensation [1901, p. 82].

4. Simple information about patterns of phenomena to be expected. The reader is given variegated information about the contingent relationships holding among various sets of phenomena—their temporal or spatial or causal relationships to one another. Relatively simple patterns of phenomena are identified on any one of the several grids on which events can make a pattern.

The pressure spots are easily fatigued; the results of the first series of experiments cannot, therefore, be immediately verified. At a later sitting, the square must be worked over in the opposite direction [1909, p. 60].

(*a*) Find a papilla which is extremely sensitive to bitter. Paint it a few times over with a 10 to 20% solution of cocaine hydrochlorate. Notice that, while the bitter taste is entirely abolished, the other tastes of which the papilla is capable remain. (*b*) If the papilla is capable of sweet and salt, or sweet and sour sensations, over and above the bitter, continue the painting. Notice that the salt (or sour) sensation persists, after sweet has undergone the same fate as bitter [1901, p. 103].

E draws a chalk line upon the floor, from a point immediately below O's ear to a point some 8 to 10 in. distant. The watch is moved out, along this line and at the level of O's ear, until the noise of its ticking is but just supraliminal; if the tick is very loud, the watch should be wrapped in a cloth. The resulting intermittences of sound are clear and are very striking. . . . The length of the attention wave, as registered in these experiments, is extremely variable. It will probably amount to 6 or 8 sec., though it may rise as high as 18 or 20 sec. The author has records in which waves of 2 and of 24 sec. durations occur. Such extreme times are suspicious; indeed in the great majority of cases, they are thrown out by the introspective account [1901, pp. 194–195].

(i) Hold two unison forks, sounding with equal loudness in opposite phase, close up to the two ears. Notice that the resulting tone is localised within the occiput in the median plane. . . . (ii) Hold two unison forks, sounding at unequal intensities, equidistant from the two ears. Note that the sound is heard exclusively by the ear on whose side is the louder fork [1901, pp. 370–371].

These manuals reflect a kind of first-order knowledge arising from the Wundt–Titchener laboratory, a knowledge that stands somewhere between practice and theory. One would ordinarily call this kind of knowledge "lore," "practical experience," "knowing how to do experiments." This kind of first-order knowledge arises immediately out of research work; anyone who has done research work instantly recognizes it; and it probably forms a platform from which that kind of second-order knowledge that we call theory then arises.

Was this all the first-order knowledge Titchener had? My guess is that he had other knowledge that he could not print or would not print. Part of Titchener's knowledge of the laboratory was motor knowledge. There is a knack to handling and fixing many kinds of laboratory apparatus, and various kinds of motor ability are involved in laboratory work. Part of Titchener's knowledge of the laboratory was via a kind of emotional and aesthetic registration responsive to patterns of experience. From all sources one gets the distinct impression that Titchener liked precision and orderliness. I would venture a guess that he liked the appearance of a room full of brass instruments, liked the process of counting and measuring, disliked those procedures where he had to resort to sloppy procedure or vague estimation. These kinds of motor, emotional, and aesthetic registrations of laboratory work deserved to be called knowledge, I believe. They are changes in the human's cognitive program arising out of experience, and they may have definite effects on a human's behavior. But this kind of first-order knowledge of Titchener could not be printed and shared among the collectivity of Wundtian researchers, and furthermore, this kind of apprehension of laboratory patterns of experience tends to be quite idiosyncratic among a community of researchers. Probably Titchener's group was as diverse in its motor, emotional, and aesthetic registrations of laboratory experience as any modern group of researchers tends to be.

There was another kind of first-order knowledge that Titchener probably had but that he would not print; it consisted of estimations of the capabilities of the colleagues with whom he was in communication. Probably Titchener held and regularly updated judgments of the following kind: "A is a good investigator, but he is ambitious and publishes quickly, and one must be a little careful about his claims"; "B has a strong interest in Brentano's theory, and his work reflects a strong interest in locating active factors in consciousness"; "C knows more than anyone else about association research"; "D has been curiously inactive lately—is something wrong?" One might call this kind of unpublishable social knowledge gossip, and certainly the collection of such knowledge reflects the inveterate human love for gossip, but it is functional scientific knowledge as well. In any collectivity of researchers each man uses the other as an instrument, and just as one wants to know the properties and biases of one's physical instruments so also does one want to know things that would help one to separate the factual from the artifactual in the communications of others.

So we have a picture of the first-order knowledge that arose from the Wundt–Titchener laboratory, estimating from what is contained within the Titchener laboratory manuals and guessing about what was probably also available. The laboratory manuals offer the public part of that knowledge and are a step toward theory. Boring's *The Physical Dimensions of Consciousness* seems to represent the next step, and in that book we arrive at something that might reasonably be called theory.

The fundamental aim of the Boring book is to arrive at dimensionalizations of experience that are completely consistent introspectively, physiologically, and physically. Fechnerian psychophysics took the dimensionalizations assigned to the world by physicists as given and sought to find mathematical equations relating those dimensions to presumptively parallel dimensionalizations of sensation. But the Wundt–Titchener group, coming out of philosophical epistemology, knew that one might just as well argue that those formats for physical phenomena that we call physical dimensions might reflect the properties of nervous system and brain and that higher order processing that we call "mind." Boring's book sets out to propose a set of dimensions of the experience of things physical that evenly reflects work on physics, work on sensory physiology, and work on introspection. If the book had succeeded, one would presumably be able to locate events of physics and of sensation on the same grid, format, or dimension system. There would be a common mapping to both domains. Boring proposes that the dimensions for such a map would be intensity, extensity, protensity, and quality.

A number of sources today speak about scientific theory as a kind of higher order perceptual learning, the statement of a pattern of phenomena. This view of theory makes sense to me. It allows one to envisage the systematizations of Darwin, of Freud, of Boring—indeed, the overwhelming majority of psychological systematizations—as theoretical, even though they do not offer an axiomatic or mathematical assumptional structure. The process of theory-making would be analogous to those processes by which adults and children make mental mappings of a large-scale geographic terrain (Siegel & White, 1975).

The "terrain" that was confronted by Titchener and Boring was the world of experience to be encountered in the Wundtian laboratory. The organization of experience in the laboratory proceeded via the identification of significant phenomena—landmarks, designated by terms of reference that single them out for discussion and that have the effect of making them stable features, "things," on the landscape. The first-order knowledge conveyed in the Titchener manuals consisted in the identification of simple patterns of the phenomena to be recurrently encountered in the terrain. This recognition of recurrent regularities, connections between things, is analogous to the learning of routes or route fragments. From assembled first-order knowledge, we then proceed, in the Boring volume, toward the construction of a survey map. This is a higher order perception of the pattern of the phenomena. Boring's book does not present a survey map of sensory phenomena, but it does take a first and essential step toward the drawing of such a map. It identifies the coordinate system for such a map as intensity, extensity, protensity, and quality.[3]

Had the Boring theory been accepted, then presumably subsequent workers would have proceeded to locate new and old phenomena on the Boring landscape—similar to the way today's biologists locate their diverse phenomena on the evolutionary map created by Darwin and psychoanalysts locate diverse phenomena on the Freudian mapping. But Boring's theory in 1932 provided a summary of a world of experience that people were no longer interested in. The Wundt–Titchener laboratory, as an organized laboratory, was largely gone, no longer of central interest to any but a handful of psychologists. We have to go back to 1900, when, very rapidly, psychologists shifted away from commitment to *a* laboratory and toward a system of multiple laboratories, multiple mappings, and a multiparadigmatic structure of scientific development.

Let us summarize for a moment the dialectic of action and thought as it seemed to take place in this system of, first, small psychology laboratories. There was no good fit between the action systems and the thought systems entertained by the early Wundtians. Their science had a good deal of ritualism to it. Productive interchange between action and thought for these philosopher—psychologists was virtually impossible, and those who expected such an interchange became frustrated and moved off. Some individuals nevertheless persevered with the procedures and, in time, we find first-order knowledge and second-order knowledge, theory, arising out of the laboratories. Boring's theory was not all grown on the soil of these laboratories. He acknowledged that important parts of his thinking came from Lashley and early neuropsychological inquiry. But the central phenomena he was attempting to map were those identified in those laboratories. The laboratories had an unanticipated but fundamentally creative effect. The theories of epistemology with which Wundt began were not debatable in his laboratory. But Boring's book is a limited species of physicalistic epistemology. And this theory is potentially debatable, at least in part, by the procedures in the laboratory.

[3] It should be noted that this image of a theory as a map seems convenient as a heuristic. A map can be represented as a set of landmarks linked by actions or operations, and if a theory is thought of in this alternate way, one has framed it in terms used by Piaget to discuss higher order thought. If the operations linking events are of a strictly algebraic or algorithmic character, then one has the strict kind of hypothetico-deductive theorizing proposed in the classical philosophy of science. However, strictly mathematical theories are so rare in psychology that it seems likely that we need a more generalized notion. Loosely linked events may be thought of as linked on maps or by operations, and the difference between these discourses may be more psychological than logical. Those who are more visual-minded might prefer one metaphor; those more auditory-minded, the other.

However, I do not mean to be completely evenhanded about the question of whether first-order human knowledge of experience is better approximated in geometric or corresponding algebraic terms. Mathematically, the question may make little difference, but psychologically there are some good reasons for believing that people find spatial metaphors more comfortable for the first-order temporal integration of experience than they do formal metaphors. In addition, they may have to assemble spatial metaphors at times as a platform for the creation of formal metaphors. Suggestions that this might be true are that: (1) presently identified systems of visual memory seem much more powerful and accessible than are systems of linguistic memory; (2) visual and spatial techniques such as the method of loci seem very useful as a mnemonic for verbal material; (3) theorists of cognitive development have regularly argued that figurative, ikonic, or eidetic organization of thought emerge before abstract, symbolic, or operational organizations; (4) one finds competent mapping of objects in space much earlier and more widely in children than one finds formal operations; and (5) the recurrent suggestion, beginning with Sir Francis Galton, that scientific training supplants "visual-mindedness" with "auditory-mindedness." All of these lines of evidence are quite argumentative, but the idea now seems worth some analytic attention (e.g., Siegel and White, 1975).

III. Some Control Cases

There were two other species of psychological empiricism before the turn of the century: one was the child study movement and the other was the mental testing movement, which grew out of Galton's anthropometry. Neither was a purely scientific effort; both had a practical thrust. Hall's child study movement was directed by concerns about education and social work. Mental testing, while not yet considered practical, was obviously directed toward the attainment of practical instruments. While neither movement was purely scientific, both were characterized by the frequent appeal to the rituals and rhetoric of science. There were journals, and papers passed back and forth. There was a community of individuals more or less dedicated to the work. There were efforts to be precise and objective. There was, at least in the case of mental testing, cross-comparison of findings and the beginning of a body of methodological knowledge. Yet neither movement seemed to develop that special internal chemistry that one associates with scientific development, and it may be useful to inquire why for a few moments.

Led by G. Stanley Hall, something called the child study movement was created in the 1890s. A rather formidable amount of publication could be collected together under the name of child study. Louis Wilson (1898–1912), librarian at Clark University, compiled bibliographies that totaled in all 4519 entries (L. Wilson, 1975). The great majority of the entries have to do with children's behavior. But the reports in these bibliographies seem to spring from a great variety of settings—the school, the home, the courts—and there is a mixture of controlled inquiry, observation, clinical case material, anecdotal material, plus speculative argument generally drawn from that loose evolutionism that Hall was later to make famous in his two volumes on adolescence (Hall, 1908). The child study movement was only partially a psychological movement. It was an interdisciplinary movement, and the modern reader can imagine the scope of these child study bibliographies if he thinks of the current journal *Child Development: Abstracts and Bibliography* and imagines it to be expanded so that it includes much more of the writing in the child service professions than that journal now does.

Still, there was a lot of information about children's behavior mixed into the child study publications, and it is interesting to ask why nothing apparently happened with that information. The child study writings appear to offer a case in which a social proof structure to energize scientific development was not possible for the group. Members wrote from different arenas of experience. Members used different terms of reference. Patterns of phenomena identified by one member of the group could not be placed beside patterns of phenomena available to others. None of those cross-comparisons that identify the factual and the artifactual were available. Common dimensions and mappings of experiences were not available to the group. So there could be no Titchener-like manual, no Boring-like theory. The findings of the child study movement, even the very existence of the movement, have been largely forgotten by contemporary psychologists.

Galton's hope of using scientific human breeding to advance human evolution, his faith in the possibility of eugenics, led him in the 1880s to introduce procedures intended to allow measurement of desirable human physical and mental characteristics. During the 1880s and 1890s there appears to be a growing exploration of the possibility of measuring individual differences in humans. Whipple's (1914–1915/1973) manuals of physical and mental tests, almost as impressive in their own sphere as is Titchener's for the psychological laboratory, give clear evidence of a considerable volume and variety of foregoing empirical work. Yet the mental testing movement of that day, and indeed to this very day, has not given evidence of what most would regard as strong theoretical development. Yet in this case, unlike the case of child study, members of the movement did confront similar arenas of experience. They used similar nomenclature. They were able to compare experiences—the Whipple manuals show that—and they were to develop a body of methodological knowledge.

Some limited theoretical development did take place in the mental testing movement when, in the 1920s and 1930s, factor analytic studies were undertaken to try to segregate dimensions of mental ability. (Again, as in the Boring effort, the first step toward theory seemed to lie in the effort to establish those dimensions along which a map of the phenomena might be laid out.) But to this day, the factor mappings of human intellect seem to be quite argumentative (R. B. Cattell, 1971). A few of the differentiations of mind offered by these analyses seem to be given general credence—for example, fluid versus crystallized intelligence, spatial versus verbal ability—but not too many. Perhaps mental testing has been too intensely practical an activity to allow for theory building. There has simply not been the effort. Or perhaps the landmark phenomena of the mental tests—statistical statements of what individuals in such and such a demographic category do on such and such a collection of items—simply do not allow for a derivation of convincing causal mappings. In any case, the present status of the mental testing movement, like that of the child study movement, appears to show that one needs something more than empiricism, nominal categorizations and ordinal scalings, and the intercommunication of objective findings among a group in order to establish a growth pattern tending toward integrative theory.

IV. The Pluralization of Psychology

Beginning around 1900, there was a sharp change in the psychological enterprise. First, psychologists began to diversify their activities sufficiently so that there was no longer one arena of psychological investigation, one laboratory sought for. Second, the initial commitment of psychologists to philosophical epistemology disappeared completely and was virtually repressed. Physically and ideologically the psychologists walked out of the philosophy departments. They took their stand on a methodological behaviorism, denying that mind, consciousness, knowing, attention, and so forth were substantive issues for psychological work. Third, the psychologists of the 20th century self-consciously tried to establish an enterprise, or enterprises, in which theory and research were designed for each other.

Introspection had not worked well as a method. There were conflicts among findings at different laboratories that did not seem easy to resolve. The work of the Wurtzburg group cast doubt on how much of the work of the mind one might actually find by searching through consciousness. Introspectionism might have been set aside because of its shortcomings, but it seems equally likely that it was swept aside by the rush to create other laboratories, other arenas of experience, for psychological investigation. Reports of the death of the Wundtian laboratory have been somewhat exaggerated, anyway. Most of the procedures of the Wundtian laboratory—the psychophysical procedures, the studies of sensory phenomena, the studies of simple and complex reaction time, the studies of association and rote memory—all survive nicely today, technologically upgraded, analyzed in different ways, but all present and in use in diverse contemporary laboratories.

New kinds of laboratories of psychology were wanted in the early 20th century. Geraldine Joncich, as quoted previously, spoke of the American rush to judge psychology applicable to education, industrial management, medicine, child-rearing, domestic relations, and the military. It would be difficult to overestimate the force of these pressures for social utilization in giving life and form to psychology as a discipline (White, 1976c).

The Wundtian procedures opened windows on sensation, reaction time, and association. But there were scientific and social pressures dictating the need to take a broader view of psychological events. What about long-term changes in human behavior and their relationship to various social support systems? There was the broad empiricism of child study. What about learning? There were the animal laboratories and the memory drum laboratories for human memory studies. What about human performance capabilities, human "intelligence"? There were the procedures for mental testing. What about human emotions and human emotional disorders? There was psychoanalysis. Whether or not these were good questions, whether or not these were good laboratories, it seems reasonable to believe that the psychologists of the early 1900s dispersed into different kinds of empiricism because they wanted to look at and think about a variety of aspects of human behavior. They wanted to aim more peepholes at the elephant—the human psychological systems—because they wanted a wider view, a broader experience with the phenomena of human behavior. Segregating themselves into distinct scientific collectivities, each group exchanging information back and forth about the view from its window, the groups gradually erected different theoretical formulations. Psychology became multiparadigmatic, with several kinds of empiricism, several collectivities, several dialectical processes, several strains of theorizing.

An awareness of this multiparadigmatic structure seemed to emerge when, in fairly short order, four books appeared to give accounts of the several psychologies that had come into existence (Murchison, 1925, 1930; Woodworth, 1931; Heidbreder, 1933). Table 1 pictures the major approaches to psychology as given by these sources and, as well, some chronological changes in the set as they were seen in later editions of Woodworth (Woodworth, 1948; Woodworth and Sheehan, 1964). Two of the three sources saw these approaches as "schools," the third as "psychologies." In fact, the groups of individuals did not seem exactly like medieval groups of school men adhering to different philosophical or theological systems of thought and engaged in disputation with one another. In part, at least, they resembled groups of people who had committed themselves to the exploration of different data bases. There was now not one laboratory, one window, but a number of laboratories.

It would be my guess that the internal chemistry of the disparate empirical groups had been schematically the same, corresponding to that suggested earlier for the Wundt–Titchener group. How does one move from one man learning and knowing to a community of knowers and learners? How does one create an *e pluribus unum* of thought? There must be a social proof structure to allow people to transmit symbolic models of experiences to one another and to permit them to hammer out agreements about what they mean. The engineering of group knowing—in science or in education—may be constrained a first time by the limitations and peculiarities of the symbol systems in which experiences and arguments must be modeled for transmission, and constrained a second time by those restrictions and organizations of the behavior of individuals necessary to maximize the efficacy of their participation in the games of a social proof structure (Harré and Secord, 1972). Scientists are, as it were, a committee of artists who paint pictures of reality in words and numbers. They are constrained by their medium and by the committee process.

We arrive, ultimately, at systematizations in public thinking that reflect both the benefits and the constraints of the cooperative process. The aggregated knowledge collected in an enterprise such as the learning theory movement lies far beyond that possible to any individual. And yet in important regards the consensual formulations of the group about learning are far more limited and "stupid" than the understandings of the private individuals who participate in the group game (White, 1970, 1976a).

Among the several paradigms of psychology after 1900 we find learning theory and psychoanalysis. They appeared to be nuclear for the two distinct clusters of activity that emerged in the three successive editions of Woodworth pictured in Table 1. Both were proclaimed as sciences of psychology by their founders, yet they looked like very different enterprises. However, if we examine the two group activities we find some general characteristics that are alike, the elements of a social proof structure. And we find aspects of group engineering that are dissimilar. The dissimilar aspects may reflect the effort of the learning-theory group to maximize the principle of proof and of the psychoanalytic group to maximize the principle of consistency.

The following general characteristics of the groups seem alike.

1. *There is a shared arena of experience.* Both learning theorists and psychoanalysts act on the world in characteristic ways. Each arranges a characteristic game by which he interacts in a formalized way with a behaving organism, the learning theorist with an animal or a human, the psychoanalyst with a human. Actually, for both the learning theorist and the psychoanalyst there is not one game but what

Table 1
Schools of Psychology in the 1930s and Later

Murchison, 1925	Murchison, 1930	Heidbreder, 1933	Woodworth, 1931	Woodworth, 1948	Woodworth & Sheehan, 1964
Behaviorism	Behaviorism, Russian	Behaviorism	Behaviorism	Associationism Behaviorism	Associationism Early behaviorism Soviet psychology Later behaviorists Behaviorism, nature of mediating process
Dynamic	Dynamic	Dynamic			
Gestalt	Configurational	Gestalt	Gestalt-configurationism	Gestalt	Gestalt 1. Lewin's field theory
Purposive	Hormic		Purposive-hormic	Hormic and holistic psychologies 1. Purposivism-hormic– McDougall 2. Holistic psychologies a. Organismic–Meyer, Coghill, Goldstein Kantor	Motivation and the unity of the person 1. Purposiveness and hormic psychology–McDougall (Lorenz, Tinbergen), R.B. Cattell 2. Organismic–Meyer, Goldstein, Maslow 3. Personalistic–Calkins, Stern

	Reaction				
"Structural"	Poststructural	Structuralism	Introspective-Existential	b. Personalistic– Calkins, Stern c. The "understanding" psychology–Spranger, G.W. Allport	4. Personology–Murray 5. The "understanding" psychology–Dilthey 6. The person as being and becoming–Rogers existentialism
	Functional	Functionalism	Functionalist	Functionalist	Functionalist

	Analytical	Psychoanalytic	Psychoanalysis
			1. Adler
			2. Jung
				Psychoanalysis
				1. Adler
				2. Jung
				3. neo-Freudians
					Psychoanalysis
					1. Ego psychology
					Other analytical schools
					1. Adler
					2. Jung
					3. Social analytical
					  a. Horney
					  b. Fromm
					  c. Sullivan

"Factor"		William James			

one might call a family of procedures. The procedures vary, but all of the learning-theory procedures have significant formal elements in common (White, 1970) so that, for example, one could never mistake a variant of a learning-theory game for a variant of a psychoanalytic game. The formal similarities between games in a family are, I believe, created by constraints on games imposed so that all will register what the particular collectivity has decided to call an event.

2. *There is a shared notion of what events, or phenomena, there are to be noticed.* Consider a half hour of a child's life. Consider, as a kind of fantasy, that we are going to look at all the child's behavior at once. We are once and for all going to encounter that "whole child" that everyone talks about. So during that half hour we will collect 20 channels of psychophysiological tracings, establish where the child stands in intelligence, creativity, spatial ability, and so forth, determine his lateralization, inquire about his Piagetian stage of development and his moral stage level, and so on, and so forth. Or, being "unobtrusive," we will observe how he gets along with his peers, the extent of his attention span in a classroom, the degree of his fear of strange situations, his use of grammatical forms in formal and informal situations, his relations with his mother, and so on. The utter impossibility of this fantasy illustrates some important issues in psychology's empiricism.

The behavior of a child, or of any organism, presents itself as an extremely complex, dynamic, never-to-be-seen-again flux of experience. In order to speak about our encounter with that episode of behavior, we have somehow to capture it in a set of things that exist, that recur, and that may be seen again and again. We find John Dewey and B. F. Skinner in agreement on this. Dewey (1900/1965) defines psychology as "The ability to turn a living personality into an objective mechanism for the time being [p. 302]." (Cf. the previously quoted passage from the Titchener laboratory manual, reproduced on p. 66, "O is, for the time being, a psychophysical machine, a reacting machine . . . .") Skinner (1935) has argued:

> In the description of behavior it is usually assumed that both behavior and environment may be broken into parts, which may be referred to by name, and that these parts will retain their identity from experiment to experiment. If this assumption were not in some sense justified, a science of behavior would be impossible [p. 50].

We must capture the flow of psychological events (what James called the "stream of consciousness," what Watson called the "activity stream") as a set of occurrences of "things." The natural language reifies a great deal of psychological experience, and psychologists capitalize on the unanalyzed terms of reference in the natural language—terms such as *motivation, need, aggression, intelligence,* and so on, and so forth. But psychological theory attempts to transcend that vague theory built into the natural language (Mandler & Kessen, 1959), and so psychologists face all the complex problems of inventing new terms of reference for behavior. They name the phenomena encountered in their arena of experience, and thus new psychological things appear. If we can establish the right set of things, then we may be in a position to portray the living personality as an objective mechanism.

The developing child may be adequately regarded, in conceptual terms, as a cluster of interrelated responses interacting with stimuli [Bijou & Baer, 1961, p. 14].

Powerful systems of choice must be exercised to capture part of the flux in fixed terms, so that the psychologist can "observe behavior." The psychologist decides what to look at, and his choice among available options is so narrow and so arbitrary that one might very well say it involves a theory of what an event is. Furthermore, any kind of looking involves managing or staging a situation for a child. One arranges things so that the child will act in certain ways. "Unobtrusive" observations do not involve overt pushing or pulling at the child's behavior so much, but such observations do still involve management by strategic selection of the child's situation. If one is going to unobtrusively observe mother–infant verbal interaction, then one wants to observe at moments when the infant and the mother are near each other, when there is apt to be conversation, when the infant is not too fretful or hungry, and so on.

In our created or contrived situation, only limited kinds and numbers of events and reactions are recorded. It seems most reasonable to me to consider all situations of empirical observations involving scientist and child as games. They are limited, formal situations. The behavior of both experimenter and child is restricted in time, space, rhythm, and contingency. There are restricted options for legal, registered moves on the part of the experimenter and the child, those moves related to each other in rule-bound ways. An item of behavior is really a move in a game. We register a pigeon's peck at a window, a child's pressing a button, a patient's verbal account of a dream, or a clipboard check against "Acts aggressively" all as units of observed behavior and treat each as physically constant configurations. But in fact there are hundreds and thousands of physically distinct ways in which a subject can perform each. What unites each set is a communality in their effect. One can say that they are united in their tending toward a common goal, the classical Hullian device for the definition of a "molar" unit of behavior. But this kind of definition obscures the fact that the "goal" is in fact an available option in a finite set offered by the experimenter and that this act of choice is set in an overall pattern of behavioral activity created or selected by the experimenter. So it seems a trifle clearer to call each event a move in a game. Moves in a game do not tell you about the patterning of behavior, not without some analysis.

Each scientific collectivity uses and creates games in which events of the kind it wants tend to appear. The learning-theory group creates games in which events such as trials, reinforcements, response times, and so on, can be noticed and recorded. So distinct scientific groups create distinct terms of reference denoting distinctive and interesting phenomena or events within their arenas of experience.[4]

---

[4] The invention of games and the selection of events cannot be actions innocent of theory since, as noted, very powerful and arbitrary selections must be exercised to arrive at them. Yet we are here trying to picture the games as platforms on which, gradually, theory gets built. Where does one get that kind of theory that must exist before looking? For the Wundtian group, the pretheory must have existed in 19th-century philosophical writings. For the

3. There is an analytic process, part individual, part collective, by which people try to reach agreement about patterns of events "out there" and about their location. As has been just noted, the record of moves in a game does not tell one about behavior, not without some analysis. What kind of analysis?

Let us consider the nature of a fact in psychological work. The most commonly occurring fact available to psychologists has something of the following form: Such and such a person, writing in a given journal, has reported that children were placed in a described situation and they showed the following patterns of behavior according to certain stipulated indices. This is reported data, but much of the analysis necessary to deal with the report applies to one's own data prior to publication.

We are not interested in this fact. What is manifest is that somebody has made a claim. We are interested in what is factual for children. So we subject the manifest fact to analysis to try to detect the latent fact. To picture the analytic process most clearly, imagine that you do not like the journal report, do not want to believe it, are committed to a belief in a very different pattern than that which the report offers. So you seek to cast coubt on the credibility of the report. You might want to see if there were decent controls, if the situation was a plausible one for children, if there was anything funny about the recording of responses, the scaling of indices, the statistics. Broadening the attack, you might very well cast a jaundiced eye at the credibility of the investigator or the reputability of the journal. You would use all of your first-order information of the kind that was proposed in our previous discussion as having been available to Titchener, the information he did print and the information he did not print. Indeed, it is exactly the possession of information or bases of judgment like this that makes one a competent or trained investigator.

Very few journal articles could survive so merciless an attack. Most psychological research is simply not that airtight. Generally speaking, you could find a way to assign the pattern of findings, tentatively, as possibly related to the procedure, the statistics, and so on. The study has told you something, but you do not know whether that something is informative about children or about the game that the experimenter has played with the children or, conceivably, about the higher order game that investigators play with each other when they exchange information in a scientific collectivity.

---

learning-theory group, the pretheory must have been the "learning theory point of view," expressed in the crude schematizations offered by Thorndike and the reflexology of Sechenov and Pavlov (White, 1970). For Freud, the pretheory lay very likely in Jacksonian neurology and in that trail of 19th-century work on hysteria and hypnosis that led toward his psychiatric practice (Ellenberger, 1970). Later in this paper, I will speak of a kind of recursive process in psychological theorizing in which old ideas get transposed to new forms, presumably to become aligned with new knowledge bases. Part of the dialectical process we are here considering might involve a reciprocal process. New looking generates new theory, but new theory generates the need for new kinds of observations.

Ideally, you would keep watching for that funny ambiguous pattern of findings. You might find that the pattern keeps recurring in the same journal or among the same circle of people, always asserted on vague or sloppy data, so that you could dismiss it as a kind of pet theory of this group, held without regard for the facts. You might find that it continually occurs only in certain kinds of procedures or only when certain statistics or controls are missing, so that you can dismiss it as a specifiable artifact: If you behave this way in an experiment, you get the pattern; if you behave that way, you don't get the pattern. Or you might find that it continually occurs everywhere. Different people using different methods continually report it so that ultimately you are reluctantly forced to conclude that it reflects a truth about children.

This process I have pictured for an individual is the basic process of the empirical dialectic that seems to go on in a scientific group facing a common arena of experience. The process seems to be dictated by the fact that one cannot directly observe the behaviors of children but rather must observe the properties of games reflecting a mixture of children's behavior and one's own behavior. One must tease apart the sources by using the kinds of analyses undertaken by our hypothetical investigator.

Note that no matter where our hypothetical investigator comes out, he learns something. He learns a truth either about a journal editor, about a group of people, about an aspect of methodology, or about children. The knowledge-building process of the scientific collectivity proceeds on several fronts, with information about methods developing as information about psychology develops. This separation of the factual from the artifactual may be a part of those higher order resolutions of egocentrism that Piaget has argued is entailed at all levels of cognitive development. One subjects the flow of experience to analysis in order to try to disentangle the acts and actors of "looking" from those of the "looked at." One does this by establishing an acts X events matrix that appears to be an analytic format common to the Piagetian sensorimotor construction of reality and the Campbell–Fiske multitrait–multimethod procedure for construct validation (White, 1976a).

The empirical dialectic of a scientific collectivity also works to locate patterns of events in frameworks of time, space, person, sex, age, and social class. One investigator reports a finding. The next cannot find it. A third, noticing that the first used lower-class children and the second used middle-class children, demonstrates that the pattern exists only at a certain class locus. Or, quite commonly in developmental psychology, a series of investigations are conducted to determine whether some feature of thought should properly be assigned to 10-year-olds, 8-year-olds, or 4-year-olds. These localizing activities of the empirical dialectic are of considerable importance because they set the stage for an overall mapping of the phenomena encountered in the arena of experience, that is, for theory.

4. *There is a social construction of reality, the projection of a pattern or picture of the interrelationships among psychological events.* The internal chemistry of a psychological group gradually generates a body of information about psychological events, patterns of phenomena plus variegated information about the localizations

of such patterns on relevant dimensions. The paradigm groups sort out the factual from the artifactual, more stringently in the case of the learning-theory group, less stringently in the case of a group such as the psychoanalytic one. Events have been found, and some others have been conjectured. Each group holds what Vygotsky (1962) would call "spontaneous concepts" and "scientific concepts," terms of reference that are defined in direct commerce with the procedure and the conjectured terms of reference. The learning-theory group has "seen" stimuli, responses, and speed of response; it has conjectured terms such as *habit, drive,* and *generalization.* The psychoanalytic group has seen reports of dreams, catharsis, transference phenomena; it conjectures terms such as *ego, id, identification,* and *the oral stage.*

The ultimate work of both groups is the projection of a map of the phenomena, a kind of map discussed earlier in conjunction with the discussion of the Titchener and Boring distillates of the earlier laboratory work. All the fragmentary information about phenomena and their relative localizations is now projected onto a unifying landscape. Ideally this unification of the diverse phenomena would be rigorous, with the kinds of mathematical linkages among terms that would allow prediction and control. In actual practice this unification is sketchy and probabilistic; one can express the gains achieved through such theorization on the intellectual side as gains of simplification of the phenomena, on the pragmatic side as marginal gains accruing from a reduction of uncertainty. Theories simplify phenomena. They allow one to look at patterns rather than isolated items. And theories give one the benefit of informed expectations about phenomena, even if they do not confer the benefits of exact predictions.

It would be too much to argue that either the learning theory of the psychoanalytic theories arose solely through commerce with the empiricism of those traditions. That would argue that people went into such activities in complete blindness, not knowing what to expect, and such was not the case. In both cases, people entered into the traditions on the basis of estimations of the promise of the activities, including estimations of the promise of the work and prefigurations of the kinds of theorizing to be expected.

V. The Principle of Proof
versus the Principle of Consistency

Learning theory and psychoanalysis were both proclaimed by their founders to be sciences of human behavior. In the view taken here, both had some reasonable basis for such a claim. Both offered procedures to their adherents, both could generate a constructive debate among members about what could be seen through the windows of the procedures, both offered theoretical sketches that, at least in principle, one might expect to be upgraded and reformulated as more and more information was crystallized through the workings of the scientific group. And, in the case of both learning theory and psychoanalysis, the theory and method were in some general sense both designed to fit together.

But there was a major difference in their establishment as a communal enterprise. Learning theory was deliberately organized to facilitate proof, the experience of one man exactly confirmable by the experience of another. The experimental study of learning has rested upon special procedures so arranged to facilitate replication, communication of procedure and findings, and systematic variation of factors. Only because we seek exact social cooperation among scientists would we ever ask a child to engage in half-hour bouts of solitary learning, with experience doled out to him in little parcels called trials, with simple little discrete events supposedly connected to simple little discrete action patterns. There is, of course, a large trade-off involved in the enhancement of the principle of proof. We trade off against complexity of reflection and analysis of experience; we want to maintain an orderly public discussion, and an orderly public discussion is greatly facilitated if we confine the discussion to what is publicly visible. So we enforce "parsimony" and we trade off against plausibility. In order to create our proof system, we are forced to create situations for children that are very unlike the natural situations in which they ordinarily learn, situations that we will have to interpret if our research is to be anything more than an empty game, if it is to have implications for the natural phenomena of human behavior.

Now, proof is of the very essence in scientific work and, on the face of it, as we maximize proof, we maximize the scientific quality of psychological work. The proof–plausibility trade-off in psychological work is very painful to those within and without the field and has been so ever since its beginning. Wundt, as has been noted, doubted that all psychology could ever be gotten into the laboratory, and there is today a significant modern movement that joins him in arguing that we must conjoin to laboratory work studies in anthropology—as modern proponents put it, work that is ethologically, ecologically, or naturalistically valid. They want more plausibility in the situations in which we observe behavior.

It is interesting in this regard to consider psychoanalysis as a case where proof structure was greatly compromised to achieve consistency in the sense of the entertaining of a broad variety of phenomena in the theory, and plausibility as a practical therapy. Freud's extensive mappings of human behavior are aligned with a method of procedure, although it seems certain that there was much more built into Freudian theory than the fruits of Freud's first ventures into psychoanalytic empiricism. In part, Freud's theories reflect the phenomena he encountered on the couch; in part, they reflect an evolutionary view of mind and brain developed in Jacksonian neurology; in part, they reflect an awareness of diverse phenomena developed in a century of antecedent work on hypnosis and hysteria (Ellenberger, 1970). Freud was not concerned, above all, to follow parsimony. He was concerned, first and foremost, to see the neurotic phenomena with which he had to deal as part of a system and to fathom the broad outlines of that system. So Freud theorized, broadly and speculatively.

The essential device used by Freud was the principle of consistency, the attempt to constrain interpretation of the phenomena of concern by the creation of a very broad common mapping of the given and of many other phenomena. Therefore

Freud filled books with vast mappings, many and diverse phenomena, and many imaginary terms and assumptions.

The theorizing offered by Freud bound together a wide variety of human phenomena in a web of plausible connections. We are today so habituated to psychoanalytic thinking, so routinely aware of its propositional structure, and so familiar with discussions of its difficulties that we tend to underestimate the initial impact of the system. At one time it seemed marvelous to people that so many odd and diverse phenomena could be made coherent, placed all together on one map. Consider Ernest Jones' (1955) description of his initial reaction to Freud's psychoanalytic work. He was describing Freud's famous case of Dora.

> This first case history of Freud's has for years served as a model for students of psychoanalysis, and although our knowledge has greatly progressed since then, it makes today as interesting reading as ever. It was the first of Freud's post-neurological writings I had come across, at the time of its publication, and I well remember the deep impression the intuition and the close attention to detail displayed in it made on me. Here was a man who not only listened closely to every word his patient spoke but regarded each such utterance as every whit as definite and as in need of correlation as the phenomena of the physical world. At the present day it is hard to convey what an amazing event it was for anyone to take the data of psychology so seriously. Yet that it should less than half a century after seem a commonplace is a measure of the revolution effected by one man [p. 257].

Jones went on to become a follower of Freud and not all who initially encountered Freud were so persuaded by him. But, still, his remarks give us a clue to Freud's indubitable appeal to many in his time. The great evidential strength of the learning theorist, following the principle of proof, is that what he sees he can discuss and debate with others. The great evidential strength of the psychoanalyst, following the principle of plausibility, is that he sees much more of what goes on in human behavior that is of natural interest to the general run of people.

Since any and all paradigms in psychology offer to their adherents programs that contain both proof and consistency, truth and beauty, the question is not which one do we want but how much of one will we give off to get the other. The answer both of the Wundt–Titchener tradition and of the learning-theory tradition was that we will give off almost everything to get strong proof structures, because the existence of proof is synonymous with science, and psychology is or must be scientific. But there was much ritualism and much anxious striving in the eager embrace of scientific status by the early psychologists. Nowadays, psychological textbooks routinely reassure students at great length on the point that psychology is scientific, although, in the end, one frequently finds great doubt about the point on the part of students, psychologists, and diverse members of the scientific community. It all depends on what one thinks science is exactly, and on whether one considers those aspects of psychology that are very close to neurophysiology or those that verge on philosophy or social commentary. Suppose one were to cease trying to establish that mysterious conceptual boundary that might tell us once and for all whether or not psychology is a science. Suppose one were to ask an easier question instead. Psychology rests on thinking about human nature aided and abetted by controlled empiricism, the experience of one man communicated to and aligned with the experience of others. How is the sharing and cross-alignment of experience best managed? The answer may very well be that for some procedures and some issues one is best served by maximizing proof, while for others—because of the relative weakness of the procedures, because of the scope of the questions—one is best served by maximizing consistency. Psychology is a collection of empiricisms, some so arranged as to advance thought about human behavior through the identification of patterns of phenomena by proof, others through the identification of such patterns of consistency.

But the sine qua non of psychology is a social proof structure. Systematic philosophy, no less than psychology, deals in facts; try to write an account of human epistemology without an appeal to perceived and received experience—it would be impossible. What distinguishes the psychologist is that he does not leave the influx of experience to chance or casual encounter. He arranges an influx of experience in some orderly manner, and he makes those compromises and arrangements that will allow him to communicate and compare experiences with others. And so we find Freud again and again insisting in his writings that the ultimate proving ground for systematic debates is in the encounter with the psychoanalytic patient, and we find him in his papers at great pains to set forth and compare his psychoanalytic experience with those of others.

Freud was a contemporary of Titchener's. He settled himself in his laboratory at just about the same time that Titchener set forth his brass instruments at Cornell. One could hardly imagine two more unlike species of psychological writings than Titchener's laboratory manuals and Freud's psychoanalytic papers. Yet, in the view taken here, both were accounts of first-order experience drawn from standardized action systems, and so one might not be surprised to find some structural similarities in nature of what is being communicated in them. In a certain social engineering sense, the problem faced by Freud was identical to that faced by Titchener and by all others who seek to participate in a cooperative construction of experience. Part of the private body of knowledge available to an individual is to be merged into a system of public knowledge. There are some less and some more complicated ways of bringing this about. Suppose we consider messages in words and numbers only. The less complicated way is for an individual to put forth models or instructions to others in a publicly available symbol system. He can write an essay, a story, or a poem. Recipients of such messages may absorb information, adapting their cognitive structure to encompass it, and thus sharing ultimately in the knowledge of the sender. This happens in the mass of symbolic communications among individuals in our society, and the social arrangements necessary to bring this about are by no means simple. However, there is a looseness in everyday written exchanges that motivates a need for more complicated social arrangements allowing for a more careful and formal process of merging knowledge.

In ordinary communication, the writer speaks from his world of experience and the reader attempts to transpose the message toward applicability to his different world of experience. What if we arrange things so that speaker and writer share an experiential world, by communicating specifications so that both can act in roughly the same way and look at roughly the same things? In ordinary communication, the writer uses the resources of the discourse system available to him as fully and as freely as he can. The ordinary writer of English is free to use whatever will have impact. What if we put restrictions on the discourse system such that whenever possible terms of reference are "operationalized," making them accessible to the observations of others. In ordinary discourse, two or more people may conduct an argument, one message contradicting another, but such debates are often blurred in the sense that it is difficult to know what the issues are and how the argument could be settled. What if we set forth rules of debate intended to maximize our ability to judge whether an argument is about observations or about inferences, and further intended to maximize our ability to judge where among the observations or inferences the exact disagreement is to be found? Finally, what if we adopt procedures for labeling and locating events such that agreed-upon entries in public knowledge may be cumulatively related to one another in synthetic maps and models?

As we move from the less complicated to the more complicated process for arriving at public knowledge, we (a) move toward social proof structures characteristic of science; and (b) we restrict and organize the way in which members of the collectivity may act and speak. We pay the price of restriction and formalization of behavior in order to get better communication. Freud seeks cooperative knowledge together with other psychoanalysts. Therefore we find him making provisions for the more complicated kind of communication.

(1) He offers procedural statements, statements of how to act in a psychoanalytic encounter. Most of the procedure that is offered is discussed with an eye to furthering the efficacy of psychoanalytic therapy. Nonetheless such procedural communication tends to direct psychoanalytic members toward a standardized and shared body of experience. This standardization is, undoubtedly, one reason why Freud speaks so frequently of a "science" of psychoanalysis. In the citations to follow, dates after Freud's name refer to the publication date of the titled essay, and roman numerals refer to the volume number in the collected papers (Freud, 1952) in which the essay is to be found.

In "On Psychotherapy" (Freud, 1904, I), we find Freud arguing that one should restrict psychoanalytic practice to those patients with a "normal mental condition," since the treatment is not intended for those with "states of confusion," severe depression, or psychoses.

In an encyclopedia article, entitled "Psycho-analysis" (Freud, 1922, V), we find him describing the "fundamental technical rule" whereby patients are urged to express thoughts objectively, freely, and calmly, regardless of the patient's personal reaction to those thoughts. Freud always observed that the subjective context of these reactions is a key to evoking hidden memories.

In "Remarks Upon the Theory and Practice of Dream Interpretation" (1923, V), Freud offers the choice of four procedures for initiating dream interpretation. One can choose: a salient element as the starting point, or, by a chronological approach, examine items in a dream element by element, asking for associations to each, or the analyst may ask about the dream in terms of the previous day's experiences, ignoring the actual dream itself, or finally, experienced patients may be encouraged to choose their own approach to interpretation.

A 1937 essay, "Analysis Terminable and Interminable" (Freud, V), defends the use of setting a goal or final date for analysis. With proper timing, Freud claims that this "blackmailing device" can be a useful therapeutic tool.

(2) The special experiential ecology of the psychoanalyst yields often surprising but characteristic phenomena, noted by special terms of reference. People who enter the land of psychoanalysis may come upon screen memories, false recalls, strategies of resistance, and overtures of love. Freud notes that some individuals, especially neurotics, remember surprisingly detailed, yet mundane childhood experiences, even though contemporaneous occurrences that, according to their parents aroused intense emotions in them as children, are forgotten ("Screen Memories," Freud, 1899, V).

Psychoanalytic patients often have a false memory (fausse reconnaisance") and vigorously insist that they have already related something to their analyst, a trick of recall that Freud likens to the *déjà vu* experience. He describes this phenomenon at length in "Fausse Reconnaisance" ("Déjà Reconte" from Psycho-Analytic Treatment, 1913, II).

In "Further Recommendations in the Technique of Psychoanalysis" (1913, II), Freud notes that some patients, especially early in their treatment, are wont to meticulously ready themselves for their analytic hour or talk over the treatment with friends. He suggests that these should be treated as devices of resistance to treatment.

A female patient may show discrete or overt signs that she is falling in love with the therapist. Freud (1915, II) discusses the phenomenon and its significance in "Observations on Transference-Love."

(3) Significant phenomena have been identified and named. Now Freud offers suggestions for disentangling the artifactual from the factual.

How can a therapist handle a number and variety of patients each day? Freud suggests "evenly hovering attention," which reduces the chance of the distortion and/or exhaustion that result from excessive concentration. If one actively attends, interprets, and analyzes, one receives only preconceptions. The true meanings become apparent only with time (Recommendations for Physicians on the Psycho-Analytic Method of Treatment, 1912, II). In this same essay, Freud warns that one endangers the therapy by seeking the new and dramatic, since this makes the therapist vulnerable to the forms of resistance a patient may bring into the session.

People undergoing treatment will spontaneously recall childhood events. In some instances, the therapist may first accept these accounts but later consider them to be confabulations inadvertently suggested by the therapist himself in the course of treatment. (See "From the History of an Infantile Neurosis," Freud, 1918, III.)

In "Constructions in Analysis" (1937, V), Freud notes that a patient's apparent concurrence with a therapist's interpretation may be misleading. It may merely be compliance, and the true consent must be substantiated by other signs appearing in the therapy.

(4) If the artifactual in psychoanalysis can be set aside, patterns of the phenomena can be identified.

Regardless of the details in any particular case, Freud felt that hysteria can always be traced back to sexual roots (see, e.g., "The Aetiology of Hysteria," 1896, I). This notion was, of course, later superseded in Freud's own writings by an argument that the inevitable source was not literal but fantasized sexual experience.

A particular obsession may stem from any action, through embellishment and/or regular repetition. Freud (1907, II) describes and provides as examples the patterned development of such varied obsessions in "Obsessive Acts and Religious Practices."

In "The Predisposition to Obsessional Neuroses" (1913, II), Freud notes that the order of severity of the principal neuroses (hysteria, obsessive neuroses, paranoia, and dementia praecox) seems to correspond to the order in which they manifest themselves in development over the life span—hysterical symptoms earliest, dementia praecox after puberty and in adult life.

A few years later, Freud noted that it is common for a girl entering a household in a domestic service to manifest fantasies about supplanting the mistress in the affections of the master of the house, becoming the wife instead. (See "Some Character-Types Met With in Psycho-Analytic Work", 1915, IV.)

These thoughts illustrate certain special features in Freud's writings designed to align his work with that of a communicating group. The communicating group develops knowledge together—even though the psychoanalytic method was not solely designed for the facilitation of knowledge gathering and arrangements were not as highly developed as they were in Titchener's communicating group.

The fundamental novelty in psychoanalysis is procedure and, flowing from the dissemination of the procedural invention, the development of a discussable new arena of experience. Freud invented a new ecology of human interaction, a kind of standardized encounter between human beings never existing in quite the same way before the late 19th century. So, also, did the originators of the new ecology provided for in the Wundt–Titchener laboratory, and so did the inventors of the procedures characteristic of the laboratories of the learning theory movement. Individuals consenting to play the specialized games of these ecologies thereby qualified for the higher-order game characteristic of a social proof structure. They began to learn together.

The evolution of the learning theory movement and psychoanalysis in the 20th century is of considerable interest, because here are not simply two rival paradigms but significant contrasting cases in the organization of a social proof structure.

Both contain the formal elements providing for cooperation, but learning theory has been strongly organized to maximize proof and psychoanalysis has been strongly organized to maximize consistency.

"Proof" in an empirical context is ultimately the ability of one man to see with his own eyes what another man says should be seen; falsification is ultimately an assertion that one has looked under the right time and place and circumstances and one has failed to see the expected. A social proof structure maximizes the availability of proofs and falsifications. However, the purpose of the social organization is not only the maximization of proof, but the projection of patterns and a consistent order in the phenomena. Scientific games that maximize proof must evolve differently from those that trade off proof for consistency.

My own analysis of the learning-theory movement would be that it rather quickly and efficiently did itself out of business in the first half of the century by repeatedly demonstrating phenomena that were not easily assimilable to the general point of view or to the specific theoretical formulations that arose in the 1930s and 1940s. There were repeated demonstrations of set effects, orienting effects, expectancy, effects, and perceptual learning effects that were not resolvable on the parsimonious behavioristic platform originally erected as a basis for theory. These findings virtually forced the tradition to abandon the behavioristic pretheory and to reopen an analysis in which consideration of behavioral phenomena is mixed with consideration of central structural variables. Some individuals predicted at the outset of behaviorism that this kind of wider outlook would be necessary, but what could not be predicted was the gradual development of instrumental capabilities in the movement that permitted the growth of an empirical cognitivism (White, 1976a). The basic questions that motivated learning theory are now pursued in the neuropsychological analysis of learning, emotion, and attention, in the information-processing analysis of the structural organization of perceptual processing, and in the developmental analyses of the organization of thought. None of these are simple elaborations of the learning-theory movement, but all benefit from those chemistries of scientific development that were created in the work of that movement. Hebb's (1960) argument makes a good deal of sense, that psychology retreated from cognitivism in order to better develop the instrumental and methodological competences that would permit a fresh and better assault.

The dynamics of empirical development have not worked as efficiently for psychoanalysis. When one teaches psychoanalysis, one still teaches Freud. It is difficult to propose minor modifications of a far-reaching system that ties many events together in a web of plausibility. Most of the modifications that have been proposed in a rather huge volume of post-Freudian publication have served to introduce minor changes in emphasis and minor elements of detail into a system that pretty much stands as it was originally projected—for example, points such as the emphasis on ego functions and defense mechanisms, or object-relations theory. But Freudian theory has benefited from another level of reconciliation, what one might call a between-paradigm dialectic.

VI. The Dialectic between Paradigms

If psychology became pluralistic and dispersed into a number of disparate ventures in the early 20th century, there still remained among the generality of psychologists a desire to find one overall system of mapping, one theory. The psychoanalytic theorists attempted to explain all psychological phenomena or, failing that, all psychologists. The stimulus–response group was explicit in the hope that eventually the behavioristic terminology might serve as a common scientific discourse for all the phenomena of psychology. So far, these hopes for a common discourse have been a prominent feature of psychological work in this century. There have been repeated large and small efforts to unify psychoanalytic and learning-theory analyses and, as the paradigms of the field have become more diverse, a variety of cross-mappings among information processing, ethology, genetic epistemology, mental testing, and neuropsychology.

The diverse groups of the field are, in a scientific and empirical sense, fundamentally out of touch with one another. They do not discuss the same world of experience. How do cross-mappings occur? It appears likely that cross-mappings are possible because one can recognize common or similar landmarks on the diverse theoretical landscapes. Probably most of the communalities exist because all species of paradigm use terms of reference in the natural language to identify entities in their theoretical discussion. The psychoanalysts talk about fear and anxiety. Students of animal behavior recognize, or can create, situations where something resembling fear and anxiety seems to make itself manifest in animal behavior. So one can align the psychoanalytic and learning-theory maps to some extent, using these and other common points, and one can then attempt further transpositions to more fully align the mappings. For development psychologists, age may offer a rather useful landmark for cross-mapping. Piaget, Vygotsky, and Freud have extremely disparate theoretical formulations. Yet, if one aligns their disparate accounts of what happens to children near the onset of schooling, one is struck by communalities in their accounts of developmental change, and one imagines one can see other points of relationship among their systems (White, 1965).

The kernel of this cross-mapping process has been interestingly discussed in Arthur Koestler's book *The Act of Creation* (1964). Koestler argues that the three fundamental domains of human creativity—humor, discovery, and art—rest alike on a bisociative process through which patterns of perceived ideas are perceived to be simultaneously capable of mapping in two different formats:

> The creative act of the humorist consisted in bringing about a momentary fusion between two habitually incompatible matrices. Scientific discovery, as we shall presently see, can be described in very similar terms—as the permanent fusion of matrices of thought previously believed to be incompatible [p. 95].

The "matrices" of the quote are elsewhere in the book referred to as "frames of reference." In the terms of this discussion, one would identify these as the localized maps of psychological phenomena created by disparate paradigm groups. Koestler's bisociative process—the recognition that a pattern of phenomena can be placed simultaneously on two maps—would be the basic source of the between-paradigm dialectic. Series of such cross-alignments, accompanied by operations on one or another map designed to bring forward the possibility of other cross-alignments, would allow major theoretical reconciliations. Thus, there arises the possibility that two pictures of psychological events resting on distinct data bases can merge so that one picture emerges, referrable to and debatable within two data bases.

It is of some interest that psychoanalytic theory has been aligned with a number of disparate data bases and theories in recent psychological writings—with genetic epistemology (Wolff, 1960), with ethology (Bowlby, 1969), and with modern neuropsychology (Pribram & Gill, 1976). Because of the broad, loose pattern of the theory, it seems to lend itself to between-paradigm mappings, to draw empirical clarification from a variety of diverse data bases, and to offer to the translators suggestions about ways to extend the scope of local mappings beyond the windows of origin. Psychoanalytic theory is thus in a kind of remote dialectical relationship with a number of existing paradigms of inquiry. One might well believe that this is compensating advantage for that looseness that makes an internal empirical dialectic not particularly efficient.

The aim of the between-paradigm dialectic is, ultimately, to tend toward that unity of theory and laboratory that, once upon a time, the Wundt group hoped for. It might be useful, as a final exercise, to consider the several dialectical processes that have been advanced in this discussion in their relation to the growth of psychology from Wundt's time until now.

VII. The Movements of Psychology

We talk about progress in psychology, about advances, about the development of psychological knowledge. How and in what way does this forward motion come about?

If one looks at scientific progress as a matter of improvement in research methods and methodology, then it is clear that psychology has advanced a great deal since Wundt's first laboratory. We have at hand all of the old procedures, and we have invented a great many more. We have technically upgraded the procedures. We have more people who are skilled in the procedures. So, generally speaking, we live in a much larger scientific *Umwelt* than did the Wundt group, capable of looking at a much wider diversity of phenomena.

But, of course, technological progress is not the progress we seek. We seek to know more, to understand more, to have theories of greater power. But in this realm, in the realm of theory, we are confronted by the puzzling problem of recursiveness in psychological theory. Anyone who glances at historical writings is struck by it and puzzles about it. Piaget's theory is a grand new theory of cognitive development, quite exciting to one and all as the fruit of 40 years of scientific development in the Geneva laboratory. But much of what seems most novel and exciting in Piagetian theory is clearly foreshadowed in the turn-of-the-century writings of James Mark Baldwin. And Baldwin's evolutionary developmentalism seems related to a cascade of earlier developmentalism (White, 1976b). Hull's theory of behavioral association in the 20th century looks much like Thomas Brown's theory of mental association in the 19th century. The ethological notion of critical periods in development seems quite novel until we find that William James takes the idea of such periods for granted in his *Talks to Teachers on Psychology* (White, 1968). One can repeatedly identify the recursion of ideas in the history of psychological writings. Do we really know more about psychology as we move forward, more in some significant sense, or do we simply rotate new-old ideas into place successively, each time adorning the old idea with new terminology?

It is my guess that this recursive pattern in psychology's history arises from the kind of dialectical process we have had under discussion here and is necessitated by it. Just as ideas must be remapped and transposed in order to move between paradigms, so also in the forward movement of psychological inquiry there must be a forward-going process of mapping and transposition.

Consider the intriguing history of the "wandering womb" theory of hysteria. Apparently, the idea that hysterical symptoms are related to female sexuality is quite old. At one time, it was thought that the womb actually moved to create hysterical symptoms of physical dysfunction. There still exist fine old medieval curses in which the womb is enjoined at length to return to its proper place, stopping not at the neck, arms, shoulder, chest, liver, and so on. Foucault (1973) traces the forward recursions of the wandering womb theory. After a time, when more was known about anatomy, it was realized that the womb cannot physically move in the body because it is held in place by connective tissue. So an argument developed that the womb shifted in place, pressing one way or another, to create hysterical symptomatology. Then, subsequently, it was understood that this process was physiologically unlikely. And so a humors-of-the-womb theory ensued in which the womb did not move, but its humors migrated to different parts of the body to cause hysteria. Humoral psychology is now discredited, but if one thinks about it, psychoanalysis still offers to the modern reader still another transposition of the wandering womb theory, the notion that psychic processes associated with female sexuality bring on hysterical symptoms.

What this evolving wandering womb theory seems to represent is the transposition of a stable conception of a patterning of events into newer and newer terminology amenable to newer and broader data bases. As the idea recurs, it remains the same, but each manifestation anchors it into consistency with a broader and broader pattern of scientific explanation of human physiology and disease processes. And in each new manifestation the idea is stated so that it can have commerce with contemporary data bases, contemporary procedures.

Let us note that we are now in the midst of a rather dramatic recursion. About 10 or 15 years ago, cognitivism and mind returned to psychology as topics. More recently, psychologists have begun talking about epistemology, at first Piaget's genetic epistemology and now Campbell's evolutionary epistemology. This present conference is in the contemporary trend to consider dialecticism in relation to psychology. It is my guess that those systematic philosophers who once hovered about the tiny Wundtian laboratory, but who could not enter, have now at last found a way to enter the contemporary dialectic between theory and method.

REFERENCES

Bergson, H. *The creative mind.* New York: Philosophical Library, 1946.

Bijou, S. W., & Baer, D. M. *Child development* (Vol. 1), *A systematic and empirical theory.* New York: Appleton, 1961.

Blumenthal, A. L. A reappraisal of Wilhelm Wundt. *American Psychologist,* 1975, **30,** 1081–1086.

Blumenthal, A. L. Wilhelm Wundt and early American psychology: A clash of two cultures. *Annals of the New York Academy of Sciences,* 1977, **291,** 13–21.

Boring, E. G. *A history of experimental psychology* (2nd ed.). New York: Appleton, 1950.

Boring, E. G. *The physical dimensions of consciousness.* New York: Dover, 1963.

Bowlby, J. *Attachment and loss* (Vol. 1), *Attachment.* New York: Basic Books, 1969.

Cattell, J. M. The psychological laboratory. *Psychological Review,* 1898, **5,** 655–658.

Cattell, R. B. *Abilities: Their structure, growth, and action.* Boston: Houghton, 1971.

Dewey, J. Psychology and social practice. In J. Ratner (Ed.), *John Dewey: Philosophy, psychology and social practice.* New York: Capricorn, 1965. (Originally published, 1900.)

Ellenberger, H. F. *The discovery of the unconscious: The history and evolution of dynamic psychiatry.* New York: Basic Books, 1970.

Foucault, M. *Madness and civilization: A history of insanity in the Age of Reason.* New York: Vintage. Pp. 143–150.

Freud, S. *Collected papers* (5 vols.) London: Hogarth Press, 1950.

Hall, G. S. *Adolescence: Its psychology and its relations to physiology, anthropology, sociology, sex, crime, religion, and education* (2 vols.). New York: Appleton, 1908.

Hall, G. S., Cattell, J. McK., Pace, E. A., Titchener, E. B., Angell, F., Warren, H. C., Angell, J. R., Stratton, G. M., Patrick, G. T. W., Judd, C. H., Urban, W. M., Tawney, G. A., Weyer, E. M., Scott, W. D., Baldwin, B. T., Arps, G. F., & Pintner, R. In memory of Wilhelm Wundt by his American students. *Psychological Review,* 1921, **28,** 153–188.

Haeberlin, H. K. The theoretical foundations of Wundt's folk-psychology. *Psychological Review,* 1916, **23,** 279–302.

Harré, R. and Secord, P. F. *The explanation of social behavior.* Oxford: Blackwell, 1972.

Hebb, D. O. The American revolution. *American Psychologist,* 1960, **15,** 735–745.

Heidbreder, E. *Seven psychologies.* New York: Appleton-Century-Crofts, 1933.

Joncich, G. *The sane positivist: A biography of Edward L. Thorndike.* Middletown, Conn.: Wesleyan University, 1968.

Jones, E. *The life and work of Sigmund Freud* (Vol 2). New York: Basic Books, 1955.

Koestler, A. *The act of creation: A study of the conscious and unconscious in science and art.* New York: Dell, 1964.

Krohn, W. O. Facilities in experimental psychology at the various German universities. *American Journal of Psychology,* 1892a, **4,** 585–595; The laboratory of the Psychological Institute at the University of Gottingen. *American Journal of Psychology,* 1892b, **5,** 282–283.

Mandler, G., & Kessen, W. *The language of psychology.* New York: Wiley, 1959.

Murchison, C. (Ed.) *Psychologies of 1925: Powell lectures in psychological theory.* Worcester,

Mass.: Clark University Press, 1926.

Murchison, C. (Ed.) *Psychologies of 1930.* Worcester, Mass.: Clark University Press, 1930.

Pribram, K. H., & Gill, M. M. *Freud's "Project" reassessed: Preface to contemporary cognitive theory and neuropsychology.* New York: Basic Books, 1976.

Sanford, E. C. Some practical suggestions on the equipment of a psychological laboratory. *American Journal of Psychology,* 1893, 5, 429–438.

Siegel, A. W., & White, S. H. The development of spatial representations in children. In H. Reese (Ed.), *Advances in child development and behavior* (Vol. 10). New York: Academic Press, 1975.

Skinner, B. F. The generic nature of the concepts of stimulus and response. *Journal of General Psychology,* 1935, 12, 40–65.

Titchener, E. B. *Experimental psychology: A manual of laboratory practice* (Vol. 1), *Qualitative experiments* (Part 1), *Student's manual.* New York: Macmillan, 1909.

Titchener, E. B. *Experimental psychology: A manual of laboratory practice* (Vol. 1), *Qualitative experiments* (Part 2), *Instructor's manual.* New York: Macmillan, 1901.

Titchener, E. B. *Experimental psychology: A manual of laboratory practice* (Vol. 2), *Quantitative experiments* (Part 1), *Student's manual.* New York: Macmillan, 1905.

Titchener, E. B. *Experimental psychology: A manual of laboratory practice* (Vol. 2), *Quantitative experiments* (Part 2), *Instructor's manual.* New York: Macmillan, 1923.

Vygotsky, L. S. *Thought and language.* Cambridge, Mass.: MIT Press, 1962.

Whipple, G. M. *Manual of mental and physical tests.* New York: Arno, 1973. (Originally published 1914–1915.)

White, S. H. Evidence for a hierarchical arrangement of learning processes. In L. P. Lipsitt & C. C. Spiker (Eds.), *Advances in child behavior and development* (Vol. 2). New York: Academic Press, 1965.

White, S. H. The learning–maturation controversy: Hall to Hull. *Merrill-Palmer Quarterly,* 1968, 14, 187–196.

White, S. H. The learning theory tradition and child psychology. In P. H. Mussen (Ed.), *Carmichael's manual of child psychology* (3rd ed.). New York: Wiley, 1970.

White, S. H. The active organism in theoretical behaviorism. *Human Development,* 1976, 19, 99–107. (a)

White, S. H. Developmental psychology and Vico's concept of universal history. *Social Research,* 1976, 43, 659–671. (b)

White, S. H. Social Implications of IQ. In S. White (Ed.), *Human development in today's world.* Boston: Educational Associates, 1976. (c)

Wilson, E. *To the Finland station: A study in the writing and acting of history.* New York: Farrar, Straus, 1972.

Wilson, L. *Bibliography of child study: 1898–1912.* New York: Arno, 1975.

Wolff, P. H. The developmental psychologies of Jean Piaget and psychoanalysis. *Psychological Issues,* 1960, 2 (Monograph 5).

Woodworth, R. S. *Contemporary schools of psychology.* New York: Ronald, 1931; 2nd ed., 1948; 3rd ed. (with M. R. Sheehan), 1964.

Wundt, W. *Psychology in kampf ums dasein.* Leipzig: Kroner, 1913.

CHAPTER 4

Behaviorism, Cognitive Psychology, and the Active Organism

CHARLES C. SPIKER

UNIVERSITY OF IOWA
IOWA CITY, IOWA

I. Introduction

In the first half of his paper (Chapter 3, this volume), Professor White provides us with a fascinating historical sketch of several aspects of introspectionistic psychology. Details aside, general agreement on the accuracy of his interpretations could easily be obtained. The interpretations he offers in the second half of his presentation for some of the psychological movements in the last 50 years are most controversial. Quite naturally, interpretations of recent history are subject to considerably more variability. I shall therefore confine my remarks to the second half of his presentation.

Implicit in this portion of his paper, although explicit elsewhere (White, 1976), is the view that psychology is currently undergoing several coexisting revolutions. The object of these alleged rebellions is the learning-theory movement that dominated experimental psychology for approximately one-third of the 20th century. The learning-theory movement is identified with "theoretical behaviorism," and it is suggested that the current revolutions arose from widespread dissatisfaction with the relatively small degree of success achieved by the learning-theory movement.

The changes that took place in psychology during the first two decades of this century were unmistakably revolutionary, as Professor White has noted. There was a fundamental change in the philosophy of psychology, which had tremendous ramifications, some of which are still being felt. Moreover, there are at present incipient, though not yet prevalent, attempts to incite revolutions against the dominant psychological establishment. Indeed, calling as they do for fundamental changes in the format of psychological explanation, as well as in the role of prediction of behavior, several papers presented at this conference represent attempts to incite such rebellion. I shall attempt to show, however, that nothing of this kind is taking place with respect to the variations of cognitive psychology to which Professor White frequently refers.

Although I am not willing to concede that the learning-theory movement has failed, there is no question that interest in the movement has declined over the past several years. For the sake of discussion, however, let us make the more extreme assumption that theoretical behaviorism has failed. In such an event, it would become important to determine whether the failure is to be attributed to the theoretical, to the behaviorism, or to both. Part of my thesis is that there are two distinct issues involved and that we confuse them at our peril. If a theory fails, scientists build a new one. Behaviorism, however, is a philosophy of psychology. Since the philosophy of a science specifies what qualifies as a theory, the failure of behaviorism would mean that we must construct a new philosophy before we can know what will constitute a theory.

My remarks are organized in the following way. First, I shall analyze the phrase *theoretical behaviorism* in order to circumscribe what it is that we are discussing. Next, I shall relate cognitive psychology to behaviorism in the context of a distinction between the "active" and the "reactive" organism. Finally, I shall consider some criteria for deciding when a theoretical movement has failed.

II. Methodological Behaviorism

Before we can make a reasonable decision as to whether behaviorism has failed, we should agree on what the term means. An appeal to the writings of John B. Watson does not provide immediate clarification of the way the term was used during the first half century of behaviorism. Under titles that contained the word, Watson wrote about his philosophy of psychology, his rudimentary theories of behavior, and his preferences for a social organization and function—his social philosophy. Now, Watson's social philosophy, reflecting as it does his personal values, does not belong in the philosophy of psychology, and it was never uniformly accepted by psychologists. Although Skinner (1971) has publicly endorsed several aspects of this social philosophy, it seems clear that he does not consider it part of the philosophy of psychology. Thus, to understand behaviorism, we must look either to the Watsonian philosophy of psychology, to his theories, or to both. Let us first consider his philosophy of psychology.

This philosophy can be stated very simply. Watson (1913) insisted that the primitive, undefined terms of the psychological language need not, and indeed should not, differ from those of the physical and biological sciences. For convenience, I shall refer to this principle as the definitional tenet. Given this basic tenet, psychology should proceed to find process laws about behavior and organize them into theories in the same manner as laws and theories are formulated in the other sciences. It is the definitional tenet, reinforced with the notion of process laws and deductively organized theory, that has become known as methodological behaviorism in order to distinguish it from Watson's other pronouncements, including his social philosophy (Bergmann, 1956).

Although the thesis of methodological behaviorism can be simply stated, the simplicity is misleading. It took the early behaviorists a long time to learn to use it properly. The definitional tenet stipulates that all *primitive* terms in psychology that refer to the private (mental) experience of subjects are taboo. Tolman, in a series of papers beginning in the early 1920s, supplied an additional wrinkle. If, for heuristic or other reasons, we wish to retain the *symbols* for mentalistic contents, the symbols may be introduced as defined terms. Thus, the symbol "fear" may be used provided that it is introduced by means of a definition that specifies which observations must be made in order to confirm or disconfirm any statement in which the word occurs (Tolman, 1923). Justification of the wrinkle is obvious: to deny the psychologist the use of certain symbols—those that refer to mental events in a natural or introspectionistic language—would be as arbitrary as denying him the use of any symbol that contained the letter x.

Watson's process laws, if discovered, would permit the prediction, from a present state of an organism and its environment, the future course of events concerning both the organism and its environment (Bergmann, 1956). This notion of the process law stood in marked contrast to the cross-sectional laws (mental chemistry) sought by the introspectionists, and it had been anticipated in the earlier writings of the functionalists. Clearly, Watson understood the notion of a process law; it is not so clear that he completely understood the structure of scientific theory. Although he definitely recommended that psychology should construct theories like those of the mature sciences, it may be that he did not know exactly what his recommendation entailed. Philosophers of science who were his contemporaries were just beginning to articulate clearly a description of scientific theory as a set of laws, deductively organized into axioms and theorems, with the axioms permitting the deduction, and therefore the prediction and explanation, of the theorems. This conception of the scientific theory was, however, clearly present in the writings of later behaviorists, particularly in those of Hull.

III. Conditioning Theories

Let us consider next what Watson offered as examples of psychological theory. Earlier, I referred to his theories as rudimentary. They were really little more than outlines of the directions that he thought would be taken in constructing psychological theories. The fundamental idea was that the more complex behavior of organisms was to be predicted, explained, and understood in terms of principles of conditioning. Watson was familiar with some of Pavlov's work and considered it fundamental. His views of complex behavior as consisting of simple chains of conditioned responses may seem naive to us today because we have seen the sophisticated theoretical constructions of the later theorists. It is erroneous, however, to consider the theoretical developments of Tolman, Guthrie, Hull, and Spence as extensions of Watson's theories of behavior. These theorists were the intellectual successors of Edward L. Thorndike, who also accepted the behaviorist philosophy of science. In addition to their philosophy, these theorists, including Thorndike, had in common one theoretical precept: they believed that a theory of behavior would have, and perhaps must have, the laws of conditioning as the basic axioms.

One can define a word as one wishes, of course, and some writers have used the term *behaviorism* to refer to the combination of methodological behaviorism and the preference for a theory with conditioning principles as axioms. Since one can take an affirmative position on the first without accepting the second, the two issues should be kept separate. Accordingly, I shall use the term *behaviorist* only for those who accept the thesis of methodological behaviorism. For brevity, I shall use the phrase *conditioning theorist* to refer to those who would construct psychological theories from conditioning axioms.

I submit that methodological behaviorism, as the term has been here circumscribed, was the core of American behaviorism, and that it was the only element of Watson's behaviorism that was ever accepted by the majority of American psychologists. It is in this sense of the word that it has been said that behaviorism "conquered itself to death [Bergmann, 1956, p. 270]." A word of qualification should be said for Skinner, who, though he seems to accept the definitional tenet and the ideal of the process law, seems to reject the use of mentalistic symbols, however introduced, and seems uncertain about the appropriate time to begin constructing psychological theories (Skinner, 1950).

Few American psychologists would claim today that they have direct access to their subjects' private experiences. Few would be willing to accept without qualification naive subjects' descriptions of such experiences. As Professor White has indicated, acceptance of methodological behaviorism effectively destroyed the introspectionistic psychology of the preceding century. This destruction was so thorough, so complete, that relatively few psychologists today even know what the classical psychologists were trying to do. Possible misconceptions, stemming from superficial similarities between classical psychology and some contemporary cognitive psychologies, may be forestalled by a few comments on certain methodological differences between introspectionistic psychology and behaviorism.

The "subject" of the introspectionist's experiment was in fact an observer—either the experimenter himself, a colleague, or an advanced student in psychology. The task of the observer was to report on the contents of his own consciousness. No one could serve as an observer unless he had been trained to use the introspectionist language in a rigorous way. This requirement meant that only carefully trained psychologists could serve as observers. No college sophomores, no man off the street, no infants or children, no infrahuman organisms could be studied by this method.

The observer might report, under some specific experimental condition, that there was a green sensation among his mental data. This report was duly recorded as a factual statement, in exactly the same way that a modern experimentalist would accept his trained research assistant's report that the rat chose the correct stimulus on a certain trial. No respectable introspectionist would have considered permitting an untrained observer to participate in his experiment, just as no respectable experimenter would today permit an untrained experimenter to collect and record his data.

Subsequent to the rejection of introspection, the early behaviorists had little problem in applying their method to the study of infrahuman subjects. Their rats, monkeys, and chimpanzees did not talk to them. If they wished to know whether a rat, for example, could distinguish between red and green, they had to conduct a discrimination experiment, making sure that different odors, positions, and other cues were not confounded with the colors. The study of inarticulate human infants was also relatively straightforward.

The language behavior of the adult human was another matter. Suppose the subject says, "I am afraid." How is the experimenter to record this behavior? Consider two alternatives. First, he may record, "The subject was afraid," as the introspectionist might have done in a similar situation with an observer in place of the subject. Second, he may record, "The subject said, 'I am afraid.' " Strictly, the behaviorist may take the first alternative only if he is willing to define "fear" as equivalent to the subject's saying, "I am afraid," which would be a behavioristically acceptable, though naive, definition. Otherwise, he must take the second option. The temptation to indulge in a new kind of anthropomorphism was very great. Even Watson suggested that the language behavior of human subjects might sometimes serve as an "abridged" method, for example, in psychophysical experiments (Watson, 1913). The methodological problem involved in a behavioristic treatment of verbal behavior is still receiving short shrift from psychologists who would nevertheless classify themselves as behavioristic in the restricted meaning I have given the term.

IV. Cognitive Psychology

The superficial similarities between classical psychology and some of the contemporary cognitive psychologies have to do with the fact that many of the terms from the two types of system *sound* alike—terms with mentalistic rings can be found in both. As Professor White points out, classical psychology dealt with "attention" and "perception." Cognitive psychologies study "selective attention" and "perceptual processing." I do not agree with the implication, however, that these superficial similarities signal a return of psychology to the mentalistic cognitivism of classical structural psychology. To the contrary, I conclude from the foregoing considerations that there is no widespread rebellion of American psychologists against methodological behaviorism. There are no reasonable alternatives for this doctrine on the horizon. The majority of American psychologists, including contemporary cognitive psychologists, consider as scientifically slovenly any of the alternatives that have been offered, including any sophisticated or unsophisticated versions of phenomenalism.

The situation is not nearly so unanimous with respect to the other issue—the role of conditioning principles in psychological theories. The difference in attitudes toward the two issues is the reason that I have insisted on keeping them separate.

In general, cognitive theorists have rejected the basic precept of the conditioning theorists. They are not at all constrained to derive their laws or propositions about behavior from conditioning principles. Indeed, the position of some cognitive psychologists seems to have reached an ideological status—they would even deny the conditioning theorist the right to waste his time. Although they accept the thesis of methodological behaviorism, many cognitive psychologists are much more relaxed and less self-conscious, compared to the leading conditioning theorists, in providing explicit definitions that relate their theoretical terms to patterns of stimulation and behavior. Yet, a careful reading of their works is generally suffi-cient to convince one that explicit definitions could be provided upon demand—that they do indeed use patterns of stimulation and behavior in order to decide whether the subject has this cognitive state, is using that cognitive strategy, or is undergoing this cognitive process. The greater relaxation of the definitional crite-rion is probably a mixed blessing. On the one hand, it encourages a greater flexibility of theoretical thinking, which is beneficial in the early stages of theory construction; on the other hand, the inevitable miscommunication contributes greatly to the clubbiness to which Professor White referred.

V. Active and Reactive Organisms

Some cognitive theorists claim, as does Professor White, that the new theoretical positions substitute the conception of an active organism for the reactive organism of the conditioning theorists (Reese, 1976; White, 1976). As the following argu-ment would demonstrate, I believe this distinction is a pseudo-issue.

It has been suggested (White, 1976) that one of the attributes of an active organism is that it exercises selective attention. Thus, though we may bombard the organism with a mass of stimulation, it selects only certain aspects of that total stimulation to attend and process. This proposition is often contrasted with the position of the conditioning theorists. A theory such as Hull's (1943, 1952) contains several mechanisms that would permit the derivation of the effect of such a filtering device, including the learning of receptor-orienting acts, differential habit loadings, and cue-producing responses. For the sake of discussion, however, let us make the unreasonable assumption that, since Hull did not specifically address this problem, it could not be addressed within the context of his theory. Does the notion of selective attention imply an active organism rather than a reactive one?

By this time it is surely incontrovertible that human subjects, including children, may attend to one relevant dimension while learning a discrimination problem and may not attend to another equally relevant dimension. We know this, operationally, because we can present postdiscrimination tests in which the two relevant dimensions are made orthogonal to each other and observe that the subjects make discriminative responses to, say, the color of the stimuli but not to their shapes. Naturally, we ask, why? One possible answer is that the subject has a *free choice* and he chooses to attend to color and to ignore shape. One meaning of the phrase free choice is that nothing the experimenter could possibly know would enable him to predict which of the two dimensions the subject will attend. This is also one possible meaning of the term *active*. The subject is free to act in an unpredictable way. It is difficult to understand why psychologists would continue their research efforts if they believed that organisms had such potential.

Rather than accept this alternative, we do what scientists have always done. We begin to manipulate variables. For example, we may give some subjects a preliminary task in which only one of the two dimensions is relevant, whereas some other subjects receive a preliminary task in which the other dimension is relevant. We then administer the task with redundant relevant dimensions, and finally we make the critical test. If we are successful, we will find that the nature of the preliminary task affects which dimension the subjects "will choose to attend." Even if successful, however, we will undoubtedly find that not all subjects were affected in the same way by the same manipulation. Hence, we look for other variables. We may consider activities that the subjects might have engaged in before they came to the experiment. No stone will be left unturned in our attempt to answer the question without resorting to the free choice alternative.

Now, if we are successful in finding variables that determine which features of the stimulus complex the subject chooses to attend, is the subject "active" or "reactive"?

What goes for selective attention also goes for the various cognitive strategies. If a subject adopts a "chunking" strategy while learning a list of words, we again ask why he does so. Cognitive psychologists seek the variables that determine which cognitive strategies their subjects adopt. Presumably they are no less diligent in their attempts than are the conditioning theorists who try to find why the rat develops a position habit or a response alternation. Why, then, should the chunking strategy, which was presumably learned and strengthened in previous learning situations, be viewed as active, while salivating to a bell is considered merely reactive?

I conclude that what the cognitive psychologists have rejected is not the methodological behaviorism of Watson and his successors but the commitment to construct psychological theories with conditioning principles as axioms. Their assumptions about the origin and function of the cognitive states, strategies, and processes are not derived from conditioning principles, and many of them would probably deny that such derivation is possible. This preference for more molar theories, however, represents a strategical judgment about the most fruitful way to proceed. It does not signal a fundamental revolution. Because the leaders of the conditioning theorists so dominated the field of psychology for nearly a third of a century, we sometimes forget that psychology was even then much broader than the territory held by the conditioning theorists. Conditioning theories did not have a firm hold on human learning and problem solving, and their impact was minimal on the field of sensation, perception, and psychophysics.

I also conclude that the differentiation between active and reactive organisms is a pseudodistinction. What might be meant by those who maintain the distinction is either that behavior is unpredictable or that some behavior cannot be explained by conditioning principles. Both alternatives are factual propositions of that peculiar sort that does not lend itself to early verification.

VI. The Rejection of Theories

Having granted earlier some issues for the sake of discussion, I would now like to take one of them back. In particular, I wish to reconsider the conclusion that the conditioning theories have failed in some fundamental way.

The success or failure of a logically consistent theory is a factual issue; that is, the question cannot be answered by sitting in an easy chair, analyzing logical principles. A theory is a deductively organized set of laws, with a subset of axioms from which the other laws (theorems) can be deduced rigorously. If the axioms permit the derivation of a statement that is empirically false, at least one of the axioms is false. Whether or not any statement deduced from the axioms turns out to be false depends on the way the world is. In brief, if a theory predicts something that is factually false, something is wrong with the theory.

What do scientists do about theories that make false predictions? There are several alternatives. The theory may be discarded and another extant theory substituted for it. Or a new theory may be developed to replace the discarded one. More frequently, however, one or more axioms of the theory will be modified so that correct predictions may now be obtained. Anyone who knows the long history of the corpuscular and undulatory theories of light in physics realizes how difficult it is to say exactly what will happen when theories make false predictions. These two theories were pitted against each other in Newton's lifetime. Newton preferred the corpuscular theory, and as a consequence, it reigned for more than 100 years. In the middle of the 19th century, the wave theory began to make a comeback. The interesting thing about these two theories is that each of them predicts correctly some phenomena that the other cannot. Moreover, there is a large body of phenomena that both predict equally well (Einstein & Infeld, 1938). The student of physics today not only must learn both theories, but he must also learn when to apply each.

When has a theory failed? One criterion commonly advocated is that a theory fails when scientists lose interest in it. By this criterion, the wave theory should have been buried during the 100-year reign of the particle theory. Another commonly advocated criterion stipulates that a theory has failed when it is unable to explain phenomena ostensibly within its scope. By this criterion, both the corpuscular and wave theories should have been discarded during Newton's time.

Philosophers of science have noted that a scientific theory is not discarded until it is replaced by a "better" one. A better theory is one that predicts and explains everything that the old theory did and, in addition, correctly predicts new phenomena that the old theory did not. It is not surprising that scientists manifest such a conservative attitude toward their theories. The extant theories of a field constitute the explanatory power of that field. Scientists are not likely to give up easily any beachhead they have won in their mission of prediction and explanation. Many psychologists display a bloodthirsty attitude toward theories, often ringing the death knell for a theory before it has fully opened its eyes. Spence's (1936, 1937) theory of discrimination learning was pronounced dead on arrival when published in 1936, again in 1937, and several times each year after that. Yet, it is questionable whether it has been replaced by a better theory, in the sense just outlined.

One reason for our savage attacks on theories is that we set goals for our theories that would not be realistic even in a mature discipline. One such goal is especially debilitating—the prediction of the behavior of the individual organism. Consider the following illustration. When I conduct a discrimination experiment, I would like to know on exactly which trial this particular child begins to attend to the relevant dimension. Moreover, I would like to be able to make a similar prediction for every child who performs on the task. If I could predict correctly, I could provide a more critical test of my theory. This aspiration is not realistic. The most important laws that we have thus far in the psychology of learning are historical in character. This means that some knowledge of the past history of the organism (e.g., reinforcement history) must be known before the laws can be applied. In the above example, I am considering a child whom I have seen for the first time only minutes ago. The laws I know tell me that the behavior of the subject in my task may be dependent on any of a wide variety of events, including some quite trivial, that took place prior to the experiment—what happened to the child at breakfast, on the way to school, in the classroom, and so on.

Now consider a comparable problem in the physical sciences. Suppose that we ask a physicist to test the law of falling bodies by predicting the exact moment that a certain brick will strike the ground. He begins to ask the questions he must have answered before he can compute the result. He finds out that the brick we have in mind is on top of the southeast corner of East Hall in Iowa City. Moreover, he finally understands that what we want him to predict is when the brick will fall as a result of the deterioration of its mortar. If he is a kindly man, he will patiently explain to us that such a prediction would require knowing when the brick was placed, what kind of mortar was used, what the weather has been like since, to say nothing of the future vagaries of the Iowa weather.

Scientific prediction and explanation require, at a minimum, one law and a statement of initial conditions. Nothing can be predicted from a law by itself. The assessment of initial conditions required for prediction can be an extremely difficult task. Let us suppose that the behavior of organisms is comprehensively lawful and that we have already discovered all the laws of this comprehensive system. Let us further suppose that some of the critical laws are historical in the sense that the assessment of initial conditions requires the determination of some facts that lie in the history of the organism. It could very well be the case that the behavior of a given organism in a given situation could not be predicted because we could not assess the initial conditions. It might well be the case that the time, energy, and expense required to predict the behavior of individual organisms would generally be prohibitive.

The foregoing comments should not be construed as an argument for the rejection of prediction as a goal of science. Scientists learned long ago to be skeptical of the utility of those explanatory systems that do not also permit prediction of the types of phenomena that they purport to explain. In a sense, science keeps its explanation honest by insisting that the same deductive schema also permit correct predictions. The argument is rather that, in psychology, the predictions need not be, and perhaps for the present, can not be the behavior of individual organisms.

There is another important reason why some psychologists summarily reject viable theories: their failure to appreciate the role and function of composition laws in the development of scientific theories. Consider Ohm's law, which states the relation among the voltage, current, and resistance of an electrical circuit. In its customary form, it applies to an elementary circuit consisting of a battery connected to a resistor by a pair of wires. If two resistors are wired in series, or wired in parallel, it is not clear how Ohm's law is to be applied. What is needed, of course, are the Kirchoff laws of current and voltage, which inform us, respectively, that the sum of currents approaching a junction point is equal to the sum of currents leaving that junction, and that the sum of voltage increases in a closed circuit is equal to the sum of voltage drops. With these two composition laws, it becomes a routine matter to analyze incredibly complex circuits in such a way that Ohm's law can be recursively applied. Without the composition laws, the "behavior" of the complex circuits is incomprehensible.

Comparable instances, although somewhat more complicated, have occurred in theories of discrimination learning. The scope of the Spence (1936, 1937) theory, for example, was greatly extended by the discovery of composition laws pertaining to the generalization of habit and inhibition. Thus, a theory constructed for simultaneous discrimination problems was extended to encompass successive discrimination problems (Spiker, 1963), as well as certain types of oddity problems and transverse patterning (Croll, 1967). There is no simple rule of thumb to tell us when the scope of a theory cannot be further extended.

VII. Summary

The thesis presented here is that present-day cognitive psychology should not be interpreted as a revolution against the philosophy of psychology that has come to be labeled methodological behaviorism. Although most cognitive psychology is fundamentally behavioristic, it has rejected the constraint, imposed by some of the early influential behaviorists, that theories of behavior must include conditioning principles as axioms. Cognitive psychology is generally no less deterministic than are conditioning theories, in that both attempt to find the factors that influence the subject variables that they define. The conception of the organism by the cognitive psychologist is therefore no more nor less active than that of the conditioning theorist. Conditioning theorists remain active and, given the inherent difficulty of evaluating the future success of a theory, it is far too early to conclude that such theories will not succeed.

REFERENCES

Bergmann, G. The contribution of John B. Watson. *Psychological Review,* 1956, **63**, 265–276.

Croll, W. L. *Oddity discrimination learning as a function of the number of dimensions along which the correct stimulus is odd.* Unpublished doctoral dissertation, University of Iowa, 1967.

Einstein, A., & Infeld, L. *The evolution of physics.* New York: Simon & Schuster, 1938.

Hull, C. L. *Principles of behavior.* New York: Appleton, 1943.

Hull, C. L. *A behavior system.* New Haven: Yale University Press, 1952.

Reese, H. W. Discussion. In H. W. Reese (Ed.), Conceptions of the "active organism." *Human Development,* 1976, **19**, 108–119.

Skinner, B. F. Are theories of learning necessary? *Psychological Review,* 1950, **57**, 193–216.

Skinner, B. F. *Beyond freedom and dignity.* New York: Knopf, 1971.

Spence, K. W. The nature of discrimination learning in animals. *Psychological Review,* 1936, **43**, 427–449.

Spence, K. W. The differential response in animals to stimuli varying within a single dimension. *Psychological Review,* 1937, **44**, 430–444.

Spiker, C. C. The hypothesis of stimulus interaction and an explanation of stimulus compounding. In L. P. Lipsitt & C. C. Spiker (Eds.), *Advances in child development and behavior* (Vol. 1). New York: Academic Press, 1963. Pp. 233–264.

Tolman, E. C. A behavioristic account of the emotions. *Psychological Review,* 1923, **30**, 217–227.

Watson, J. B. Psychology as the behaviorist views it. *Psychological Review,* 1913, **20**, 158–177.

White, S. H. The active organism in theoretical behaviorism. *Human Development,* 1976, **19**, 99–107.

CHAPTER 5

Cohort, Age, and Time of Measurement: Biomorphic Considerations[1]

HARVEY L. STERNS AND RALPH A. ALEXANDER

UNIVERSITY OF AKRON
AKRON, OHIO

I. Introduction

Earlier discussions of models and theories of human development by Reese and Overton (1970), Overton and Reese (1973), Looft (1973), and Riegel (1973a) attempted to analyze the major "party lines" and explicate assumptions of the mechanistic and organismic world views. The questions often asked are: Where do I fit in the categorization? What kind of a psychologist am I? The reaction of many has been: Don't bother me with philosophy, I'm busy doing research or developing sophisticated methodology. It is interesting that these discussions took place in the earlier life-span volumes (Baltes & Schaie, 1973a; Goulet & Baltes, 1970; Nesselroade & Reese, 1973), since the clarification of these issues came to be important in setting the stage for a life-span psychology. Perhaps one of the most valuable contributions of those early volumes was to take existing child models and push them into the realm of the adult portion of the life span.

Riegel (1972b, 1973a, 1973b, 1975b, 1975c), Looft (1973), and others were already suggesting a movement toward a more dialectical approach to the behavior of organisms, and that approach has recently been acknowledged by Baltes and Willis

[1] The preparation of this paper was partially supported by funds from the Andrus Foundation and the University of Akron Institute for Life-Span Development and Gerontology.

(1977) and others. Riegel (1973a) argued that much was to be gained from an examination of Soviet psychology in that it incorporates the views of development either as an accumulation of external information by a passive organism or as a spontaneous emergence of new modes of operation drawing from the environment in a selective way. Wozniak (1975) stated, "The world must be understood in its continual change and development." Or, ". . . man, in other words, has control over his own destiny. He is an active cognizer of the world rather than a passive receiver of sensations. He is capable of directing his own actions [p. 28]."

It has been advanced that a dialectical theory of development is concerned with the simultaneous progressions of events along the interdependent dimensions of inner-biological, individual-psychological, cultural-sociological, and outer-physical, and that a dialectical view of development is based on the interactions of these four dimensions (Riegel, 1975c). Dialectical philosophy is one of movement, development, and interaction. "As such it is opposed to the metaphysical which focuses on the static and defines objects in isolation from one another [Lawler, 1975, p. 3]."

Although these writers have served to focus the attention of developmental psychologists on the organism as an active, growing, and changing entity, they have failed to produce, or have been counterproductive, in at least two major ways. First, while arguing that the essence of growth is the synthesis of seemingly incompatible opposites, they continue to portray themselves as representing one side of each of several "controversies" and leave the task of resolution to others. For example, they declare themselves to be antireductionistic, whereas writers such as Simon (1969) and Luchins and Luchins (1965) begin bringing the wholist–reductionist positions into resolution. The dialecticians set themselves out as antimechanistic and leave it to writers such as Alston (1974) and Lave and March (1975) to reconcile the mechanistic–organismic views of the proper science of behavior. They see their views as dynamic and ignore the works of writers such as Simon (1969), Serebriakoff (1975), Pribram (1971), Piaget and Inhelder (1969), and Diesing (1971), who are attempting to develop the necessary conceptual and formal framework for treating systems that display both static and dynamic characteristics. In short, they have failed to take their own rhetoric seriously.

In addition, dialecticians continue to emphasize the distinction between qualitative and quantitative differences, whereas contemporary measurement theory defines quantification as the process of assigning symbols (usually numbers) to objects or events on the basis of qualitative observations of attributes by some consistent set of rules (Krantz, Luce, Suppes, & Tversky, 1971). The qualitative–quantitative distinction, then, hinges on the discovery and specification of relevant dimensionality and the rules of symbol assignment. For any science, the practical distinction is hazy indeed.

The second major failure has been of a more pragmatic nature. Several authors, including White (Chapter 3, this volume), have pointed out that one of the most pressing problems for any science is the selection or the development of a suitable language that is both accurate and meaningful for the subject matter. The importance of having suitable language in which to phrase one's science can easily be demonstrated. If we consider the greater ease of thinking about and development of a logic of number systems in Arabic as opposed to trying to do the same with Roman number symbols, it can readily be seen how great the effects of notation are on the development of a science and how crippling a poor language can be for those who are trying to use it. Natural language, of course, is the early favorite and logical first choice of a science and is still the most prevalent in psychology. However, as a science begins to mature, it must develop methods and concepts much more precise than can be expressed in the common idiom.

A most important step is the process of developing a formal language that is appropriate insofar as its central concepts and semantic and syntatic structure are homomorphic with the theory to be formalized. It is in this area that the dialectical school has been particularly sterile. A serious effort was made by Kosok (1966), who attempted to develop a formalization of the concepts of dialectics; yet, even he finally admitted that the attempt was substantially a failure. The usefulness and applicability of dialectics to the systematic study of the behavior of organisms remain to be demonstrated (Van den Daele, 1975). One of the more extreme views of the pragmatic value of dialectics is a statement, attributed to Gilbert Ryle: "Hegel did not deserve to be studied, even as error [Findlay, 1972, p. 2]."

II. A Biomorphic Approach to Human Behavior

The human organism must respond to a spectrum of stimulation in an ever-changing environment. In fact, there is a large body of evidence and wide agreement that for the human (as well as for other living systems) stimulus change is the salient environmental feature that the organism is predisposed to detect. As a biological system with a genetically determined life span, the human has a developmental history that begins with conception and ends with death. This life span is generally characterized by much of contemporary developmental psychology as being possessed of the basic principle of continual change in the biological, psychological, and social functioning of the individual.

We will first undertake to show that this indiscriminate questioning for change, which reaches its zenith (or nadir, depending on one's opinion) in the writings of dialectical psychologists is no better a description of, nor more useful a guide to, the study of living systems than that of the "staticists" these writers hope to discredit. We will propose a biomorphic representation of human development, which can be found in the contemporary writings of areas of inquiry such as information theory, biology, the theory of adaptive or self-inquiring systems, the foundling science of design, and developmental theory such as Piaget and Inhelder (1969, p. 157). The prevailing theme of that literature over the past two decades has been the reconciliation of two apparently contradictory principles—entropy and homeostasis.

A first look at living systems seems to characterize them as being in a constant state of flux, actively growing and changing. It is this feature more than any other that characterizes the emphasis of dialectical psychology. "Dialectic Psychology is committed to the study of *activities* and *changes*. Therefore both Hegel and Marx have their roots in Heraclitus's notion of 'ceaseless flux' . . . [Riegel, 1975a, p. 8]. The logical endpoint of such a view was expressed by Norbert Wiener (1961) when he characterized the stable or steady state of living organisms as death. One need only spend a few days in the presence of both a corpse and a living person to question the wisdom of Wiener's view.

This contradiction is at once spotlighted and resolved by looking at the definition of change. Change, for the physical scientist, is expressed in the second law of thermodynamics, which establishes that disorder (entropy) increases over time and that, with increased entropy, systems degenerate toward more probable states. Arranged, ordered, organized, sorted, patterned objects or events tend to become mixed, disordered, disorganized and lose pattern over time. It is precisely by this loss of organization that one can tell an earlier from a later moment in time, and it is the universal tendency toward entropy that permits the prediction of future states.

A second look, then, at living systems indicates that they appear to behave as though they were designed to locally resist or minimize such change (disorder, entropy) in themselves. This apparent stability seeking of organisms is well known under the concept of homeostasis. There are, however, two specific features of homeostasis that serve to provide the basis for a biomorphic representation of living entities. Both are most often ignored by the so-called "organismic" dialectical critics of the concept. The first is that homeostasis is defined as the process of minimizing irreversible changes in, or maintaining invariance of, form. *Form* as distinct from content or structure! It is an important property of adaptive systems that the inner and outer environments are insulated from each other in such a way as to preserve a maximally invariant relation between the organism's inner environment and its goals, independent of a wide range of variations in most external parameters (Simon, 1969). A morphostatic entity, then, appears to resist or avoid forces that threaten continuity of form, which would act to change the interrelationships between its parts. Homeostasis distinctly does *not* imply the seeking of stability of structure, content, or physical constituents; rather it implies the stability of arrangement or interrelationship of the entity's parts.

The second principal feature of homeostasis that is germane to this discussion is that three primary processes have been identified by which adaptive systems maintain at least temporary quasi-independence from the "universal pressure" toward increased entropy. These are reactive negative feedback (most often discussed, particularly by psychologists, as response to environmental stimuli), passive insulation, and predictive adaptation. It is the last of these that may prove to be most crucial to the life-span developmental psychologist. It is this process by which an organism either permits or initiates irreversible change that will increase its future ability to resist or minimize irreversible change.

Thus, such a biomorphic representation of living entities is in a position to propose a potentially useful definition of an organism as "a member of that class of systems which are so arranged as to minimize irreversible changes in their form other than those changes which increase their power to minimize future changes" (Serebriakoff, 1975). Thus, while adaptive systems behave as if to achieve stability, they also accept, and often contain subsystems whose purpose is to generate a special type of irreversible change, namely, those changes that are intended to move the organism toward higher orders of stability.

This view sees life as that small bit of the universe that is moving the "wrong way"; against entropy toward greater order, more patterned systems, less probable arrangements. It sees death as the surrender to entropy, the *resumption of change.* Thus, Heraclitus's notion that nothing abides was an accurate description of the inanimate universe that is immutably ruled by the law of entropy. In one minor but highly significant way he was absolutely wrong. A small part of the universe—life— abides. It is in this sense that dialecticists present at least as mechanomorphic a representation of living systems as the "physicalists" they seek to supplant.

It is interesting to note than even in such recent works as Lerner (1976) the "unity of science" view is portrayed as holding the position that there are "basic and common laws that govern *all things in the universe* [p. 23, emphasis added] ." The biomorphic view implies something quite different. It implies that living systems are indeed governed by the same set of laws that govern the inanimate universe, but that there are an additional set of laws that apply only to living entities. This is anything but a trivial distinction.

The primary advantage to the developmental psychologist of such a biomorphic view, though, is not necessarily in its logical congruence; the advantage is in the pragmatic value of its assumptions and in its potential utility for research and for understanding observed phenomenon. Such a view, for example, necessitates re-linquishing the indescriminate quest for change of any kind and enables us to focus on a different conceptualization of human behavior. The identification of the fundamentally different processes by which adaptive systems achieve self-preserva-tion appears to provide a useful framework for the study of human behavior. Reactive negative feedback is the process by which the adaptive organism responds to environmental change in such a way as to preserve stability of form. Thus, much of classical and traditional psychological theory and research is preserved as the legitimate study of one of the basic processes of the organism.

A fundamentally different process, however, is that of predictive adaptation, the process by which the organism permits or initiates changes in form. It seems that this latter process is an especially powerful construct for developmental psycholo-gists, particularly with respect to growth, stages of development, terminal change, and related phenomena.

It provides us with the conceptual framework for coherently dealing with a variety of diverse forms of behavior that are particularly intractable in more molar theories of behavior except through painfully convoluted logic. For example, response to environmental stimuli is likely to continue to be directed toward maintenance of present form until such stimuli reach sufficient frequency, dura-tion, or intensity to cause the organism to passively permit or actively initiate a change in its form. In addition, since stability of form is conceived in terms of the interrelationship between the organism's parts, any change by addition, disruption, or deletion of the structural makeup of the organism, by definition, result in a change in form. Thus, a person who is blinded becomes a functionally different organism, as does the tadpole that grows up to be a frog. It is also the case that any change in the goals of the organism must, of necessity, be accompanied by a change in form.

Finally, the concept of predictive adaptation provides a basis for considering organismic change undertaken in anticipation of, or as the result of, predicted, future environmental events. One interesting implication of this model is that all changes in form are intended to provide *higher order* stability for the organism. Thus, while some changes may appear (to the "outside observer") to be either lateral or even regressive, each form change represents for that organism an attempt at an order of stability higher than the stability represented by its present form.

Although a full discussion of the assumptive network and ramifications of this biomorphic representation is well beyond the scope of this paper, it does appear to be rich in its implications for both theory and observation in psychology, and the interested reader is directed to the body of literature referred to earlier. We will, however, endeavor to place the concepts, discourse, and data regarding the variables of age, time, and cohort into this framework. We further propose the consideration of fairly recent conceptual, formal models that are beginning to evolve from such thinking and that seem to have promise for the future of developmental psychology.

III. Age, Cohort, and Time

The research designs of Schaie (1965) and Baltes (1968) did not explicitly come out of a particular scientific theory or approach. In fact, much of the discussion was directed at assumptions made about developmental change in an empirical atmosphere. These approaches were attempting to understand developmental change and what factors affect it. The lack of congruence between cross-sectional and longitudinal studies was the impetus. It is now obvious that development reflected numerous factors besides chronological age, most especially generational-cohort change and time of measurement—cultural change (Nesselroade & Baltes, 1974; Riegel, Chapter 1, this volume; Schaie, 1970).

Current discussions of generation or cohort differences have made us take another look at the meaning of existing data and consider whether developmental models and theories have been altered in their meaning. Nesselroade and Baltes (1974) advanced that a rapprochement between evolutionary sociological, anthropological, and psychological world views relative to the nature and etiology of human development is in order. The present focus on the interactive relationship between individual and historical change is going on in a number of disciplines, especially sociology (e.g., Bengston & Black, 1973; Buss, 1974a, 1974b; Keniston, 1970, 1971; Neugarten & Datan, 1973; Riley, 1973).

Riegel (1972a, 1972b, 1975c) has called not only for developmental psychology to become less culture centered and more sensitive to historical factors, but also for the basis of short-term and long-term developmental change to be given greater consideration. The focus on the interactions between inner-biological, individual-psychological, cultural-sociological, and outer-physical reminds us of the overwhelming number of potential influences that affect an organism's development.

The issue of individual and cultural changes has become a major focus of study in psychological gerontology by the elaboration of developmental research designs (Baltes, 1968; Buss, 1973a, 1973b, 1974a, 1974b; Cattell, 1970; Schaie, 1965, 1970, 1973). Riegel (1975c) states that these designs allow for analysis of change along the inner-biological and individual-psychological, represented by the dimensions of age and time of measurement, and along the cultural-sociological and outer-physical, representing generational-cohort differences and historical changes. The focus, according to Riegel, must be placed on the interaction of any two of the four dimensions.

All of these researchers are correct to emphasize the importance of these change dimensions and to point out that developmental science was remiss in not being sensitive to these change dimensions. However, at the same time we must remember that on some variables there are no differences between cross-sectional and longitudinal studies, even in the face of large environmental and cultural changes. Also, for many variables, if there are no generational-cohort differences and if there are no time of measurement—cultural change effects, then cross-sectional and longitudinal studies should give us similar results.

Schaie (1975) has, in his recent work, been focusing on models of cognitive development that emphasize that adult developmental stages occur in response to experiential events. He feels that:

> most age differences in cognitive functioning are not ontogenetic but related to the comparison of individuals belonging to generations differing in asymptotic level of acquisition of acculturated materials in young adulthood. But even if there is little change of age on measures validated for the young, this does not tell us that the young and the old are cognitively alike [p. 2].

Schaie advances that the acquisition of cognitive structures in childhood and during the early adult phase may not be relevant to the maintenance of functions and that the reorganization of cognitive structures may be required to meet the demands of older adulthood. Schaie further proposes adult stages going beyond formal operations and requiring different models. All of his adult stages have the organism readapting to new demands for that stage of the life span.

The reintegrative stage of older adulthood (the "why should I know" phase of life) occurs at a time when the complexity of the adult cognitive structure has reached an overload stage and demands simplification. The resulting cognitive response does not lead to disengagement; it is a response of more selective attention to cognitive demands which remain meaningful or attain new meaning. New problem-solving approaches requiring meaning and purpose within the immediate life situation become dominant. Thus, as we said earlier, some changes may appear to be lateral or even regressive. However, each form change represents for that organism an attempt at an order of stability higher than the stability represented by its present form. Schaie and Parham (1976), in their most recent discussion of personality, have emphasized that, based on their data analysis, stability is the rule rather than the exception.

The point that should emerge here is that data-gathering techniques which are able to separate environmental change, behavioral change, behavioral (interindividual) difference, and form change may lead to a better understanding and greater appreciation of behavior as a stability-seeking device.

> Mainly, principally, and essentially, living things seem to be "set" to defy change. They behave as if they were "designed" to resist or minimize changes in their form through time. I say "form" because in all living things the contents change while the form remains relatively stable. The morphostasis of a fountain not the stability of a stone [Serebriakoff, 1975, p. 14].

Cultural change and environmental change may be like a wind that blows the water in the fountain to the left or right. The organism maintains its basic form but is affected by the environmental influences. Developmental designs such as sequential strategies give us an opportunity to try to capture these change components (Baltes, 1968; Buss, 1973b, 1974b; Lawton & Nahemow, 1973; Schaie, 1965, 1970; Schaie & Baltes, 1976).

There has been extensive discussion of the merits of the sequential designs (e.g., Baltes, 1968; Buss, 1973a; Schaie, 1965, 1973; Schaie & Baltes, 1976; Wohlwill, 1970a, 1970b, 1973). A growing number of research studies (e.g., Baltes & Reinert, 1969; Nesselroade & Baltes, 1974; Nesselroade, Schaie, & Baltes, 1972; Schaie, 1970; Schaie, Labouvie, & Buech, 1973; Schaie & Labouvie-Vief, 1974) all show the pervasiveness of cohort differences and time differences. Such data clearly imply that generational or historical differences contribute significantly where self-reported personality and ability dimensions are examined. Nesselroade and Baltes (1974) have demonstrated that such cohort/time differences must be considered in adolescence in addition to middle and older adulthood. Even one year may be enough of a time span for "generation" differences to emerge. The interactive effects of individual versus historical change components affect not only average scores but intraindividual change as well.

The foregoing results lead up to the need to simultaneously examine the time-related changes of the organism and of the environment (Baltes & Nesselroade, 1973; Eckensberger, 1973; Nesselroade & Baltes, 1974; Willems, 1973), and emphasize that research must be carried out that allows us to go beyond simply attributing differences to cohort and time effects. We must move to a detailed explication of the cohort and time effects.

It becomes obvious from these considerations that progress has been made in explicating age. Age relations "are invariably in transition to being explained by other variables without recourse to the use of the term age [Birren, 1959, p. 8]." Development reflects numerous factors besides chronological age, and this emphasizes the need to have a "dynamic" approach to developmental analysis. Order and regularity in behavior change are produced by the interacting influence patterns of ontogenetic and biocultural systems. Chronological age is a useful parameter if intraindividual change patterns are sufficiently homogeneous to yield a high correlation between chronological age and behavioral change. However, when individual differences are large in the age–behavior change function, it is not useful to focus on the age-change model. An age-irrelevant but sequence-relevant approach to development may be more appropriate (Baltes & Willis, 1977).

That there can be such transient changes in the development of organisms should not surprise us. Serebriakoff (1975) advances that morphostats with more flexible efferent and afferent sensory and control systems are capable of short-term adjustment ontogenetically within a single generation. Ontogenetically intelligent creatures can be highly flexible, but they have to pay "the price of having to start each new generation anew with fewer built-in know-how patterns and less built-in power to classify significant events. They will need to build up stimulus–response systems anew in each animal (p. 30).

The biological nature of the organism will, of course, set limits to the possibilities and pacing of change. "The normal course of life is partially determined by inner-biological factors that find expression in the normative age-grading of any society (Neugarten & Datan, 1973) [Riegel, 1975b, p. 101]." Perhaps the most pervasive example of biological set limits is terminal drop (Riegel & Riegel, 1972). Terminal drop suggests a determinate chain of behavior changes that are less related to *age* per se than to time of death. The phenomenon shows an onset that varies widely for different people. Such changes in biologically older individuals should not surprise us, since older organisms "must be defective because of the law of entropy; any given event has a much greater probability of disturbing than of improving a complex entity. And time brings more events, more chance of disturbance, more chance of incorrigible disturbance [Serebriakoff, 1975, p. 40]." The organism maintains form as long as it can but, when overwhelmed by potential disaster, may move to what appears to be a lower level of functioning.

IV. Experimental and Analytic Approaches

As stated earlier, we must move away from descriptive approaches, even those of a sophisticated sequential nature, and move to a detailed explication of the cohort and time effects as well as the age effects. Dissatisfaction with the concept of age and with its utilization in developmental research as an independent variable (Baltes & Goulet, 1970; Wohlwill, 1970a, 1970b, 1973) has focused research efforts on the investigation of developmental variables by means of experimental manipulation (e.g., Baltes & Goulet, 1971; Birren, 1970).

An experimental study of development involves the manipulation of an independent variable or variables in such a manner that the age–performance function is altered. Such changes in the age–performance function should be directed at approximating the change in individuals associated with chronological age or should be used in determining the degree of change possible at various points of the life span. This approach represents the process-analytic strategy, which centers on explicating performance differentials by specification of the antecedents and processes involved.

The goal of scientific explanation is the determination of necessary and sufficient antecedent conditions for the occurrence of events. Manipulative experiments are the major tool for examining the validity of assumed causal relationships. The possibility of manipulating antecedents implies that age—performance functions are not fixed and irreversible but are subject to modification (Labouvie, 1973). Short-term experiential manipulations are a first step to isolating relevant dimensions for designing successful intervention strategies (Sterns, 1972).

The manipulation approach in the experimental situation provides the base for intervention in developmental settings. Researchers now realize that what have been assumed to be age-related deficits may be principally generational differences. As a result of current methodological advances, current research and theoretical discussions (Baltes & Labouvie, 1973; Labouvie-Vief, Hoyer, Baltes, & Baltes, 1974; Sanders, Sterns, Smith, & Sanders, 1975; Sterns, Barrett, Alexander, Greenawalt, Gianetta, & Panek, 1975) indicate that developmental changes, especially deficits, may be a function of nonuniversal, experientially based antecedents. Such a view of development leads to process-oriented research that focuses on identifying and modifying those factors associated with lower levels of performance. Reduced performance may be the result of inhibitory behavior components that are mediated and maintained by environmental contingencies (Labouvie-Vief et al., 1974). Short-term experiential manipulation can be seen as mini-interventions that will be instructive in designing ways to remove inhibitory behavior components maintained by unfavorable environmental contingencies or as a reduction in the impact due to genetically controlled maturation. What is needed is a better understanding of the interaction of the individual and the environment.

Riegel (1972b, 1973a, 1975b), Buss (1974b), and Atchley (1975) emphasize the dialectical relationship between the changing individual and the changing environment: The individual determines and sets limits for environmental change, and the environment determines and sets limits for individual change.

Buss (1974b) presents this view explicitly:

> The key concept "fresh contact" summarizes explicitly the idea that each successive biological generation (continuously emerging and therefore aging) comes into contact anew with existent cultural heritage. Each new generation interprets reality without the years of commitment to a previous ideology and, therefore, transforms that reality. The biological given that there is a continuous emergence of new generations does not guarantee the transformation of social structures, but it does serve as a vehicle for social change....
>
> The interaction between the individual and society referred to above consists of an interaction between cause and effect—where each may serve as both cause and effect. Introducing the time dimension into this paradigm serves to complicate matters consider-

ably since the interaction between the individual and society (reciprocal causation) will interact with historical time [p. 67].

What Buss calls reciprocal causation is a complex but potentially solvable situation. In fact, as research scientists, we have been having this problem for a very long time. The growing research on ability-extraneous factors in intelligence responsible for apparent decline in ability is a good example. Researchers following suggestions offered by Birren (1970), Baltes and Goulet (1971), and Baltes and Schaie (1973b) have been able to tease apart some of these relationships of reciprocal causation (Baltes & Labouvie, 1973).

The result has been to move to manipulative research and attempt to see how modifiable, within given limits, is the behavior of older adults. This does not yet allow us a clear understanding of what factors are responsible for inhibitory behavior components; but this leads us toward an attempt to better dimensionalize assumed causal antecedents.

The limitations of understanding age and cohort interaction do not come from the analysis models used as suggested by Wohlwill (1973) and Buss (1974b) but rather from our ability to ask the right questions. We have not really explored many existing suggestions (Schaie, 1973).

"Past descriptive research has frequently collected the wrong data to answer the right question or even worse collected the right data in ignorance of the questions to be asked appropriately from such data [Schaie, 1973, p. 264]."

It may therefore be timely to stress unequivocally that a proper research approach involves the following: (1) asking the right question; (2) asking the question so that we can collect data; (3) knowing something about sources of error in our instruments.

If the research is framed in a meaningful way, then many relatively unsophisticated approaches may still have much utility for our future work. At some point statistical models will have to be abandoned (Stevens, 1968), and a strong move to paradigmatic approaches taken.

Schaie and Baltes (1976) emphasize that some researchers will judge models and assumptions to be acceptable, while others will reject them for their failure to match with explanatory hypothesis. At this point in time, a pluralistic approach to explication and model building seems most appropriate provided that these approaches give us a meaningful context in which to do research.

A concluding reemphasis of a strong cautionary nature is clearly in order regarding the burgeoning literature (particularly in developmental psychology) on multivariate statistical methods. There appears to be little doubt that multivariate methods are capable of meeting most, if not all, of the promise ascribed to them by their advocates as *inferential, hypothesis-testing* statistical methods. There is, however, a growing body of both empirical and theoretical evidence that as sophisticated descriptive analyses of human behavior they are of very limited practical value.

The fields of educational and industrial psychology have widely employed multiple-regression and multiple-discriminant analysis in selection research for the past 30 years. Several results from that literature leave the techniques as being highly questionable at best, and at worst seriously misleading. Several authors (e.g., Lawshe, 1969; Marks, 1966) have demonstrated both theoretically and empirically that regression and discriminant weights are so unstable that both unit and random weights hold up at least as well on cross validation. In addition, recent investigations into the statistical power of multiple regression indicate that even with relatively few independent variables, sample sizes must generally be substantially larger than those typically employed in order to make reasonable estimates of either the weights or the correlation coefficients (Gross, 1973; Schmidt, Hunter, & Urrey, 1975). The most serious practical problems with the model, however, probably arise from two sources. Attenuation of correlation coefficients as a result of restriction of range is well documented in the literature (Barrett, Alexander, O'Connor, Forbes, Balascoe, & Garver, 1975). Lumsden (1976), on the other hand, has recently discussed the debilitating effects of violation of the random uncorrelated error assumption on correlation regression and has pointed out that in practice most psychological tests are differentially accurate across their range. As serious as these factors are to the general linear model, where relatively few variables are typically involved, a moment's reflection will show that they render the factor-analytic data-reduction approach virtually useless. Any real-world sample on which data are likely to be collected is virtually assured of displaying *differential* restriction of range on the variables. For either longitudinal or cross-sectional samples, this restriction is also very likely to change, differentially across the variables, from sample to sample. Since it is the intercorrelation (or covariance) matrix resulting from such samples that forms the basis of factor analysis, it should come as no surprise that Nunnally (1973) commented that these methods have to date produced nothing of substance for developmental psychology. Nor has that situation changed in the past 3 years.

In a slightly different vein, it must be remembered that multivariate statistics and factor analysis (as well as similar systems, such as cluster analysis, multidimensional scaling, etc.) are first and foremost taxonomic statistics, developed by taxonomists for constructing ordered classification systems (Gregson, 1975; Sokal, 1974). As Eisler (1967) has carefully pointed out, there is a great deal of difference between data reduction or data collapsing models and models that are descriptive of the theoretical—empirical relationships among variables.

The field might be well advised to spend less effort contorting the interrelationships of human behavior to "fit" existing statistical (particularly linear additive) models and begin the search for models that better fit the empirical and theoretical relationships of interest. An excellent starting place for such a search would be in parallel processing models such as Serebriakoff's (1975) polyhierarchical model, holographic theory as applied to human behavior by researchers such as Pribram (1971), or the recent promising work in the mathematics of Thomian topology (Zeeman, 1976) exemplified in Feedle's chapter (Chapter 17) in this volume.

REFERENCES

Alston, W. P. Conceptual prolegma to a psychological theory of intentional action. In S. C. Brown (Ed.), *Philosophy of psychology.* London: Macmillan, 1974.

Atchley, R. C. The life course, age grading, and age-linked demands for decision making. In N. Datan & L. H. Ginsberg (Eds.), *Life-span developmental psychology: Normative life crises.* New York: Academic Press, 1975.

Baltes, P. B. Longitudinal and cross-sectional sequences in the study of age and generation effects. *Human Development,* 1968, 11, 145–171.

Baltes, P. B., & Goulet, L. R. Status and issues of a life-span developmental psychology. In L. R. Goulet & P. B. Baltes (Eds.), *Life-span developmental psychology: Research and theory.* New York: Academic Press, 1970.

Baltes, P. B., & Goulet, L. R. Exploration of developmental variables by manipulation and simulation of age differences in behavior *Human Development,* 1971, 14, 149–170.

Baltes, P. B., & Labouvie, G. V. Adult development of intellectual performance: Description, explanation, and modification. In C. Eisdorfer & M. P. Lawton (Eds.), *The psychology of adult development and aging.* Washington, D.C.: American Psychological Association, 1973.

Baltes, P. B., & Nesselroade, J. R. The developmental analysis of individual differences on multiple measures. In J. R. Nesselroade & H. W. Reese (Eds.), *Life-span developmental psychology: Methodological issues.* New York: Academic Press, 1973.

Baltes, P. B., & Reinert, G. Cohort effects in cognitive development of children as revealed by cross-sectional sequences. *Developmental Psychology,* 1969, 1, 169–177.

Baltes, P. B., & Schaie, K. W. (Eds.) *Life-span developmental psychology: Personality and socialization.* New York: Academic Press, 1973. (a)

Baltes, P. B., & Schaie, K. W. On life-span developmental research paradigms: Retrospects and prospects. In P. B. Baltes & K. W. Schaie (Eds.). *Life-span developmental psychology: Personality and socialization.* New York: Academic Press, 1973. (b)

Baltes, P. B., & Willis, S. L. Toward psychological theories of aging. In J. E. Birren & K. W. Schaie, (Eds.), *Handbook of psychology of aging.* New York: Reinhold-Van Nostrand, 1977.

Barrett, G. V., Alexander, R. A., O'Connor, E., Forbes, J. B., Balascoe, L., & Garver, T. *Public policy and personnel selection: Development of a selection program for patrol officers* (Tech. Rep. 1). Akron: University of Akron, Department of Psychology, Industrial/Organizational Psychology Group, 1975.

Bengston, V. L., & Black, K. D. Intergenerational relations and continuities in socialization. In P. B. Baltes & K. W. Schaie (Eds.), *Life-span developmental psychology: Personality and socialization.* New York: Academic Press, 1973.

Birren, J. E. Principles of research on aging. In J. E. Birren (Ed.), *Handbook of aging and the individual: Psychological and biological aspects.* Chicago: University of Chicago Press, 1959.

Birren, J. E. Toward an experimental psychology of aging. *American Psychologist,* 1970 25, 124–135.

Buss, A. R. A conceptual framework for learning effecting the development of ability factors. *Human Development,* 1973, 16, 273–292. (a)

Buss, A. R. An extension of developmental models that separate ontogenetic changes and cohort differences. *Psychological Bulletin,* 1973, 80, 466–479. (b)

Buss, A. R. A general developmental model for interindividual differences, intraindividual differences, and intraindividual changes. *Developmental Psychology,* 1974, 10, 70–78. (a)

Buss, A. R. Generational analysis: Description, explanation and theory. *Journal of Social Issues,* 1974, 30, 55–71. (b)

Cattell, R. B. Separating endogenous, exogenous, ecogenic, and epogenic component curves in developmental data. *Developmental Psychology,* 1970 3, 151–162.

Diesing, P. *Patterns of discovery in the social sciences.* Chicago: Aldine, Atherton, 1971.

Eckensberger, L. H. Methodological issues of cross-cultural research in developmental psychology. In J. R. Nesselroade & H. W. Reese (Eds.), *Life-span developmental psychology: Methodological issues.* New York: Academic Press, 1973.

Eisler, H. *Multidimensional similarity: An experimental comparison between vector, distance, and set theoretical models.* Unpublished manuscript, University of Stockholm, 1967.

Findlay, L. N. *The contemporary relevance of Hegel;* In A. MacIntyre (Ed.), *Hegel: A collection of critical essays.* Garden City, N.Y.: Anchor, 1972.

Goulet, L. R., & Baltes, P. B. (Eds.). *Life-span developmental psychology: Research and theory.* New York: Academic Press, 1970.

Gregson, R. *Psychometrics of similarity.* New York: Academic Press, 1975.

Gross, A. L. Prediction in future samples studied in terms of the gain from selection. *Psychometrika,* 1973, **38**, 151–172.

Keniston, K. Postadolescence (youth) and historical change. In J. Zurbin & A. M. Freedman (Eds.), *The psychopathology of adolescence.* New York: Grune & Stratton, 1970.

Keniston, K. Psychological development and historical change. *Journal of Interdisciplinary History,* 1971, **2**, 330–345.

Kosok, M. The formalization of Hegel's dialectual logic. *International Philosophical Quarterly,* 1966, **6**, 596–631.

Krantz, H. H., Luce, R. D., Suppes, P., & Tversky, A. *Foundations of measurement* (Vol. 1), *Additive and polynomial representations.* New York: Academic Press, 1971.

Labouvie, G. V. Implications of geropsychological theories for intervention: The challenge for the seventies. *Gerontologist,* 1973, **13**, 10–15.

Labouvie-Vief, G. V., Hoyer, W. J., Baltes, M. M., & Baltes, P. B. Operant analysis of intellectual behavior in old age. *Human Development,* 1974, **17**, 259–272.

Lave, C. A., & March, J. G. *An introduction to models in social sciences.* New York: Harper, 1975.

Lawler, J. Dialectical philosophy and developmental psychology: Hegel and Piaget on contradiction. *Human Development,* 1975, **18**, 1–17.

Lawshe, C. H. Statistical theory and practice in applied psychology. *Personnel Psychology,* 1969, **22**, 117–124.

Lawton, M. P., & Nahemow, L. Ecology and the aging process. In C. Eisdorfer & M. P. Lawton (Eds.), *The psychology of adult development and aging.* Washington, D.C.: American Psychological Association, 1973.

Lerner, R. M. *Concepts and theories of human development.* Reading, Mass.: Addison-Wesley, 1976.

Looft, W. R. Socialization and personality throughout the life span. An examination of contemporary psychological approaches. In P. B. Baltes & K. W. Schaie (Eds.), *Life-span developmental psychology: Personality and socialization.* New York: Academic Press, 1973.

Luchins, A. S., & Luchins, E. H. *Logical foundations of mathematics for behavior scientists.* New York: Holt, 1965.

Lumsden, J. Test theory. *Annual Review of Psychology,* 1976, **27**, 251–280.

Marks, M. *Two kinds of regression weights which are better than betas in crossed samples.* Paper presented at the 74th annual meeting of the American Psychological Association, New York, August, 1966.

Nesselroade, J. R., & Baltes, P. B. Adolescent personality development and historical change: 1970–1972. *Monographs of the Society for Research in Child Development,* 1974 39(1, Serial No. 154).

Nesselroade, J. R., & Reese, H. W. (Eds.). *Life-span developmental psychology: Methodological issues.* New York: Academic Press, 1973.

Nesselroade, J. R., Schaie, K. W., & Baltes, P. B. Ontogenetic and generational components of structural and quantitative change in adult behavior. *Journal of Gerontology*, 1972, 27, 222–228.

Neugarten, B. L., & Datan, N. Sociological perspectives on the life cycle. In P. B. Baltes & K. W. Schaie (Eds.), *Life-span developmental psychology: Personality and socialization*. New York: Academic Press, 1973.

Nunnally, J. C. Research strategies and measurement methods for investigating human development. In J. R. Nesselroade & H. W. Reese (Eds.), *Life-span developmental psychology: Methodological Issues*. New York: Academic Press, 1973.

Overton, W. F., & Reese, H. W. Models of development: Methodological implications. In J. R. Nesselroade & H. W. Reese (Eds.), *Life-span developmental psychology: Methodological issues*. New York: Academic Press, 1973.

Piaget, J., & Inhelder, B. *The psychology of the child*. New York: Basic Books, 1969.

Pribram, H. H. *Languages of the brain: Experimental paradoxes and principles in neuropsychology*. Engelwood Cliffs, N.J. Prentice-Hall, 1971.

Reese, H. W., & Overton, W. F. Models of development and theories of development. In L. R. Goulet & P. B. Baltes (Eds.), *Life-span developmental psychology: Research and theory*. New York. Academic Press, 1970.

Riegel, K. F. The influence of economic and political ideology upon the development of developmental psychology. *Psychological Bulletin*, 1972, 78, 129–141. (a)

Riegel, K. F. Time and change in the development of the individual and society. In H. W. Reese (Ed.), *Advances in child development and behavior* (Vol. 7). New York: Academic Press, 1972. (b)

Riegel, K. F. Developmental psychology and society: Some historical and ethical considerations. In J. R. Nesselroade & H. W. Reese (Eds.), *Life-span developmental psychology: Methodological issues*. New York: Academic Press, 1973. (a)

Riegel, K. F. On the history of psychological gerontology. In C. Eisdorfer & M. P. Lawton (Eds.), *The psychology of adult development and aging*. Washington, D.C.: American Psychological Association, 1973. (b)

Riegel, K. F. A manifesto for dialectical psychology. *Newsletter for Dialectical Psychology*, 1975, 1, 8–11.

Riegel, K. F. Adult life crises: A dialectic interpretation of development. In N. Datan & L. Ginsberg (Eds.), *Life-span developmental psychology: Normative life-crises*. New York: Academic Press, 1975. (b)

Riegel, K. F. Toward a dialectical theory of development. *Human Development*, 1975, 18, 50–64. (c)

Riegel, K. F., & Riegel, R. M. Development, drop, and death. *Developmental Psychology*, 1972, 6, 306–319.

Riley, M. W. Aging and cohort succession: Interpretations and misinterpretations. *Public Opinion Quarterly*, 1973, 37, 35–49.

Sanders, J. A., Sterns, H. L., Smith, M., & Sanders, R. E. Modification of concept identification performance in older adults. *Developmental Psychology*, 1975, 11, 824–829.

Schaie, K. W. A general model for the study of developmental problems. *Psychological Bulletin*, 1965, 64, 92–107.

Schaie, K. W. A reinterpretation of age-related changes in cognitive structure and functioning. In L. R. Goulet & P. B. Baltes (Eds.), *Life-span developmental psychology: Research and theory*. New York: Academic Press, 1970.

Schaie, K. W. Methodological problems in descriptive research on adulthood and aging. In J. R. Nesselroade & H. W. Reese (Eds.), *Life-span developmental psychology: Methodological issues*. New York: Academic Press, 1973.

Schaie, K. W. Old wine into new bottles; a stage of theory of adult cognitive development. In P. Baltes (Chair), *Cognitive behavior and problem solving*. Symposium presented at the meeting of the 10th International Congress of Gerontology, Jerusalem, 1975.

Schaie, K. W., & Baltes, P. B. On sequential strategies in developmental research and the Schaie-Baltes controversy: Description or explanation? *Human Development,* 1977, in press.

Schaie, K. W., Labouvie, G. V., & Buech, B. Generational and cohort-specific differences in adult cognitive functioning: A fourteen-year study of independent samples. *Developmental Psychology.* 1973, 9, 151–166.

Schaie, K. W., & Labouvie-Vief, G. Generational versus ontogenetic components of change in adult cognitive behavior: A fourteen-year cross-sequential study. *Developmental Psychology,* 1974, 10, 305–320.

Schaie, K. W., & Parham, I. A. *Stability of adult personality: Fact or fable?* Unpublished manuscript, Ethel Percy Andrus Gerontology Center, University of Southern California, Los Angeles, 1976.

Schmidt, F. L., Hunter, J. E., & Urrey, V. W. *Statistical power in criterion-related validation studies* (PS-75-7). Washington, D.C.: Personnel Research and Development Center, U.S. Civil Service Commission, 1975.

Serebriakoff, V. *Brain.* London: David-Poynter, 1975.

Simon, H. A. *The sciences of the artificial.* Cambridge, Mass.: MIT Press, 1969.

Sokal, R. R. Classification: Purposes, principles, progress, prospects. *Science,* 1974, 185(4157), 1115–1123.

Sterns, H. L. *Short-term experimental manipulations in geropsychological research.* Paper presented at the annual meeting of the Gerontological Society, San Juan, December 1972.

Sterns, H. L., Barrett, G. V., Alexander, R. A., Greenawalt, J. P., Gianetta, T. E., & Panek, P. E. Improving skills of the older adult critical for effective driving performance. In L. Pastalan (Chair), *Maintaining the (personal) mobility of older persons.* Symposium presented at the 28th annual meeting of the Gerontological Society, Louisville, 1975.

Stevens, S. S. Measurement; statistics, and the schemapiric view. *Science,* 1968, 161, 849–856.

Van den Daele, L. D. Ego development in dialectical perspective. *Human Development,* 1975, 18, 129–142.

Wiener, N. *Cybernetics: Or control and communication in the animal and machine.* Cambridge, Mass.: MIT Press, 1961.

Willems, E. P. Behavioral ecology and experimental analysis: Courtship is not enough. In J. R. Nesselroade & H. W. Reese (Eds.), *Life-span developmental psychology: Methodological issues.* New York: Academic Press, 1973.

Wohlwill, J. F. The age variable in psychological research. *Psychological Review,* 1970, 77, 49–64. (a)

Wohlwill, J. F. Methodology and research strategy in the study of developmental change. In L. R. Goulet & P. B. Baltes (Eds.), *Life-span developmental psychology: Research and theory.* New York: Academic Press, 1970, (b)

Wohlwill, J. F. *The study of behavioral development.* New York: Academic Press, 1973.

Wozniak, R. H. A dialectical paradigm for psychological research: Implications drawn from the history of psychology in the Soviet Union. *Human Development,* 1975, 18, 18–34.

Zeeman, E. C. Catastrophy theory. *Scientific American,* 1976, 234, 65–83.

CHAPTER 6

The Status of Dialectics in Developmental Psychology:
Theoretical Orientation versus Scientific Method

PAUL B. BALTES AND STEVEN W. CORNELIUS

PENNSYLVANIA STATE UNIVERSITY
UNIVERSITY PARK, PENNSYLVANIA

I. Introduction and Objective

During the last few years we have witnessed a growing enthusiasm among behavioral scientists, especially among developmentalists, for the perspectives provided by a dialectical orientation (e.g., Huston-Stein & Baltes, 1976; Nesselroade & Baltes, 1974; Riegel, 1975, 1976; Rychlak, 1976a). The present conference and the volume resulting from it are an indicant of this development. In our view, the rationales for the increasing interest in a dialectical orientation among behavioral scientists are numerous. We observe, however, that the concept of dialectical orientation is often used in such an expansive and nebulous manner that the intrinsic power and attractiveness of dialectics may not find the fruition it deserves.

In the present chapter we will briefly summarize our views of the historical context that has led to the surge of interest in a dialectical orientation in relation to issues in developmental psychology. Subsequently, we will examine the logical status of dialectics within the framework of empirical scientific methodology. Our main conclusion will be that the questions raised by the advocates of a dialectical approach are important ones. However, advancements in a dialectical psychology will be less likely to come from efforts to use dialectics as a specific methodology than from efforts to employ dialectics as a general theoretical orientation. A corollary conclusion will be that a dialectical orientation can be implemented through a variety of research paradigms, including those developed within the "separate" metacontext of mechanistic or organismic world views (Overton & Reese, 1973; Reese & Overton, 1970); that is, we will argue that the empirical translation of dialectical questions does not necessarily require the formulation of a new paradigm, as suggested by Riegel (1976). On the contrary, our viewpoint concurs with that of Hook (1953). The effort to link dialectics as a philosophical theory with specific implications for the scientific method and unique empirical research strategies is a conceptual trap that empirically oriented behavioral scientists are advised to avoid.

II. The Research Issues in Developmental Psychology

In our view, the major reasons for the advent of dialectics in the behavioral sciences are related to a number of problems that current research and theory has difficulty resolving. Some of these problem areas have attracted prominent attention in developmental psychology. Developmental psychology is a prime candidate among the behavioral sciences for identifying such "dialectical" problem areas because it shares with dialectics a focus on change and process.

The salient problem areas that developmental research has identified as critical to the study of development and that lend themselves to a dialectical approach include the following: (a) the nature of change, (b) the role of transitions and discontinuity, (c) the nature of structure and structural transformation, (d) the nature of interaction and interactive relationships, (e) the relationship between ontogenetic and evolutionary perspectives, (f) the notion of contextual, multiple, and bidirectional causality, and (g) the notion of relative, nonabsolute predictability and probabilistic models.

Each of these problem areas or salient issues in developmental research exhibits some surface "phenotypic" convergence with the prototypical features of dialectical philosophy and dialectical materialism. Our position, however, is that none of these problem areas necessarily requires a basic "genotypic" alignment with a specific model or particular theory.

It is beyond the scope of this brief chapter to delineate in detail each of the problem areas listed above. Various recent reviews of theory construction and research in developmental psychology (e.g., Baltes & Willis, 1977; Huston-Stein & Baltes, 1976; Reese & Overton, 1970; Riegel, 1973, 1976) can be consulted for that purpose. To illustrate the nature of the issues, only a few examples will be offered.

For instance, one central issue is the nature and logical status of *behavioral change*. The question is whether change is considered as a primary phenomenon or whether it is a secondary phenomenon derived, for example, from differences between observations made at different points in time. Similarly, in discussing the issues of *transition* and *discontinuity,* a salient question is whether or not contemporary developmental theory (including Piaget's cognitive theory and the sociological role theory) is too "stage-static" and does not account at all for the mechanisms of transitional processes themselves. Furthermore, an important issue is to what degree the concept of *structure* or organization is essential to the study of developmental change not only at the level of extrapersonological–environmental analysis but also at the intrapersonological or intrapsychic level of analysis (e.g., Riegel & Rosenwald, 1975). Similarly, in examining the logical status and definition of an *interaction* such as nature–nurture relationships, it has become more and more apparent that there are multiple conceptions of interaction (e.g., Overton, 1973) and that most formulations are excessively vague. Furthermore, in regard to *ontogenetic* and *evolutionary* perspectives, research on cohort effects (e.g., Baltes, Cornelius & Nesselroade, 1977a; Baltes & Schaie, 1976; Nesselroade & Baltes, 1974) and in sociobiology (e.g., Campbell, 1975; Wilson, 1975) has rekindled interest in conjointly studying interactive principles and mechanisms of evolutionary and ontogenetic development.

As to the notions of *causality* and *relative predictability,* greater recognition is being given to the distinction between and the usefulness of multiple concepts of causality in attempts to explain developmental change. Researchers have advanced, for instance, distinctions between proximal and distal causality (Baltes, Reese, & Nesselroade, 1977c) and between unidirectional-and bidirectional-conjoint causality (Overton & Reese, 1973; Riegel, 1976). These distinctions among types of causality have attracted considerable attention in efforts to account for salient developmental issues such as those related to time-lag explanations of sleeper effects (distal causality) or the conceptualization of dialogues (bidirectional causality). Finally, there is an acknowledgement that future trends in environmental conditions (eco-psychologies) are not likely to be fully predictable (e.g., Toffler, 1970). This recognition has led some researchers to embrace the notion of relative predictability and to conclude that behavioral development is, therefore, in principle, never fully predictable. Accordingly, notions of incomplete determinancy and probabilistic models (see also Labouvie, 1975) are gaining in prominence among developmental researchers.

It might be useful to note that the field of life-span developmental psychology has been in the forefront of developments in each of the problem areas listed. This is not surprising since the life-span approach, which focuses on long-term change, is apt to stretch the boundaries of existing developmental theories and, thereby, to be sensitive to the identification of basic and salient issues in theory and methodology (e.g., Baltes & Schaie, 1973; Huston-Stein & Baltes, 1976).

In the following sections, some basic tenets of dialectics will be briefly reviewed. In the process, it will be shown why it is likely that many developmentalists concerned with the problem areas listed above are attracted to dialectics as a philosophical theory or as a theoretical orientation. As indicated previously, however, whether the convergence of research issues in developmental research with the propositions of dialectics is more than a temporary courtship is another question.

III. Dialectics and Scientific Inquiry

Dialectics, of course, has become a multifaceted and nonmonolithic conception. Therefore, the present exposition will need to be sketchy and perhaps exceedingly narrow; the discussion will focus on those aspects of dialectics that easily relate to the issues of developmental research, as outlined. A recent monograph edited by Rychlak (1976a) provides in its introductory chapter (Rychlak, 1976b) a good overview of the many historical roots and meanings of dialectics. Similarly, Hook (1953) emphasizes the importance of distinguishing between (a) dialectics as a metaphor for the nature of change; and (b) dialectics as a method of understanding change.

A. The Basic Tenets and Assumptions of Dialectics

The dialectical perspective originated in the philosophical writings of Hegel, and some would argue that the germinal seeds of it may be found in Platonic (e.g., Eastman, 1940) and Aristotelian (e.g., Hook, 1953) thought (see also Rychlak, 1976a). Two of the basic notions espoused by Hegel were that (a) reality consists not of things but of ideas that (b) are in a state of flux or process of dialectical unfolding (Eastman, 1940). Marxist dialectical materialism is a descendant of Hegelian philosophy but renounces the notion that reality is constructed through ideas; rather reality is inherent in material things (Eastman, 1940). The materialist view suggests that the dialectical process consists of a contradiction that "is objectively present in things and processes" and is an "actual force as well [Engels, 1923, cited in Hook, 1957, p. 7]."

The introduction of a dialectical perspective into American developmental psychology (e.g., Riegel, 1973; Rychlak, 1976a) has been preceded by its entrance into some sister sciences, such as sociology (e.g., Boudon, 1975), anthropology (e.g., O'Laughlin, 1975), and Soviet psychology (e.g., Graham, 1971; Wozniak, 1975). However, the status of dialectics, and particularly of Marxist dialectical materialism, with regard to science and the scientific method has been for many years a subject of considerable debate among philosophers (e.g., Eastman, 1940; Hook, 1953, 1955, 1957). The debate has not been resolved and continues in the current literature (e.g., Geymonat, 1973; Kupers, 1973). The proponents' and critics' continual discussions of dialectics and the scientific method reflect in part the confusion associated with the multiple meanings and conceptions assigned to dialectics (e.g., Hook, 1953; Rychlak, 1976b).

Hook (1957), in the context of dialectical materialism, examined three laws of dialectics: (a) *contradiction;* (b) *negation of negation;* (c) *quantity and quality* (see Rychlak, 1976b, for a more restricted view of the "core" propositions of dialectics). The law of contradiction expresses the belief "that contradiction is objectively present in things and processes [Hook, 1957, p. 7]." The focus in the dialectical materialism version is on the internal sources for change, though Hegel would maintain that the contradiction of which he speaks is one of ideas about things and not of things themselves (Eastman, 1940).

Second, the law of negation of negation assumes that "things change in time, that every distinction within a temporary process may be regarded as an opposition, and that every opposition in time loses its defining character and assumes the traits of its converse [Hook, 1957, p. 15]." The implication of this assumption is that change or development is an incessant aspect of thought (Hegel) or things (Marx).

Third, the law of quantity and quality asserts that quantitative change, after a certain limit is surpassed, produces qualitative change or a qualitative-structural transformation. The transformation of phenomena occurs by the cumulative quantitative changes. "This law is so formulated as to suggest that quality first comes into existence as a result of variations in quantity [Hook, 1957, p. 20]."

The three laws of the dialectic outline the metatheoretical assumptions that are espoused from a dialectical perspective. It is these laws of contradiction, negation of negation, and quantity and quality that developmental psychologists (e.g., Riegel, 1976; Wozniak, 1975) are attracted to. The laws are used as generic principles for, or representations of, issues such as that change and interaction are "primary," that change is intrinsically quantitative *and* qualitative, and that the sequel of change might be discontinuous. The phenotypic similarity between some salient issues of developmental research and dialectics is apparent. The textbook by Schmidt (1970; see also Baltes, 1971) perhaps makes most explicit the linkage between dialectics and theory construction in developmental psychology.

B. Dialectics and Scientific Method

The key question is whether the core ideas of dialectics are directly linked to, and/or lend themselves to, a direct translation into principles of the scientific method. In examining this question, it is important to distinguish, as Hook (1953; see also Rychlak, 1976b) does, between dialectics as "the pattern of existential change [p. 702]" and dialectics as "a method of understanding change [p. 705]." This distinction is similar to the one Rychlak (1976b) makes between dialectics as a "world principle" and dialectics as a "valid organon," that is, between a metatheoretical paradigm (world view) and a correct means or manner of coming to know truth (valid organon).

In the present context, a critical examination of the assumption of dialectics as a general world view is of less concern. In fact, the potential usefulness of such a world view for heuristic purposes is acceptable, in our view, as long as there is a clear recognition that the assumptions of this world view are likely to be untestable. However, the examination of dialectics as an empirical method aimed at generating scientific knowledge about change is of utmost concern. The contributions of Mehlberg (1955) and Hook (e.g., 1953, 1955, 1957) are particularly helpful in illustrating the basic points related to the use of dialectics as a scientific method.

In a prelude to the examination of the usefulness of dialectics for the scientific method, Mehlberg (1955) makes a distinction between questions of *verification* and *proof,* on the one hand, and questions of *discovery,* on the other. He argues that the scientific method deals with procedures for verification (or falsification) and proof in the general context of empiricism. The necessary procedures are fairly clear and established. On the contrary, however, Mehlberg argues that there has never been a systematic method of discovery (see, however, Maxwell, 1974a, 1974b); discovery—while in the end necessarily linked to methods of proof—follows multiple procedures and therefore cannot be described a priori and in any universal fashion. Rychlak (1976b) apparently agrees with the core contention of Mehlberg (1955): He states that "to make dialectic into a method of proof *per se* is surely risky business, considering the potentials it has for sophistical and erroneous commentary [p. 12] ."

Similarly, Hook (e.g., 1957) provides an extensive examination of the usefulness of the three laws of dialectics (contradiction, negation of negation, quantity and quality) for the scientific method and includes in this discussion examples drawn from the literature on growth (p. 15). From his view of the scientific method as representing a set of procedures for establishing proof in the context of empiricism, Hook concludes that "the dialectic method can claim to have meaning and validity only when it is understood to be synonymous with scientific method, and that therefore there is no need to talk about dialectic method at all [p. 27] ." Further-more, Hook concludes that "since the traditional formulation of this method [dialectic] is burdened with many misleading and mistaken conceptions, it would be more conducive to clear thinking if the phrase were dropped [p. 27] ." Finally, Hook comments that the retention of dialectic "engenders a mythical philosophy of nature and prepares the way for a doctrine of 'two truths'—one ordinary, scientific and profane, the other esoteric, 'dialectical' and 'higher' [p. 27] ."

Hook's (1953, 1955, 1957) complete refusal to accept dialectics as a useful method for generating scientific knowledge portrays a quite extreme position. However, his arguments are persuasive if one considers them from, and clearly links them to, the aspect of knowledge generation that deals with verification and proof (Mehlberg, 1955). There are other aspects of theory construction, however, that extend beyond the use of the scientific method and that give the application of dialectics an important role in the search for knowledge.

C. Dialectics and Theory Construction

Theory construction is a multifaceted process that includes, but also stretches beyond, principles of the scientific method(s). Within the framework of empirical sciences, theories involve statements about the relations that are believed to prevail in a comprehensive body of facts. The key elements of a theory can be identified, for example as Reese and Overton (1970) have shown, to include: (a) general laws and principles that serve as axioms or assumptions; (b) other laws that are deducible from the general axioms or assumptions; and (c) coordinating definitions relating theoretical terms to observational (empirical) sentences.

Following Kaplan (1964), we also take the position that "truth itself is plainly useless as a criterion for the acceptability of a theory. . . . We must proceed conversely . . . and characterize truth as the outcome of inquiry, suitably carried out [p. 313] ." It is the pattern of the process by which (a–c) are formulated and coordinated that defines whether an inquiry is acceptable and leads to statements of truth.

Although it is not possible to align specific and distinct methodologies with each of the three elements of a theory, it is suggested that the *scientific method*—as seen by Hook (1955) and Mehlberg (1955)—involves primarily element (c), namely, the formulation of coordinating definitions relating theoretical terms to observational sentences. The scientific method thus deals with *general* procedures for the establishment of empirical knowledge. These procedures are applicable to a wide variety of assumptive contexts and substantive territories (elements [a] and [b]). The procedures associated with the application of the scientific method, then, provide general (content-free) guidelines in the process of knowledge generation to be applied in the context of a specific empirical situation.

In addition to these general guidelines inherent in the scientific method, there are a variety of methods more specific than the generic criteria (such as research designs, data collection methodologies, and data analysis techniques) that can be utilized within the general rules dictated by the scientific method. The adoption or invention of one or another specific research methodology (rather than the scientific method) is influenced by the metatheoretical and theoretical context in which research questions are formulated. Thus, attributes of the scientific method should be distinguished from more specific aspects of research design, methodology, and data analysis, as applied to a specific content area.

The scientific method, then, can be seen as dealing primarily with element (c) of our definition of a theory. The application of this view leads to the following conclusion when it comes to the status of dialectics: Dialectics, especially if defined in relation to philosophical arguments, might serve as a context for specifying the first element (a)—that is, general laws and principles that serve as axioms or assumptions—in our attempt at defining a theory. Conversely, since the virtue of dialectics does not reside in its power as scientific method, our conclusion is that dialectics is not an important part of element (c), that is, of the procedures requisite for the development of coordinating definitions relating theoretical terms to observational (empirical) sentences. A dialectical orientation, however, can lead to a different set of substantive questions that may be investigated by means of generic principles of the scientific method.[1]

The structural definition of a theory just presented can be further elaborated by considering theories in a sociological context and as hierarchical systems. First, the formulation of metatheoretical assumptions does not occur in a vacuum but is

[1] After the manuscript was completed, it was brought to the authors' attention that the interpretation and argument contained here had been presented in a more general context by Schwartzman (1975).

influenced by the sociohistorical context of the individual scientist. Riegel (1972, 1973), for example, has clarified the importance of recognizing sociohistorical factors as they alter the dominant models of man and the conduct of scientific research. Likewise, Kantor (1973) has argued that one must not neglect the influence of cultural institutions on the development of scientific theories.

Second, if one accepts a hierarchical system in which theories are constructed (see Reese & Overton, 1970), a differentiation of substantive theories from the metatheoretical assumptions and influences that underlie them is possible. The relationships between levels of a theory can be manifold. It is an interesting question whether the metatheoretical context is better construed as structurally (and completely) independent from the theory, or whether the metamodel assumptions are functionally interdependent with the axiomatic content of the theory. The degree to which one emphasizes the interdependence, exchange, and reciprocal influence between the various levels of a theory determines the kind of relationship between theory construction and scientific method that one adopts.

The most general and inclusive metamodels or metatheoretical orientations are metaphysical systems that specify the nature of all phenomena and include cosmological and ontological components. One may also include epistemological systems (i.e., rationalism-empiricism, metaphorism, metaphorism-rationalism; see Royce, 1970) as an aspect of the world view which is orthogonal to the metaphysical systems. Thus, Reese and Overton (1970; Overton & Reese, 1973; Reese, Chapter 11, this volume) have described three dominant metaphysical paradigms: mechanistic, organismic, and contextual (also see Maruyama, 1974). These paradigms, in our view, do not influence the nature of the scientific method. *The scientific method, associated with the rationalist–empiricist epistemological position, is applicable to each of the metaphysical paradigms.* Although the content of knowledge and the format of specific research methodologies differ according to specific metaphysical paradigms and theoretical orientations, the general criteria of the scientific method are identical or at least highly similar across metaphysical paradigms.

The implication resulting from this discourse concerning both the elements of a theory and the hierarchical structure of the relationships among levels of theory is that dialectical perspectives are relevant in the formulation of the axiomatic and assumptive context, that is, for the formulation of a theoretical orientation. It is within this context that the empirical process of knowledge generation and theory construction proceeds: such a metacontext will influence the nature of research questions selected, the interpretation of data, and the coordination of data chosen for the development of a given theory. However, a dialectical orientation will not prescribe modifications in the use of the scientific method. The latter is defined by generic principles aimed at proof and verification (or falsification) in the public domain. *A dialectical orientation will, however, influence the substance of research questions, the scope and structure of theoretical concepts, and the format of "lower-level" research methodology associated with research design and data analysis.*

The proposition that it is important and useful to distinquish between the metacontext of theory construction (or a general theoretical orientation) and scientific methodology is similar to a position advocated by Willems (1973) when he discussed the theoretical and methodological merits of behavioral ecology. Dialectics, then, is potentially quite useful as a metatheoretical orientation. It is less likely to be useful and, indeed, more likely to be confusing when one attempts to employ it as a substitute for or supplement to well-established canons of the scientific method. Specific implications of this conclusion for the use of dialectics in developmental psychology will be discussed in the following section.

IV. Dialectics and Developmental Psychology

A. Methodological Paradigm vs. Theoretical Orientation

The central theme of our argument is that dialectics and dialectical psychology are not associated with or identical to a specific unique feature of the scientific method. Dialectics is more likely to be a potentially useful approach in the behavioral sciences if it is viewed as a general, high-level (in the hierarchical sense) theoretical or metatheoretical orientation suggesting specific or unique formats of lower-level research methodology. Those aspects of dialectics involving implications for logic or for a strategy for arriving at truth statements (valid organon à la Rychlak, 1976b) have doubtful validity, especially in the framework of empirical sciences.

From the viewpoint of a theoretical orientation, dialectical approaches may be useful in the process of theory construction. First, a dialectical orientation can lead to a specific class of metamodels which are unique in their defining assumptions and thereby permit different kinds of uncertainties (Labouvie, 1975). Second, a dialectical orientation may result in a particular set or pattern of research questions and in particular emphases and parsimony in the interpretation and organization of empirical statements. At present, the uniqueness of such a dialectical orientation is not yet well explicated. Thus, it is open to question whether this emerging theoretical orientation can acquire the degree of distinctiveness and acceptance necessary to qualify as a paradigm, in the sense of Kuhn (1970). Next to be discussed is whether dialectics (though not having implications for the scientific method) might have unique implications for lower-level research methodology.

It may be helpful to illustrate the potential role of dialectics as a theoretical orientation for this issue with a couple of comparative examples. It was previously mentioned that the situation of dialectics is similar to the one in behavioral ecology. In a methodological evaluation of ecology, Willems (1973) argued that the association of an ecological perspective with an ecological methodology (naturalistic, nonexperimental methodology) was an unfortunate historical coincidence.

Behavioral ecology is a perspective, an orientation, or a set of theoretical principles in terms of which the investigator formulates questions about behavior and its habitat and the context in particular ways. . . . That [ecological] perspective is elusive and difficult to define . . . . It is not a theory or a method. It is just what I have suggested—a general orientation or viewpoint which leads one to view behavior and development and research upon them in certain ways [pp. 196, 206–207].

In addition to the situation in ecology, a similar argument has been made in connection with phenomenology. MacLeod (1970), for example, stated:

Psychological phenomenology is a useful propaedeutic to a science of psychology, i.e., that it serves to define problems and to point the way to possible answers. It does not, as such, provide answers nor is it relevant to all questions commonly termed psychological. It does, however, bring into a focus a good many problems which are frequently neglected in contemporary psychological research and theory. Psychological phenomenology is not a theory, not a system or school, not a philosophy; it is an approach [p. 247].

We tend to agree with the essence of both Willems' and MacLeod's positions. Dialectics as a theoretical orientation implies that some lower-level research methodologies are more useful than others (see, for instance, the need for lower-level methodologies that permit the study of structure or interaction). However, such a view does not imply a specific isomorphic relationship between dialectics and a specific lower-level research methodology. Rather, methodological pluralism is encouraged. For example, the concept of structure can be approached usefully both from an organismic and a mechanistic format (e.g., Baltes, Nesselroade, & Cornelius, 1977b).

A theoretical orientation, thus, has a different status in the process of theory construction than the requirements of a scientific method, which is aimed at the development of empirical statements of proof. A theoretical perspective may serve a number of functions; the primary one is to delineate the metacontext for the formulation of research questions and the organization of data interpretation. In this sense, a theoretical perspective does not mandate a unitary methodological or procedural approach that need be adopted for investigating research questions emanating from a particular perspective. Indeed, it seems that if a specific methodology (e.g., dialectic as a valid organon) is attached to a given theoretical perspective, it either is a coincidental aspect of the thrust of the perspective or will likely hinder the full potential of the thrust of the orientation.

In order to implement a dialectical perspective, pluralistic but systematic methodological procedures are necessary. A dialectical perspective need not be linked with a specific metaphysical (i.e., mechanistic, organismic, contextual, etc.) paradigm nor with a specific epistemological (i.e., rationalism-empiricism, metaphorism, metaphorism-rationalism) model but may be better implemented by the utilization of multiple world views or metaparadigms and lower-level research methodologies.

In summary, then, two conclusions have been advanced concerning the status of dialectics vis-à-vis psychological research:

1. Dialectics may best be regarded as a perspective or an orientation in the sense of a metaphor. It is not an acceptable procedure or prescriptive method for knowledge generation in the empirical sciences.

2. Viewing dialectics as an orientation and not as a method in the empirical sciences leads to a refutation of any monolithic method of research implementation.

It follows that a dialectical orientation can be conceived of within each of the different world views and that in principle pluralism in lower-level research methodology is useful. However, it might be that certain lower-level formats of research methodology prove to be more useful than others.

B. Application to Developmental Psychology

This chapter was begun by outlining a series of research issues currently faced by developmental psychologists: the nature of change, the notions of structure, transition, interaction, and so on. What are the implications of the position that dialectics is better viewed as a general theoretical orientation and not as a specific research methodology for the discussion of these issues?

The dialectical orientation may aid researchers in identifying and organizing a number of research issues in developmental psychology with the goal of producing a new pattern of knowledge and/or research. In our view, however, it is false to argue that one of the major aims of dialectics should be "to convince social scientists that something like the dialectic might be really going on in this world of interpersonal, social, and historical forces [Rychlak, 1976b, p. 12]." Such a conclusion is ill-advised since it confounds the assumptive (nontestable) characteristics of the dialectical orientation with an assessment of its usefulness for the process of theory construction. How research issues, which are suggested by a dialectical orientation, are translated into empirical-observational sentences is not tied to a unique dialectical method. As Hook (1953, 1955, 1957) has shown most persuasively, a dialectical method which is separate from the scientific method does not exist in the framework of empiricism.

The usefulness of dialectics as a general theoretical orientation can be best served by investigating research questions derived from it with multiple methodological paradigms. For example, the concepts of structure, interaction, and bidirectional causality can be studied fruitfully by use of either mechanistic or organismic paradigms. Simulation studies of structural transformations in the development of intelligence presented by Baltes and Nesselroade (1973; Baltes et al., 1977b) are a good case in point, as is the study of cohort effects (Baltes et al., 1977a; Nesselroade & Baltes, 1974; Schaie, 1970). All these projects have involved a concerted effort to demonstrate the usefulness of "dialectical" ideas such as structural transformation and interaction. Perhaps they resulted in novel knowledge, but it was not because a dialectical methodology was used. Rather, it is likely that the contrary is the case: Whatever success is accredited to these studies was a result of using *existing* procedures in the translation of a general pattern of coordinated "dialectical" questions into concrete research programs.

In our view, whenever dialectically oriented researchers (e.g., Riegel, 1976; Rychlak, 1976b) argue or suggest that unique designs and empirical methodologies are needed, the arguments are neither cogent nor appealing; in fact, the illustrative examples chosen are occasionally inelegant and not persuasive. The strength of a dialectical approach lies in its power to suggest different research questions programmatically and to highlight novel combinations or coordinations of empirical-observational sentences in the process of theory construction. The quicker researchers recognize that dialectics does not lead to unique empirical strategies involving the scientific method, the sooner will they join in our efforts to investigate in a concerted manner an important set of theoretical issues.

ACKNOWLEDGMENTS

We would like to acknowledge many helpful comments by, and discussions with, Margret M. Baltes, John R. Nesselroade, Stanley H. Rosen, and Carol D. Ryff. The writing of this chapter was also facilitated by a grant from the National Institute of Education (Grant No. NIE-C-74-0127).

The second author was supported by a National Science Foundation graduate fellowship during the completion of this chapter.

REFERENCES

Baltes, P. B. Heinz Werner smiles—Should he? *Contemporary Psychology,* 1971, **16,** 444–445.
Baltes, P. B., & Nesselroade, J. R. The developmental analysis of individual differences on multiple measures. In J. R. Nesselroade & H. W. Reese (Eds.), *Life-span developmental psychology: Methodological issues.* New York: Academic Press, 1973.
Baltes, P. B., Cornelius, S. W., & Nesselroade, J. R. Cohort effects in behavioral development: Theoretical and methodological perspectives. In W. A. Collins (Ed.), *Minnesota symposia on child psychology* (Vol. 11). New York: Thomas Crowell, 1977, in press. (a)
Baltes, P. B., Nesselroade, J. R., & Cornelius, S. W. Toward an explanation of multivariate structural change in development: A simulation. In J. Shanan (Ed.), *Transitional phases in human development.* 1977, in preparation. (b)
Baltes, P. B., Reese, H. W., & Nesselroade, J. R. *Life-span developmental psychology: Introduction to research methods.* Monterey, Calif.: Brooks-Cole, 1977, in press. (c)
Baltes, P. B., & Schaie, K. W. On life-span developmental research paradigms: Retrospects and prospects. In P. B. Baltes & K. W. Schaie (Eds.), *Life-span developmental psychology: Personality and socialization.* New York: Academic Press, 1973.
Baltes, P. B., & Schaie, K. W. On the plasticity of intelligence in adulthood and old age: Where Horn and Donaldson fail. *American Psychologist,* 1976, **31,** 720–725.

Baltes, P. B., & Willis, S. L. Toward psychological theories of aging and development. In J. E. Birren & K. W. Schaie (Eds.), *Handbook of the psychology of aging*. New York: Van Nostrand Reinhold, 1977.

Boudon, R. The three basic paradigms of macrosociology: Functionalism, neo-Marxism and interaction analysis. *Theory and Decision*, 1975, 6, 381–406.

Campbell, D. T. On the conflicts between biological and social evolution and between psychology and moral tradition. *American Psychologist*, 1975, 30, 1103–1126.

Eastman, M. *Marxism: Is it science?* New York: Norton, 1940.

Geymonat, L. Neopositivist methodology and dialectical materialism. *Science and Society*, 1973, 37, 178–194.

Graham, L. R. *Science and philosophy in the Soviet Union*. New York: Knopf, 1971.

Hook, S. Dialectic in society and history. In H. Feigl & M. Brodbeck (Eds.), *Readings in the philosophy of science.* New York: Appleton, 1953.

Hook, S. Science and dialectical materialism. *Science and freedom*. London: Martin Secker & Warburg, 1955.

Hook, S. *Dialectical materialism and scientific method*. Manchester, Eng.: Special Supplement to the Bulletin of the Committee on Science and Freedom, 1957.

Huston-Stein, A. C., & Baltes, P. B. Theory and method in life-span developmental psychology: Implications for child development. In H. W. Reese & L. P. Lipsitt (Eds.), *Advances in child development and behavior* (Vol. 11). New York: Academic Press, 1976.

Kantor, J. R. System structure and scientific psychology. *Psychological Record*, 1973, 23, 451–458.

Kaplan, A. *The conduct of inquiry*. San Francisco: Chandler, 1964.

Kuhn, T. S. *The structure of scientific revolutions* (2nd ed.). Chicago: University of Chicago Press, 1970.

Kupers, T. Historical materialism and scientific psychology. *Science and Society*, 1973, 37, 81–90.

Labouvie, E. W. The dialectical nature of measurement activities in the behavioral sciences. *Human Development*, 1975, 18, 396–403.

MacLeod, R. B. Psychological phenomenology: A propaedeutic to scientific psychology. In J. R. Royce (Ed.), *Toward unification in psychology*. Toronto: University of Toronto Press, 1970.

Maruyama, M. Paradigmatology and its application to cross-disciplinary, cross-professional and cross-cultural communication. *Dialectica*, 1974, 28, 135–196.

Maxwell, N. The rationality of scientific discovery: Part I. The traditional rationality problem. *Philosophy of Science*, 1974, 41, 123–153. (a)

Maxwell, N. The rationality of scientific discovery: Part II. An aim oriented theory of scientific discovery. *Philosophy of Science*, 1974, 41, 247–295. (b)

Mehlberg, H. The method of science, its range and limits. *Science and freedom*. London: Martin Secker & Warburg, 1955.

Nesselroade, J. R., & Baltes, P. B. Adolescent personality development and historical change: 1970–1972. *Monographs of the Society for Research in Child Development*, 1974, 39(1, Serial No. 154).

O'Laughlin, B. Marxist approaches in anthropology. *Annual Review of Anthropology*, 1975, 4, 341–370.

Overton, W. F. On the assumptive base of the nature–nurture controversy: Additive versus interactive conceptions. *Human Development*, 1973, 16, 74–89.

Overton, W. F., & Reese, H. W. Models of development: Methodological implications. In J. R. Nesselroade & H. W. Reese (Eds.), *Life-span developmental psychology: Methodological issues*. New York: Academic Press, 1973.

Reese, H. W., & Overton, W. F. Models of development and theories of development. In L. R. Goulet & P. B. Baltes (Eds.), *Life-span developmental psychology: Research and theory*. New York: Academic Press, 1970.

Riegel, K. F. The influence of economic and political ideologies on the development of developmental psychology. *Psychological Bulletin,* 1972, 78, 129–141.

Riegel, K. F. Developmental psychology and society: Some historical and ethical considerations. In J. R. Nesselroade & H. W. Reese (Eds.), *Life-span developmental psychology: Methodological issues.* New York: Academic Press, 1973.

Riegel, K. F. (Ed.). The development of dialectical operations. *Human Development,* 1975, *18*(1–3).

Riegel, K. F. From traits and equilibrium toward developmental dialectics. In W. Arnold (Ed.), *Nebraska Symposium on Motivation.* Lincoln: University of Nebraska Press, 1976.

Riegel, K. F., & Rosenwald, G. C. (Eds.). *Structure and transformation: Developmental and historical aspects.* New York: Wiley, 1975.

Royce, J. R. The present situation in theoretical psychology. In J. R. Royce (Ed.), *Toward unification in psychology.* Toronto: University of Toronto Press, 1970.

Rychlak, J. F. (Ed.). *Dialectic: Humanistic rationale for behavior and development.* New York: Karger, 1976. (a)

Rychlak, J. F. The multiple meanings of dialectic. In J. F. Rychlak (Ed.), *Dialectic: Humanistic rationale for behavior and development.* New York: Karger, 1976. (b)

Schaie, K. W. A reinterpretation of age related changes in cognitive structure and functioning. In L. R. Goulet & P. B. Baltes (Eds.), *Life-span developmental psychology: Research and theory.* New York: Academic Press, 1970.

Schmidt, H. D. *Allgemeine Entwicklungspsychologie.* Berlin: Deutscher Verlag der Wissenschaften, 1970.

Schwartzman, D. W. Althusser, dialectical materialism and the philosophy of science. *Science and Society,* 1975, **39,** 318–330.

Toffler, A. *Future shock.* New York: Bantam, 1970.

Willems, E. P. Behavioral ecology and experimental analysis: Courtship is not enough. In J. R. Nesselroade & H. W. Reese (Eds.), *Life-span developmental psychology: Methodological issues.* New York: Academic Press, 1973.

Wilson, E. O. *Sociobiology: The new synthesis.* Cambridge, Mass.: Belknap Press of the Harvard University Press, 1975.

Wozniak, R. H. A dialectical paradigm for psychological research: Implications drawn from the history of psychology in the Soviet Union. *Human Development,* 1975, **18,** 18–34.

CHAPTER 7

Stability, Change, and Chance in Understanding Human Development

KENNETH J. GERGEN

SWARTHMORE COLLEGE
SWARTHMORE, PENNSYLVANIA

As a social psychologist my contribution to understanding life-span development is open to reasonable suspicion. Social-psychological research over the past three decades has been peculiarly divorced from developmental considerations of any kind. Research on attitude change, social perception, attraction, prejudice, aggression, altruism, group behavior, and so on has proceeded under the assumption that if the emerging theories manifest predictive validity, proper developmental theory must eventually prove corroborative. The task of social understanding, it is felt, can scarcely await a fully elaborated theory of human development. This self-satisfied separatism is perhaps characteristic of any paradigmatic discipline (Kuhn, 1962). Provided there are a set of credible assumptions concerning the task of the scientist and these assumptions are welded to the power and prestige structures of the field, simultaneous developments in fields not sharing in the agreement pool can be disregarded. And if such developments are antithetical to the dominant paradigm, as in the case of dialecticism, exposure may even pose an undesirable threat. In any case, the possibility of shared dilemmas within developmental and social psychology has been little explored. It is my present contention that traditional pursuits in both social and developmental psychology are in similar peril and that mutual deliberation is essential.

It is said that present-day social psychology is in a state of crisis (Elms, 1975). Serious doubts concerning the efficacy of the traditional paradigms are emerging on every side (cf. Armistead, 1974; Harré & Secord, 1972; McGuire, 1973). My own particular concern has been with the central positivist assumption that social knowledge can be accumulated across time in much the same manner enjoyed in the physical sciences (Gergen, 1973, 1976, 1977). Research in social psychology has largely been predicated on the assumption that through careful empirical inquiry a firm data base can be constructed upon which sound principles of social behavior can be established. Through the rigorous testing of hypotheses, poor theories can be cast aside and better theories continuously improved. Should this assumption prove erroneous, the entire positivist program is threatened. The hypo-thetico-deductive juggernaut comes grinding to a halt. An examination of developmental psychology within the past several decades reveals that the supposition of accumulation is essential to this tradition as well. Further, it appears that the life-span movement, if it may be so called, has begun to emerge as a vital revolutionary force. At stake is not simply an alteration or expansion of theoretical perspective but rather the entire positivist tradition of developmental psychology. Of pivotal concern is, again, the supposition of accumulation.

It will be the aim of this paper to elaborate on the emerging challenge to the positivist program as represented by the interlocking arguments within the social and life-span frameworks. The elaboration may begin with a consideration of four criteria for the evaluation of theoretical models of development. These particular criteria have been selected for their relevance to the paradigmatic revolution mutual to our disciplines. Once the criteria have been detailed, we may proceed to evaluate three central models of human development. Two of these models have virtually dominated the field of developmental psychology since the turn of the century. The third has emerged primarily within the life-span developmental domain and may be viewed as a central challenge to the earlier traditions. This discussion should not only elucidate a number of major strengths and weaknesses in each approach but should lend itself to clarification of the emerging revolution.

I. Toward Theoretical Evaluation

Over the years considerable attention has been given to the question of theoretical evaluation. Dozens of criteria for comparing theories have emerged from such discussion. However, most of these criteria need not concern us at this juncture. Sufficient agreement (or disagreement) exists such that little is to be gained from mere enumeration. Rather, four criteria for evaluating models of human development have been especially selected for their relevance to the shared crises within social and developmental psychology. Each demands attention.

A. Comprehensive Understanding

Few would contest the desideratum that theories should enable one to understand the course of human development. At best, a good theory should provide us with (1) a broadly inclusive description of developmental sequence, and (2) an efficient rationale or explanation for those sequences included within the description. Thus, we may hold one theory as superior to another if a greater range of facts is described and a more complete explanation relating these facts is provided.

Although the criterion of comprehensive understanding is widely accepted, it may be further argued that the criterion deserves independent status. Traditionally, the criterion of understanding has been intimately linked with a second benchmark, that of predictive capability. As it is commonly said, the task of science is to "understand and predict," and it is commonly assumed that such tasks are virtually inseparable. Thus, the scientist first attempts to describe and explain and then tests his or her theoretical account against newly accumulated facts. Such testing is essentially viewed as a predictive operation. The scientist makes predictions based on hypotheses derived from the theoretical superstructure. Should the predictions be confirmed, confidence in the initial description and explanation is strengthened; should the predictions fail, the exactitude of the initial description and the adequacy of the initial explanation may both be called into question. It is my contention, however, that the close connection maintained between the criteria of explanation and prediction has been most unfortunate for the sociobehavioral sciences, and that independent consideration is essential.

The unfortunate consequences of this linkage will become manifest as the argument proceeds. For the present it is sufficient to note that theoretical understanding may play a number of highly valuable functions independent of prediction, and that prediction may proceed with great efficacy without the aid of elaborated theory. Independent of its predictive validity, theoretical understanding first serves to *organize experience*. Normal experience furnishes us with highly variegated, diverse, and often incoherent inputs; through the analytic process various inputs are singled out and treated as equivalent, while others are treated as nonexistent. Theory allows us to treat a virtual infinity of events as a simple sequence, and to organize responses to a broad pattern over and above discrete experiences.

Theory may also play a very important *sensitizing role*. Although it may seldom serve as a basis for precise prediction, theory may provide an indication of what is possible in social life, what has occurred in the past, and possible reasons for its occurrence. For example, if faced with the behavior problem of a young adolescent, psychoanalytic theory may sensitize us to possible early antecedents in the life of the individual, role theory may direct our attention to influences of the peer group, social-learning theory might prod us into considering reinforcement contingencies currently supporting the problem behavior, and so on. Theoretical understanding may further provide us with a *sense of coherence*. At least within Western culture, a certain degree of anxiety accompanies events not subsumed within existing theories. To "know" something within our culture is to embed it within an analytic framework. Possibly this need for theoretical embedding is related to the common belief that theory is the first step toward gaining power over a phenomenon and reducing its potential danger. Whatever the origin, the sense of coherent understanding is widely valued, and theory does provide a basis for this sense.

Finally, over and above the question of prediction, theory is vital as a means of *decomposing common understanding.* All theories must be viewed as artificial templates of experienced reality. Regardless of sophistication, theories are fundamentally incapable of describing the essence of their subject matter. Concepts treat as equivalent that which is essentially distinct; they call attention to similarities among stimuli while disregarding the multifarious differences. Analytic concepts are also ill equipped to deal with a qualitative difference among entities and with events in flux. And yet, with all their imperfections, theories are both useful and inevitable. Thus, a premium is to be placed on theories counterposed to what passes for theoretical knowledge at any given point. Theories that unsettle common conceptions of "what" and "why" provide an invaluable service in preventing an unmerited commitment to any single, but flawed, conception. Theories that challenge our common understandings enable us to maintain a healthy state of scepticism and to remain open to change and sensitive to the relativity of conception.

Virtually all of these important functions may be served by theory without reference to their predictive validity. In fact, it may be said that over the past century the most significant theories of human behavior have prevailed without benefit of predictive validation. The theories of Darwin, Marx, Freud, and Skinner, for example, have immense intellectual challenge, and have proved useful as well on all the above grounds. Yet, systematic empirical validation is lacking in every case.

B. The Need for Prediction

As suggested, the task of prediction can proceed quite effectively apart from the development of formal theory. We must daily make thousands of predictions, and generally do so with a moderate degree of success. Each time we speak, we engage in a silent wager that others will comprehend the meaning of our communications. We make such predictions with little in the way of formal communications theory. Many auto and life insurance actuarials are outstanding in their role as prognosticators of the future, and their predictions are seldom articulated with major theoretical permises. However, even though prediction may proceed quite adequately without theory, we need not conclude that understanding should always be irrelevant to the process of prediction. We may continue to apply the traditional criterion of predictive validity, realizing full well that valuable theoretical contributions may be made independent of prediction and that theories poor in their provision for general understanding may contribute to excellence in prediction. In the application of the predictive criterion, a further distinction must be made between extrapolation-based prediction and emergent prediction.

1. Extrapolation-Based Prediction

On the most primitive level, predictions can be made on the basis of past observations. In this case we simply assume a redundancy of pattern: that which happened in the past will be replicated in the future. In this case, the better theory is one that most accurately describes events of the past. The greater the number of events "post-dicted" by the theory, the greater its potential utility in extrapolation to the future.

2. Emergent Prediction

Most traditional theories within the sociobehavioral sciences are designed for extrapolation-based prediction; that is, most assume that future conditions will remain sufficiently stable such that the past is a reasonable forecaster of future events. However, if there is reason to believe that the future will provide a novel configuration of conditions, a more sophisticated variety of theory is required, one that allows for logical derivations to novel conditions. Such emergent prediction is possible within certain branches of the physical sciences. For example, given the current state of chemistry, it is possible to make accurate predictions about the character of a wholly novel compound. A special premium may thus be placed on theories with emergent predictive value.

C. Prescriptive Valuation

Max Weber (1949) once maintained that in social science theories without prescriptive value were an impossibility. Even in the simple selection of phenomena for study, we invest them with value and reduce the unselected to obscurity. Weber's arguments have been subject to periodic debate (cf. Runcinan, 1972), but his essential message was largely shunted aside in the wave of positivist enthusiasm. From the positivist perspective, it seemed possible to separate out the descriptive and prescriptive aspects of theoretical understanding. Theories could describe and explain, it was held, without advocating. The prime exemplar of theory without prescriptive implication was mathematics, and since translation into mathematical notation was viewed as the desirable end state of all theorizing, prescriptive problems seemed remote. Yet, with the rebellious fervor of the 1960s, the linkage of the social sciences with prevailing institutions and ideologies came under renewed critical scrutiny. The results of such scrutiny (cf. Gouldner, 1969; Myrdal, 1969; Poole, 1972) have become increasingly and compellingly clear and provide striking vindication of Weber's initial line of argument. No investigation is without implicit valuational implication. What the theorist singles out for study, the terms in which it is described, the commitment of causal analysis, the employment of abstraction, the objectification of subject matter, the attempt at dispassionate observation, the obviation of some theories in the elaboration of others, the implications for social change, and the very attempt to avoid value statements may all have significant effects on one's conception of the good, the moral, or the desirable.

At this juncture it may be argued that as scientists we can no longer afford to treat the problem of value loading as a minor irritant. Theories of human behavior have the potential to unleash untold brutality and to foster a common bond among people. In light of earlier arguments advocating a relativistic orientation to theoretical "truth," the criterion of valuational implication must be considered on an equal footing with its aforementioned competitors. What a theory implicitly advocates is as important as its contribution to understanding and its predictive capability.

D. Scientific Promise

Most of us do not wish to jettison the scientific orientation to human behavior. We retain an investment in rational understanding and in discovering systematic means of improving our condition. Yet, there are also intimate connections between theoretical understanding and metatheoretical commitments; that is, depending on our metatheoretical understanding of what we are about, certain theoretical orientations are prescribed and others obviated; in turn, our theoretical conceptions have vital implications for metatheoretical outlook. Thus, for example, if we accept the metatheoretical premise that all events may be understood in terms of their antecedents, we can scarcely embrace a theory proposing that people are the origins of their own actions. And investment in a theory of psychological dynamics is inconsistent with a metatheoretic assumption that science must concern itself solely with observables.

Our final criterion, then, concerns the implications of theory for conducting the scientific enterprise. In what degree are the major theoretical views supportive of, or consistent with, the traditional positivist conception of science? To what extent do they suggest modifications of the tradition or its abandonment? These are significant questions that must be asked of the available theoretical forms.

II. Theoretical Forms for Understanding Human Development

The primary task is at hand. Given these four criteria of evaluation, what may be said of the major theoretical forms presently existing within the developmental domain? Although no compelling nosology of theoretical form is at hand, we may consider three major orientations, each of which encompasses a variety of more specific models of development. Each demands attention in terms of the four evaluative criteria just described.

A. The Stability Template

For many years the dominant theoretical form within developmental psychology placed greatest emphasis on the stability of behavior patterns over time. In this case the overarching analytic template has essentially registered stability and eschewed the transitory. The Freudian theory of character formation provides the classic exemplar of the stability orientation. As Freud maintained, the first 6 years of life are critical in determining adult personality. As a result of early psychosexual history, and particularly the configuration of repression, the foundation for adult psychodynamics is firmly established. Without massive intervention (ideally through psychoanalysis) the same psychobehavioral patterns will relentlessly repeat themselves throughout the life cycle. Much the same view was adopted by early learning theorists. Here it was maintained that the effects of early learning experiences are of greater strength than later experiences. Early learning thus provides the basic orientation toward later experience. Whatever exists tends to endure. A similar orientation is nicely represented in the Sterns and Alexander contribution to the present proceedings. As they argue, living systems appear to be designed to resist or minimize change. However, alterations in the environment do cause organismic change, but such change is always "intended to provide *higher order* stability for the organism."

Given this brief description of the stability orientation, we may turn to the problem of evaluation.

1. Understanding through the Stability Template

In spite of the general antagonism toward the stability orientation represented in much of the life-span literature, I believe the orientation can be well defended on the basis of its contribution to general understanding. As the psychoanalytic profession continues to demonstrate, the stability orientation is highly effective in organizing one's experience. There are virtually no life history data, however inchoate, that cannot be organized within this framework. The orientation is also highly sensitizing. The assumption that present behavior patterns can always be traced to early antecedents sensitizes one to the potential effects of early socialization. Observational strategies are thus sharpened, and countless hypotheses can be mounted regarding the long-term influence of various parental, sibling, sociocultural, or environmental factors. The stability orientation also furnishes an excellent sense of coherence. In reviewing one's life history, one can discern the morphological similarities among highly disparate behaviors and come to believe in the continuity of his or her identity over time. In light of Erik Erikson's (1950) argument that one's feelings of well-being are vitally dependent on his or her sense of personal continuity, it might be said that the stability orientation has played a powerful therapeutic role. Further, the orientation may also be viewed as highly catalytic in its effects on common understanding. Its special drama lies in its capacity to transform what appears to be novel or newly formed behavior into yet another instance of a long-standing pattern. We often believe ourselves to be confronting an ever-emerging pattern of events. Yet, if we reconsider reality through the conceptual lens of the stability theorist, we find that "the more things change, the more they remain the same."

2. The Predictive Capacity of Stability Theory

A brief assessment of the predictive capacity of stability theory is impossible. Over the years an immense wealth of data has been amassed favoring the orientation. Case studies number in the thousands; longitudinal research is typically dedicated to the discovery of continuity; animal experimentation has often demonstrated the long-term effects of early learning experiences; studies of adult psychopathology often reveal systematic differences in early experience between hospitalized and normal populations; and so on. Yet, so immense is the volume of supportive data that in spite of the current hegemony of the ordered-change orientation (to be discussed shortly), the stability orientation has remained relatively free of direct assault. It may fairly be said that contemporary culture has almost fully accepted the assumption that early experience is vital in shaping adult behavior. The immense concern with child-rearing practices, early education, enriched environments for the young, and so on, indicates a deep-seated belief in the stability orientation.

Yet, a challenge to the stability assumption must be mounted. The data base upon which it rests is far less substantial than it might appear. The case analyses garnered from the therapeutic and analytic journals are largely worthless as "proofs." The events of most people's lives are sufficiently variegated and multifarious that virtually any theoretical template can be validated. The case study simply allows the investigator freedom to locate the facts lending support to his or her preformulated convictions. Longitudinal support is also less convincing than it might initially appear. Perhaps the most significant of these investigations has been undertaken by Kagan and Moss (1962) in their analysis of the Fels Institute data. This study followed a sample of some 80 men and women from early infancy to a period some 30 years later. Over 100 objective assessments were made of various behavior tendencies at 4 separate intervals over the 20-year period. Correlations were then carried out to detect continuity across the various periods. The investigators asked, for example, whether individuals tended to retain roughly the same ranking in the sample with respect to achievement motivation, aggression, dependence, passivity, heterosexuality, and so on. Although continuities in such areas as aggressiveness and dependency were demonstrated, it is noteworthy that careful screening of the data was required in order to mount such demonstrations; that is, nonsignificant results abound within the data matrix, and the case for continuity is made by selecting out those particular findings providing confirmation. Careful inspection of the data further reveals that virtually no relationships beyond chance exist between behavior patterns in the first 6 years of life and the same or related patterns during adulthood. In effect, the study provides no support whatever for the assumption that the first 6 years of life are crystallizing in their effects on individual character.

Results from infrahuman research are equally questionable. Perhaps the most frequently cited evidence supporting the stability assumption is that of Harlow and Harlow (1965) on maternal deprivation in the infant monkey. As the Harlows so dramatically demonstrated, when a rhesus monkey is deprived of all social contact during the first 6 weeks of life, and then reintroduced into the monkey colony, the deprived animal is permanently debilitated. The animal continues indefinitely to display aggressive, antisocial, and otherwise aberrant characteristics. Of course, it is unclear whether results of infrahuman research can ever be applied on the human level. However, even if we do accept the implications of this work for human functioning, more recent research by Suomi and Harlow (1972) indicates that these effects need not be permanent and are easily reversed. A 6 week retraining program in which the deprived monkey continuously associates with a somewhat younger animal is sufficient to reverse all the ill effects of early deprivation.

Additional research within social psychology strongly indicates that whatever habits are acquired during development do not generally seem to persist across diverse circumstances. For example, because of our extensive training, most of us do not believe that we could be induced to torture another human being to the point of death; we loathe the thought and believe that our socialization has insulated us against such heinous behavior. Yet, as Stanley Milgram (1974) has demonstrated, adults of all ages and from diverse backgrounds can rather easily be coerced into delivering the most painful shocks to an innocent victim of circumstance.

In a related vein, at Swarthmore my colleagues and I were curious about what kind of relations would develop among total strangers placed in an altogether anonymous circumstance for a single hour (Gergen, Gergen, & Barton, 1973). Volunteers for research on environmental psychology were thus invited to the campus from diverse locales. Each arrived separately at the laboratory, and each was told that he or she would be spending approximately an hour in an unlighted room with "some other people." There were no instructions as to how the hour was to be spent; however, all subjects were required to remove their shoes and deposit their valuables before entering the darkened chamber. They were told that they would never have the opportunity to meet the persons in the chamber after the hour was over. I suspect most of us generally feel that we would not engage in physical intimacies with total strangers; such reluctance seems fundamental to the manner in which we have been socialized. Yet, as we learned from biographies and ratings completed after the experience, over 90% of the participants engaged in purposeful touching; only 20% indicated that they ever prevented anyone from touching them. Over 50% engaged in hugging, and 80% said that they were sexually aroused during the experience. As one participant wrote:

> As I was sitting, Beth came up and we started to play touchy face and touchy body and started to neck. We expressed it as "love to each other." Shortly before I was taken out, we decided to pass our "love" on, to share it with other people. So we split up, and Laurie took her place. We had just started touchy body and kissed a few times before I was tapped to leave [p. 130].

Behavior in the control condition, in which the chamber was illuminated, was in sharp contrast; under these circumstances participants sat at a safe distance and talked quietly for the entire hour. Clearly, whatever lessons have been acquired from early socialization are limited to very specific situations.

Such studies as these are only illustrative of a massive volume of research in social psychology and cast additional doubt on the predictive validity of stability theory.

3. The Ethics of Stability

Although psychoanalytic theory is possibly an exception, it may be ventured that the stability framework generally prescribes stable behavior. The normal, and thus desirable, person is one who remains roughly the same from one day to the next. We are typically disturbed when someone behaves inconsistently and equate maturity with coherent patterning in behavior (see Gergen, 1968). More general rationalizations are used to buttress the stability ethic. Stable behavior is necessary, it is argued, because without it society would be chaotic. People would be unable to place themselves within the social system, unable to predict others' actions, and unable to act functionally. Stability is thus essential to the viability of the society. Although this line of thinking seems eminently reasonable, it may be challenged on the grounds of the mediocre predictive capability of various forms of stability theory. If people do not generally display stability, can the ethic remain unchallenged?

4. Science and Stability

The construction of scientific principles in the positivistic mode ultimately depends on the stability of events in nature. If the facts of nature are not recurring, science must be replaced by history. Thus, the success of the physical sciences depends in large measure on the selection of subject matter. Selected are phenomena that demonstrate reliable "behavior" regardless of the period of history in which they are examined. In similar manner, if the patterns of human behavior demonstrate marked stability over time, we may anticipate construction of knowledge according to the positivist program. The stability orientation is highly compatible with traditional views of scientific conduct.

B. The Template of Ordered Change

The second major orientation to human development centers on change as opposed to stability. In particular it is assumed that development is constituted by patterned or orderly change across time. Typically such change is said to be invariant both across the human species and throughout history; exceptions to the basic sequence may be accounted for in terms of extrinsic factors impinging on the human organism. Again, Freud provides the initial exemplar of this orientation; the theory of psychosexual development elaborates a natural history of libidinal development. Although Freud's theory is limited primarily to the first 6 years of life, revisionists have fruitfully extended the theory to account for later developmental crises. Erik Erikson (1950, 1968) has of course been seminal in this respect. With the possible exceptions of Loevinger's (1966) work on ego development, such psychodynamic interests have largely been shunted aside in recent years as concern with cognitive development has taken center stage. The impact of Piaget's (cf. 1926, 1930, 1955, 1970) theory of cognitive growth cannot be underestimated, and most major theoretical contributions since Piaget's hegemony have adopted some form of stage theory consistent with Piagetian theory. It may fairly be said that the ordered-change orientation in general, and Piagetian theory in particular, has become the guiding paradigm within contemporary developmental psychology. For the present it is not important to distinguish among contributions emphasizing quantitative as opposed to qualitative change, or change through accretion as opposed to change through crisis. It is sufficient for now to recognize a class of theories similar in respect to their focus on orderly, replicable change in human development. What may be said for such theories in terms of the present criteria?

1. Understanding through Ordered Change

Earlier stability theories were defended with respect to their contribution to comprehensive understanding. However, this defense is in no way to denigrate the ordered-change orientation. The latter template enables one to organize wide-ranging experiences into a coherent whole. It is perhaps more convenient in application than the stability orientation in that differences are recognized among distinct classes of behaviors, and such differences roughly correspond to chronological age. Thus, childhood behavior may be dealt with separately from adult behavior and the difficult search for underlying similarity obviated. The orientation has also proved valuable as a sensitizing agent. It focuses one's observations on differences in behavior over the life span and, in its most catalytic form, demands that we attend to underlying (structural) differences among behaviors that are ostensibly similar. Although ordered-change theories do not provide a special sense of coherence, they do engender the experience of growth. Change can often be singled out as an indication of enhanced maturity. Finally, the ordered-change approach can effectively unsettle common understanding. It is perhaps less successful in this endeavor than stability theory inasmuch as it accepts the possibility that what we perceive to be dissimilar is so in fact. In contrast, stability theory constantly challenges us to reconceptualize as different that which is perceptually similar.

2. Prediction and Ordered Change

In the case of the stability orientation, distinguishing among particular theories according to predictive capability was not essential. Theories emphasizing stability all tend to make similar predictions; the major differences lie in the manner of explanation. However, in the case of the ordered-change orientation, the assessment of predictive validity is far more complex. Theories focus on different types of change and make differential predictions regarding developmental sequence and the relationship of chronological age to such sequence. Space limitations fortunately prevent a complete review of predictive studies falling within each theoretical domain. It is thus necessary to rely on a limited number of summary remarks regarding the major theoretical domains.

With respect to classic psychoanalytic theory, continued study has done little to increase one's confidence in Freud's particular characterization of the stages of psychosexual development. Innumerable disconfirmations have emerged over the years. Although defenders of the tradition have often argued that such disconfirmations were either ill conceived or irrelevant to the central tenets of the theory, this line of defense has implied that the theory is sufficiently rich, complex, qualified, murky, and abstract such that it is not open to empirical validation. In any case, the once zealous attempts to validate psychoanalytic theory (cf. summaries by Barnes, 1952; Blum, 1953; Sears, 1944) are no longer in evidence, and little confidence in its description of early development seems warranted. In the case of neoanalytic revisions, few have received systematic study. Loevinger's (1966) theory of ego-development is rapidly proving an exception, but in this case it is too early to draw confident conclusions.

Piagetian theory has generated an immense welter of research (cf. summaries by Brown, 1970; Inhelder & Matalon, 1960; Kohlberg, 1969b), and much of this work has been very promising. However, such work may also be considered exploratory, in the sense that investigators have largely searched for relevant contexts in which support may be maximized rather than pursuing broad-scale assessment of behavior patterns. Further, the Piagetian stages have not been subjected to systematic cross-cultural study; existing cross-cultural research yields ambiguous results; and many studies indicate that cognitive capabilities may be subject to a host of environmental influences (see summary in Dasen, 1972). Attempts to link the stage theory to chronological age have proved less than promising, as great variability is evidenced in the cognitive capabilities manifested within any given age group. Many of these same remarks apply as well to the Kohlberg extension of Piagetian theory to the realm of moral development (cf. Kohlberg, 1969a, 1969b, 1973). Kohlberg's work has also been seriously criticized on methodological grounds (cf. Kurtines & Grief, 1974).

In the case of both cognitive and moral development, ample evidence for "regression" or reversal in sequence has been discovered, and such evidence raises serious questions concerning the predictive capability of the basic theoretical structures. The most prevalent defense against reversals in what should otherwise be fixed sequences is that they reflect only superficial behavioral changes. They are not indicative of alterations in basic cognitive structure or stage of moral thought. One form of this argument is contained in the familiar competence versus performance distinction. Rapid alterations in performance may be evidenced without necessary implications for basic competence. Although such defenses may be quite reasonable, they do raise the same problems concerning cognitive development that investigators of psychosexual sequence encountered during the preceding era; that is, if all behavioral disconfirmations are dismissed on the grounds that they do not capture the relevant psychological processes and no firm definitions linking psychological process with externally observed behavior can be provided, then the theory essentially remains untestable. The defense of inadequate realization of psychological constructs may be considered a hazardous resort, as it ultimately discourages systematic investigation.

In sum, none of the major theories within the ordered-change orientation have proved exceptional with respect to predictive validity. Much research is suggestive, much is promising. However, in the applied arena, only the grossest predictions are permissable, much variability prevails, and strong confidence is not yet warranted.

3. The Prescription of Ordered Change

Within the ordered-change orientation, three prominent evaluative biases are evident. The first is that change *should* occur. The individual who is stabilized at a given stage is typically viewed as a deviant, subject to special attention, if not contempt. The Freudian concept of "fixation" provides the boldest statement of the bias. Fixation, in Freudian terms, is a serious form of neurosis, subject to cure through analysis. However, being arrested in a Piagetian preoperational state or the second stage of moral development in the Kohlbergian framework would carry with it the same pejorative implications. The second prominent bias is that the individual should not return to previous behavior patterns. Change should be unidirectional. The Freudian concept of regression serves as the evaluative cornerstone for subsequent theorizing. Regression in psychoanalytic terms is a defensive maneuver through which the individual avoids realistic confrontation with his or her problems. Regression within the schemes of Piaget and Kohlberg is viewed as a special anomaly and requires extensive theoretical defense. When one has transcended an inferior status, how is return to be justified?

Both of these prescriptive biases must be qualified by a third, the "middle adulthood prejudice." Although forward change is generally viewed as positive, this demand is attenuated once the individual has reached "maturity." Generally speaking, within Western culture middle adulthood provides the model for optimal comportment, and the more remote one's behavior from the optimum, the more questionable. Thus, if an adult regresses to teen-age behavior, he or she may be tolerated (if such behavior is limited to specific periods set aside for "immaturity"); however, to behave like an early adolescent is more deplorable, and to act childishly is wholly culpable. Such approbation cannot be accounted for in terms of simple age grading (i.e., everyone should act their age). If a child begins to demonstrate adult characteristics, the parents are typically congratulated for either the rich environment they have provided or their genetic constitution. The preference for middle-adult behavior patterns is again manifest when we consider models of aging. Generally, the more removed one's behavior from the middle-adult norm, the more inferior its evaluative status. For example, a negative value is thus built into the process of disengaging from society (Cumming & Henry, 1961; Neugarten, 1968). Indeed, the very concept of development, with its intimations of "forward" movement, is applied with hesitancy to the later years.

It should finally be noted that stability and change ethics coexist within society and typically within the same person. The coexistence is not always a happy one, and much strife within relationships may be traced to such conflict. On the one hand, most of us strive for some degree of stability within our lives and within those about us. We feel that the mature individual is one who displays consistency, coherence, and an enduring identity. Yet, we also value growth, as we call it, and chastise ourselves and those to whom we are attached if change is not apparent. Discerning the difference between stability and stasis, and between growth and impulsivity is often tortuous. Given the arbitrary character of such constructions, one might view the entire value conflict as dispensable.

4. Science and Ordered Change

Frameworks centering on ordered change lend themselves very well to the construction of knowledge in the positivist mold. As we have seen, theories within this domain assume that patterns of development are reliable and replicable; they may be found throughout the species and may be duplicated in virtually any historical era. To the extent that such assumptions are valid, it should be possible to accumulate knowledge about such patterns and to improve this knowledge through continued research.

C. The Aleatory Change Template

A third orientation to human development demands attention. It is an orientation that has been less fully elaborated than either the stability or the ordered-change template, but is one that lies implicit in much life-span literature in general, and within the dialectical domain in particular. Central to this orientation is the assumption that there is little about human development that is "preprogrammed;" that is, we enter the world with a biological system that establishes the limits or range of our activities but not the precise character of the activities themselves. Like computer hardware, the biological system informs us as to what operations are possible but does not determine the nature of processing at any given moment. For such determination to be made one must examine the character of the inputs to the system. In the case of human development, the system inputs may be viewed as a confluence of potentially interacting factors or processes, a confluence that is in a state of continuous change. In effect, the confluence may be viewed as a cross-time emergent. Thus, just as we cannot derive psychological principles from physiological knowledge, or one phase of development from a preexisting phase, we cannot be certain of the nature of the confluence at time$_2$ from our knowledge at time$_1$. In other words, the relationship between any x factor and y response is potentially unreliable; all relationships between antecedent factors and responses are fashioned in part by historically specific conditions. In the broadest sense it may be said that the determining confluence is subject to chance, and thus aleatory in nature.

D. Aleatory Thinking in Life-Span Developmental Psychology

This conception of human behavior obviously requires amplification and support. Let us first trace its existence within the life-span developmental movement. Substantial support for the aleatory orientation is derived from the movement's concern with development during adulthood. In this instance, ontogenetic sequences are difficult to discern, and primary attention has been paid to environmental influences. The latter are widely evident and much explored. To the extent that such influences predominate, the aleatory position gains strength. Environmental factors are subject to gross modification over time; they do not evolve on a constitutionally based schedule. In this vein, Neugarten (1968) has discussed the alterations in life-cycle patterns for females as they depend on labor needs. For example, the proportions of women in the labor force at various stages of adulthood have undergone dramatic differences between 1870 and 1966, with consequent alteration of the adult female life pattern. As Neugarten and Datan (1973) conclude, "Changes in the life cycle [such as these] have their effects upon personality, and it is likely that the personalities of successive age cohorts will, therefore, be different in measurable ways [p. 68]."

This emphasis on shifting sociohistorical circumstances is amplified by Lieberman (1975) in his discussion of the effects of environmental stressors in adult life, and by explorations of Pearlin (1975) and Schlegel (1975) into the environmental sources of the oft-observed differences in depression between males and females. A similar orientation has been adopted by investigators into adult sex role development. David Gutmann (1975), for example, has expressed deep concern over the effects of new life styles on sex role differentiation in parenting; Meda Rebecca (1975) has developed a model of sex role development that specifically singles out the current sociohistorical context for its importance in shaping contemporary sex role patterns.

Equally as important as the emphasis on environmental circumstance has been the extensive empirical and conceptual exploration of cohort effects in the development of human abilities (Baltes & Reinert, 1969; Nesselroade & Baltes, 1974; Schaie & Strother, 1968) and personality characteristics (Baltes & Nesselroade, 1973; Woodruff & Birren, 1972). As these explorations have demonstrated, different developmental trajectories are found among cohorts born in different eras within the same culture. As Buss (1974) has concluded from his review of this literature, "Each new generation interprets reality without the years of commitment of a previous ideology and thereby transforms that reality [p. 66]." The practical implications of such findings have been of major concern to Birren and Woodruff (1973) and to Baltes and Schaie (1973), as they have noted the difficulties in predicting the effects of educational intervention. Such effects may vary depending on the particular cohort selected for attention. As Baltes and Schaie

(1973) suggest, "it is questionable whether behavioral scientists will ever be able to demonstrate the type of treatment and prevention effects that characterize much of the classical biological and medical sciences [p. 380] ."

On a broader theoretical level, Amhammer's (1973) application of social-learning theory to life-span development makes an important contribution to the aleatory approach. As she demonstrates, patterns of adult change can be explained in terms of differential learning experiences embedded within varying environmental circumstances. Looft's (1973) relational orientation to development is also consistent with this orientation. His concern with sociological and demographic inputs to development within their historical context leads him to conclude: "No longer should developmental psychologists focus so exclusively on ontogenetic age functions; each new generation will manifest age trends that are different from those that preceded it, and thus, previous empirical endeavors are reduced to exercises in futility [p. 51] ." Such sentiments gain additional support from Stein and Baltes's (1975) "multidirectionality" theory of development. As they argue, developmental change is subject to a host of varied and changing factors, and the particular set of factors to which the individual is exposed may change from one historical period to another. Thus, developmental sequences may take many different forms; universality and unidirectional sequences are outmoded concepts.

Finally, dialectical theory makes a vital contribution to the aleatory framework. The impact of Riegel's (1972, 1973, 1975) contributions in this area cannot be underestimated. His elaboration of the four planes of development—the inner-biological, individual-psychological, cultural-sociological, and outer-physical—along with their dynamic of continuous conflict, can usefully integrate much of the work just described. Kvale's explorations (Chapter 9, this volume) cast additional doubt on the classic assumptions of development, particularly regarding the innate character of human memory. As he shows, human memory processing is vitally dependent on the social institutions in which one is enmeshed. As he concludes, "the meaning of the past is continually understood through new retrospectives, which involves a principal undeterminedness of the context for understanding." Much the same emphasis is found in Reese's probing (Chapter 11, this volume) of the dialectical development of discriminative learning and transfer. The character of various cognitive operations importantly depends on individual incentives, which, in turn, depends on the event structure in contemporary society. Rebecca's (1975) dialectical analysis of sex-role socialization has already been alluded to.

III. Constitutional and Cultural Contributions
to an Aleatory Orientation

Support for the aleatory orientation is hardly limited to the life-span literature. If we consider the biological nature of the human organism and persistent valuational investments within the culture, the strength of the position becomes further apparent. In the case of biological makeup, comparative study first makes it clear that as the physiological system gains in complexity, behavioral dependency on specific stimuli is progressively reduced (Ford & Beach, 1951). Thus, in simple organisms (e.g., flatworms, mollusks, and anthropods) behavior is reliably related to surrounding conditions. The presence of a specific environmental condition (heat, light, sound, etc.) will consistently elicit a specific behavior from the organism. Depending on the simplicity of the mechanism involved, we speak in such cases of taxes, tropisms, reflexes, and instincts. However, as organisms gain in physiological complexity, and particularly with the development of the cerebral cortex, such dependable reactions are progressively diminished. Thus, in primate colonies, certain mating and power relations seem to be under instinctual control, but the major share of primate behavior cannot be accounted for on this basis. In the case of human behavior, "automatic" reactions of the instinctual or reflex variety are scarcely in evidence. In almost no way is the human being "stimulus bound."

This argument may be coupled with a second. In large measure human behavior seems dependent on internal, symbolic capabilities. Further, such capabilities essentially cut us away from the stimulus as given. A given environmental condition thus has the capacity to stimulate virtually any symbolization, and such symbolizations may be rapidly altered over time. Thus, at any point we may symbolically reconstruct our past, present, or future—with resounding consequences for our social conduct. In the case of symbolic transformations of the past, both Kvale's and Riegel's contributions to the present volume provide ample documentation. With respect to the reconstruction of the present, my colleagues and I have been especially concerned with the ways in which people come to reconceptualize their own being within various social settings (see Gergen, in press, for a summary). We have found, for example, that the mere presence of someone with socially desirable features is sufficient to cause a debilitating devaluation of self; the presence of a seeming inferior may have exactly the opposite consequences (Morse & Gergen, 1970). Enhancement of self-conception may also be achieved through egotistical role playing (Gergen & Taylor, 1966) or through another's positive regard (Gergen, 1965). In effect, self-conception is constantly being reshaped as the individual engages in relations with others. Views of the future may be similarly altered. How much of the future one takes into account, one's articulation of specific future events, and the affective associations to one's symbolization of the future may be altered over time and sometimes very rapidly so (see reviews by Cottle & Klineberg, 1974; Doob, 1971).

We must add to this case for constitutional flexibility, with its supportive implications for an aleatory orientation to human development, a consideration of recurring values within society. In particular we may consider a cluster of values that mitigate against the formation of stable patterns of human behavior. For one, strong investments in freedom are found in many cultures of the world. People often value the capacity for unrestrained action and strongly resent restrictions placed on their behavior (cf. Brehm, 1966; Wicklund, 1974). At times, such valuational investments are sufficient such that large numbers of people will give up their lives in their defense. When we consider the relationship between scientific theory and such investments, it is clear that the quest for freedom may often be at odds with science. In their prescriptive capacity, scientific descriptions often sanction certain forms of behavior and relegate other behavior patterns to a deviant class. In effect, scientific description may itself serve to rigidify certain patterns of conduct and in this way poses a threat to the individual's sense of freedom. A case in point is the resentment of many women at the implications of research and theory on the women's movement. Such investigation has a strong liberal to radical bias, and women (e.g., mothers, housewives) who are denigrated by such investigations often react with an increased affirmation of their own life-styles.

A similar argument can be made with respect to the value of uniqueness. As Fromkin (1970, 1972) has shown, within Western culture people often desire to see themselves as unique. The experience of reward is greater when received by the individual him or herself than when diffused among a group; further, the likelihood of being replaced is greater when one is a replica of others. Scientific activity essentially aims at destroying such uniqueness. Professional rewards are garnered by the investigator who can account for the conduct of the greatest number with the fewest abstractions. In this sense, traditional science may be viewed as dehumanizing, and the quest for uniqueness at loggerheads with its goals. In the same way that black Americans have often resented the stereotypes emerging from research of black family life, psychodynamics, self-esteem, and intelligence, so one may challenge encapsulation by developmental stage designations.

In sum, we find that both biology and recurring social values lend strong support to an aleatory view of human development. They suggest that behavior patterns may undergo constant modification over time and counsel against the likelihood of discovering principles or laws of transhistorical significance. They indicate that at any point in time individual behavior may be subject to multiple influences, both internally and externally engendered. Various determining confluences may be operative for various segments of the culture and for differing segments at different points in history. Given highly stabilized social conditions, any particular confluence may remain relatively unchanged for long periods of time; in other eras, the confluence may alter with wrenching rapidity.

We are now in a position to examine the aleatory orientation in the light of our critical criteria.

A. Aleatory Understanding

In terms of comprehensive understanding, the aleatory orientation proves unique. The orientation itself does not favor a single domain or class of relevant theories. Rather, it prompts a strong theoretical relativism. From the aleatory viewpoint, virtually any theory may be applicable to some segment of the population at some point in history. Thus, a multiplicity of theories is invited by the orientation, while commitment to any single account is discouraged. The orientation has excellent sensitizing potential, inasmuch as it encourages the individual to maintain constant surveillance over a wide range of potentials. Dialectical operations are particularly useful in this respect, as they prompt investigation of opposing factors or processes. From the dialectical standpoint, the isolation of any potential determinant is sufficient to posit the existence of a counterforce. Existence demands consideration of negation.

Depending on one's viewpoint, it may be said that the aleatory orientation provides either the maximum or the minimum sense of coherent understanding. Understanding behavior in terms of evolving confluences invites a wholistic perspective, in which events possess an ever-emerging interrelatedness. The experiential world is one, wholly coherent. Yet, because this relatedness can never be encompassed in a single analytic framework, one is bereft of explanatory certainty. Analytic coherence is unavailable. Finally, the aleatory orientation fully lends itself to the unsettling of common understanding. In its emphasis on theoretical relativity, it invites a sceptical reaction to all theoretical formations. At its most dramatic, is suggests that any theoretical statement may be countered with its opposite, and with equal claims to validity. Statements such as "behavior is a function of available reinforcement contingencies," "behavior is determined by the state of the phenomenological field at the moment of its inception," or "development takes place in a series of recognizable and discriminable stages" may all be countered with a negation of equal validity.

B. Prediction in the Aleatory Mold

From the aleatory viewpoint, there is little merit in attempting to prove competing theoretical formulations. Findings may be generated to suit any reasonable theory (see Gergen, 1975). In this sense, the aleatory orientation lends itself to the earlier argument for independent evaluation of theory and prediction. At the same time, the aleatory orientation does not rule out the task of prediction. Behavioral phenomena are under the influence of antecedent conditions at any given point in history; however, the relationship between observable antecedents and resulting consequences may not remain stable. Although there may be no fundamental ordering of behavior patterns over time, at any given point ordered patterns may be discerned. Thus, from the aleatory position, prediction is optimally viewed as a continuous process in which the predictive formula are constantly monitored for waxing and waning efficacy. We may find, for example, that enriched environments, early educational intervention, early speech acquisition, and so on all have effects on later cognitive skills. However, such findings may be vitally dependent on historical circumstancess, and the predictive validity of such statements must be monitored across time.

Special note must be made of the relationship between dialectical theory and the problem of prediction. Until now the dialectical perspective has largely played a catalytic role within the behavioral sciences. It has described fundamental shortcomings or biases in the prevailing paradigms and argued for an alteration in thinking about behavior. However, in many such writings one discerns a tendency to codify the dialectical perspective, that is, to transform it to a set of principles that might function in a predictive role. Statements to the effect that all change depends on conflict, that conflict inevitably leads to progress or enhanced consciousness, or that all elements are in conflict with their contradictions are exemplary. Each suggests an underlying order, which order may be more fully elaborated and empirically tested over time. This attempt at codification is inconsistent with the aleatory orientation. In this mold, dialectics becomes simply another form of ordered-change theory.

C. Aleatory Prescription

Within the aleatory domain, dialectical theory has clearly had the strongest valuational impact. As dialecticians maintain, positive change depends on confrontation of thesis and antithesis; progress thus depends on crisis. This descriptive analysis has lent powerful support to revolutionary forces throughout the world. However, as we have seen, dialectical theory in rigidified form is not fully aleatory. From the aleatory perspective, conflict is not a necessary harbinger of positive change. Even the concept of positive change or progress is open to question, as the validity of such a concept depends on a theoretical framework, and all frameworks are defective. More consistent with the aleatory position is an ethical relativity. Differing ethical systems may be functional within various sociohistorical contexts. The solidification of any ethical system may have deleterious consequences over time. Continuous reassessment of prescription must be undertaken, and avenues established for "unfreezing" institutional safeguards of tradition. Further, the aleatory orientation invites creative consideration of change. Given the maleability of the human organism and the emerging confluence of circumstance, one is encouraged to inquire into the adequacy of present circumstances and means for their alteration. Since past solutions are not necessarily applicable to the ever-emerging character of the existing problems, a special premium is placed on the novel solution.

D. Toward an Aleatory Science

Clearly the aleatory orientation to human development does not lend itself to the accumulation of knowledge in the positivist mold. Human behavior will not generally display the same type of stability characteristic as phenomena within the physical sciences. To be sure, certain ontogenetic patterns of development may occur in virtual disregard of the particular sociocultural context. Such processes may be "wired in" and thus more successfully treated within the traditional scientific framework. Required by the aleatory orientation, however, is a revision of the traditional scientific program. The essential elements of this revision are implicated within the preceding discussion. At a minimum, an aleatory science would entail the following:

1. *Theory Construction.* Such theory would primarily be dedicated to historically sensitive description and explanation, sensitization, and the disruption of

common understanding. Since all reasonable theories may be valid for some portion of the people at some period, research stemming from such theory would primarily be used for illustrative purposes.

2. *Prediction.* In a world of changing behavior patterns, the task of prediction becomes frought with difficulty. In this respect we are in a position similar to that of the weather forecaster. Broad physical principles allow for a *posthoc* understanding of all weather conditions but do not enable us to make definitive predictions on any given day. The task of the behavioral scientist is far more perplexing, however, inasmuch as the number of variables and the relationship among them may be continuously evolving. Although immensely complex, the task of prediction is still an important one. A premium is to be placed on predictive formulae with built-in feedback devices for theoretical revision and correction. Such prediction would ideally be concerned with problems of pressing importance within the society.

3. *Advocacy.* Rather than adopting the traditional pretense of nonprescription, an aleatory science would ideally be one continuously exploring the value implications of any theoretical or empirical endeavor. The relativity of understanding implied by the aleatory program suggests that our adaptive potential is maximized when conflict of interest prevails. Danger lies in unanimity concerning what is known and what it implies for human comportment. Thus, a premium is to be placed on advocacy, for in the bold elaboration of investment, conflict among assumptions is made manifest.

REFERENCES

Amhammer, I. M. Social-learning theory as a framework for the study of adult personality development. In P. B. Baltes & K. W. Schaie (Eds.), *Lifespan developmental psychology: Personality & socialization.* New York: Academic Press, 1973.

Armistead, N. (Ed.). *Reconstructing social psychology.* Middlesex, Eng.: Penguin Books, 1974.

Baltes, P. B., & Nesselroade, J. R. The developmental analysis of individual differences on multiple measures. In G. R. Nesselroade & H. W. Reese (Eds.), *Life-span developmental psychology: Methodological issues.* New York: Academic Press, 1973.

Baltes, P. B., & Reinert, G. Cohort effects in cognitive development of children as revealed by cross-sectional sequences. *Developmental Psychology,* 1969, 1, 169–177.

Baltes, P. B., & Schaie, K. W. On life-span developmental research paradigms, retrospects and prospects. In P. B. Baltes & K. W. Schaie (Eds.), *Life-span developmental psychology: Personality and socialization.* New York: Academic Press, 1973.

Barnes, C. A. A statistical study of Freudian theory of levels of psychosexual development. *Genetic Psychology Monographs,* 1952, 45, 105–175.

Birren, J. E., & Woodruff, D. S. Human development over the life span through education. In P. B. Baltes & K. W. Schaie (Eds.), *Life-span developmental psychology: Personality and socialization.* New York: Academic Press, 1973.

Blum, G. S. *Psychoanalytic theories of personality.* New York: McGraw-Hill, 1953.

Brehm, J. W. *A theory of psychological reactance.* New York: Academic Press, 1966.

Brown, R. *Cognitive development in children.* Chicago: University of Chicago Press, 1970.

Buss, A. R. Generational analysis: description, explanation, and theory. *Journal of Social Issues,* 1974, 30, 55–71.

Cottle, T. J., & Klineberg, S. L. *The present of things future.* New York: Free Press, 1974.

Cumming, M. E., & Henry, W. E. (Eds.). *Growing old: The process of disengagement.* New York: Basic Books, 1961.

Dasen, P. R. Cross-cultural Piagetian research: A summary. *Journal of Cross-Cultural Psychology,* 1972, **3**, 23–40.

Doob, L. W. *Patterning of time.* New Haven: Yale University Press, 1971.

Elms, A. C. The crisis in confidence in social psychology. *American Psychologist,* 1975, **30**, 967–976.

Erikson, E. *Childhood and society.* New York: Norton, 1950.

Erikson, E. Identity and identity diffusion. In C. Gordon & K. J. Gergen (Eds.), *The self in social interaction* (Vol. 1). New York: Wiley, 1968.

Ford, C. S., & Beach, F. A. *Patterns of sexual behavior.* New York: Josiah Macy, Jr. Foundation, 1951.

Fromkin, H. L. Effects of experimentally aroused feelings of undistinctiveness upon valuation of scare and novel experiences. *Journal of Personality and Social Psychology,* 1970, **16**, 521–529.

Fromkin, H. L. Feelings of interpersonal undistinctiveness: an unpleasant affective state. *Journal of Experimental Research in Personality,* 1972, **6**, 178–185.

Gergen, K. J. Interaction goals and personalistic feedback as factors affecting the presentation of self. *Journal of Personality and Social Psychology,* 1965, **1**, 413–424.

Gergen, K. J. Personal consistency and the presentation of self. In C. Gordon & K. J. Gergen (Eds.), *The self in social interaction* (Vol. 1). New York: Wiley, 1968.

Gergen, K. J. Social psychology as history. *Journal of Personality and Social Psychology,* 1973, **26**, 309–320.

Gergen, K. J. *Experimentation in social psychology: Death & transfiguration.* Invited address, Division 9, American Psychological Association, Chicago, September, 1975.

Gergen, K. J. Social psychology, science and history. *Personality and Social Psychology Bulletin,* 1976, **2**, 373–383.

Gergen, K. J. Social exchange theory in a world of transient fact. In R. L. Hamblin (Ed.), *Behavioral theory in sociology.* Edison, N.J.: Transaction Books, 1977.

Gergen, K. J. The social construction of the self. In T. Mischel (Ed.), *The self in psychology.* Oxford: Blackwell, in press.

Gergen, K. J., Gergen, M. M., & Barton, W. Deviance in the dark. *Psychology Today,* October 1973, **7**, 129–130.

Gergen, K. J., & Taylor, M. G. *Role-playing and modifying the self concept.* Paper presented at the meeting of the Eastern Psychological Association, New York, March 1966.

Gouldner, A. *The coming crisis in western sociology.* Glencoe, Ill.: Free Press, 1969.

Gutmann, D. Parenthood: A key to the comparative study of the life cycle. In N. Datan & L. Ginsberg (Eds.), *Life-span developmental psychology: Normative life crises.* New York: Academic Press, 1975.

Harlow, H. F., & Harlow, M. K. The affectional systems. In A. M. Schrier, H. F. Harlow, & F. Stollnitz (Eds.), *Behavior of nonhuman primates.* New York: Academic Press, 1965.

Harré, R., & Secord, P. F. *The explanation of social behavior.* Oxford: Blackwell, 1972.

Inhelder, B., & Matalon, B. The study of problem solving and thinking. In P. H. Mussen (Ed.), *Handbook of research methods in child development.* New York: Wiley, 1960.

Kagan, J., & Moss, H. A. *Birth to maturity: A study in psychological development.* New York: Wiley, 1962.

Kohlberg, L. Continuities and discontinuities in childhood and adult moral development. *Human Development,* 1969, **12**, 93–120. (a)

Kohlberg, L. *Stages in the development of moral thought and action.* New York: Holt, 1969. (b)

Kohlberg, L. Continuities in childhood and adult moral development revisited. In P. B. Baltes &

K. W. Schaie (Eds.), *Life-span developmental psychology: Personality and socialization.* New York: Academic Press, 1973.

Kuhn, I. S. *The structure of scientific revolutions.* Chicago: University of Chicago Press, 1962.

Kurtines, W., & Grief, E. The development of moral thought: Review and evaluation of Kohlberg's approach. *Psychological Bulletin,* 1974, 81, 691–704.

Lieberman, M. A. Adaptive processes in late life. In N. Datan & L. Ginsberg (Eds.), *Life-span developmental psychology: Normative life crises.* New York: Academic Press, 1975.

Loevinger, J. A. Models and measures of developmental variation. *Annals of the New York Academy of Sciences,* 1966, 134, 585–590.

Looft, W. R. Socialization and personality throughout the life span: An examination of contemporary psychological approaches. In P. B. Baltes & K. W. Schaie (Eds.), *Life span developmental psychology: Personality and socialization.* New York: Academic Press, 1973.

McGuire, W. J. The yin and yang of progress in social psychology. *Journal of Personality and Social Psychology,* 1973, 26, 446–456.

Milgram, S. *Obedience to authority.* New York: Harper, 1974.

Morse, S., & Gergen, K. J. Social comparison, self-consistency and the concept of self. *Journal of Personality and Social Psychology,* 1970, 16(1), 148–156.

Myrdal, G. *Objectivity in social research.* New York: Pantheon, 1969.

Nesselroade, J. R., & Baltes, P. B. Adolescent personality development and historical change: 1970–1972. *Monographs of the Society for Research in Child Development,* 1974, 39(1, Serial Number 154).

Neugarten, B. L. *Adaptation and the life cycle.* Paper presented at the meeting of the Foundations Fund for Research in Psychiatry, Puerto Rico, June 1968.

Neugarten, B. L. (Ed.), *Middle age and aging: A reader in social psychology.* Chicago: University of Chicago Press, 1968.

Neugarten, B. L., & Datan, N. Sociological perspectives on the life cycle. In P. B. Baltes & K. W. Schaie (Eds.), *Life span developmental psychology: Personality and socialization.* New York: Academic Press, 1973.

Pearlin, L. I. Sex roles and depression. In N. Datan & L. Ginsberg (Eds.), *Life-span developmental psychology: Normative life crises.* New York: Academic Press, 1975.

Piaget, J. *The language and thought of the child* (M. Warden, trans.), New York: Harcourt, 1926.

Piaget, J. *The child's conception of physical causality.* New York: Harcourt, 1930.

Piaget, J. The development of time concepts in the child. In R. H. Hock & J. Zublin (Eds.), *Psychopathology of childhood.* New York: Grune & Stratton, 1955.

Piaget, J. *Genetic epistemology.* New York: Columbia University Press, 1970.

Poole, R. *Towards deep subjectivity.* New York: Harper, 1972.

Rebecca, M. *A dialectical approach to sex-role socialization.* Unpublished paper, University of Michigan, 1975.

Riegel, K. F. Time and change in the development of the individual and society. In H. W. Reese (Ed.), *Advances in child development and behavior* (Vol. 7). New York: Academic Press, 1972.

Riegel, K. F. Dialectic operations: The final period of cognitive development. *Human Development,* 1973, 16, 346–370.

Riegel, K. F. From traits and equilibrium toward developmental dialectics. In W. Arnold (Ed.), *Nebraska Symposium on Motivation.* Lincoln: University of Nebraska Press, 1975.

Runcinan, W. G. *A critique of Max Weber's philosophy of social science.* London & New York: Cambridge University Press, 1972.

Schaie, K. W., & Strother, C. R. The effects of time and cohort differences on the interpretation of age changes in cognitive behavior. *Multivariate Behavioral Research,* 1968, 3, 259–294.

Schlegel, A. Situational stress: A Hopi example. In N. Datan & L. Ginsberg (Eds.), *Life-span developmental psychology: Normative life crises.* New York: Academic Press, 1975.

Sears, R. R. Experimental analyses of psychoanalytic phenomenon. In J. McV. Hunt (Ed.), *Personality and the behavior disorders* (Vol. 1). New York: Ronald Press, 1944.

Stein, A. H., & Baltes, P. B. Theory and method in life-span developmental psychology. *Society for Research in Child Development,* 1975.

Suomi, S. S., & Harlow, H. F. Social rehabilitation of isolate-reared monkeys. *Developmental Psychology,* 1972, 6, 487–496.

Weber, M. *The methodology of the social sciences.* Glencoe, Ill.: Free Press, 1949.

Wicklund, R. A. *Freedom and reactance.* New York: Halsted Press, 1974.

Woodruff, D. S., & Birren, J. E. Age changes and cohort differences in personality. *Developmental Psychology,* 1972, 6, 252–259.

CHAPTER 8

Another Look at the Issue of Continuity versus Change in Models of Human Development

STANLEY H. COHEN

WEST VIRGINIA UNIVERSITY
MORGANTOWN, WEST VIRGINIA

Professor Gergen (Chapter 7, this volume) has called on us to reexamine two major, current models of development—that of stability or continuity and that of ordered change—and to replace them with his proposed dialectical aleatory model. His call to battle is indeed a Kuhnian revolution of the first order! While I recognize the limitations of these two suspect models, I shall argue the position that we need to extend these models further, not relegate them to ancient history.

The critical test for the stability model is the continuity of development as the individual organism ages. Individual differences are assumed to exist, but these differences should be maintained over the lifespan. Hence, the correlation between a given behavior at time$_1$ and at time$_2$ should be large, if not approaching 1.00 in magnitude. Many major and carefully undertaken longitudinal studies report mixed results. Time-lag correlations vary from 0 to .5 and are occasionally negative.

One is tempted to dismiss the stability model in light of this prima facie evidence. However, this would ignore many inherent problems in measuring behavior over the life span and, more importantly, fail to take into account the interaction between the organism and its environment. In his monumental work, Bloom (1964) found consistent support for a stability model from dozens of longitudinal and cross-sectional studies. In fact, one is amazed at the convergence of the findings, after problems such as measurement unreliability and restriction of range in the sample are adjusted for. Other researchers (cf. Nesselroade, 1970) have proposed more sophisticated stability models that incorporate the subtleties and complexities of changing factorial measurement structures, generational effects, and time of measurement. Their reanalysis of longitudinal data tends to resurrect the fundamental viability of the stability model.

The ordered-change model has its immediate origins in the writings of Piaget and its primary alliance to epigenetic processes that posit universal sequences of development. Unlike the stability model, the ordered-change model predicts qualitative changes in the form of behavior over the life span. But like the stability model, the ordered-change model holds that these sequences are an invariant (and irreversible) progression of stages that occur in every organism, albeit with slight temporal individual variability. Professor Gergen finds this model to be deficient on two points. First, there are virtually no systematic data on prediction (but there are data on reversals and regressions), and, second, its status as a set of general laws is debatable. A quick reply here would be to enumerate a large body of within-culture and cross-cultural literature that, at the very least, demonstrates the universality of the model and the patterned sequence within individuals. I do concur, however, with Professor Gergen's concern about the generality of the model across the life span and its applicability to noncognitive psychological domains. Recent work (cf. Looft, 1972) is beginning to advance the model into "personality-like" variables such as egocentrism and into the adult and old age segments of the life span.

With the stability model and the ordered-change model aside, I now turn to the new proposal put forth by Professor Gergen: the aleatory model of development. My remarks are aimed at several of his conclusions about the developmental process, and I shall discuss each in turn.

First is his notion that much of behavior does not "appear" to be "preprogrammed," as is suggested by the stability and ordered-change models. Indeed, the individual exhibits complex, spontaneous action seemingly freed up from reactive stimulus-bound behavior. In part, Gergen attributes this to our symbolic capacities. His statements are obviously strongly directed against the mechanistic assumptions underlying certain versions of the stability model and, to some degree, the ordered-change model (cf. Reese & Overton, 1970). My contention is that there *are* machine models of the organism that permit and predict "complex, spontaneous" action. The analogy here is to general purpose versus special purpose computers. While the general purpose computer is prewired, it is designed to accept many programs. The continuity of behavior follows from the regularity in which these programs are executed and the precise specification of output that results from a given input plus the machine's state of configuration. Ashby (1963) provides many illustrations of these cybernetic models.

Another feature of the aleatory model centers around autonomous change during development. The organism, in its environment, is "invited" to change and, more fundamentally, can change. It is the dynamic environment and our response to it that goes unnoticed in traditional continuity models. I believe, however, that for continuity models this is an error of omission, not commission. The experimental method has locked psychology into the study of reactive arrangements and with it some rather circumscribed principles of behavior. But there is a light at the end of the tunnel! Bijou (1975) has recently written about the operant analysis of concepts like novelty and curiosity. Skinner (1971) has analyzed freedom and autonomy from the perspective of radical behaviorism. Even though these are only first approximations, it is clear that these phenomena are subject to explication by traditional models.

At the very core of Professor Gergen's proposal is the irreplicability of causal patterns among variables over time. That is, because of the nature of the process we study, historical context is the prepotent intervening variable between cause and effect. And unless history is constant, our laws of behavior are transient or, at the very least, reduce to a study of the psychohistory underlying the shaping of mankind. What I want to underscore is whether history can be viewed as an antecedent variable or as an intervening (and interacting) variable in our theories. If history is "simply" an antecedent, then we must include it in our existing models and proceed to measure it for prediction purposes. Econometric models routinely employ this procedure. However, if history interacts with our laws of behavior and historical substance is transitory, then our traditional models and methods are obsolete.

But before rushing into replacement paradigms, we should consider some circumstantial evidence contrary to the second view of history. Schaie (1970) and his colleagues have presented results in support of the position that history or generation effects are additive, not interactive. Gergen himself, in a series of articles (1973, 1976) reviews evidence taken almost exclusively from laboratory settings. I am not convinced that history intervenes to the extent he cites in psychological processes outside the laboratory. But in his defense, I agree that we must redesign those methods that capitalize on "artificial," nongeneralizable aspects of behavior.

The debate over these three models will continue long after this conference adjourns. The evolution of development theory, like our own biological evolution, requires both time and mutation. It is hoped that the fittest will survive, and the others will have contributed heuristic value.

REFERENCES

Ashby, W. R. *An introduction to cybernetics.* New York: Wiley, 1963.
Bijou, S. W. Development in the preschool years: A functional analysis. *American Psycologist,* 1975, **30**, 829–837.
Bloom, B. S. *Stability and change in human characteristics.* New York: Wiley, 1964.
Gergen, K. J. Social psychology as history. *Journal of Personality and Social Psychology,* 1973, **26**, 309–320.
Gergen, K. J. Social psychology, science and history. *Personality and Social Psychology Bulletin,* 1976, **2**, 373–383.

Looft, W. R. Egocentrism and social interaction across the life-span. *Psychological Bulletin,* 1972, 78, 73–92.

Nesselroade, J. R. Application of multivariate strategies to problems of measuring and structuring long-term change. In L. R. Goulet & P. B. Baltes (Eds.), *Life-span developmental psychology: Research and theory.* New York: Academic Press, 1970.

Reese, H. W., & Overton, W. F. Models of development and theories of development. In L. R. Goulet & P. B. Baltes (Eds.), *Life-span developmental psychology: Research and theory.* New York: Academic Press, 1970.

Schaie, K. W. A reinterpretation of age related changes in cognitive structure and functioning. In L. R. Goulet & P. B. Baltes (Eds.), *Life-span developmental psychology: Research and theory.* New York: Academic Press, 1970.

Skinner, B. F. *Beyond freedom and dignity.* New York: Knopf, 1971.

RESEARCH APPLICATIONS

Dialectics and Research on Remembering

STEINAR KVALE

UNIVERSITY OF AARHUS
AARHUS, DENMARK

Remembering is a relationship of a developing individual to a developing world. Remembering is, within a dialectical perspective, studied as an activity, and the notion of memory as a thing or as a storehouse of things has been discarded.

I shall here first discuss our access to remembering activity, in its consciousness and behavioral aspects, by contrasting the radical phenomenological approach of Husserl with the radical behaviorist approach of Skinner. Their focus on remembering as a relationship is then confronted with the reification of memory in psychoanalytic theory and in the verbal-learning tradition. The assembly-line model of memory, after Ebbinghaus, and the current cognitive bureaucratic memory models are criticized and related to the general reification of human behavior in a technological society.

Bartlett's studies of remembering as an activity, as a search for meaning in a natural world, are compared with the artificiality of memory in current psychological research. Finally, I shall indicate some research applications of a dialectical perspective on the social functions of remembering within a material and historical world.

I. Dialectics

Dialectics focuses on development and interaction and studies the internal relations between phenomena that exist as aspects of a totality. These relations involve contradictions between aspects mutually implying and excluding each other. The focus is upon the qualitative development of phenomena, of one quality changing into another. Dialectics is the concrete study of concrete relations, investigating psychological phenomena in their internal relations to a broader social and historical totality. Thinking and action are two internally related aspects of man's practice in the world (Mao Tse-tung, 1968).

Dialectics emphasizes the interdependence of man and world, of the observing subject and of the observed object. Men act upon the world, change it, and are again changed by the consequences of their actions. The contradictions of men's thinking and action are to be traced to the contradictions of the material basis of society, primarily to the modes and relations of production.

Dialectics discards the empiricist philosophy that conceives of consciousness and behavior as consisting of isolated atoms, or data, tied together by external, mechanical, and quantitative relations. A dialectical approach to psychology rejects the subject–object dichotomy and the dualism of an inner consciousness and an outer behavior haunting current memory research.

Dialectics is a general conception of man's relation to the world; it is neither a psychological theory nor a psychological method. No new theory of memory or research method will be given here. But in presenting an alternative framework—remembering conceived as a dialectical relation to the world—some old problems of memory research may lose their relevance, and some new issues may become central.

The study of remembering as an aspect of a dialectical interaction with a sociohistorical milieu, in the Soviet Union, has been reviewed by Meacham (1972). In an earlier paper (Kvale, 1975), I criticized the metaphysical nature of current empiristic memory research and pointed out aspects of a dialectical understanding of remembering by psychoanalysis, Gestalt psychology, Bartlett, and Piaget. Here I shall discuss some further implications of a dialectical perspective on remembering.

II. A Phenomenological and a Behavioral Approach
to Remembering

A. A Dialectic of Consciousness and Behavior

A dialectical approach to remembering shall first be depicted through the apparent detours of a phenomenological and a behavioral analysis of remembering activity. A radical phenomenology conceives of human action as a perpetual debate with a material and social world. It discards the spatial metaphor of behavior and consciousness as having separate existences somewhere "outside" and "inside," respectively, and takes as its subject matter man's relation to the world (Giorgi, 1970; Merleau-Ponty, 1967; cf. also the general emphasis on the unity of action and consciousness in Soviet psychology; Rubinstein, 1963).

Behavior and consciousness relate respectively to a third- and a first-person perspective on human action. A third-person approach involves someone observing the "public" and "visible" remembering activity of another person. A first-person approach involves a person remembering, who observes and describes his own "private" and "invisible" remembering consciousness. On the basis of Merleau-Ponty's analysis of the dialectic embedded in human action, Romanyshyn (1975) suggests a complementarity principle in psychology: "Thus what is behavior from one point of view, that of the observer of the other, is experience from another point of view, that of the actor toward himself [p. 4]."

The study of remembering as behavior and the study of remembering as consciousness mutually imply and exclude each other. A third-person approach presupposes a first-person remembering something. Access to his remembering activity may be obtained by observing his behavior, for example, his frantic searching activity and emotional expressions, and, more common, through his own verbal accounts, spontaneous or in reply to questioning.

A first-person approach involves a systematic reflection upon an unreflected conscious act of remembering (Sartre, 1961). A reflection upon one's own immediate consciousness presupposes, though, a third-person approach. It is necessary to have obtained a distance from one's own activity; one must have learned, in G. H. Mead's expression, to take the attitude of the other toward oneself. Also, the language applied in the description of one's own consciousness is learned in a verbal community, and the oral or written report implies a communication of the experience to others.

Methodologically, both a first- and a third-person approach are required to give full knowledge of remembering as a subject's relation to the world. A systematic application of each perspective to remembering activity will now be presented: Husserl's phenomenological analysis of internal time consciousness and Skinner's radical behaviorist conception of the behavior of recall. It should be noted that Husserl's phenomenology is quite different from the Gestalt phenomenology known in the United States and that Skinner's radical behaviorism departs from classical behaviorism (Day, 1969; Giorgi, 1975; Kvale & Grenness, 1967; Malone, 1975).

B. Husserl—Internal Time Consciousness

Husserl (1859–1938) is the founder of phenomenological philosophy. He took over and developed Brentano's concept of intentionality. For Husserl, consciousness is no inner box, as it is for the introspectionists. Consciousness is an intentional relation; it is always directed toward something. In his later works he emphasized the basis of consciousness in the life world—"Lebenswelt"—a theme further developed by Heidegger's analysis of man as being-in-the-world.

Husserl (1964) worked out the implications of James' conception of the stream of consciousness to involve also a memory in a continual flux (Kvale, 1974c). Consciousness is to Husserl a living-in-the-face-of, a living from one "now" to the next. The unity of the stream of consciousness is constituted by its basic intentionality, not to be confounded with explicit and purposive intentions. Every now has its intentions, which lead from one now to the new now, the intentions toward the future and, on the other side, the intentions toward the past. The formal structure of the stream of consciousness consists of a now constituted through an impression and joining a train of *retentions* and a horizon of *protentions*. As the retentions refer to the "just gone," the immediate memory, the protentions refer to the "not yet" of the immediate future. The retentions and protentions are in general not explicitly experienced as such; they are given in the mode of a "temporal background."

The flux of consciousness constitutes its own unity. As every new phase of consciousness keeps the just preceding phase in a retentional consciousness, an inherent unity of consciousness becomes possible. At the forward end of the present now the protentions—as open, undetermined intentions—constitute a unity of consciousness. Every consciousness of a temporal event contains an expectation and is a fulfillment.

In *recollection,* the protentions are not only present as voidly constituting and intercepting what is coming, they have also intercepted. They have been fulfilled, and we are aware of this fulfillment in recollection. An original silence has in recollection become the silence-before-the-thunder; the silence is now remembered "through" the thunder.

Merleau-Ponty (1962, p. 417) has summarized Husserl's retentionalizing of impressions, as shown in Figure 1. The horizontal line represents a series of nows—A, B, and C. The vertical lines represent the successive retentions of one now—A, A', and A", and so on. The oblique lines show the series of nows seen from a further now. Thus, from the new now C, the previous now B appears in a retention B', and the previous now A in a retention of a retention A" seen through the intermediate B'. Thus A is remembered "through" its "fulfillment" B, the "not knowing what comes next" in perception has become a "knowledge of what came next" in remembering.

In remembering an event, a subject does not step outside the stream of consciousness, but implicitly the whole stream of consciousness up to the living present is reproduced:

This means that as an essential *a priori* phenomenological formation memory is a continuous flux because conscious life is in constant flux and is not merely fitted

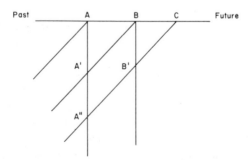

Fig. 1. Retentionalizing of impressions. [From Merleau-Ponty, 1962, p. 417.]

member by member into a chain. Rather, everything new reacts on the old; its forward-moving intention is fulfilled and determined thereby, and this gives the reproduction a definite coloring. An *a priori,* necessary retroaction is thus revealed here [Husserl, 1964, pp. 77–78].

One aspect of the issue of *memory change* was made the subject of experimentation as an attempt to investigate the empirical implications of Husserl's phenomenological analysis of an a priori necessary retroaction of memory. The phenomenon, which may be termed *meaning retroaction,* can be exemplified by the listening to, and remembering of, a sentence, as, for example, *In order to illuminate this better I shall give yet another example.* Recollection of the first words of the sentence necessarily occurs through the later words of the sentence. And in recall, the word *illuminate* will obtain a different coloring, or meaning, if it is part of another sentence, such as *In order to illuminate this better, I shall find another lamp for you.* The meaning of the word *illuminate* (A) has been retroactively determined or modified by the succeeding words *example/lamp* (B); and in remembering (C) the original *illuminate* cannot be reached except through this retroactively determined meaning (Kvale, 1974c).

When remembering is conceived as a search for meaning, it would also be expected that the remembered meaning and form of the ambiguous word (illuminate) would be different in the two sentences. The experimental results showed that when not reproduced verbatim, the reproduction of the "same" word (illuminate) was markedly different in the two sentences: as "clarify," "explain" versus "light up." The finding of meaning retroaction influencing reproduction was also demonstrated in other sentences and for ambiguous visual figures succeeded after various time intervals by defining names (Kvale, 1974a, 1974b). These results do not prove Husserl's a priori analysis, but do point to its relevance for observable remembering behavior.

The experimental design used may appear familiar as an instance of a *retroactive interference* study: learn A → learn B → remember A. Traditionally these experiments have used externally related elements as stimulus material, often nonsense syllables or words as list A and list B, and the quantitative amount of list A reproduced has been measured. In contrast, the present design involves internal relations between A and B, and a qualitative analysis of the reproductions showed qualitative changes in the reproductions related to meaning retroaction.

The intentionality of consciousness, with its internal relations of protentions and retentions, is no theoretical construction imposed upon consciousness, but appears to an open observation as embedded in conscious activity. James' critique (1963) of introspective psychology for neglecting the fleeting and vague internal relations of the stream of consciousness may still be valid for current memory research: "If to hold fast and observe the transitive parts of thought's stream be so hard, then the great blunder to which all schools are liable must be the failure to register them, and the undue emphasizing of the more substantive parts of the stream [p. 154]." In part due to the introspective difficulty of grasping the vague relations, the empiricists as well as the intellectualists only came to recognize separate and distinct elements, which then had to be externally reconnected by mechanical associations or higher mental activities.

The phenomenological rejection of the introspectionist view of consciousness as a chain of atoms or as the pearls of a necklace, tied together by external bonds, involves the dismissal of memory as a storehouse of isolated and permanent memory traces. The conception of an internal stream of consciousness necessarily leads to a memory in a continuous flux.

C. Skinner—The Behavior of Recall

Skinner as well as the phenomenologists rejects the doubling of the world in the representational copy theories of perception, and the construction of some inner man, or homunculus, to account for action. Skinner dismisses the notion of memory as a thing, as an inner storehouse of memory traces, and instead studies the behavior of recall. His conception of behavior, while somewhat ambiguous, involves aspects of a dialectical concept of action (Kvale, 1976c). Skinner (1975) focuses on the relation between the organism and the environment, defining radical behaviorism as the scientific investigation of the relation between behavior and environment. Men act upon the world, change it, and are again changed by the consequences of their actions. Behavior operates upon the world to generate consequences: "... operant behavior is the very field of purpose and intention. By its nature it is directed towards the future: a person acts *in order that* something will happen, and the order is temporal [Skinner, 1974, p. 55]."

Skinner has not worked out systematically the radical consequences of his temporal conception of operant behavior for remembering. Some statements on the behavior of recall may, however, indicate the implications of his relational conception of behavior. Skinner criticizes the reification of memory into a place where things reside and points to the many difficulties created by the belief in a memory where copies of stimuli—faces, names, texts, and so forth—are stored as some form of engrams, to be retrieved at later occasions. Storage is particularly hard to imagine for the memory of temporal events, such as a musical composition or a story. For Skinner (1974) "The contingencies which affect an organism are not stored by it. They are never inside it; they simply change it [p. 109]." Referring to the work of Penfield, where remembering activity is aroused by electrical stimulation of the brain, Skinner (1969) finds it unnecessary to postulate some copies of early environmental events that the subject looks at or listens to. It is simpler to assume that it is behavior of seeing, hearing, and so on that is aroused.

A behavioral approach to remembering is also given in the *interbehavioral psychology* of Kantor (Kantor & Smith, 1975). Remembering is not a faculty but a way in which persons interact with objects and situations. Under ordinary circumstances an individual's remembering is systematically organized and related to the various persons and objects constituting his human environment. One's remembering activity is open to observation, and involves basically different types of activity, such as the forward-looking activity of remembering an appointment tomorrow, the reminiscence of past events, and the memorizing activities of the school and the psychological laboratory. The danger of reducing the variety of remembering activities to one type is pointed out; remembering is to be observed and studied as one aspect of a person's interactions with a world of things and people.

D. The Temporality of Behavior

Not only is remembering an activity, the activity of other people is an important topic of remembering. In contrast to the remembering of spatial objects such as a house, the remembering of temporal events, such as a sequence of speech, involves a temporality of its own. The temporality of behavior has been recognized in descriptive studies of behavior in natural settings, where the stream of behavior constitutes its own unity. According to Barker (1963), the directionality of behavior, the end toward which it moves, is almost as immediately perceived as the unity of a visual form or an auditory pattern. The apprehension of behavior-in-progress gives the behavior stream its unity. In a phenomenological and experimental analysis of the perception of the behavior of other people, From (1971) has described how we usually experience the intentions of an acting person as inherent in his behavior. We experience the meaning of an action in its future-directedness, and through future developments of the context of an action its meaning may become retroactively modified, the new meaning acting backward, in a sense. A retroactive reordering of experience takes place, and later remembering of the action encompasses this meaning retroaction. Applying Husserl's analysis of internal time consciousness, we may state that the forward-going intentions of the behavioral act are no longer open and indeterminate; they have become fulfilled, and we remember the behavioral act through its later fulfillment. Thus, the remembered act cannot, in principle, be the same as the perceived act.

Skinner (1974) rejects a mechanical stimulus–response psychology. The principle of reinforcement and the functional descriptions of radical behaviorism involve a temporality of behavior, as stated in Skinner's description of operant behavior as purposive and future-directed. In functional descriptions, a behavior sequence is described in the terms: discriminative stimulus → operant behavior → reinforcing stimulus. The punctuating of the continual sequence of behavior into these phases is arbitrary, and the reinforcing stimulus of one behavioral act becomes the discriminative stimulus for the next sequence.

The principle of reinforcement has been criticized as being empty and circular. The interpretation of an event as reinforcing can only be determined by observing the succeeding events: whether the frequency of a given behavior increases or decreases. The description of an event as a reinforcer can only be given after observation of the succeeding future events. The later remembering of the original event occurs through the hindsight of knowing whether it was an effective reinforcer or not.

Our actions upon the world may change its meaning for us. This observation was used by Dewey (1896) in a "prenatal" critique of a mechanistic stimulus–response behaviorism. By means of James' example of a child's relating to a candle, Dewey argued that stimulus and response are not isolated entities but correlated phases of an individual's relation to the environment. The child sees a candle, the meaning of which to the child may be "light." The child reaches for the flame, touches it, and is burned. By this simple act the meaning of the candle to the child has been transformed to the "seeing-of-a-light-that-means-pain-when-contact-occurs." Stimulus–response psychology fails to recognize the unity of action and has to create an inner soul or a mechanical push and pull to reconnect the disconnected series of jerks. In contrast, to Dewey the reflex arc is a circuit, involving a "continual reconstitution" of a stimulus through new responses "into it."

Dewey's conception of a continual reconstitution of our experience through our actions upon the world may possibly provide a "meeting point" for Husserl's phenomenological analysis of the intentionality of consciousness and Skinner's functional analysis of operant behavior. Applying Husserl's analysis of remembering consciousness, we may say that from a later now (C) the original light (A) is remembered through the pain-when-touched (B). In Skinner's terms, the original discriminative stimulus, light (A), is remembered "through" the succeeding operant behavior and the negative reinforcing stimulus of pain (B); the negatively reinforcing quality of the light-that-means-pain-when-touched has, in remembering, become a quality of the candle.

The implications of the temporality of behavior for remembering and the issue of how the world appears to the remembering subject have been given little attention within radical behaviorism. Although Skinner (1974) analyzes private events as imagining from a first-person perspective, it is a third-person approach that has dominated radical behaviorism (cf. Malcolm, 1964).

Psychological research has often passed over one step. It has studied an inner entity termed "memory," constructed theories about its nature, but neglected some principal problems of how we can obtain knowledge of a memory. The validity of our inferences about a memory need to be related to their basis in the observation of remembering activity. Theoretical difficulties arise when the results of a first- and a third-person approach are accredited separate spatial existences. The observational results of a first-person approach have often been placed within an inner box of consciousness, and those of a third-person approach in an external world of behavior. The consequences of this dualism have further been complicated by locating meaning and intentions inside the box of consciousness and regarding behavior as mechanical responses or outer manifestations of the inner intentions.

From both a radical phenomenological and a radical behaviorist perspective, the conception of memory as an inner storehouse or a mental apparatus is discarded as an unnecessary explanatory fiction. In a dialectical conception, man exists in and as his relation to the world; consciousness and behavior are two aspects of this unitary relation. Meaning is located neither inside nor outside, but exists in man's continual dialogue with the world.

E. Remembering in Psychoanalysis

In psychoanalytic therapy a first-person approach to remembering is of central importance, in sharp contrast to the anonymous third-person processes of current memory experimentation. Psychoanalysis involves a reliving, a reinterpretation, and a reworking of a life history within a personal patient–therapist relationship. By overcoming repressions of the patient's conflicts, the therapist attempts to bring about emotional insights that lead to a correction of the neurotic development. The material to be remembered is the patient's own life history; he is to search for the meaning of his present neurotic behavior and is given ample time to seek the deeper meaning of what he remembers. The psychoanalytic therapy may be seen as involving a continual meaning retroaction: "It must not be forgotten that the meaning of things one hears is, at all events for the most part, only recognizable later on [Freud, 1963, p. 118]." The aim of the therapy is, through qualitatively changing the patient's understanding of his past, to alter his present neurotic modes of relating to the world.

Psychoanalytic *therapy* need not only be understood from the psychoanalytic *theory* of an inner mental apparatus, but may be subjected to a phenomenological and behavioral reinterpretation. Habermas (1971), who discards the "scientistic self-misunderstanding" of psychoanalytic theory, has even supported the psychoanalytic situation as a research paradigm for a critical social science, as it involves a dialectic of understanding and explanation subordinated to an emancipatory knowledge interest.

From a phenomenological viewpoint, Laing (1961) rejects the elaborate constructions by psychoanalytic theory of an inner mental apparatus. He dismisses the dualism of an inner, mental and an outer, physical world and points to the many imaginary problems that arise when attempting to explain a continual shuttle service between an inner and an outer world by theoretical constructions such as "introjection," "projection" and "conversion." Laing suggests that the spatial inner–outer model be replaced by a distinction between a private and a public mode of experience.

On the basis of Heidegger's philosophy of existence, Boss (1963) criticizes the psychoanalytic understanding of neurotic behavior as mere outer manifestations or symptoms of some inner repressed ideas. A person's mental state is not hidden in some inner psychic locality but presents itself in the relations of a person to his world. One fulfills one's existence in and as one or the other mode of behavior in regard to an object or a person. One is fundamentally "out in the world" and with the "things" he encounters. "The patient is 'outside' from the start, i.e., he exists from the outset within and as his neurotic behavior to the world [from *Psychoanalysis & Daseinsanalysis* by Medard Boss, translated by Ludwig B. Lefebre, © Basic Books Inc., Publishers, New York]."

"Transference" is to Boss no unconscious transfer of some stored childhood perceptions and feelings to the therapist. Rather, the patient is limited to childlike modes of experiencing the world and acting upon it. His human situation is constricted and similar to a child's; he is open only to the father- and mother-like aspects of the men and women he encounters; and he behaves toward the therapist as if he or she were his parent. In the transference relation of the psychoanalytic situation the patient thus reactivates certain childlike ways of behaving.

To Skinner (1953, 1961) the subject matter of psychoanalytic therapy is neurotic behavior. The radical behaviorist position does not accept neurotic behavior as mere behavioral expressions or symptoms of some more basic postulated inner states, as, for example, a conflict between the id and the superego. Such a reified conception of neurosis has encouraged the therapist to avoid specifying the behavior that is to be corrected or stating why it is disadvantageous. The constructive contribution of psychoanalysis is the demonstration that many features of behavior that appeared meaningless could be explained as the product of circumstances in the history of the individual. And this history is not stored in some mental apparatus inside the person, but exists here and now as a behavioral repertoire. "What has survived through the years is not aggression and guilt, later to be manifested in behavior, but rather patterns of behavior themselves [Skinner, 1961, p. 191]."

Both radical phenomenology and behaviorism discard the notion of memory as some inner mental apparatus and instead focus on remembering as an activity of a subject in the world. Phenomenology has mainly analyzed the consciousness of a remembering person from a first-person view, and radical behaviorism has mainly treated the behavior of recall from a third-person view; emphasizing, respectively, the intentionality and the functionality of remembering activity.

III. The Reification of Memory

Before turning to some research applications of a dialectical perspective, I shall contrast the relational conception of remembering to the reification of memory in current psychological research. The internal unity of the stream of behavior and consciousness is fragmented into isolated elements to be assembled mechanically. Remembering as a relation of a subject to the world is dichotomized into an inner memory apparatus and its external behavioral manifestations.

The temporal and social aspects of remembering as a dialectical interaction with the world, when recognized at all, have generally been relegated to either a naive, artistic, or a philosophical, speculative sphere. I shall now point out some philosophical and social presuppositions of two conceptions that have dominated psychological memory research: the assembly-line model and the bureaucratic model of memory.

A. The Assembly-Line Model of Memory

The work at an assembly line consists of mechanical operations upon isolated fragments of a larger project, the worker is often without insight into the totality that his monotonous and repetitive work enters; he is controlled by the time pressure of the assembly line; individual creativity is a source of error; what matters is the quantitative output of standardized products.

The psychological research on memory, instigated by Ebbinghaus, has often "preformed" the experimental subjects' remembering activity, in correspondence with the workers' behavior at the assembly lines of industry, by techniques such as: (1) *fragmentation*—the learning and remembering required of the subjects are usually mechanical responses to isolated fragments, often lists of nonsense syllables and words; (2) *indoctrination*—the experimental instructions demand that the subjects learn mechanically by rote and refrain from contextualizing the material to be remembered; (3) *time pressure*—learning and remembering take place under the time pressure of a memory drum, making any search for meaning difficult; and (4) *quantification*—the products of the subjects' remembering activity are quantified and combined into anonymous group averages, while possible qualitative and creative changes are dismissed as sources of error (Kvale, 1975). However, while the fragmented work at the assembly line results in a final integrated product, the nature of the final result of the mechanical memorizing is more vague.

Those aspects of remembering that are essential in a dialectical perspective are systematically sliced away by the assembly-line techniques of tailoring the empirical data to an empiricist conception of consciousness and behavior. The empiricist philosophers postulated some elementary, meaningless sense data of consciousness, which were sought by the introspectionist psychologists. Ebbinghaus externalized these sense data as nonsense syllables and made them the subject of experimental investigation. James' critique of introspective psychology for neglecting the fleeting and vague internal relations of the stream of consciousness still appears valid to the externalized introspection of the memory laboratories. Within the verbal-learning tradition classical behaviorists and cognitivists are engaged in controversies about how the paired associates learned at the memory drums are stored—by mechanical associations or by a hierarchical organizing. Their common basis is the conception of memory as a collection of isolated and finished things, which have to be combined by external connections.

If the empiristic sense-data theory of consciousness were true, the assembly-line research would have a certain validity as giving access to the pure sense data and the ensuing memory traces as the basic atoms of memory, undisturbed by the complexities of remembering in daily life. If, however, this atomistic philosophy of consciousness is discarded in favor of a conception of remembering as a dialectical interaction with the world, a large share of psychological memory experiments are reduced to a collection of laboratory curiosities.

The assembly-line approach has dominated memory research for a long time. As recently as 1972, nearly 80% of the memory experiments reported in the *Journal of Verbal Learning and Verbal Behavior* were based on the assemblage of fragmented units, such as lists of words, nonsense syllables, letters, and so forth. The mechanical assembly-line model is, however, gradually becoming outdated and is today being replaced by more sophisticated cognitive bureaucratic models.

B. The Bureaucratic Model of Memory

Bureaucracy is characterized by fixed structures and stable elements. Written documents make out a basic element in bureaucratic work, documents that may be stored and retrieved from the archives when required for a specific case. A bureaucracy is divided into separate and distinct departments, with formal lines of communication between departments. Bureaucratic processes are impersonal and anonymous. Work in a bureaucracy is regulated by fixed schedules and formal operations, with quantification as a general trait. The time of the bureaucracy is clock time—one-dimensional, divisible into the smallest elements, and quantifiable.

Current memory research often involves the conception of memory traces stored in some inner mental apparatus, with separate boxes for a short-term and a long-term memory. The bookkeeping models involve a hierarchical organization of memory, from which the traces required for a specific case may be obtained by complex retrieval procedures. The remembering subject is absent in these models or replaced by some inner homunculi. Remembering consists of the stimulating of anonymous third-person processes that produce certain responses. The psychology of memory has become the science of a mental bureaucracy.

> We view the cognitive processing structure as one that consists of a multilayered assemblage of experts. Each expert is a process that knows how to handle the data and suggestions provided it. . . . The entire system consists of a multiplicity of hierarchies of experts, each expert working on its own aspect of processing, interpreting and predicting the data which are available to it, shipping requests to higher processes, and expectations of inputs to lower ones [Bobrow & Norman, 1975, pp. 145–146].

The existence of separate memory traces resting permanently in an inner warehouse has been a central postulate of the bureaucratic models.

> A special implication of the inhibition hypothesis is that memory is permanent—forgetting is only a matter of building inhibition, and the traces themselves are left completely intact [from *Human Memory* by J. A. Adams. Copyright 1976 by McGraw-Hill. Used with permission of McGraw-Hill Book Company].

> The theory of the permanent storage is a logical extension of EPAM suggested to the theorist as a resolution of certain difficulties with the present model [Feigenbaum, 1970, p. 467].

The *permanent storage of memory traces* is the result of theoretical speculations; the authors admit that there is not much empirical evidence to support it, and "the ways of testing it are foggy at the moment" (Adams, 1967, p. 37). The permanent memory hypothesis may in principle be unrefutable, as all empirical evidence of reproductions changed from the original stimuli can be attributed to either the perceptual process or interference with the reproduction process, while the pure permanent memory traces reside undisturbed in an inner, inaccessible storehouse (cf. e.g., the dispute over the effect of language upon the reproduction of ambiguous visual figures after the experiment by Carmichael, Hogan, & Walter, 1932; see Kvale, 1974a). The observed activity is reduced to external manifestations of some supposed inner entities, which have hardly any empirical evidence and which may in principle be untestable. The requirements of speculative theories have, in the empiristic tradition, obtained priority over the empirically observable remembering activity.

The concept of memory traces appears to involve circular reasoning. The only access we have to memory traces is through remembering activity, and the evocation of memory traces to explain this activity gives no extra information. The belief in memory traces may in part be due to a contamination of a first- and a third-person perspective. To the remembering person there exists no memory traces that are retrieved from a storehouse. He is not searching and reading memory traces in some inner library (Straus, 1967, 1970). He is in an imaginary relation directed toward a not-present situation or object; he is "imaginary present" by the content he is remembering (Sartre, 1961). An observer cannot directly "share" the content of the other person's remembering activity, but he can learn about the remembered object through his verbal account. The observer may then make the error of believing that the final product of the other's remembering activity has been stored all the time as a memory trace in an inner container. The observer's error consists of taking the final product of a remembering process (or the "building blocks" of this product)—the reproduction—as its starting point.

In a dialectical conception of remembering as a relationship there are no memory traces, no things or copies stored in an inner bank. Rather, a person's behavioral repertoire and possibilities have been altered by his past experiences. This involves, of course, physiological changes in the organism, but these need not be in the form of a library or picture album the remembering person is inspecting. The person has been changed through his experience so that he may re-produce, re-construct, re-cognize more or less vivid and accurate earlier experiences and also communicate them to others. By systematic investigations of remembering as a subject's interaction with the world, applying phenomenological descriptions and experimental studies, the recourse to an inner bureaucracy as explanation of observable remembering activity may become superfluous.

While a main contribution of assembly-line research has been to make the psychology of memory an arid desert, there are some trends within recent computer-oriented research toward investigating more interesting phenomena closer to the remembering of daily life. The effects of instructions, the remembering of stretegies, and the coding of processes for prose passages are increasingly coming into focus in research. The confrontation of computer simulation with the complexities of understanding and remembering natural language brings up aspects of remembering that are central in a dialectical approach, such as the temporal dimension of understanding, the issue of when an interpretation is final, and the problem of continual changes of contexts for understanding (Schank & Colby, 1973; Bobrow & Collins, 1975). In common with psychoanalysis, however, the focus on important phenomena of the lived world has been accompanied by a theoretical flight to some substantialized inner mental bureaucracy.

It is sometimes difficult to know how metaphorical and realistic the bureaucratic memory models are intended (cf. Reese, 1973). In some cases the inner bureaucracy has lost its status of a hypothetical model and obtained a reality of its own. The remembering activity from which it was inferred in the first place is reduced to mere outer manifestations of some more basic inner entity. While Freud explicitly stated the real existence of the mental apparatus he was studying, current cognitive theories are often more vague on the reality status of their mental bureaucracies.

From the present viewpoint, a main critique of bureaucratic memory models—regardless of whether they are intended metaphorically or realistically—is not the many logical problems they create, but the diversion of intensive research efforts into guessing about the structure and functioning of metaphysical memory castles. With some minor exceptions, research is led away from studying remembering as an interaction with a social and historical world and the practical possibilities of influencing remembering activity.

More than 25 years ago Skinner posed the question "Are theories of learning necessary?" and concluded that the ruling theories of learning were irrelevant for understanding and improving learning. Today the question "Are theories of memory necessary?" may be answered in a similar way. It is rather difficult to find any substantial practical contributions of the enormous output generated by the assembly-line and bureaucratic models of memory. With respect to school learning, it has even been maintained with the well-rehearsed findings of rote learning and retroactive interference in memory are not only irrelevant, but may also be directly erroneous if applied to the meaningful learning and remembering in the school situation (Ausubel & Robinson, 1969). It is possible that theories of learning may have mainly provided an ideological legitimation of a technological approach to learning (Kvale, 1976b).

C. The Material Context of the Reification of Memory

Because the long history of scientific arguments against the empiricist reification of experience and remembering has had so little influence, it becomes relevant to investigate possible extrascientific contexts supporting this tradition. We may ask about the nature of an epoch that should choose to conceive of memory as a mechanical apparatus, as a warehouse, or as a bank box.

Empiricist and positivist psychology has tended to regard mental life as the manifestations of some ahistorical and asocial inner entities. Ancient philosophers, however, conceived of an internal unity of reason and society. One example may be indicated: the concept of *hierarchy,* which is rather central in current cognitive models of memory. Hierarchy meant originally a rule by priests and was developed as a philosophical concept by Dionysios Aeropagitas (1911) in the fifth century A.D. Hierarchy depicts a rigidly organized pyramidal structure, with knowledge and power distributed from top to bottom. Dionysios conceived of a hierarchy as a holy structure, a holy unity of reason and action. He postulated a hierarchical structure in heaven and on earth. The society of angels was divided into nine levels of drones, cherubs, serafs, and the like. The society of men was organized in an analogous hierarchy, and the higher the position in the earthly hierarchy, the greater the quotient of reason.

It would be an interesting task to analyze the possible relations of the current hierarchical models of cognition in terms of Dionysios' hierarchies of angels, men, and reason. In the present context, the main point is that previous thinkers saw a relation between social structure and thought, a connection that has been lost in current positivist psychology. However, the founder of positivist philosophy and the science of sociology, Comte, explicitly advocated positivism as a mode of thought for a hierarchical society (Samelson, 1974). Comte's "sociocracy" was to be ruled by industrialists and bankers and with a positivist scientist priesthood taking care of ideology and seeing to it that the workers were kept in their place. In contrast to later adherents of positivism, Comte emphasized the inner unity of positivist politics and methodology, conceiving both as weapons against rising communism.

Positivist psychology is characterized by a fetishization of facts, where human activity is transformed to reified, fixed, and isolated data (Kvale, 1976a). According to Lukacs (1971), the facts represent a crystallization of capitalist development into an ossified, impenetrable thing alienated from man. The products of human activity appear as something objective, as independent of human action; essentially socially determined relations are presented in a disguised form as relations between things.

Current memory research often involves a transformation of a socially determined remembering activity into a thing or to fragmented and anonymous processes taking place in some inner mental apparatus from which the remembering subject disappears. The modeling of memory after the computer is today openly stated in the bureaucratic memory models. The assembly line has not been an explicit paradigm for memory research. Some structural similarities between the mechanical laboratory study of nonsense syllables, in the Ebbinghaus tradition, and the human engineering developed by the engineer Taylor in American factories before the turn of the 19th century may, however, be indicated (Kvale, 1975). Starting with systematic "time and motion" observations of the workers' behavior, Taylor developed a system of scientific management by fragmenting and isolating the work operations, by transferring the mental parts of the tasks from workers to management (working out minutely detailed job cards for the workers to be followed at a prescribed speed), and by strictly quantifying both the operations and the outcome. The Taylorization of industry was later perfected by Ford's invention of the assembly line.

I am not positing any conscious adjustment of the psychologists of the Ebbinghaus tradition to the assembly line of industry; I am suggesting merely that empiricist philosophy, the mechanical natural science method of psychology, and the human engineering of industry are all aspects of a general technologizing of society, where the development of the material forces and relations of production are of primary importance (Kvale, 1973). In correspondence with the gradual change of industrial work from the mechanical, repetitive operations on the assembly line to the more complex organizational and computerized work today, the assembly-line paradigm in psychology is gradually being replaced by the bureaucratic computer models of mental life. In short, this tentative material situating of memory research, which needs to be supported by systematic historical studies, indicates that it is not natural science, but the history of industry that has provided the basic paradigm for memory research.

The apparent artificiality of psychological memory research, then, needs to be reconsidered. It is possible that rote learning at the memory drum is not so unrepresentative of the daily work situation at an assembly line, nor are the bureaucratic computer models so artificial when compared with the job situation of an office employee. The assembly-line and the bureaucratic memory models may reflect, in a transformed mode, essential aspects of the world of modern work. Empiristic memory research reflects the technological world, however, in a concealed form; that is, as an ahistoric and asocial technical approach to a "natural" memory conceived as a mental apparatus.

IV. Research Applications of a Dialectical Perspective

Dialectical thinking also reflects a social and historical context. In contrast to empiricist and positivist psychology, however, dialectics attempts to make the relations of social conditions and remembering activity—and memory research—conscious, and attempts to study these relations, and to work for change in the social conditions that reinforce repressive human relations.

A. Some Aspects of a Dialectical Approach

Some general aspects of a dialectical approach to remembering may be outlined in eight points:

1. Dialectics conceives of remembering as a *relation* of a subject to a world, the subject affecting and being affected by this interaction.

2. Dialectics studies the *consciousness* and the *behavioral* aspects of remembering activity. The private, invisible aspect of remembering from a first-person perspective and the public, visible aspect of remembering activity from a third-person perspective are considered as mutually implying and excluding each other. Both aspects are included in a dialectical approach; neither is reduced to the other.

3. Dialectics does not imply that philosophical speculation replaces empirical investigations. On the contrary, a *propaedeutic* contribution of a dialectical approach would be to relieve the psychology of memory of the many pseudoproblems brought up by the metaphysical empiristic models of memory.

4. A dialectical analysis proceeds by *dividing a totality into parts,* but in contrast to the empiricist reification of the parts as finished and isolated things—or facts—in themselves, dialectics conceives of the parts as aspects of a broader and developing totality, to which they must again be related.

5. Dialectics does not involve a new or specific *research method* but may, in the investigation of man's interaction with a historical and social world, include

phenomenological descriptions and experimental investigations, and qualitative analysis and quantitative studies.

6. The *temporality* of remembering, with its net of past, present, and future relations, is studied in relation to a developing, historical world.

7. The *social* shaping and functions of remembering within a conflicting social world is a main theme of study.

8. Remembering activity, as well as research on memory, is related to the contradictions of the *material basis* of society.

I am not in a position to present a systematic dialectical analysis of remembering in terms of this tentative outline. I shall only indicate some areas where dialectics may be applied, such as the "error sources" of the empiricist tradition, Bartlett's study of remembering as a search for meaning, and finally some implications of remembering conceived as an interaction with a historical and social world.

B. Empiristic Sources of Error Reinterpreted

From a dialectical perspective, the multitude of sources of error in the Ebbing-haus tradition may be read as an open book in essential aspects of remembering. The ingenious methods to rid laboratory studies of meaning point to a search for meaning as a major trait of remembering. The systematic techniques to prevent the subjects from contextualizing disconnected material suggests contextualizing as an important aspect of remembering. The attempt to rule out the influence of individual history by construction of nonsense syllables indicates that remembering is internally related to an individual's life history.

It is possible that by a more systematic *figure/ground reversal* of error sources of the empiristic tradition, they may no longer appear as noise disturbing the research of a pure memory but rather as essential aspects of remembering situated in a social and historical world. These error sources and the empiricist resistance techniques against seeing remembering as a search for meaning in a social and historical world may perhaps be read as indications of more general techniques of the fragmentation of the meaning of experience and behavior in a technological society.

C. Bartlett—Remembering as a Search for Meaning

In Bartlett's (1932) studies of remembering in natural settings, the error sources of the empiristic tradition appear as main aspects of remembering as a search for meaning, embedded in the individual's life history and social situation. Bartlett criticizes the tendency to use the psychological experiment chiefly as a buttress to some all-embracing philosophical theory. To Bartlett, remembering is a function of daily life and has developed to meet the demands of the life world. Remembering serves a biological function in a ceaseless struggle to master and enjoy a world full of variety and rapid change. In accordance with this functional approach, Bartlett investigated remembering outside the artificial laboratories by realistic experimentation close to daily situations and firsthand social observation, including ethnographical investigations. He studied remembering as a specific reaction of a whole subject reacting, considering recall as a form of behavior as well as including the images reported by the subjects.

Remembering is essentially an effort after meaning, an attempt to connect what is given with something else, a characteristic of every human cognitive reaction. The notion of memory as a storehouse of past impressions is merely an unpleasant fiction. Remembering is not the reexiting of fixed, lifeless, and fragmented traces, but rather an imaginative reconstruction. Literal reproduction is the exception in the remembering of daily life; it is mainly an artificial construction of the armchair or of the laboratory. Bartlett conceives of remembering as consisting of "schemas," as organizations of past reactions and past experiences, and as active, living, and developing patterns. The remembering we are able to study always occurs in some social setting, except, maybe, for that which occurs in certain rather abstract psychological experiments. Both the manner and the matter of recall are influenced by social conditions, alike with the individual and with the group; the past is being continually remade, reconstructed in the interests of the present.

Although Bartlett's empirical findings are easily reproducible and have considerable ecological validity, they have not instigated any major research tradition comparable, for example, to the verbal-learning tradition after Ebbinghaus. This may be due to the contrast of his conception of remembering as an activity with the empiristic reification of memory. The study of remembering as a search for meaning contrasts with the mechanical natural science experimentation of the verbal-learning tradition. Some aspects of Bartlett's approach to remembering come close to the hermeneutic method of the humanities. Hermeneutics concerns procedures for the methodical interpretation of the meaning of written texts in relation to a social and historical context (Giorgi, 1970; Radnitzky, 1970). A further reason for the relative neglect of Bartlett's study of remembering, except insofar as he is quoted as a classic, may be the lack of a systematic framework for investigating the consciousness and behavioral aspects of remembering as an interaction with a changing social world. Such a systematic framework may be provided by Husserl's phenomenological analysis of a remembering consciousness and by Skinner's functional analysis of operant behavior, both understood as giving access to different aspects of remembering as a dialectical relation to a social and historical world.

Within the psychological tradition of memory research, several investigators have focused on some aspects of Bartlett's comprehensive approach to remembering. Hunter (1964) and Miller (1966) conceive of remembering as an activity; Miller criticizes the common reification of memory into a warehouse, while still retaining an information-storage model of memory. Neisser (1967) also conceives of remembering as an activity, and he criticizes, in relation to James, empiricism's "reappearance" hypothesis of memory, suggesting that it be replaced instead by a "utilization" hypothesis. Paivio (1971) has investigated imagery and meaning in memory; Bobrow and Norman (1975) have criticized the context-independent linkage of the common list structures, emphasized context-dependent descriptions, and postulated "event-driven" schemata. Jenkins (1974) discards the empiricist associationism, which he maintains has become almost coextensive with the experimental method in American psychology. Jenkins advocates a contextualist, pragmatist approach to memory, which comes close to the dialectical approach advocated here but misses the emphasis on contradictions and the social and material context of remembering.

These trends in memory research deal with important aspects of remembering as an active search for meaning. They reject the empiricist assembly-line approach. Some apply the bureaucratic memory models, while others reject them. While involving important trends toward a more ecologically valid memory research, these forms of "meaning revisionism" have generally been confined to the experimental laboratory. They have stopped short of Bartlett's more comprehensive understanding of the functions of remembering within a changing social world.

From a dialectical perspective, Bartlett's analysis of remembering as an interaction with the world has not been carried far enough. His biological functionalism has neglected the specific temporality of remembering in relation to a historical world as well as the possibilities of remembering that serve socially oppressive, and liberating, functions. I shall now conclude by giving some examples of remembering as an aspect of the complex "interactions between psychoindividual and sociocultural changes" (Riegel, 1973).

D. The Temporality of Remembering in a Historical World

The above analyses of the stream of consciousness and of behavior both led to the conception of a memory in continuous flux. The complexities involved in the temporality of our relating to past events appear to be more recognized with respect to autobiographies and the writing of history than they are to the psychology of memory.

Autobiographical memory is part of a person's present projects. Berger and Luckmann (1967) discuss meaning retroaction in respect to personal remembering after a conversion. Everything preceding the radical conversion is now apprehended as leading toward it, which involves a reinterpretation of past biography *in toto*. Frequently this indicates the retrojection into the past of present interpretative schemata that were not subjectively present in the past but are now necessary for the reinterpretation of what took place then.

G. H. Mead (1932) has analyzed the writing of the history of the universe in relation to current physical and astronomical research. There exists no real past independent of the reconstruction from present scientific activities. Past and future refer to the activity that is central to the present. And the novelty of every future demands a novel past. The present accepts that which is novel as an essential part of the universe and from that standpoint rewrites its past. For instance, the present history of the sun is relevant to the present understanding of the atom, and given another analysis of the atom, the sun will have another history, and the universe will be launched into a new future. To Mead "the import of all histories lies in the interpretation and control of the present [p. 28]." In G. Orwell's *Nineteen Eighty-Four* (1954) history is continually rewritten, as the mutability of the past has become a technique of political manipulation. " 'Who controls the past' ran the Party slogan, 'controls the future: who controls the present controls the past' [p. 31]."

For historical understanding it has been emphasized that the meaning of past texts and events cannot be understood independently of the succeeding events (Habermas, 1967). The historian's hermeneutic understanding recognizes that the meaning of the past is continually understood through new retrospectives, which involves a principal undeterminedness of the context for understanding. Also for the ordinary citizen remembering historical events, this retroactive reordering of originally ambiguous events through later knowledge may take on an "automatic" character, for example, when recalling the original news of the Tet Offensive today, it may be difficult to suppress the hindsight that it was the beginning of the communist victory in Vietnam.

Some implications of such hindsight for remembering of political events have been investigated empirically. Thus, a person's remembering of an original uncertain and upcoming event, such as the outcome of Nixon's trip to China, was found to be subject to retroactive influence from the later knowledge of how the trip actually turned out (Fischhoff, 1975; Fischhoff & Beyth, 1975). The influence of later events upon the remembering of earlier events has been given due emphasis in the psychology of testimony, for example, in connection with the problem of leading questions (Lofthus & Palmer, 1974). Such studies have, however, generally been relegated to some "mere" applied psychology and have been considered irrelevant to the scientific studies of a "pure" and "permanent" memory. A related attitude has been displayed toward studies of the social functions of remembering.

E. The Social Shaping and Functions of Remembering

The social functions and shaping of different types of remembering activity may be exemplified by Schachtel's psychoanalytic study of childhood amnesia, by Freire's banking concept of education, and by the forms of remembering reinforced by examinations.

Schachtel (1959) explicitly relates forms of remembering and forgetting to conflicts in man and society, treating especially the marked adult forgetting of childhood experiences. He dismisses the impersonal and artificial memory experimentation as more appropriate for investigations of a mental apparatus than for understanding the function of memory in a living person; the human function of remembering was not developed in order to make possible the recall of nonsense.

On the basis of Proust's and Freud's studies of autobiographical memory, Schachtel interprets childhood amnesia as due to the cultural repression of the freer mode of experiencing in childhood. In a repressive technological society it is necessary that the remembrance of a time in which a fuller, freer, and more spontaneous life be extinguished. The conventionalized memory schemata of adults are not suitable for the recall of a radically different childhood mode of experience. Schachtel here points to Bartlett's findings of the gradual distortion of experience into stereotyped and conventionalized reproductions.

Schachtel posits the repression of individually and culturally tabooed experiences studied in psychoanalysis as subordinated the gradual and insidious process of education. The conventionalized experience schemata provided by education make it difficult to recall the transschematic experience of childhood, which contains the potentiality of a free personality but which would be a threat to a repressive society.

Freire (1973) has given a sharp critique of the repressive forms of Western education. On the basis of Husserl's and Sartre's phenomenological analysis of consciousness and of Marx's political analysis he attacks the *banking concept of education,* which comes rather close to what has been described here as the bureaucratic memory model. The pupils are thought of as containers, with a consciousness similar to an empty vessel waiting to be filled with knowledge. This "eating epistemology" implies a dichotomy between man and world, where knowledge is considered to be a reception of deposits from the outer world to be stored somewhere inside the pupil. It implies a mechanical and static container conception of consciousness and conceives of reality as static, compartmentalized, and predictable. The teacher makes deposits of information in the pupil's memory bank, which the student passively receives, memorizes, and repeats.

The banking approach to education turns pupils into automatons, into adaptable and manageable beings, and hampers the development of a critical consciousness and a liberating praxis: the action and reflection of men upon the world in order to transform it. The dialectical relation of men with the world involves

> men as beings in the process of *becoming*—as unfinished, uncompleted beings in and with a likewise unfinished reality. . . . The banking method emphasizes permanence and becomes reactionary; problem-posing education—which accepts neither a "well-behaved" present nor a predetermined future—roots itself in the dynamic present and becomes revolutionary [Freire, 1973, p. 56–57].

It is possible that the bureaucratic memory models of psychological research are not merely metaphysical castles in the air but may rather, in a concealed form, reflect a repressive reality of education, which they may again support, albeit in a minor way, by providing this repression with a scientific legitimation.

The banking concept of education is not just a metaphor. Today the structure of the educational system is increasingly being formed from the perspective of the "economics of education" (Blaug, 1968), with educational technology as one important means of reducing investments in education. One aspect of the more comprehensive "Taylorization of education" (Bruder, 1971) shall be discussed here—the effects of multiple choice tests upon remembering activity.

A pupil's success in the educational system depends upon his remembering activity in a well-controlled examination situation (Kvale, 1977). It is thus conceivable that the content and form of an examination may reinforce specific forms of remembering. Standardized testing with multiple choice tests has acquired a strong position in education. It has been estimated that in the United States about 200 million standardized tests are taken by about 45 million pupils a year, making an average of about four tests per pupil per year (Kirkland, 1971). These tests generally measure isolated bits of knowledge, to be checked as either true or false, often under time pressure, and with the number of correct items quantified. When examinations function as the goal of learning, the examination behavior determining access to further education, the structure of the multiple choice tests may reinforce an atomistic and mechanical learning. There does not exist much empirical research on this issue, but some observations and a few experiments suggest that the multiple choice tests reinforce a superficial rote recognition of disconnected items of knowledge, whereas essay examinations reinforce a search for broad concepts and general principles (Ausubel & Robinson, 1969; Balch, 1964; Kirkland, 1971).

The contingencies of reinforcement involved by multiple choice tests would appear to be a central subject for recent trends in radical behaviorism toward the study of behavior modification in natural settings. While Skinner's general approach implies a relational concept of remembering, it is possible that the programmed teaching he instigated may reinforce a mechanical remembering of fragmented items. It appears somewhat remarkable that the effects of such common and socially important remembering situations as examinations have not been investigated as intensively as has, for example, the serial position effect in the learning of nonsense syllables.

Discarding the laboratory studies of list learning in favor of remembering in natural environments need not imply a reliance on subjective impressions and anecdotes. It is precisely the well-controlled examination situation, where the natural world has become adapted to the experimental laboratory, as with TV-administered and computer-scored multiple choice tests, that should secure experimental rigor. Perhaps this form of natural laboratory situation has been ignored, because it was considered irrelevant to the search for a "pure" memory, uncontaminated by the social and historical context of remembering. Or perhaps the remembering behavior reinforced by the multiple choice tests has gone unnoticed because it is in harmony with the assembly-line model of memory and the banking concept of education.

Further relevant topics for research on the social functions of remembering would be the recall of *news* and *advertisements*. One hypothesis for investigation would be whether the common presentation of news preforms the material in accordance with the assembly-line model of remembering, with fragmentation, indoctrination, time pressure, and quantification as main techniques. In the United States, newspapers, radio, and television are financed by advertisements, based on the presupposition that the commercials are remembered in a form that leads to significant increases in buying behavior. However, the types of remembering involved by news and commercials have received little attention within academic memory research.

V. Conclusion

I have not been able to present here a systematically developed dialectical perspective on memory research. Some aspects of a dialectical approach have been indicated, starting with a possible complementarity of radical phenomenological and behavioral approaches to remembering. The reification of remembering in the common assembly-line and bureaucratic approaches to memory were discarded in favor of the conception of remembering as one aspect of man's dialectical relation to the world. The inner mental memory apparatuses of the psychoanalytic and cognitive theories of memory were argued to be no more empirically based than the angels and devils of medieval theology, also believed to interfere with human affairs. Perhaps one major contribution of a dialectical approach would be the abandonment of the many imaginary problems created by the belief in heavenly or inner entities, such as the scholastic disputes of how many angels can dance on a pin point or how many memory compartments exist in the inner mental apparatus. The existence of such hypothetical entities cannot be falsified empirically, but they may lose general interest as empirical knowledge is increased regarding how human action is formed by an environment that is largely of our own making. Within this dialectical perspective, the functions of remembering in a social and historical world become a major research topic, with a focus on the repressive and progressive aspects of specific remembering activities. The basic alternative to the reification of memory in psychology is not a new theory of memory, but a society where it no longer appears natural for a science to conceive of remembering as a mere external manifestation of an inner mental apparatus, warehouse, or bank box.

REFERENCES

Adams, J. A. *Human memory.* New York: McGraw-Hill, 1967.
Ausubel, D. P., & Robinson, F. G. *School learning.* New York: Holt, 1969.
Balch, J. The influence of the evaluating instrument on students' learning. *American Educational Research Journal,* 1964, **1**, 169–182.
Barker, R. A. *The stream of behavior.* New York: Appleton, 1963.
Bartlett, F. C. *Remembering: a study in experimental and social psychology.* Cambridge: University Press, 1932.
Berger, P. L., & Luckmann, T. *The social construction of reality.* New York: Doubleday, 1967.
Blaug, M. (Ed.). *Economics of education.* London: Penguin Books, 1968.
Bobrow, D. G., & Collins, A. *Representation and understanding.* New York: Academic Press, 1975.
Bobrow, D. G., & Norman, D. A. Some principles of memory schemata. In D. G. Bobrow & A. Collins (Eds.), *Representation and understanding.* New York: Academic Press, 1975.
Boss, M. *Psychoanalysis and Daseinanalysis.* New York: Basic Books, 1963.
Bruder, K.-J. Taylorisierung des Unterrichts. Zur Kritik der Instruktionspsychologie. *Kursbuch,* 1971, **24**, 113–130.
Carmichael, L., Hogan, P. H., & Walter, A. A. An experimental study of the effect of language on the reproduction of visually perceived form. *Journal of Experimental Psychology,* 1932, **15**, 73–86.

Day, W. F. Radical behaviorism in reconciliation with phenomenology. *Journal of the Experimental Analysis of Behavior,* 1969, **12**, 315–328.

Dewey, J. The reflex arc conception in psychology. *Psychological Review,* 1896, **3**, 357–370.

Dionysios Aeropagitas. *Angebliche Schriften über die beiden Hierarchien.* Munich: Käsel, 1911.

Feigenbaum, E. A. Information processing and memory. In D. A. Norman (Ed.), *Models of human memory.* New York: Academic Press, 1970.

Fischhoff, B. Hindsight ≠ foresight. *Journal of Experimental Psychology: Human Perception and Performance,* 1975, **1**, 288–299.

Fischhoff, B., & Beyth, R. "I knew it would happen." *Organizational Behavior and Human Performance,* 1975, **13**, 1–16.

Freire, P. *Pedagogy of the oppressed.* London: Penguin Books, 1973.

Freud, S. *Therapy and technique.* New York: Collier, 1963.

From, F. *Perception of other people.* New York: Columbia University Press, 1971.

Giorgi, A. *Psychology as a human science.* New York: Harper, 1970.

Giorgi, A. Convergences and divergences between phenomenological psychology and behaviorism: A beginning dialogue. *Behaviorism,* 1975, **3**, 200–212.

Habermas, J. Zur Logik der Sozialwissenschaften. *Philosophische Rundschau,* 1967, Sonderheft.

Habermas, J. *Knowledge and human interests.* Boston: Beacon Press, 1971.

Hunter, I. M. L. *Memory.* London: Penguin Books, 1964.

Husserl, E. *The phenomenology of internal time consciousness.* Hague: Nijhoff, 1964.

James, W. *Psychology–briefer course.* Greenwich, Conn.: Premier Books, 1963.

Jenkins, J. J. Remember that old theory of memory? Well, forget it! *American Psychologist,* 1974, **29**, 785–795.

Kantor, J. R., & Smith, N. W. *The science of psychology–an interbehavioral survey.* Chicago: Principia Press, 1975.

Kirkland, M. C. The effects of tests on students and schools. *Review of Educational Research,* 1971, **41**, 303–350.

Kvale, S. The technological paradigm of psychological research. *Journal of Phenomenological Psychology,* 1973, **3**, 143–159.

Kvale, S. Permanence and change in memory, I. Reproduction and cognition of visual figures. *Scandinavian Journal of Psychology,* 1974, **15**, 33–42. (a)

Kvale, S. Permanence and change in memory, II. Reproduction of words in sentences. *Scandinavian Journal of Psychology,* 1974, **15**, 139–145. (b)

Kvale, S. The temporality of memory. *Journal of Phenomenological Psychology,* 1974, **5**, 7–31. (c)

Kvale, S. Memory and dialectics: Some reflections on Ebbinghaus and Mao Tse-tung. *Human Development,* 1975, **18**, 205–222.

Kvale, S. Facts and dialectics. In J. F. Rychlak (Ed.), *Dialectic: Humanistic rationale for behavior and development.* Basel: Karger, 1976. Pp. 87–100. (a)

Kvale, S. The psychology of learning as ideology and technology. *Behaviorism,* 1976, **4**, 97–116. (b)

Kvale, S. *Some notes on radical behaviorism and dialectical materialism.* Unpublished manuscript, Psykologisk Institut, Aarhus Universitet, 1976. (c)

Kvale, S. Examinations–from ritual through bureaucracy to technology. *Social Praxis,* 1977, **3**, 185–204.

Kvale, S., & Grenness, C. E. Skinner and Sartre: Towards a radical phenomenology of behavior? *Review of Existential Psychology and Psychiatry,* 1967, **7**, 128–150.

Laing, R. D. *The self and others.* London: Tavistock, 1961.

Lofthus, E. F., & Palmer, J. C. Reconstruction of automobile destruction: an example of the interaction between language and memory. *Journal of Verbal Learning and Behavior,* 1974, **13**, 585–589.

Lukacs, G. *History and class consciousness.* London: Merlin, 1971.

Malcolm, N. Behaviorism as a philosophy of psychology. In T. W. Wann (Ed.), *Behaviorism and phenomenology—Contrasting bases for modern psychology.* Chicago: Chicago University Press, 1964.

Malone, J. C. William James and B. F. Skinner: Behaviorism, reinforcement, and interest. *Behaviorism,* 1975, **3**, 140–151.

Mao Tse-tung *Four essays on philosophy.* Peking: Foreign Languages Press, 1968.

Meacham, J. A. The development of memory abilities in the individual and society. *Human Development,* 1972, **15**, 205–228.

Mead, G. H. *The philosophy of the present.* Chicago: Open Court, 1932.

Merleau-Ponty, M. *Phenomenology of perception.* London: Routledge & Kegan Paul, 1962.

Merleau-Ponty, M. *The structure of behavior.* Boston: Beacon Press, 1967.

Miller, G. *Psychology—the science of mental life.* London: Penguin Books, 1966.

Neisser, U. *Cognitive psychology.* New York: Appleton, 1967.

Orwell, G. *Nineteen eighty-four.* London: Penguin Books, 1954.

Paivio, A. *Imagery and verbal processes.* New York: Holt, 1971.

Radnitzky, G. *Contemporary schools of metascience.* Goeteborg: Scandinavian University Books, 1970.

Reese, H. W. Models of memory and models of development. *Human Development,* 1973, **16**, 397–416.

Riegel, K. F. The recall of historical events. *Behavioral Science,* 1973, **18**, 354–363.

Romanyshyn, R. D. *Phenomenological psychology and dialectical thinking.* Unpublished manuscript. Institute of Psychology, University of Dallas, 1975.

Rubinstein, S. L. *Prinzipien und Wege der Entwicklung der Psychologie.* Berlin: Akademie-Verlag, 1963.

Samelson, F. History, origin myth and ideology. *Journal for the Theory of Social Behaviour,* 1974, **4**, 217–231.

Sartre, J.-P. *The psychology of imagination.* New York: Citadel Press, 1961.

Schachtel, E. G. *Metamorphosis.* New York: Basic Books, 1959.

Schank, R. C., & Colby, K. M. *Computer models of thought and language.* San Francisco: Freeman, 1973.

Skinner, B. F. *Science and human behavior.* New York: Macmillan, 1953.

Skinner, B. F. *Cumulative record.* London: Methuen, 1961.

Skinner, B. F. *Contingencies of reinforcement.* New York: Appleton, 1969.

Skinner, B. F. *About behaviorism.* New York: Knopf, 1974.

Skinner, B. F. The steep and thorny way to a science of behavior. *American Psychologist,* 1975, **30**, 42–49.

Straus, E. On memory traces. In N. Lawrence & D. O'Connor (Eds.), *Readings in existential phenomenology.* Englewood Cliffs, N.J.: Prentice-Hall, 1967.

Straus, E. Phenomenology of memory. In E. Straus & R. M. Griffith (Eds.), *Phenomenology of memory.* Pittsburgh: Duquesne University Press, 1970.

CHAPTER 10

"Remembering" Is Alive and Well (and Even Thriving) in Empiricism[1]

ALEXANDER W. SIEGEL

UNIVERSITY OF PITTSBURGH
PITTSBURGH, PENNSYLVANIA

I. Introduction

Kvale's dialectical analysis of "remembering" and criticism of "memory" is both intellectually impressive and emotionally provoking. On a nonrational (some might argue subcortical) level, there is a feeling or quality rarely found in typical scholarly and critical analyses—passion. The passion is both exciting and irritating. Hegel (1956) argued that passion produces activity: "Passion—is that which sets men in activity, that which effects 'practical' realization [p. 38]." Furthermore, Hegel argued that nothing great is accomplished without passion:

> We assert then that nothing has been accomplished without interest on the part of the actors; and—if interest be called passion, inasmuch as the whole individuality, to the neglect of all other actual or possible interests and claims, is devoted to an object with every fibre of volition, concentrating all its desires and powers upon it—we may affirm absolutely that *nothing* Great in the World has been accomplished without passion [p. 38].

Using a kind of quasi-logic, I felt that indeed I had possibly read or heard something "great." Kvale's passionate plea for looking at remembering within a

[1] This paper was made possible by Grant No. HD-09694 from the National Institute of Child Health and Human Development.

dialectical perspective, as an activity, as a relation of the person to the world, as a dynamic search for meaning, resonates with my own frame of reference. A lucid presentation and critique of such diverse theoretical positions on remembering as those of Husserl, Skinner, Freud, and Bartlett is combined with a solid argument for the fruitfulness of the joint utilization of both first- and third-person approaches to the study of remembering. The paper flows—it persuades, it convinces. One's first thought upon reading it quickly is: "Of course. How obvious. How logical! How could things be otherwise?"

After letting the paper sink in and upon a more careful reading, I began to be able to articulate that which irritated me—a polemic, evangelistic tone that promises me forgiveness for my sins if I repent, go out into the real world, look at real-world activities, forsake my use of word lists and serial position procedures, and terminate my subscription to the *Journal of Experimental Child Psychology* forthwith. Not that I would not want to embrace *the* world view most comprehensive in scope and precise in nature. But somehow, in a paper dealing with the purported logical or cognitive bases for understanding and interpreting which are the "reals" of remembering (or memory), I find a polemic and dogmatic tone rather disturbing and unwarranted.

II. Dialectics and World Hypotheses

In a remarkable little book, Pepper (1970) argues that presently there are four world hypotheses of about equal adequacy: formism, mechanism, contextualism, and organicism. If my interpretation of Kvale's position is correct, then the world hypothesis Kvale has adopted, and from which follow his analyses, is fundamentally that of contextualism. The world hypothesis that Kvale cannot accept, and against which he directs his criticism, is mechanism.

Kvale spends a great deal of time arguing that the factors that are sources of "error" for researchers in the "empirical" tradition are those same phenomena that are the real, or essential, aspects of remembering from a dialectical perspective. Insofar as the cognitive grounds for Kvale's beliefs are equivalent to those for the mechanists' belief, to pretend otherwise is misleading. Pepper (1970) has argued this point most eloquently:

> It is illegitimate to disparage the factual interpretations of one world hypothesis in terms of the categories of another—if both hypotheses are equally adequate. . . . The . . . refined evidence of every one of these rather reliable world hypotheses has traditionally been presented and accepted as indubitable by the believers in these hypotheses. . . . One reason they have been so sure of themselves is that whichever of these hypotheses they have espoused, they have been able to give relatively adequate interpretations *in their* own terms of the refined evidence and categories of the other hypotheses. "You see," they say, "we are able to explain what these other mistaken philosophers have thought to be facts, and to show where the errors of their observations lay, how they rationalized their prejudices, accepting interpretations for acts and missing the real facts. Our hypothesis includes theirs and is accordingly the true account of the nature of things."

This would be a good argument if the other hypotheses were not equally well able to make the same argument. . . . What are pure facts for one theory are highly interpreted evidence for another [pp. 98–101. Copyright © 1970 by Stephen C. Pepper; reprinted by permission of the University of California Press.]

Kvale's criticisms of the mechanistic world view are cogent, and he correctly points to its shortcomings in terms of comprehensiveness. Nonetheless, it is not legitimate to assume that the claims of his (i.e., the contextualistic or dialectical) world hypothesis are established by the exhibition of the shortcomings of the mechanistic world view. Pepper refers to this fallacy as "clearing the ground":

It assumes that if a theory is not perfect it is no good, and that if all other suggested theories are no good, then the ground is clear for whatever one's own theory can produce. . . . This is so obvious a fallacy that it is remarkable it should be so frequently used and to such persuasive effect. Yet a great proportion of philosophical—and not only philosophical—books give a large part of their space to polemic, finding the faults in rival theories with an idea that this helps to establish the theory proposed. The cognitive value of a hypothesis is not one jot increased by the cognitive errors of other hypotheses. The only reason for referring to other theories in constructive cognitive endeavor is to find out what other evidence they may suggest, or other matters of positive cognitive value. We need all world hypotheses, so far as they are adequate, for mutual comparison and correction of interpretative bias [p. 101].

In short, although my own metatheoretical predilections are far closer to dialectics than to mechanism, I object to a mode of argument that insists that "that which my model specifies as not being a primary construct (e.g., a structure) is at best an 'epiphenomenon,' and at worst an 'unnecessary explanatory fiction.' " Thus, while I am impressed with the scholarly dissections and passion of the paper, for me to reject on the bases of polemic all theories of memory based on a mechanistic metaphor would run the serious risk of throwing out the baby with the bath water.

III. On the Necessity for Structure

I agree wholeheartedly with Kvale that Bartlett's (1932) emphasis on remembering as an activity occurring within a changing sociohistorical context is a critical one, and an emphasis frankly missing in psychology (until recently). I agree with Kvale's earlier comments (1975) that one of the greatest disservices to psychology was the labeling of Bartlett's studies as "classic" (implying that they are done, have somehow lost vitality, and thus have become ignored). It is important to recognize that memory is *not* a stagnant entity, the traces of which, forever immutable, reside somewhere in the cerebral neocortex. Demonstrations of this, whether by Husserl's "retentionalizing of impressions," Bartlett's "meaning retroaction," or Tulving's "encoding specificity," point clearly to the phenomenon of memory change. However, the conception of, and emphasis on remembering, "memory," and the stream of consciousness being in a continual flux appears to constitute far too drastic a figure/ground reversal. Somewhere, somehow there has to be constancy and stability in the system—even if this fixity is momentary. One of the miracles of human beings with operative nervous systems is that we are able to extract regularities and construct constancies from the flux—the question is not how constancy or stability breaks down, but how it is created in the first place!

I would argue that humans are both neurologically and phenomenologically predisposed to create such constancies, or momentary states or points of permanence, in the flow of consciousness. Bergson (1911) elaborates on this point:

> Our activity is fitted into the material world. . . . In order that our activity may leap from an *act* to an *act,* it is necessary that matter should pass from a *state* to a *state,* for it is only into a state of material world that action can fit a result, so as to be accomplished. . . . The primal function of perception is precisely to grasp a series of elementary changes under the form of a quality or of a simple state, by a work of condensation. . . . In short, the qualities of matter are so many stable views that we take of its instability [p. 302].

> We take snapshots, as it were, of the passing reality, and as these are characteristic of the reality, we have only to string them on a becoming, abstract, uniform and invisible, situated at the back of the apparatus of knowledge, in order to imitate what there is that is characteristic in this becoming itself . . . *the mechanism of our ordinary knowledge is of a cinematographical kind.* . . . Action is discontinuous, like every pulsation of life; discontinuous, therefore, is knowledge [pp. 306–307].

The notion of constructing constancy from the flux is also a main tenet of holistic structuralism, a theory having close connections with an antireductionistic or contextualistic metaphor. As Overton (1975) has argued, the problem for holistic structuralism is to:

> impose order and organization on the activity, thereby establishing a workable stability, or momentary constancy in the face of change. This does not in any way deny the basic dialectic nature of the universe, but rather it asserts the necessity of introducing organization for complete understanding. The significance of the introduction of an organization or system should be immediately apparent for form or organization is the "structure" to which structuralism makes reference [p. 8].

Indeed, "structure" and "order" are introduced by holistic structuralism as primitive constructs that play a necessary role in explaining and understanding objects and events. For holistic structuralism, structure is primitive and not ultimately reducible to more basic constructs. Holistic structuralism, which seems closely allied both to a general systems theory and a dialectical perspective, thus does imply an "inferred entities" approach, positing structures, even if only momentary. (Activity, not the object, is still basic, however; not so the case in mechanistic formulations or "elementaristic structuralism"; see Overton, 1975.)

From the perspectives of Bergson and Overton, as well as from my own first-person introspection, then, it is essential that humans seek constancies in daily life and that scientists seek regularities and propose structures so as to better explain and make order out of the variety of phenomena observed both in the real world and in the laboratory.

Dialectics keeps reminding us, however, that constancy or stability is an illusion. But it is an illusion that helps us bring order out of chaos. If it is an illusion, it is one that man is philosophically, neurologically, and probably phylogenetically canalized to create. Structure, or inferred entities, or schemata are real. In fact, the "new now" and "previous now" of Husserl and Kvale's "past experiences" seem every bit as inferred, as structural, as Bartlett's schemata.

It would appear that there is a dialectical contradiction—structure and flux both imply and exclude each other. My main concern is that, analogously, the figure/ground reversal also be continual and dynamic. It seems that in both human thought and in the study of memory, structure and flux time-share and that there is a reciprocal interweaving of the two. Activity has both synchronic and diachronic dimensions. The diachronic refers to the development of the phenomena under consideration, and in its essence is the organization of the phenomena through its history; the synchronic refers to the momentary structure or organization. Indeed, structures are not static but can be defined, as Piaget does, as the "organizational forms of mental activity [Piaget, 1967, p. 5]." Structures are primitive postulates. Whether the particular structures described are adequate representations of the activity is an empirical issue (Overton, 1975).

IV. The Historical-Social Context
of the "Empirical Tradition"

I would like now briefly to consider the historical context within which the Ebbinghaus tradition—what Kvale refers to as the assembly-line model of memory—developed. During the last 40 years of the 19th century, psychology was in the middle of a "paradigm" shift. Starting with the work and writings of Alexander Bain, European psychology began to move from solely epistemological concerns to an empirical science. Bain was probably the first modern thinker whose primary concern was with psychology itself. (He founded *Mind* in 1876, the first psychological journal in any country; Young, 1970.) The associationist movement, borrowing heavily from the evolutionary associationism of Herbert Spencer, was a powerful force, whose primary thrust was to capitalize on the advances in knowledge made in the physical sciences, and it represented an attempt to apply that philosophy and rigor to a new science of mental life. Ebbinghaus was the eloquent leader of the anti-Wundtians (according to Boring, 1957, he wrote the first readable text in psychology). He argued strongly that the higher mental processes *are* amenable to scientific study in the laboratory. His model of the experiment was, indeed, that of the physical sciences. Ebbinghaus created the conception of the serial learning procedure, and saw in Fechner's "elements of psychophysics" its possibilities for measuring the strength of mental associations. He attempted to make the procedures as clean as possible and to eliminate what he took to be possible contaminating sources of error.

Something, or someone, was needed at this period in history to make the study of mental processes a "legitimate" science and to free it from its (at the time, unwanted) philosophical and metaphysical encumbrances. If Ebbinghaus had not lived and done the work, European society would have, within only a few years, invented him. The tradition built around Ebbinghaus encompassed a variety of kinds of activity and served a number of scientific and social functions. It provided an instrumental base—the memory drum; it elaborated a methodology—a knowledge about procedures, materials (nonsense syllables), and data designed to assist in deciding what was "objective fact" and what was "artifact"; it accumulated a large body of objective facts and coherences in the findings; and it served some personal and social functions for participants in the tradition—people needed and wanted some way to engage in "scientific" study in psychology, to become "legitimate."

The Ebbinghaus tradition had its problems. And if science is considered merely a set of ideological explorations, then perhaps Kvale is correct when he argues that research stemming from the Ebbinghaus tradition was mainly an unfortunate waste of time and resulted in the collection of a large variety of "laboratory curiosities." As White (1976) has argued, if in the beginning, everyone had been as sensitive to the metatheoretical restrictions of stimulus–response analysis (as were, for example, Hering, Brentano, and Stumpf), then the not-so-bright individuals in the area would not have had to invest 40 years of work to discover the problems the "bright" individuals foresaw at the beginning.

Perhaps it was not all a waste of time if a deeper view is taken of any tradition in psychology (what Kuhn, 1970, calls a "paradigm"). In one major sense, a tradition or paradigm exists to provide a social support system for a group of scientists who agree with one another about how to discuss psychology (White, 1976). In another sense, the tradition provides a unique lens through which one can experience reality. This lens consists of, at least, accepted apparatus and procedures and a set of basic events—the "data" to be recorded. The paradigm draws a following, and from what is seen through the lens the members of the group socially construct a reality (Berger & Luckmann, 1967).

Psychological theories and experimental paradigms hold within them the seeds of their own eventual demise. Ebbinghaus' were no exception. The original paradigm—rote learning of lists of nonsense syllables (the data derived from which were quantified measures of time, savings, etc.)—was eventually abandoned because it defied an atomistic analysis—the "stimulus" could not be identified. And if this were so, then how could one be sure one had a handle on stimulus–response "associations?" In its place grew up paired-associate learning in which the stimulus, supposedly, was readily identifiable. A further justification for paired-associate learning was that it represented an analog to the animal conditioning procedures in vogue at the time and could be used to study association—which was believed to be the mechanism of all higher mental processes. The paired-associate methodology survived well into the early 1960s and, in a strictly "knowledge-accrual" sense, probably contributed relatively little to our understanding of memory or remembering activity.

However, what the paired-associate methodology did produce was equally as important, in a scientific sense, as what it did not produce. It produced anomalies—interesting and reliable findings that were fundamentally unexplainable by stimulus–response analysis stretched to any reasonable limit. These anomalies, whether formalized or not in the literature, provided demonstrations that, try as experimenters would, it was almost impossible to prevent subjects from "using their heads" during an experiment. These anomalies were recalcitrant to stimulus–response analysis and forced researchers to look not only at the inadequacies of their theoretical formulations but quite possibly challenged their beliefs in the mechanistic world view (cf. Jenkins, 1974).

V. The Figure/Ground Reversal in Contemporary Memory Research

I believe that the empirical tradition and researchers in it are not as myopic and inflexible as Kvale would make them. Only someone deeply familiar with an apparatus and a set of procedures can turn that apparatus and set of procedures on its head and perform the figure/ground reversal that Kvale demands. To a large extent this figure/ground reversal is well under way. The old procedures, which produced anomalies, are currently being used to study fruitfully what Kvale refers to as the "real" phenomena of remembering activity. It looks like you *can* teach an old dog new tricks.

Investigators have recently used serial learning to look at "subjective organization"–the extent to which subjects in experiments actively organize for themselves novel and initially unrelated material (Laurence, 1967; Tulving, 1962). Paired-associate learning is being used to study the flexibility of remembering activity (Martin, 1972), the strategies that subjects invent or construct, and the imagery and other mnemonics they can invent or utilize (e.g., Reese, in press). We are now, within these same paradigms, studying individual differences in remembering (once considered statistical artifacts and lumped into the error term) (e.g., Hunt, Lunneborg, & Lewis, 1975). We are also beginning to utilize first-person approaches by asking little children (and bigger children) what they know about their own remembering ability (e.g., Kreutzer, Leonard, & Flavell, 1975).

The field of memory research in the 1970s is not "sterile," and indeed, the contextualistic world view is becoming more and more the dominant one. It seems to me that hardly anyone working on child or "adult" memory really believes anymore that a stimulus can be defined independently of the activity of the remembering organism (White, 1970) or that a memorial representation is a mere "copy" of an event (Kail & Siegel, in press).

Although Bartlett's approach (the study of remembering activity) is not *yet* the dominant research paradigm, it is becoming increasingly a more and more popular one (cf. Brown, 1975; Flavell, 1971; Neimark, 1975; Paris & Lindauer, in press). Let me play a quick numbers game. Kvale reports that "as recently as 1972 nearly 80% of the memory experiments reported in the *Journal of Verbal Learning and Verbal Behavior* were based on the assemblage of fragmented units, such as lists of words, nonsense syllables, letters, and so forth [Chapter 9, this volume]." Although I cannot precisely say where memory begins and language perception leaves off, of the 58 papers in the 1975 volume of the same journal, 45% of the experiments used sentence or prose material, and only 10% used lists of letters, numbers, or nonsense syllables. The remaining studies used lists of words, but in only 17% of these studies were the words unrelated.

The sterile characterization of the field of memory research that Kvale provides seems to me to have been accurate in 1966 but is inaccurate in 1976. More and more studies are moving away from atomized lists (nonsense syllables, lists of numbers, letters, etc.). More and more studies are encouraging, instructing, and even demanding that the subject *not* memorize mechanically (Neimark, 1975). The subjects are encouraged to contextualize the material to be remembered (cf. Bower, 1970; Paris & Lindauer, in press). Most current studies do not use time pressure. Finally, qualitative analysis of a person's remembering activities are being used, in addition to quantitative analyses (cf. Butterfield, Wambold, & Belmont, 1973; Flavell, Friedrichs, & Hoyt, 1970). When one looks at the changes in (the representation of) a person's "semantic space" over development or after particular prose manipulations (e.g., Henley, 1969), surely these must be looked at as qualitative analyses. More and more researchers are seriously looking at comprehension of prose passages and how this comprehension changes with time (Kintsch, 1975). Not only do investigators record the number of sentences remembered, but they try to analyze the extent to which the theme has been extracted from the story and how it has been qualitatively distorted, reconstructed, and otherwise changed.

Even the language in which memory is described has been transformed. For example, in recent formulations by Norman and Bobrow, the notions of "static memory traces" and "atomized storage" are foreign. Norman (1975), Norman and Bobrow (1976), along with Bartlett and Piaget, talk of "schemata":

> The notion of structural frameworks or schemata is central to our ideas. These notions are not novel. The concepts play a fundamental role in Bartlett's (1932) work, and it is from him that we have borrowed the term. Piaget uses schemata as a major theoretical concept. Norman uses the terms *structural framework* and *knowledge frames* to help explain why subjects make conceptual distortions in drawing such things as the floor plan of the apartment in which they have lived for two years [Cofer, 1976, p. 119].

In short, what I am arguing is that in using old methodologies for new purposes, in the use of free recall, sentence and prose comprehension, and inference-making techniques, the field of memory research is well into the business of performing the figure/ground reversal for which Kvale so eloquently argues. It appears that Bartlett is alive and well in 1976; terms such as *remembering, activity, schemata,* and *context* are here to stay.

VI. New Directions

But, lest this entire discussion be perceived as a negative critique of a provoking, thoughtful, and scholarly analysis, let me argue that most of what Kvale says makes good scientific sense, and the research directions he specifies seem to be exceptionally fruitful. I certainly agree that future research will be much more productive if first- and third-person approaches are viewed as complementary and used concomitantly. One of the tricks will be to devise clever techniques to engage a young child in giving us his first-person account of his own remembering activity. As Kvale argues, "the socially conventionalized schemata of adults are unsuitable for the recall of the radically different childhood mode of experience [Chapter 9, this volume]."

I would agree with Kvale that the effects of essay and multiple choice examinations on the organization of subsequent remembering activity is an important topic that deserves study. However, care must be taken that we pay attention not only to the categorical nature of the test items, that is, whether they are "objective" or "essay" items, but also to the kind of remembering activity that the items demand. I seriously question whether *all* multiple choice items reinforce "an atomistic and mechanical learning." I give you the following multiple choice item (see Figure 1).

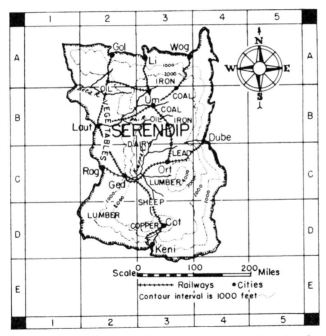

Which of the following cities would be the best location for a steel mill?

(A) Li   (3A)

(B) Um   (3B)

(C) Cot   (3D)

(D) Dube   (4B)

Fig. 1 Multiple choice item. From *Multiple choice questions: A close look.* Copyright © 1963 by Educational Testing Service. All rights reserved. Reprinted by permission.

Even though the cities in Figure 1 are labeled with nonsense syllables, I seriously doubt that this item reinforces atomistic, rote, and mechanical learning. Indeed, I can think of several types of *essay* questions that reinforce atomistic and mechanical learning. For example, "Provide a chronology of the major land battles of World War II, and which side won each." In short, the extent to which either multiple choice or essay examinations tap into deep thematic knowledge or reinforce rote and mechanical learning is item-dependent.

There is a variety of other memory phenomena that fit well within an active-organism-in-a-sociohistorical-context approach and that have received little, if any, empirical attention. Two of these phenomena will now be described.

A. Remembering and Forgetting Social Agendae

Consider the following situation: Assume that, as is often the case in Pittsburgh, every morning when you drive to work, you park your car in a different place. You park the car, go to the office, work, lecture, write, read, fill out forms until 6:00 p.m., and then go, typically unerringly, to your car for the trip home. The location of the car was not in "working memory" during the day, and yet you remembered where it was 8 hours later with little difficulty. The next morning you park the car in a different location, and the process repeats itself. There is no retroactive interference from one day to the next. You "dump" the location of your car from memory as soon as you have completed that particular social agenda. Similarly, I could probably ask every one to write out a list of "things that you have to do within the next week." (I have tried this informally, and the lists generated often contain over 50 agendae.) People report that after they have accomplished one agenda item, they seem to check it off on the list and forget it; if they have not accomplished it, they remember that they have to do it. How is this selective remembering and forgetting accomplished? It would be interesting to devise a set of procedures to study this more formally in children as well as in adults.

B. Spatial Memory

Much current psychological and neurological theory, especially "developmental" theory, assumes a plurality of human knowledge systems, for example, Piaget's several levels and kinds of thought, Bruner's several systems of representation, the information-processing theorists' variety of very-short, short-, and longer-term memory systems, mental testings' number of intellectual factors or abilities, and neurological analysis' set of semidifferentiated knowledge and action organization in the nervous system (Jackson, 1884; Luria, 1973). The human information—processing system seems to consist of an interorganized *set* of knowledge subsystems, each incorporating experience in characteristically different ways and processing it according to its own "laws of learning" (Novikoff, 1945; White & Siegel, 1976).

There is increasing evidence within the child and adult literatures for the existence, at the very least, of knowledge and memory systems for processing verbal-acoustic, visual, and spatial events. Within each system, knowledge, comprehension, and remembering can be viewed as outcomes of the assembly of meaning over real time. In the successful "comprehension" of textual materials, chessboard positions, or road maps, children and adults do extend thought and action over real time.

It is not novel to argue that figurative knowledge is the substrate for verbal-symbolic knowledge (Piaget, 1971; Werner & Kaplan, 1963). On the one hand, some children have difficulties in learning to read and in comprehending written text—there is some deficit or dysfunction in their strategy, capacity, or motivation to extend their thought and action within a verbal-acoustic-symbolic knowledge system over real time; their extraction and assembly of meaning within this system over time is impaired. On the other hand, most children rarely get lost in the real world—they get from home to school successfully, without a road map, compass, or adult to lead them. They are capable of "way finding" and in so doing demonstrate few troubles in extending their thought and action within a visual-spatial knowledge system over time. Why?

Visual-spatial knowledge is essentially figurative and is the fundamental substrate on which symbolic or operative knowledge is developed (in the child's cognitive growth, in the microgenesis of thought in adults; Flavell & Draguns, 1957, and in the evolution of *Homo sapiens;* Fishbein, 1976). Research on understanding and remembering within this substrate and optimally functioning visual-spatial knowledge system seems to be a natural partner of research on comprehension and remembering within the verbal-symbolic system.

The field of psychology is overinvested in the language/verbal system. According to such investigators as Tulving, Werner, and Kaplain, and Huttenlocher, the field has invested considerable effort looking at verbal-symbolic knowledge, while visual-spatial knowledge has received little systematic consideration. Spatial knowledge, the spatial representation system, and the remembering of spatial environments are barely tapped in either adults or children. An understanding of this visual-spatial knowledge and remembering system is important for several reasons (see Siegel & White, 1975, for a fuller explication of this argument): (1) for its own sake and for what its understanding can contribute to general psychological-developmental theory; understanding the systemic properties of the visual-spatial knowledge system will contribute to the understanding of the properties of other knowledge systems and of comprehension and remembering within those systems; and (2) there are a large number of nonspatial domains of experience that we comprehend or understand primarily through the use of spatial metaphor: sequential memory (Siegel, Allik, & Herman, 1976), syllogistic reasoning (Huttenlocher, 1968), models of analysis of variance, the semantic differential, and so on. Understanding the rules and underlying processes of visual-spatial remembering should provide useful substrates for our understanding of comprehension within more formalized symbolic knowledge systems.

This kind of research is amenable to both first- and third-person approaches and is compatible with both a dialectical and an experimental perspective.

REFERENCES

Bartlett, F. C. *Remembering*. Cambridge, Eng.: University Press, 1932.

Berger, P. L., & Luckmann, T. *The social construction of reality*. Garden City, N.Y.: Doubleday, 1967.

Bergson, H. *Creative evolution*. New York: Holt, 1911.

Boring, E. G. *A history of experimental psychology*. New York: Appleton, 1957.

Bower, G. H. Organizational factors in memory. *Cognitive Psychology*, 1970, **1**, 18–46.

Brown, A. L. The development of memory: Knowing, knowing about knowing, and knowing how to know. In H. W. Reese (Ed.), *Advances in child development and behavior* (Vol. 10). New York: Academic Press, 1975.

Butterfield, E. C., Wambold, C., & Belmont, J. M. On the theory and practice of improving short-term memory. *American Journal of Mental Deficiency*, 1973, **77**, 654–669.

Cofer, C. N. (Ed.), *The structure of human memory*. San Francisco: Freeman, 1976.

Fishbein, H. D. *Evolution, development and children's learning*. Pacific Palisades, Calif.: Goodyear Pub. Co., 1976.

Flavell, J. H. What is memory development the development of? *Human Development*, 1971, **14**, 272–278.

Flavell, J. H., & Draguns, J. A. A microgenetic approach to perception and thought. *Psychological Bulletin*, 1957, **59**, 197–217.

Flavell, J. H., Friedrichs, A. G., & Hoyt, J. D. Developmental changes in memorization processes. *Cognitive Psychology*, 1970, **1**, 324–340.

Hegel, G. W. F. *The philosophy of history*. New York: Dover, 1956.

Henley, N. M. A psychological study of the semantics of animal terms. *Journal of Verbal Learning and Verbal Behavior*, 1969, **8**, 176–184.

Hunt, E., Lunneborg, C., & Lewis, J. What does it mean to be high verbal? *Cognitive Psychology*, 1975, **7**, 194–227.

Huttenlocher, J. Constructing spatial images: A strategy in reasoning. *Psychological Review*, 1968, **75**, 550–560.

Jackson, J. H. Evolution and dissolution of the nervous system (Croonian Lectures). Published in parts in the *British Medical Journal, Lancet,* and *Medical Times and Gazette*, 1884. Reprinted in J. Taylor (Ed.), *The selected writings of John Hughlings Jackson* (Vol. 2). New York: Basic Books, 1958. Pp. 45–75.

Jenkins, J. J. Remember that old theory of memory? Well, forget it! *American Psychologist*, 1974, **29**, 785–795.

Kail, R. V., & Siegel, A. W. The development of mnemonic encoding in children: From perception to abstraction. In R. V. Kail, Jr. & J. W. Hagen (Eds.), *Perspectives on the development of memory and cognition*. Hillsdale, N.J.: Lawrence Erlbaum Associates, in press.

Kintsch, W. Memory representations of text. In R. L. Solso (Ed.), *Information processing and cognition, the Loyola Symposium*. Hillsdale, N.J.: Lawrence Earlbaum Associates, 1975.

Kreutzer, M. A., Leonard, S. C., & Flavell, J. H. An interview study of children's knowledge about memory. *Monographs of the Society for Research in Child Development*, 1975, **40**(No. 1, Serial No. 159).

Kuhn, T. S. *The structure of scientific revolutions* (2nd ed.). Chicago: University of Chicago Press, 1970.

Kvale, S. Memory and dialectics: Some reflections of Ebbinghaus and Mao Tse-tung. *Human Development*, 1975, **18**, 205–222.

Laurence, M. W. A developmental look at the usefulness of list categorization as an aid to free recall. *Canadian Journal of Psychology*, 1967, **21**, 153–165.

Luria, A. R. *The working brain*. London: Penguin Books, 1973.

Martin, E. Stimulus encoding in learning and transfer. In A. W. Melton & E. Martin (Eds.), *Coding processes in human memory*. Washington, D.C.: Winston, 1972.

Neimark, E. D. The natural history of spontaneous mnemonic activities under conditions of minimal experimental constraint. In A. D. Pick (Ed.), *Minnesota symposium on child psychology.* (Vol. 10). Minneapolis: University of Minnesota Press, 1975.

Norman, D. A. Memory, knowledge, and the answering of questions. In R. L. Solso (Ed.), *Information processing and cognition, the Loyola Symposium.* Hillsdale, N.J.: Lawrence Erlbaum Associates, 1975.

Norman, D. A., & Bobrow, D. G. On the role of active memory processes in perception and cognition. In C. N. Cofer (Ed.), *The structure of human memory.* San Francisco: Freeman, 1976.

Novikoff, A. B. The concept of integrative levels and biology. *Science,* 1945, **101,** 209–215.

Overton, W. F. General systems, structures and development. In K. F. Riegel & G. C. Rosenwald (Eds.), *Structure and transformation: Developmental and historical aspects.* New York: Wiley, 1975.

Paris, S. G., & Lindauer, B. K. Constructive aspects of children's comprehension and memory. In R. V. Kail, Jr. & J. W. Hagen (Eds.), *Perspectives on the development of memory and cognition.* Hillsdale, N.J.: Lawrence Erlbaum Associates, in press.

Pepper, S. C. *World hypotheses.* Berkeley: University of California Press, 1970.

Piaget, J. *Six psychological studies.* New York: Random House, 1967.

Piaget, J. *Biology and knowledge.* Chicago: University of Chicago Press, 1971.

Reese, H. W. Imagery and associative memory. In R. V. Kail, Jr. & J. W. Hagen (Eds.), *Perspectives on the development of memory and cognition.* Hillsdale, N.J.: Lawrence Erlbaum Associates, in press.

Siegel, A. W., Allik, J. P., & Herman, J. F. The primacy effect in young children: Verbal fact or spatial artifact? *Child Development,* 1976, **47,** 242–247.

Siegel, A. W., & White, S. H. The development of spatial representations of large-scale environments. In H. W. Reese (Ed.), *Advances in child development and behavior* (Vol. 10). New York: Academic Press, 1975.

Tulving, E. The effect of alphabetical subjective organization on memorizing unrelated words. *Canadian Journal of Psychology,* 1962, **16,** 185–191.

Werner, H., & Kaplan, B. *Symbol formation: An organismic-developmental approach to language and the expression of thought.* New York: Wiley, 1963.

White, S. H. The learning theory tradition and child psychology. In P. H. Mussen (Ed.), *Carmichael's manual of child psychology* (Vol. 1). New York: Wiley, 1970.

White, S. H. The active organism in theoretical behaviorism. *Human Development,* 1976, **19,** 99–107.

White, S. H., & Siegel, A. W. Cognitive development: The new inquiry. *Young Children,* 1976, **31,** 425–435.

Young, R. M. *Mind, brain, and adaptation in the nineteenth century.* London & New York: Oxford University Press (Clarendon), 1970.

CHAPTER 11

Discriminative Learning and Transfer: Dialectical Perspectives[1]

HAYNE W. REESE

WEST VIRGINIA UNIVERSITY
MORGANTOWN, WEST VIRGINIA

I. Introduction

A. Alternative Approaches to Discriminative Learning and Transfer

Discriminative learning and transfer are strongholds of stimulus–response behaviorism. The best articulated behavioristic theories are those formulated to deal with discriminative performance, and a vast experimental literature indicates that these are also the most successful behavioristic theories (for reviews, see House, Brown, & Scott, 1974; House & Zeaman, 1963; Reese, 1963, 1964, 1976a; Reese & Lipsitt, 1970; Spiker, 1963, 1970, 1971; Spiker & Cantor, 1973; Zeiler, 1967). Nevertheless, behavioristic analyses of discriminative performance are not trouble-free, and the troubles are of sufficient magnitude to warrant a search for alternative methods of analysis that may be more satisfactory.

One alternative is the dialectical approach, which for several reasons was selected for examination in the present paper. One reason is that the dialectical approach resolves major problems of the behavioristic approach, including problems of the behavioristic approach to development. In addition, dialectical perspectives on psychological development, particularly memory development, have been worked

[1] I am indebted to Drs. Michael Cole, Barry Gholson, and John A. Meacham, who read and commented upon a previous version of this contribution.

out in considerable detail, not only in the Soviet Union (see Meacham, 1972, in press; Zaporozhets & Elkonin, 1971b), but also by non-Soviet psychologists (Kvale, 1975, Chapter 9, this volume; Meacham, Chapter 13, this volume; Reese, 1976b, 1976d). Given the categorical presupposition (Overton & Reese, 1973; Reese & Overton, 1970) in dialectical views that developments in different psychological domains are strongly interrelated, it follows that developments in the domain of discriminative performance should parallel developments in other psychological domains. One purpose of the present paper is to determine whether the data support this parallel.

The competing approaches are described in Section II, the research evidence is surveyed in Section III, and finally the implications of the dialectical approach are discussed in Section IV. Before proceeding to these sections, however, it may be useful to characterize the general models from which the competing approaches are derived in order to explicate the nature of the competition among the approaches.

B. The Underlying Models

1. General Comments

Reality cannot be known directly; hence, it must be constructed or represented conceptually. It can be represented, or modeled, in various ways, each of which has different implications about the nature of evidence and the explanation of evidence (e.g., Kuhn, 1962; Pepper, 1942). The most general modes of representation are called world views or world hypotheses (Pepper, 1942) or paradigms (Kuhn, 1962), which are cosmologies differentiated by the "root metaphor" (Pepper, 1942) by which reality is represented. The currently most popular root metaphors in psychology are the machine, the growing organism *qua* organism, and the historical event developing in its historical context. The respective cosmologies are mechanism, organicism, and contextualism, but in psychology mechanism reflects Newtonian mechanics rather than the mechanics of modern physics, organicism reflects a naive conception of the growing organism rather than genetic embryology, and contextualism reflects a commonsense analysis of history rather than historiography.

In mechanism, substance is particulate, and change is in the direction or speed of movement of the particles. Change is caused by the application of external forces; that is, causes are immediate and the cause–effect relation is antecedent–consequent. In psychology, the mechanistic model is reflected by the reactive model of the organism. In the reactive organism model, the organism is like the machine, reactive to forces and incapable of transforming forces except through mechanisms that are themselves reactive to forces. For example, purpose cannot be a cause unless it has a concurrent status: The end cannot determine the means unless the end is part of the antecedent of the means. The end might be represented by an antecedent such as "expectancy" or "fractional anticipatory goal response" (see J. S. Brown, 1961, pp. 176–180; see also Lambert, 1971); but then purpose is a derived concept rather than a basic concept.

In organicism, the essence of substance is activity, process rather than substrate. Change is given, and the aim is to identify the rules of change, the transitions from one form into another, and the system in which the changes occur. The process is the unit. It is expressed in multiple forms ("unity is found in multiplicity") and the present form or state is explained by the rules of change, not by static rules ("being is found in becoming"), but the rules of change are immutable ("constancy is found in change") (quotations from Reese & Overton, 1970, p. 133). In addition to antecedent-consequent causality, which is analogous to the effect of ingesting and metabolizing nutrients, organicism requires final or teleological causality, explaining the direction of development toward the mature form of the organism. In psychology, the organismic model is reflected by the active organism model, in which the organism actively participates in the construction of known reality. The organism can know the world only through transformations actively imposed by the organism upon its experiences, but imposed because of its experiences. "Activity generates meaning, and meaning generates activity [Rappoport, 1975, p. 195]."

In contextualism, as in organicism, the essence of substance is activity, or change, and the aim is to identify the rules of change and to describe transitions and the contexts in which they occur. In contextualism, unlike organicism, there is no end state of change—no mature form toward which development progresses. Hence, antecedent-consequent causality is assumed in contextualism but teleological causality is not. (Both contextualism and organicism also assume *formal* causality—determination by the nature of a form.) In psychology, the contextualistic model is reflected by an active organism model, in which not only the organism but also the context actively transform reality as known, each at the same time influencing the nature of the transformation. (For a more detailed discussion of the issues outlined in this subsection, and related issues, see Overton & Reese, 1973; Reese & Overton, 1970.)

2. The Behavioristic Model

Stimulus–response behaviorism clearly incorporates the reactive organism model, and in other ways as well is consistent with the mechanistic model (see Overton & Reese, 1973; Reese & Overton, 1970, 1972). One implication is a limitation on the way *response* can be defined, a limitation that is especially important when the response is an unobservable private event. Responses can be defined as specific patterns of muscular activity—the "particles" are the muscles reacting to specific stimuli—or responses can be defined by their effects upon the environment (e.g., Spence, 1956, pp. 42–43). With the latter type of definition, responses are differentiated not by the muscle group involved but by another concrete attribute, effect on environment. With both types of definition, it is implied that responses have concrete existence.

Unobserved responses have the same ontological status as observed responses; they are in principle concrete and differentiated by concrete attributes. Thus, for example, an unobserved verbal response has the same properties as an overt verbal response except for observability. Such concepts as "rule," "strategy," and the like are not analogous to overt responses, and hence are not definable as unobserved responses. They are also not analogous to stimuli and other forces, hence are not definable in behaviorism or any other model derived from the mechanistic cosmology.

3. Cognitive Models

Cognitive models in psychology have been derived from organicism (e.g., Piaget's genetic epistemology) and from contextualism (e.g., Jenkins', 1974, model of memory). These models deal with behavior, of course, but the emphasis is on the transformations or processes that underlie behavior and on the system that organizes the processes. Thus, for example, Piaget describes the organizing system as changing in form during the course of development (change in form requires a stage model, each form defining a different stage), and describes the emergence of new processes in new stages and changes in the meaning or function of processes that are retained from earlier stages. The sequence of stages is explained teleologically in Piaget's model, consistent with organicism.

An example of a contextualistic model is the Soviet model of memory. It is derived from materialistic dialectics, which lacks the "absolute truth" of idealistic dialectics, hence lacks the teleological principle of idealistic dialectics (and organicism in general). Development proceeds by stages and is characterized by strong reciprocal influences of person and environment. The environment includes not only physical events but also a sociohistorical context. The dialectical model emphasizes the opposition of conflicting or contradictory principles and their resolution through emergent consequences. Knowledge is social, created by the activities of society; but it is also individual, acquired by the individual through his own activities. Thus, there is a dialectical relation between the individual's activities and the activities of the society, and the result is the individual's knowledge, which may, however, change society's knowledge.

II. Developmental Models of Discriminative Performance

A. Stimulus–Response Models

In discriminative-learning theories developed from the Hullian model, the materials presented are conceptualized as potential stimuli, and the choice made by the subject is conceptualized as an approach response. Discriminative learning consists of increasing, through reinforcement, the habit strength of the association between the positive stimulus and the approach response and increasing, through nonreinforcement or punishment, inhibition of the association between the negative stimulus and the approach response. However, as a result of generalization, positive stimuli acquire inhibition as well as habit strength, and negative stimuli acquire habit strength as well as inhibition. Theoretically, habit or inhibition conditioned to a stimulus generalizes to similar stimuli, the amount of generalization decreasing as stimulus similarity decreases.

The tendency to approach a stimulus is defined as the excitatory potential of the stimulus and is related to the difference between the habit and inhibition (conditioned and generalized) of the association between the stimulus and the approach response. (Excitatory potential also includes the effects of other variables: drive level, excitatory threshold, general inhibition that oscillates from moment to moment, and work inhibition.) The probability of a correct discriminative response—approach to the positive stimulus—is a mathematical function of the difference between the excitatory potentials of the positive and negative stimuli.

One complication in the theory is that the positive and negative stimuli are defined as *effective* stimuli, which are transformations of the potential stimuli actually presented. The transformations may be as simple as transductions of energy, or they may be so complex that there is little isomorphy between the potential and effective stimuli. Even in the latter case, however, a degree of isomorphy is maintained, and the transformations are accomplished by mechanisms identified as responses, specifically, attentional responses.

Another complication is that the approach response may be controlled not by the putative effective stimulus but rather by an intervening stimulus, which is, however, produced by another response under the control of the putative effective stimulus. This complication refers to the role of mediating responses and the stimulation they produce.

Finally, a third complication is that stimulus similarity is a complex concept in the most highly articulated version of Hullian discriminative-learning theory, the theory formulated by Spiker (1963, 1970, 1971; Spiker & Cantor, 1973). In this theory, stimulus similarity depends not only upon the discriminability of stimulus elements but also upon the configuration, compound, or context of the elements.

The three complications are not independent, because, for example, a mediating response can mediate an attentional response and at the same time add an element to the stimulus context. Furthermore, stimuli that are distinctively different in a psychophysical task may be functionally equivalent in a discriminative task, and stimuli that are highly similar in a psychophysical task can become functionally distinctive in a discriminative task, as demonstrated in studies of the acquired equivalence and distinctiveness of cues and in studies of transposition.

The mathematized versions of discriminative-learning theory include individual-difference parameters in equations defining the intervening variables. For example, the growth of habit strength is a function of the number of reinforced trials:

$$_SH_R = A[1 - (1 - F)^n] \qquad (1)$$

where $_SH_R$ is habit strength, A is the limit to which habit will grow, F is the rate of approach to this limit, and n is the number of reinforced trials (Spence, 1951, footnote 4, p. 251). The constants A and F are individual-difference parameters.

For a developmental analysis, it would be reasonable to hypothesize that the values of these parameters are related to age, and developmental research could be conducted to determine the nature of the relation.

Another example is the principle of stimulus generalization:

$$s'\bar{H}_R = {_S}H_R \times 10^{-ad} \tag{2}$$

where $s'\bar{H}_R$ is generalized habit, $_SH_R$ is conditioned habit, a is an individual-difference parameter, and d reflects the difference between the conditioned stimulus (S) and the generalized stimulus (S') (e.g., Spiker, 1963, p. 236). Developmentally, one might expect age differences in the value of a and perhaps in the value of d.

In short, basic discriminative-learning theory provides a set of individual-difference parameters that can be hypothesized to change in value developmentally. The three complications discussed above provide additional opportunities for developmental change. An example can be derived from the Zeaman and House (1963) theory of the role of attentional responses in discriminative performance. In this theory, the probabilities of various attentional responses are ordered hierarchically, and changes in the probabilities are related mathematically to reinforcement and nonreinforcement. Research evidence indicates different initial hierarchies at different ages (e.g., Lee, 1965), presumably because of different preexperimental experiences, and indicates developmental differences in the parameters of the change equations (see Eimas, 1970). Another example, from mediation theory, is provided by an application of equations reflecting the effects of mediation, yielding quantitative estimates of developmental changes in the probability of mediation (e.g., Kendler, 1972). A final example is provided by Spiker's previously cited theory of the effects of context upon stimulus generalization, which includes individual-difference parameters and hence is suitable for a developmental analysis.

B. Cognitive Models

In cognitive models, performance is represented as a product of transformational processes. The processes are referred to as hypotheses (e.g., Krechevsky, 1932; Levine, 1963), strategies (e.g., Campione & Brown, 1974), rules (e.g., Gagné, 1974), plans (G. A. Miller, Galanter, & Pribram, 1960), and so on. Details differ among the cognitive models, but most of the models can be characterized as information-processing models, and therefore it is convenient to utilize the information-processing terminology.

The basic information-processing model of discriminative performance relates this performance to processing operations, or "hypotheses." A hypothesis is an attempted solution to the task, presumably transferred from previous experience on the basis of situational similarity (Campione & Brown, 1974) and the subject's understanding of the task demands or "meaning" of the task. Elaborate theories of hypothesis sampling and testing have been developed (e.g., Levine, 1975; G. A. Miller et al., 1960; Restle, 1962).

Developmentally, one would expect to find differences in the hypotheses available, the subject's understanding of the meaning of the task, and perhaps the sampling and testing routines. For example, the young child may have a limited set of hypotheses available but may require extensive disconfirmation for rejection of an incorrect hypothesis and may sample with replacement. The older child, in contrast, should have a larger set of hypotheses available, may require little disconfirmation, and may sample without replacement. Another developmental shift, discussed next (Section II,C,1), is in the efficiency of producing and utilizing hypotheses. Further details of hypothesis theory are presented in Section III, in connection with specific research topics.

C. Eclectic Models

1. Introduction: Mediational Deficiencies

Deficiencies and inefficiencies in the production and use of mediators are well documented in the developmental literature, although insufficient research has been aimed at determining the causes of their relation to age and, particularly, their relation to task characteristics (Cole & Medin, 1974; Gollin & Rosser, 1974). In the more interesting cases, the potential mediators are in the child's repertoire but are not utilized at all or are utilized inefficiently. These cases reflect a dialectical contradiction: The mediator is available but is not utilized. This contradiction is one of many instances of a more general contradiction, the competence–performance distinction, which appears in language, cognition, verbal learning and memory, and, as we shall see, discriminative learning and transfer.

As originally formulated (Reese, 1962), the concept of mediational deficiency referred to discriminative performance. In subsequent refinements of the concept, a distinction was made between the production and use of mediators, referred to as "production" deficiency and "mediation" or "control" deficiency (Flavell, Beach, & Chinsky, 1966; Kendler, 1972). In addition, a distinction was made between failures and inefficiencies in the production and use of mediators, adding the concepts of production and control "errors" or "inefficiencies" (Jeffrey, 1965; Zeiler, 1967; see also Reese, 1970a). Throughout these conceptual developments the concepts retained their reference to discriminative performance, in which the presumed mediators are relatively simple responses, such as individual words or the push of a button. During the period of development of the concepts, however, they began to be applied to more complex mediators, such as strategies, hypotheses, rules, information-processing operations, and cognitive operations in general (e.g., Flavell, 1970; Meacham, 1972), and this extension of the application of the concepts has since become routine (e.g., Bearison & Isaacs, 1975; A. L. Brown, 1975; Reese, 1976d).

The change in application is not a simple extension, however, because the application of the concepts to discriminative performance was behavioral, and the more recent applications are cognitive; that is, the concepts were originally interpreted within behavioristic theories, which, as already noted (Section I,B), are consistent with the mechanistic world view; and in their newer applications they are interpreted within cognitive theories, which are inconsistent with the mechanistic world view. One implication of the difference is that a failure to produce an appropriate word—the problem originally dealt with—is now interpreted to reflect a failure to produce a "naming strategy" or a failure of this strategy to be implemented.

During the period of development of the concepts, there were also developmental changes in the two types of theory, in that many behaviorists attempted to deal with evidence for complex organismic determinants of behavior by introducing such concepts as "strategies," "rules," and "higher-order habits" (see previously cited references; see also Reese, 1976c; White, 1976). Other behaviorists attempted to deal with this evidence by outright rejection of the behavioristic approach and adoption of the cognitive approach. The first trend was a liberalization of behaviorism, which often came dangerously close to useless, confusing eclecticism (cf. Pepper, 1942). The second trend was a growing popularity of the cognitive approach. This second trend is seen in the currently dominant position of cognitive, information-processing theories in the areas of verbal learning and memory, the strong position of Piagetian theory in the area of intellectual development, and the increasing influence of general systems theory in the area of community mental health. The trend is also seen in the area of discriminative performance, with analyses in terms of hypothesis testing and decision processes. Finally, the currently small but increasingly widespread interest in dialectical approaches in developmental psychology is another expression of the trend.

The dialectical approach, as already noted, is cognitive rather than behavioral, in that it is consistent with either the contextualistic or the organismic world view (see Lawler, 1975; Reese, 1976d). Therefore, the extended concepts of deficiencies and inefficiencies in mediation—referring to cognitive operations rather than to response elements—are relevant.

2. White's Stage Model

Riegel (1973) proposed a stage of "dialectical operations" in intellectual development, appearing in adulthood after Piaget's stage of formal operations. At maturity, according to Riegel, all of the developmentally earlier modes of thought coexist, and the mature adult can select any one of these modes for action to suit present needs or task demands. Similarly, White (1965) proposed what is here designated a dialectical stage in the development of learning processes. White's model deals with the developmental changes in mediation. According to White, there are two major stages in the development of learning processes, with a transition around 5 to 7 years of age. In the pretransition, or "associative" stage, learning is consistent with the laws of stimulus—response association. In the posttransition, or "cognitive" stage, learning may follow the associative laws or may be controlled by cognitive processes. Because of this opposition (of learning processes), the cognitive stage can be characterized as dialectical.

The analogy between Riegel's and White's dialectical stages is not close. One distinction is that Riegel's stage characterizes adulthood and White's characterizes childhood. This distinction is trivial from the point of view of metatheory, in which no systematic importance is attached to age. Another distinction is that although both conceptions involve the contradiction of coexisting levels of operations with different ontogenetic orders, Riegel's stage involves only operations that are defined consistently with the organismic world view, while White's stage involves one set of operations defined consistently with the mechanistic world view (those related to associative laws) and another set of operations defined consistently with either contextualism or organicism (the cognitive operations). Thus, Riegel's dialectic does not mix world views, but White's does.

A problem when world views are mixed is that the resulting eclectic model is apt to be confusing, to give the illusion of understanding rather than real understanding (see Kuhn, 1962; Pepper, 1942; Reese & Overton, 1970). White's analysis included two models, the mechanistic, reactive organism model and the contextualistic or organismic active organism model. The problem is that if the organism is simultaneously reactive and active, the model may be confusingly eclectic.

One way to deal with the eclecticism in White's model is to take the position that the organism simultaneously has the *potential* for reactive and active operation, but that at any given moment only one of these potentials is actualized; that is, the organism can be *either* reactive or active, but never is *both* reactive and active. In this model the ideal is to specify rules for determining, independently of the subject's behavior, whether the reactive or the active model is currently applicable—that is, to predict how the subject will operate in a given situation. White speculated that eliciting conditions and stress might be relevant. In this connection, Peterson (1973) produced mediational deficiency in adults by pacing the task so rapidly that mediation did not have time to occur; and Kendler (1974) has speculated that production deficiency in young children may result from the strain of symbolic coding, the difficulty of suppressing sensorimotor processing, or the failure to realize the advantages of symbolic coding—all of which could presumably be manipulated experimentally by appropriate pretraining.

An alternative to this model is that the organism can be simultaneously reactive and active, but *not in the same domains of operation.* Anecdotally and experimentally, this alternative model seems reasonable. A person can drive his car along a familiar route while mentally solving a problem unrelated to the driving; but he cannot cognitively monitor his mechanical behaviors without making them deliberate instead of mechanical. If a person is walking along in an habitual gait and begins to attend to the walking, the gait changes. An experimental example (Fry & Hampson, 1976) is that if an older child is asked to give a verbal description of a projected stimulus, he adjusts the loudness of his voice directly according to changes in the background noise level. However, a young child modulates his voice only when the stimulus is simple; when the stimulus is complex, the young child is unresponsive to changes in background noise. Thus, it appears that intense cognitive activity (interpreting the stimulus) can interfere with mechanical activity (modulating voice level). Along a similar line, automatization of a behavior is believed to occur when the behavior does not entirely absorb the person's attention (Lisina &

Neverovich, 1971, p. 308). Also in agreement, Bugelski (1971) has argued that activity interferes with imaging (although certain kinds of activity, such as appropriate eye movements, may facilitate certain kinds of imaging—Antrobus, Antrobus, & Singer, 1964; Moore, 1903; Slaughter, 1902; see also Washburn, 1916).

With respect to task-oriented behaviors, the two models just discussed are indistinguishable. In both, the organism is either reactive or active, and the eventual problem is to predict which kind of operation will be exhibited in a particular situation. At present, the problem is to describe conditions that are associated with the two kinds of operation in order to provide a data base for the theorizing that will eventually permit the predictions to be made. Both models are dialectical in dealing with and resolving the reactive—active contradiction.

White's (1965) original model was also dialectical in another way, in that he speculated that the associative level in an adult is "more sophisticated, more grown up, better developed" than that of the child (p. 216). Thus, White was suggesting that the associative system continues to develop during the "cognitive" stage, which would be consistent with the principle of the negation of the negation (see Wozniak, 1975): The associative level is negated by the cognitive level, which, however, incorporates the associative level at a higher plane.

D. The Dialectical Approach

1. White's Model Reinterpreted

Even as modified by the two models proposed above, White's model would be inconsistent with Soviet dialectical psychology. Lisina and Neverovich (1971) characterized this type of hierarchical model as "eclectic, . . . arising from the treatment of . . . stages in terms of different and, in essence, mutually exclusive theories. It does not provide an adequate explanation of the problems being examined [p. 319]." In their own model, they referred to developmental changes resulting from an increased effectiveness of verbal mediation and changes in the "orienting" activity. These changes yield qualitative changes in the learning process (p. 321), but although White also postulated qualitative changes in the learning process, his shift from the behavioristic model to the cognitive model would be rejected by Soviet psychologists.

Consistent with the Soviet view, and following a suggestion by Overton (1973) in another context, one can modify White's model by adopting the active organism model throughout and treating the reactive organism component of White's model as a "convenient fiction" that represents performance in a useful way when the reciprocal interaction of person and context is weak enough to be modeled as unidirectional, linear causality.[2] The continuing development of associative opera-

---

[2] According to the model under consideration here, the organism is always active and reciprocally interacting with the environment. However, the reciprocal interaction is sometimes weak enough that a linear analysis will be satisfactory. In the linear analysis the organism and environment alternate as causes of effects in each other, permitting a turn-by-turn analysis of

tions assumed in White's model would be expected in the model proposed here, in that the "associative operations" would actually be automated or "weak" forms of cognitive operations. The ability of a person to select between weak and strong forms of cognitive operations would also be expected, reflecting the person's initial analysis of the task requirements and his plan for meeting these requirements.

2. The Soviet Model

According to Lisina and Neverovich (1971, p. 284), behaviorists limit themselves to descriptions of the external aspects of learning: Learning is the appearance of a response to a stimulus that without training would not arouse the response. The specific content of the learning activity—that which produces the change in overt responding—is ignored, according to Lisina and Neverovich, and learning becomes the same in animal and human organisms—the means of adaptation to the immediately surrounding environment.

In a sense, this particular criticism of behaviorists is unjustified. Although it may be warranted when leveled against the radical behaviorists—the neo-Skinnerians—the criticism is unwarranted in the case of the learning-theory behaviorists, who have introduced a number of complicating processes such as selective attention (e.g., Zeaman & House, 1963), mediation (e.g., Kendler, 1972), and stimulus interaction (e.g., Spiker, 1963). In another sense, however, the criticism is justifiably leveled against both kinds of behaviorist, who ignore the cognitive nature of learning processes assumed in the Soviet model. However, in still a third sense even this justifiable criticism is unjustified in that it reflects a debate between paradigms, the mechanistic for behaviorists and the contextualistic for the dialectical model of the Soviet psychologists. Between-paradigm debates are fruitless (Kuhn, 1962; Pepper, 1942; Reese, 1976c).

For animals, in the Soviet view, environment is a *condition* of development; for the child, it is a *cause* of development; "if for animal offspring environment is only the sum of conditions to which it has to adjust, then for the child his specific social environment is not merely an external condition, but a source of development [Zaporozhets & Elkonin, 1971a, p. xx]."

---

cause—effect relations (M. M. Baltes & Reese, 1977). The linear analysis is consistent with a reactive organism model but is a "fiction" in the proposed model, in which the organism is actually always active and the cause—effect relation is actually simultaneous and not linear. It is a "convenient" fiction if it works, that is, if it does not yield anomalous results and accounts for a substantial portion of the variability in performance with no unexpected and unexplainable interactions (in the analysis-of-variance sense). Thus, in the proposed model the successful use of the linear reactive organism analysis indicates that although the true relation between organism and environment is a reciprocal interaction (by assumption), this reciprocal interaction is weak. In contrast, if the linear analysis yields anomalous results, then from the perspective of this model the relation must be a *strong* reciprocal interaction, or else, as Gewirtz suggested (personal communication, March 29, 1976), there may be no orderliness in the phenomenon.

Psychological development consists of acquiring the content of the social environment—historically acquired social experiences. Mastery of this social experience is an active, complex process. It involves the development of "leading activities," "actions," and "operations." A leading activity has the selective or directive function of motives as conceptualized in behaviorism, but not their energizing function. The term *motive,* in this restricted sense, may be less confusing than leading activity, and therefore is substituted for the latter phrase in this chapter. It must be remembered, however, that motive in this sense refers to a conscious mental activity. An action is a means of achieving a goal; it may be physical or mental, but it is always under conscious control. An operation supports implementation or utilization of an action, somewhat the way a subroutine supports the functioning of a programmed routine in a computer (J. A. Meacham, personal communication, May 6, 1976). An operation may be either physical or mental and can be carried out without conscious effort.

In this model a motive (e.g., do well in school) leads to the selection of actions (e.g., remember the contents of a report), which in turn lead to the selection of operations (e.g., memorize the report) (Meacham, in press). An action can become a motive (e.g., the action of remembering a report may be converted to the motive to understand psychology), or it can become an operation (e.g., remembering as an action in the service of doing well in school, as contrasted with remembering as an operation in the service of solving a problem, which may be an action in the service of doing well in school). According to this model, an operation appears first as a conscious goal-directed action. After it is well developed as an action and can be carried out without conscious control, it can become an operation, that is, it can be subordinated as a means of accomplishing some other action. For example, the use of a hammer to drive a nail is more efficient if attention is directed to the nail rather than to the swinging of the hammer. Thus, the action of driving a nail can become efficient when the action of moving the arm is well enough practiced that it can be done without conscious control, that is, when the arm movements have become operations (J. A. Meacham, personal communication, May 6, 1976; see also Lisina & Neverovich, 1971).

The development of mental actions occurs in the context of other developing actions, conditions of life, and training. At first, development is related to physical action, in the purely practical sense of goal attainment. However, new modes of mental actions and new spheres of application develop, in increasingly complex structures including other types of actions and contexts. At the same time, new demands on the child's thinking emerge and "mediate the transition to qualitatively new, distinctive stages of intellectual development [Zaporozhets, Zinchenko, & Elkonin, 1971, p. 208]." Motives also undergo development, reflecting transformations of actions into motives as a result of changes in demands on the child's thinking. The mental actions develop in a sequence reflecting increasing complexity and greater organization. The sequence is determined by external demands and training, which select certain actions for practice. As the actions become well established and capable of being performed without conscious control, they can be subordinated as operations in the service of more complex actions, which arise because of new demands and new motives. Thus,

at each qualitatively distinct level of development a dominant role is assumed by a specific type of leading activity, which determines the form of mastery and to a large extent the character and extent of the acquired content. Such leading types of activity at an early age are object manipulations; for preschool-age children, games; and for school-age children, learning combined with various types of practice in mutually useful tasks [Reprinted from *The psychology of preschool children* by A. V. Zaporozhets & D. B. Elkonin (Eds.) by permission of the MIT Press, Cambridge, Massachusetts. P. xx].

While different activities, or motives, are dominant at different levels of development, they do not necessarily appear only at the levels in which they are dominant. Rather, they may be present at different levels as nondominant components in a system of motives. The system of motives determines the formation of the dominant motives and the mode of executing them. Cognitive processes are formed and develop as "individual exploratory acts" that fulfill the orienting and regulating functions of dominant motives, but always in context of the system of motives.

A task becomes meaningful when it is interpreted consistently with a motive, but the interpretation also depends in part on the system of motives. Motives and their systematic structure change with age; hence, a task may have different meanings or validities at different ages (see also P. B. Baltes, Reese, & Nesselroade, 1977; Reese, 1976b). For the young child, "winning" may be unimportant (Zaporozhets *et al.,* 1971, p. 250). The dominant motive for the preschool child is play (e.g., Lisina & Neverovich, 1971, p. 295), although the play motive can be social (Yendovitskaya, 1971b, p. 93). For the elementary-school child, according to the Soviet view, the dominant motive is goal-directed educational activity (Lisina & Neverovich, p. 295; Zaporozhets & Elkonin, 1971a, p. xx). However, the elementary-school child, in America at least, is also a collector; the peak age for collecting is at about 10 to 11 years (Hurlock, 1964, pp. 460–461). For the American elementary-school child, then, the dominant motive may be economic (collect material gains). For the college student the dominant motive may be intellectual (outwit the experimenter), and for the old person, social (interact with the experimenter). If so, then a discriminative-learning task, for example, might be interpreted as a game by the preschooler, as labor by the elementary-schooler, as a puzzle by the college student, and as a nuisance by the old person (or the old person might interpret it as a guessing game, a part of the social interaction implying taking turns at hiding the token). The appropriate action, then, would be to have fun for the preschooler, disregarding winning and losing; to work hard for the elementary-schooler, with less emphasis on winning than on trying hard; to solve the problem for the college student, emphasizing winning; and to avoid the task or to guess for the old person, in either case in the context of socializing.

In modest, anecdotal support of these hypothesized changes in dominant motives, (a) preschool children often appear to be unconcerned with winning (Zaporozhets *et al.,* 1971; see also Meacham, in press), which is not surprising when one notes that American researchers have often explicitly told the children that the task is a game; (b) L. B. Miller and Estes (1961) found that when monetary rewards were used in a discriminative-learning task, elementary-school children performed relatively poorly, apparently because they were preoccupied with their gains, tending to "gloat, count, and worry" about the money rather than attend to the task (see also McGraw & McCullers, 1974; Tindall & Ratliff, 1974); (c) Levinson and Reese found that college students sometimes refused to eat the consumable rewards gained—small chocolate candies—and returned them to the experimenter at the end of the task, perhaps because solving the task was sufficient reward (Levinson & Reese, 1967, previously unreported observation); and finally (d) Levinson and Reese (1967) reported that old persons were sometimes so preoccupied with socializing with the experimenter that they were inattentive to the task and became task-oriented only when told that a social period would follow completion of the task.

All forms of psychological development are interrelated, in the Soviet view, and development in all cases is attributed to the same underlying processes. Verbal processes, for example, are involved in the development of voluntary attention (Yendovitskaya, 1971a), voluntary memory (Yendovitskaya, 1971b), imagination (Repina, 1971), imitation (Lisina & Neverovich, 1971), and motor development (Lisina & Neverovich, 1971, pp. 328–341). Verbal development itself is related to the development of thinking (Zaporozhets et al., 1971) and speech (Elkonin, 1971). For example, voluntary attention begins to appear in the preschool age, and its development is closely related to the development of verbal regulation, including verbal instruction from an adult and verbalizations by the child (Yendovitskaya, 1971a). Further, "The participation of speech ['verbal mediation'] in the establishment of semantic connections within the material being remembered is one of the central factors in memory development during preschool age [Yendovitskaya, 1971b, p. 102]."

A distinction is made between situational and contextual speech (Rubenshtein, cited in Elkonin, 1971, pp. 113ff). The difference between these forms is in the objective, semantic content of speech. The content of situational speech is clear only when the situation being discussed and paralinguistic accompaniments are taken into consideration. It reflects an involuntary tendency of the child "to construct his speech on the basis of what he directly knows and understands [Rubenshtein, cited in Elkonin, 1971, p. 116]." The content of contextual speech is clear independently of taking the situation into account. Situational speech appears ontogenetically earlier than contextual speech, but the two forms coexist by about 7 years of age, when either form is used depending on which is appropriate (Leushina, cited in Elkonin, 1971, p. 114).

Early in speech development, relational expressions are understood only in reference to concrete, perceived object relationships—situational speech. Later, relational expressions acquire symbolic meaning—contextual speech—"becoming a grammatical form expressing object-relationships apart from concreteness [Elkonin, 1971, p. 144]."

3. A Dialectical Model of Discriminative Performance

In the Soviet model of psychological development, a distinction is made between voluntary and involuntary actions. Voluntary memory, for example, requires a motive that makes the mnemonic goal meaningful and depends on the availability of appropriate actions and operations subordinated to the mnemonic goal. Involuntary memory also requires a motive, but not one that makes the mnemonic goal meaningful, and it also depends on appropriate actions and operations, but not ones that are directed to a mnemonic goal. (A. L. Brown's, 1975, strategic–nonstrategic distinction is similar to the voluntary–involuntary distinction, in that Brown's distinction seems to refer to whether or not *deliberate* selection of a strategy is needed rather than to whether or not any kind of strategic intervention occurs.) Paradoxically, an intention to remember—having the mnemonic goal—may interfere with recall in young children. The intention to remember may lead to inappropriate actions in the young child, yielding neither voluntary nor involuntary memory, while an appropriate action may occur without the intention to remember, yielding involuntary memory.

The distinction between voluntary and involuntary actions should also be encountered in discriminative performance. Both types of action in this extension of the distinction could involve speech. Voluntary discriminative learning would require voluntary attention to the discriminative cues. In the Soviet model, attention depends on identifying the goals and conditions of a task and the situational elements forming the context of the task (Yendovitskaya, 1971a). In a problem-solving task, the child considers the conditions of the problem, forms an intention, and then executes it. The child's initial intellectual solutions consist of the application of earlier formed actions to new situations (cf. Kendler & Kendler, 1967). The older child uses more complex actions involving the construction of a solution method (actions and operations) appropriate to the new problem.

According to Lyublinskaya (cited in Elkonin, 1971, pp. 129–130), speech functions to formulate the problem and to plan a course of action. In its latter function, speech represents a prototype of internal planning, which is ineffective unless speech also has a regulatory function leading to execution of the plan.

By analogy to the developments in speech, there should be situational and contextual discriminative actions, differing in generalized *meaning*. A situational discriminative action would be adduced to suit a specific task, that is, the directly experienced stimulus dimensions in specific locations, and so on. A contextual discriminative action would be independent of the specific situation; it would refer to generalized problem-solving approaches of sufficient scope to be applicable in a variety of situations. For specific application, however, the contextual form would require activation of subordinated versions of the ontogenetically prior situational discriminative actions.

Situational and contextual discriminative actions also have analogies in the realm of motor development, specifically, analogies to visual demonstration and verbal instruction. For example, "a habit developed from verbal instruction is more flexible than one formed on the basis of visual demonstration [Lisina & Neverovich, 1971, p. 339] ." Additional evidence is that young children tend to respond to perceptual cues more than to conceptual cues, while older children can respond with equal ease to whichever type of cue is more appropriate (Ingison & Levin, 1975; see also Gollin & Schadler, 1972; Schadler, 1973). Perceptual cues, according to the present analysis, would be expected to be more effective when the discriminative actions are situational, conceptual cues when the discriminative actions are contextual.

The emergence of contextual speech parallels the emergence of verbal mediation in memory (cf. Yendovitskaya, 1971b). Hence, it is reasonable to suppose that the emergence of contextual discriminative actions should parallel these developments; that is, contextual discriminative actions are presumably indentifiable as verbal mediators in the form of contextual speech. A difference is that both situational and contextual speech serve the goal of social interaction, while the discriminative actions seem to serve a problem-solving goal. However, an implication of the present analysis is that the problem-solving goal may itself be subservient to the more general goal of social interaction, in this case social interaction between subject and experimenter (see also Bronfenbrenner, 1974; Riegel, 1975). In this connection Syrkina (cited in Elkonin, 1971, pp. 125ff) found that children's requests for help in problem solving were least frequent when the child was with an unfamiliar adult experimenter, intermediate in frequency when with a group of unfamiliar children, and most frequent when with a group of familiar children, indicating a relation between mutual collaboration in problem solving and the probability of social interaction.

Just as the unit of speech is not the word but the sentence (Elkonin, 1971), so the unit of discriminative performance is not the single-trial response but the pattern of responses across trials. The pattern of performance reflects actions and operations intended to satisfy the problem-solving goal, which is determined by the dominant motive of a particular stage of development. If the task is interpreted as a discriminative-learning task, then presumably the discriminative actions will be voluntary; if it is interpreted as a game or as labor, for example, then the discriminative actions should be involuntary, and may or may not lead to problem solution. In both cases, however, the actions may be predominantly verbal. For the young preschooler, these actions should be situational, closely tied to the concrete, physical present; and for the older preschooler, the actions should be contextual, referring to generalized problem-solving routines and attempted solutions, which in turn would refer to subordinated actions and operations derived from the ontogenetically prior situational discriminative actions.

III. Theory and Research on Discriminative Performance

In the present section, selected domains of data on discriminative learning and transfer are surveyed, together with relevant theoretical analyses. The selected domains are a small subset of the data set on discriminative performance, but they clearly reflect the kinds of troublesome problems that arise in behavioral analyses and that make the dialectical approach a reasonable alternative. From the domain of discriminative learning, the selected problems are simultaneous discrimination and transverse patterning. From the domain of discriminative transfer, the selected problems are the acquired distinctiveness and equivalence of cues and discriminative learning set.

A. Simultaneous Discrimination

1. Stimulus–Response and Cognitive Theories

Spiker's stimulus-interaction theory (1963, 1970, 1971) is the best articulated and most successful stimulus–response theory of discriminative performance. Nevertheless, it is not entirely successful. For example, Spiker assumed response only to absolute cues, and the theory seems to yield incorrect predictions when performance can be facilitated by response to relational cues (Berch, 1972). However, this problem is of no systematic importance because even strict behaviorists do not need to deny the possibility of effective relational cues (e.g., Bergmann, 1957; Spence, 1952), and Reese (1968) has shown that relational cues can be incorporated in a strict stimulus–response learning theory similar to Spiker's.

Another problem is more serious. Spiker and Cantor (1973) noted two points at which the theory encounters difficulty: Performance changes more rapidly than predicted, and the amount of transfer is sometimes greatly underestimated. Fitzgerald (1974) and Reese and Porges (1976) considered these problems to challenge the basic tenets of the theory because the effects on learning and transfer appear earlier than expected in stimulus–response theory but not earlier than expected in cognitive theory.

According to learning theory, memory is a product of learning; and in cognitive models, such as the information-processing models of memory and of discriminative performance, learning is a product of memory (e.g., Reese, 1973). More formally, memory is a derived phenomenon in stimulus–response associationism, attributed to the development of habit strength through reinforcement in the Hullian version; and learning is a derived phenomenon in cognitive theory, attributed to memory traces that are created and maintained by coding and other processing operations. One implication of this difference is that acquisition is expected to be gradual in stimulus–response theories, reflecting gradual increments in habit strength through reinforced repetitions of the stimulus–response association, while acquisition can be saltatory in cognitive theories if optimum processing operations are used.

The intent here is not to single out Spiker's theory for criticism. Another well-developed stimulus–response theory—the attention theory of Zeaman and House (1963)—is at least equally susceptible to criticism (see Adams & Shepp, 1975; Reese & Porges, 1976). One alternative to stimulus–response theories such as these is the cognitive model referring to strategies or hypotheses rather than to stimulus–response associations (e.g., Casey, 1975; Reese, 1976a; Reese & Porges, 1976).

Levine and his colleagues have developed a well-articulated hypothesis-sampling theory of discriminative learning (e.g., Levine, 1975). According to the theory, subjects sample hypotheses from the set in their repertoire and may test them against the feedback provided by rewarded and nonrewarded choices. The hypotheses are classified as "response-set" hypotheses or as "prediction" hypotheses. A response-set hypothesis reflects bias and is relatively insensitive to disconfirmation. This category includes position preference, position alternation, stimulus preference, and stimulus alternation. A prediction hypothesis is considered to be an attempted solution to the task instead of merely a transfer from previous experience.

Hypotheses may be sampled unsystematically or systematically. Unsystematic sampling means that hypotheses are sampled at random; systematic sampling means that when the hypothesis being tested is disconfirmed, there are rules for selecting the next hypothesis to be tested (e.g., the hypothesis selected is "locally consistent"—it explains why the last-rewarded response was rewarded). Systematic sampling is "stereotypic" when it involves response-set hypotheses, and is "strategic" when it involves prediction hypotheses (Gholson, Levine, & Phillips, 1972; Levine, 1975). The strategic hypothesis-sampling systems include "hypothesis checking," or trying out each of the possible prediction hypotheses successively and systematically; "dimension checking," or trying out each dimension to test its relevance, again successively and systematically; and "focusing," or simultaneously testing all possible hypotheses and eliminating all logically disconfirmed ones. Hypothesis checking and dimension checking require local consistency, and focusing requires global consistency. Local consistency means that the hypotheses now sampled are consistent with stimulus cues included in the immediately preceding correct stimulus complex; global consistency means that the hypotheses now sampled are consistent with cues included in all previously correct stimulus complexes. Global consistency, and hence the focusing strategy, requires perfect memory; and perfect memory is also required for hypothesis checking and dimension checking if sampling is without replacement.[3]

---

[3] This scheme refers specifically to performance in a multidimensional discriminative task that is set up to require concept identification in a small fixed number of trials. Since focusing requires perfect memory and global consistency, it will always yield the solution in the fewest logically possible trials. Hypothesis checking involves arranging the hypotheses into sets, each including all hypotheses referring to a particular dimension, then systematically testing each hypothesis within a set before proceeding to the next set. This system will lead to solution, but requires a large number of trials unless the subject is lucky and checks the hypotheses referring to the correct dimension early. Dimension checking leads to relatively rapid learning in most tasks, since all dimensions can be tested very quickly. In a task with two values per dimension, for example, only one value per dimension is actually tested, because the subject using the dimension-checking system realizes that the complementary value is disproved at the time of locally consistent sampling; that is, the presently tested value is locally consistent, and therefore its complement has already been disproved. (The foregoing analysis is based on a personal communication from B. Gholson, May 2, 1976.) In other kinds of discriminative tasks,

Developmental research by Gholson and his colleagues has shown that unsystematic hypothesis sampling is relatively rare even in children in the preoperational stage of cognitive development (Gholson, 1976), that local consistency increases with age, that "zero memory" (sampling with replacement) declines, that the use of a stereotyped system decreases, and that the use of a strategic system increases (e.g., Gholson & Danziger, 1975). To account for these data, and others, Gholson, O'Connor, and Stern (1976) suggested a synthesis of Piagetian and hypothesis-sampling theory. A "processor" or "executive system" changes qualitatively with development, perhaps as in the "developmentally related groupings described by Piaget [p. 74]." In addition, cognitive subprocesses such as stimulus differentiation and attention are sequentially organized, and their availability and interrelations change quantitatively with development. Several studies have demonstrated a relation between Piagetian concepts and discriminative performance. For example, Buss and Rabinowitz (1973) demonstrated that seriation training increased intermediate-hue transposition in first- and second-graders; and Fitzgerald (1974) demonstrated a relation between preschoolers' classification ability and their performance in the acquired-distinctiveness–acquired-equivalence task.

Nevertheless, a better approach might be to merge the hypothesis-sampling theory with the dialectical model. The executive system is presumably the system of motives, and the cognitive subprocesses are the actions and operations that serve the learning goals, reflecting task interpretations made within the system of motives. In the dialectical model, the hypotheses may be actions, carried out with conscious intent, or they may be operations, carried out in the service of some conscious action. In either case, a hypothesis must be supported by operations such as remembering the previous choice and—for prediction hypotheses—the outcome of the previous choice. In the rest of this chapter, hypotheses are assumed to be actions, that is, under conscious control. The hypothesis-sampling systems are best interpreted as actions, superordinate to the hypotheses in the structure of actions. The hypothesis-sampling system used, and the hypotheses used in the selected hypothesis-sampling system, will presumably depend on the dominant motive as well as on previous experience with each hypothesis-sampling system, each hypothesis, and the operations that support the hypotheses.

An example of the dialectical approach is the interpretation of unsystematic hypothesis sampling. By Levine's definition, the strategic hypothesis-sampling systems require local (or global) consistency and sampling without replacement. In the dialectical model these restrictions refer to the level of operations and not to the level of performance. Suppose that a child's structure of motives is such that he elects to use a particular strategic hypothesis-sampling system, but suppose that at his level of development the required memory operations are not yet well practiced, hence not yet capable of being fully subordinated to the goal of the concept-identi-

---

different sets of hypotheses are used, but in general they are separable into "response sets" and "prediction hypotheses," and hence "stereotyped" and "strategic" hypothesis-sampling systems are possible, and there may be subdivisions among the strategic systems.

fication task. The child intends to use the local consistency rule, which is part of the structure of operations in any strategic hypothesis-sampling system, but local consistency requires that he remember the stimulus that was positive on the last feedback trial. Thus, the child's imperfect memory, resulting from incomplete subordination of the relevant memory operations to the problem-solving goal, interferes with local consistency in his hypothesis sampling. Memory operations are also needed for sampling without replacement, which requires remembering the hypotheses that have already been tested and rejected. With inefficient memory operations, the child will have imperfect avoidance of these hypotheses. In short, unsystematic hypothesis sampling is conceptualized as an attempt at systematic hypothesis sampling that fails because of a deficiency in the operative system, specifically in memory operations that are needed for local consistency and sampling without replacement, thus yielding the paradox of systematic sampling with replacement.

The above example deals with a discrepancy between competence at the action level and performance, and the discrepancy is attributed to incompetence with respect to the operations that serve the actions. The dialectical approach can also deal with other competence–performance discrepancies, or decalages, and seems to explain them more readily than does the Piagetian approach. In the dialectical approach, decalages are attributed to changes in operations rather than to task variables per se. The structure of motives changes developmentally, leading to changes in the interpretation of a task and consequently to changes in the goals of the task, leading in turn to changes in the actions that are mobilized, hence determining which actions will become well-enough established to be capable of being subordinated as operations to enhance performance.

2. Decalages in Performance

It is known that intercorrelations of performance across different learning tasks are low in children (Ash, 1975; Friedrichs, Hertz, Moynahan, Simpson, Arnold, Christy, Cooper, & Stevenson, 1971; Martin & Blum, 1961; Stevenson, 1970; Stevenson, Friedrichs, & Simpson, 1970; Stevenson, Hale, Klein, & Miller, 1968; Stevenson & Odom, 1965). Even when the tasks are methodologically similar, the correlations are not high. For example, Stevenson and Odom (1965) found that three discrimination tasks had an average intercorrelation (among grades and sexes) of only about .40, and two verbal tasks had an average intercorrelation of only about .42 (there was no correlation between the two types of tasks, average about .05).

Across methodologically different tasks that have a similar theoretical basis the interrelations are even lower. Ash (1975) gave third-grade children four tasks that are theoretically related to mediational processes—reversal shift in the optional discriminative-shift task, free recall of a categorized list, mediated association in paired-associate learning, and far-test intermediate-size transposition. The relationships among the tasks were found to be unsystematic, weak, and statistically nonsignificant. Unfortunately, Ash's empirical analysis was not fine grained: (a) subjects were classed as mediating versus not mediating on the optional-shift task, but no distinction was made among the latter subjects between those with production deficiency and those with control deficiency; and (b) mediation in the other three tasks was assessed as a continuous variable (clustering score in free recall, trials to criterion on the critical paired-associate list, number of transposition responses) rather than as even the gross dichotomy between mediating and nonmediating subjects. Thus, the Ash results are not definitive. They are, however, suggestive that a decalage exists among tasks in which mediation should affect performance.

Reese (1962) suggested that such a decalage might reflect the level of learning of the potential mediators. According to this interpretation, there is one mediational process, and deficiencies in its operation are determined by characteristics of the mediating responses.

3. Dialectical Interpretation of Decalages

An alternative interpretation is provided by dialectical theory, according to which there is not one mediational process but rather a variety of hypotheses, or actions, that can mediate between stimulation and behavior. Deficiencies in the evocation of these actions depend upon whether the actions are available to the relevant goal and whether the subject interprets the task in such a way as to make that goal relevant. Deficiencies in the utilization of the actions that are evoked depend upon whether the supporting operations have already been subordinated to their service.

Both the relevant interpretation of the task and the availability of the relevant actions and operations are related to age, in that the interpretation of the task and the acquisition of actions depend on the structure of motives, which changes developmentally, and the subordination of operations depends on the structure of motives, the structure of societal demands, and the complexity of the actions to be subordinated—all of which are related to age.

If the subject interprets the tasks used by Ash in the ways that are intended, then the relevant actions are (a) for optional shift, "same dimension is relevant, switch choice"; (b) for the categorized list, "observe the categories, sort the words mentally, and retrieve by categories"; (c) for mediated association, "note the A–B, B–C relation, and use it to relate A and C in List 3"; and (d) for transposition, "ignore the change in absolute size and choose the same relative size." (Note, however, that these actions are stated contextually. Stated situationally, as they perhaps would be in practice, the actions might be, for example, "size is relevant, switch to small," "sort the words into numbers, parts of the body, etc.," "table goes with desk, desk with vag, therefore table goes with vag, etc.," and "choose the middle-sized one.") These actions are obviously different from one another, and it should not be surprising if they are in different stages of acquisition, or evocability.

Thus, even if these actions served the same superordinate goal-action—"use a verbal mediating process"—the same level of performance would not necessarily be expected in all four tasks.

Actually, the hypothesis-actions probably serve different goal-actions, strengthening the expectation of different performance levels. The optional-shift and transposition tasks both begin as multidimensional discrimination problems. In the optional-shift task, the initial problem is a two-stimulus simultaneous discrimination with five dimensions (absolute and relative dimensions of brightness and size, plus position), and the initial problem in the transposition task is a three-stimulus simultaneous discrimination with three dimensions (absolute and relative size, plus position). In spite of the differences between these problems, the goal is the same ("solve the discrimination"), and the relevant action may be the same ("use a strategic system of hypothesis checking"). The subordinate actions—sampling and testing prediction hypotheses about dimensional values—would be somewhat different because of the difference in the numbers of values on the dimensions (two vs. three). Suppose, however, that the outcome is the same in the sense that the action eventually selected includes "choose relative size," plus "choose larger" for the optional-shift task and "choose middle-sized" for the transposition task. In the next phase of the optional-shift task, the relevance of the selected action is disconfirmed, and the subject must decide whether to retain part of the action, leading to "choose relative size, shift to smaller," the *reversal shift,* or to try "choose brightness," the *nonreversal shift.* The reversal shift might reflect hypothesis checking, and the nonreversal shift dimension checking, but if so, the developmental trends seem to be anomalous. Human subjects generally exhibit the reversal shift, but young children often exhibit nonreversal (e.g., Eimas, 1970). A sample of the type of analysis needed to explain differences such as these is presented later (Section III,A,4).

In the transposition test in Ash's study, the subject should notice the change in the situation (because it was a far test with a 2:1 ratio of stimuli—see Reese, 1968) and must decide whether to retain the action selected in original learning, "choose relative size, choose middle-sized," yielding a *transposition response,* or to try a different action, "choose absolute size, choose most similar to positive training stimulus," yielding an *absolute response.* College students will try one of these, and if it is disconfirmed (response nonreinforced), will shift to the other (Zeiler, 1964). It is worth noting that other changes in actions are possible, such as "choose relative size, try largest," or "choose absolute size, avoid similarity to positive training stimulus," but these actions are not intuitively reasonable, and the evidence indicates that they rarely occur (for review, see Reese, 1968).

The goal of the other two tasks used by Ash, free recall and paired associates, is mnemonic and therefore different from the goal of the two discrimination tasks. Hence, the relevant actions are not the same as in the discrimination tasks. The action selected for the two memory tasks may be the same for both tasks—"use a mnemonic strategy"—but the mnemonic strategy that is most efficient will not be the same—"categorize" versus "elaborate imagined referents of the words" (e.g., Paivio, 1971).

The conclusion, then, from the dialectical perspective is that the lack of interrelatedness among different learning tasks, even ones that are methodologically or theoretically related, is certainly not unexpected and can easily be explained by identifying differences in goals, actions, or operations associated with the different tasks.

4. Sample of Needed Analysis

The kind of analysis needed for a dialectical interpretation is illustrated by an examination of a study by Cole (1976) dealing with discriminative learning and reversal shift. In this study Cole used a technique he had developed for identifying the cues to which children respond. The stimuli, presented two at a time, were three-dimensional, and the two stimuli presented on any one trial differed on all three dimensions. Four of the eight possible stimuli were used for learning, and the other four were reserved for testing. For example, with form relevant, the four training stimuli were a large black square (+) versus a small white triangle (−), and a small white square (+) versus a large black triangle (−). After the child attained a learning criterion, trials with the test stimuli were interspersed among further training trials. In the example, the test stimuli would be large white square versus small black triangle, and small black square versus large white triangle. A subject who is responding on the basis of the form dimension, whether because of selective attention (e.g., Zeaman & House, 1963) or mediation (e.g., Kendler, 1972), should consistently choose the square on the test trials (in the example); but a subject who is responding to compounds or objects as wholes should not choose any one of the test compounds consistently because none of the test compounds was encountered during training.

Using this method, Cole found that 54% of 3-, 4-, and 5-year-old lower-class children were responding to compounds, and the other 46% were mediating (or using selective attention). After the initial discrimination was learned to a new criterion, a reversal shift was given, again with interspersed test trials. In this transfer task, 66% of the children responded to compounds, and only 34% used mediation (or selective attention). Thus, the children were more likely to respond to compounds in the transfer task than in the initial task—in fact, 56% of the children who initially exhibited mediation switched to compounding, while only 26% switched from compounding to mediating.

The results fit neatly, but of course tentatively, with the dialectical theory outlined in the present chapter. Given that the children in Cole's study were young and from the lower class, they should be in the Piagetian preoperational stage of cognitive development (e.g., Morello, Turner, & Reed, 1976). In the dialectical model, they should be characterized by "situational" discriminative actions rather than by "contextual" actions (see Section II,D,3). Both compounding and mediating appear to reflect situational actions, in that both are specific to the presented objects and their physical attributes, and therefore the appearance of both kinds of responding is consistent with the dialectical model. However, within the dialectical model it seems reasonable to infer that compounding reflects a more primitive form of situational action than does mediating or selective attending in the sense that the former is lower in the complexity hierarchy and is ontogenetically prior. Responsiveness to compounds, or wholes, is primitive according to Gestalt theory and research (see Reese, 1968), the probability of mediation increases ontogenetically (e.g., Kendler, 1972; Reese, 1962; White, 1965), and selective attention increases ontogenetically (e.g., Yendovitskaya, 1971a). In the standard discrimination task, mediating is more efficient than responding to compounds, because with response to elements a single discrimination solves the problem, while with response to compounds several discriminations must be learned, one for each compound containing the positive cue. Presumably, children tend to use the most advanced action that is available and consistent with their interpretation of the task. A final consideration is that in the reversal shift the subject's initial basis of responding is abruptly and mysteriously disconfirmed (in the typical procedure, as in Cole's study, there is no break between the initial learning and transfer tasks).

Given these assumptions, Cole's results indicate that when the mediational action was initially used and subsequently disconfirmed, the children tended to reject this action and shift to the compounding action, which, being lower (more primitive) in the hierarchy of actions, was readily available. Conversely, when the compounding action was initially used and subsequently disconfirmed, the children tended to retain the compounding action because the more advanced mediational action tended not to be available in the hierarchy (having not yet been acquired).

The analysis of Cole's results in terms of the hierarchy of actions implies that there should be age differences in performance on a task even when the same motives and actions are involved, as would be expected when the age range covered is small. Across large age ranges, there should be age differences in performance not only because of changes in the available actions and operations but also because of changes in the dominant motives, with consequent changes in the goals of a task and changes in the actions that can be and are brought to bear upon the task.

5. Age Differences

A sample of the research on age differences in discriminative learning was summarized by Reese (1968, Table 5-9, p. 162). The 22 studies cited included 12 covering relatively small age ranges (median 2.2 years, range 1.0–3.3 years) within the span from 1.7 to 9.5 years, and 10 covering large age ranges (median 6.5 years, range 4–14 years) within the span from 0.7 years to college age. All the studies dealt with two-stimulus simultaneous discrimination, and age differences were assessed cross sectionally. Among the studies covering small age ranges, 75% indicated that learning speed increased with age (but not significantly in one-third of these studies), and the other 25% indicated no change with age. The trend was not clear in two of the studies covering large age ranges, but among the other eight, 50% indicated an increase in learning speed with age, 25% no change, and 25% mixed effects. Thus, learning speed tends to increase with age over small ranges, but may increase or exhibit mixed effects over large ranges. In one of the large-range studies showing mixed effects (Shirai, 1951) learning speed increased between 2 and 4 years, then decreased from 5 through 13 years. In the other study showing mixed effects (Stevenson, Iscoe, & McConnell, 1955) learning speed increased from preschool to the fifth grade, then decreased through college age.

The developmental changes in speed of acquisition are psychologically important, but the main reason is that they lead to the question of why the changes occur. The slower learning speed at the older age levels has been attributed to the use of more complex hypotheses by the older subjects (e.g., Kendler, Kendler, & Learnard, 1962, pp. 583–585; Rabinowitz & Cantor, 1967; Shirai, 1951; Stevenson et al., 1955). A similar effect was obtained by Osler and Trautman (1961), comparing normal and intellectually gifted children. The superior children outperformed the normal children on a simple two-dimensional task, but were inferior to the normal children on a multidimensional task, apparently because the gifted children tried out unnecessarily complex hypotheses in the latter task while the normal children used simpler hypotheses in the two tasks (on which they performed equally well, incidentally).

The young child's poor discriminative performance may result, in part, from perceived social norms: The solution may require actions the child has not performed or that he believes he is not permitted to perform. When the child reaches the preschool age, adults begin to demand that he exhibit greater independence, but he is still encouraged to seek adult aid in the natural environment, and therefore he has a tendency toward collaborative and cooperative interaction with adults (Elkonin, 1971, p. 129). Consequently, "the child constantly orients himself toward an adult, turns to him with requests, demands and quite often attains the necessary results only directly through another human being [Zaporozhets et al., 1971, p. 211]." However, in the usual laboratory-learning study in American research, the experimenter is cast as an *imago incognito*, forbidden to interact with the subject after the task begins, except, in some studies, to provide verbal rewards or punishments. The intent, of course, is to prevent the "Clever Hans" error (cf. Katz, 1937, pp. 2–10). However, in the Soviet view the Clever Hans phenomenon is not an error but rather is the essence of the child's performance. Thus, as Bronfenbrenner (1974) also noted, a naturally social situation becomes asocial or even antisocial. Consequently, the child is not only bewildered by the adult experimenter's refusal to give help, but may also inhibit his own intellectual actions, in order not to violate the norm that he may believe has prohibited these actions (apparently prohibited in the past by adults who gave aid before it was requested—as is perhaps usually the case—and apparently prohibited now by the experimenter's suppressing his own actions).

In line with the above suggestion, the speech of a 3- to 4-year-old child is likely to be about the task and associations to it rather than about its solution (the latter type of comment being apparently prohibited). In addition, Levina (cited in Zaporozhets *et al.*, 1971, pp. 214–215) found that when the experimenter asked task-relevant questions, such as "How are you going to reach that?" or "What is broken?" the actions of the child were more organized and goal-directed. The mutual actions of the child and adult, without the adult's providing the solution, were natural enough to encourage the child to use his own mental actions and to direct them toward the problem at hand.

With respect to questioning by an experimenter, the relevance of the child's answer depends at least in part on whether the questions seem reasonable or natural to the child. Blank (1975) noted that the usual form of questioning a young child about his discriminative performance is to ask, with the discriminanda in view, "How did you know which one to choose?" This question is much less reasonable than "Which one had the candy?"; but even the latter is not sensible if the discriminanda are in view, because the experimenter can see them as clearly as the child and therefore knows as well as the child which one had the candy. More reasonably, the experimenter could ask "Which one had the candy?" with the discriminanda removed from view. Blank found that under the last condition 81% of 3- and 4-year-olds gave relevant answers, while essentially none gave relevant answers to the same question when the discriminanda were in view, nor to the "How" question whether or not the discriminanda were in view.

B. Transverse Patterning

1. Definition of the Task

A conditional discrimination is one in which no stimulus *element* is consistently positive but some stimulus *combinations* are consistently positive. The combinations can be cue–position compounds or cue–cue compounds. Cue–position compounds are relevant in the simplest kind of conditional discrimination, the successive-discrimination problem in which two stimuli are presented, one at a time, and a different positional response is associated with each stimulus. Warren (1960) identified this task as a "sign-differentiated positional" problem. Children can solve this kind of conditional discrimination problem, although it is generally more difficult than the two-stimulus simultaneous-discrimination problem (Horowitz & Armentrout, 1965; for review, see Rieber, 1970).

Another kind of conditional discrimination involves cue–cue compounds. Two sets of stimuli are used, typically with two stimuli per set. The two stimuli in one set are presented simultaneously, and those in the other set are presented successively. The successive stimuli determine which of the simultaneous stimuli is positive. For example, given a choice between a triangle and a circle, the triangle might be positive if both shapes are white and the circle positive if both are black. In this type of conditional discrimination, identified by Warren (1960) as a "sign-differentiated object" problem, as in the sign-differentiated positional problem the two sets of cues may be spatially overlapping; that is, in the sign-differentiated positional problem a trial generally consists of presenting two instances of one stimulus, and the correct response is to the instance in one of the two locations. Thus, the conditional or sign cue overlaps spatially with the positional cue. Similarly, in the sign-differentiated object problem, the conditional or sign cue—black versus white, for example—overlaps spatially with the object cues.

In another kind of conditional discrimination involving cue—cue compounds the two sets of cues do not overlap spatially (Eimas & Doan, 1965). This is the "transverse-patterning" problem (Spence, 1952) in which the positive stimulus is conditional upon the stimulus pairing, which varies from setting to setting. For example, if Stimuli A and B are presented, A is correct; if B and C are presented, B is correct; and if A and C are presented, C is correct. Each stimulus is correct in one of the three pairings, incorrect in a second pairing, and absent from the third pairing. The differences between this problem and the other kind of cue—cue compounding problem (sign-differentiated object problem) are so striking that it seems desirable to use a different label for the compound involved, and Spence's (1952) term, transverse pattern, seems appropriate.

Spiker's theory predicts successful performance in the sign-differentiated positional problem and the sign-differentiated object problem, but predicts that the transverse-patterning problem is unsolvable (Croll, 1967). Spence (1952), however, predicted not only that the transverse-patterning problem is solvable but that it should present no particular problem to infrahuman subjects: "Presumably white rats should be able to learn such a pattern discrimination problem; certainly it should be possible of solution by monkeys or chimpanzees [p. 92]." The discrepancy between these predictions arises because Spiker assumed only responsiveness to stimulus components, while Spence was assuming responsiveness to compounds, specifically transverse patterns.

2. Survey of Research

Thompson (1953) found that chimpanzees could solve the transverse-patterning problem, but it was far from easy. One of five chimpanzees failed to solve the problem in 2100 trials (this chimpanzee had extensive brain damage, however), and the other four solved it in from 358 to 1031 trials, averaging about 718. Furthermore, even when they had solved the problem, errors were relatively frequent, averaging about 9% in the 60-trial criterion run. Finally, no other researcher has had as much success in bringing the majority of a group to criterion on this problem without special training techniques, even when the subjects were college students. In the studies with human subjects, however, no researcher has given as many training trials as were required by the average chimpanzee in Thompson's study, and Thompson's training procedure was used in only one study.

Thompson trained the subjects to criterion on Pair 1, next trained them to criterion on Pair 2, and then trained them to criterion on both pairs. Next, the subjects were trained to criterion on Pair 3, with "retention" trials on Pairs 1 and 2, and finally the subjects were trained on Pairs 1, 2, and 3, presented at random with no one pair presented more than twice in succession. The final training was continued to a criterion of at least 90% correct responses in 60 trials, with a maximum of 3 errors on any one pair.

Paden and Soto (1967) used a procedure essentially the same as Thompson's, testing 4-year-old children. Of 13 children, 1 solved the problem in 170 trials, and the other 12 failed to solve it within 400 trials, although 1 of the 12 was given additional trials and solved the problem within 440 trials.

In all of the other studies with human subjects, the pairs were presented at random from the beginning of training, thus requiring simultaneous learning on all three pairs rather than learning on each pair sequentially. Zeaman and House (1962) used this random-presentation procedure with retarded children and allowed a maximum of 600 trials, at a rate of 30 trials per day, to reach a criterion of 9 correct in 10 trials on each pair for at least 2 of 4 consecutive days. None of the 19 children tested solved the problem.

Berch and Israel (1974) used the random procedure with fourth-graders, allowing a maximum of 90 trials to reach a criterion of 12 consecutive correct responses. None of the 15 children tested solved the problem. (Berch and Israel also included other groups in which substantial numbers of subjects met criterion, but modifications in the task made transverse patterning unnecessary for problem solution, and therefore these groups are irrelevant here.) Berch and Israel (1971) used the same procedure with college students and found that only half of the group solved the problem in the 90 trials allowed.

The same procedure was used by Franks, Reese, and Kohn (1974), except that a maximum of 72 trials was allowed and the criterion was verbalization of the problem solution (probed periodically). The subjects were college students. Only 2 of 16 reached criterion. In another group, trained with a fading technique, only 1 of 15 met criterion; and in a third group, provided with paper and pencil and told to write down whatever might help them, only 4 of 16 met criterion. Most of the subjects in the paper-and-pencil group either wrote nothing or recorded incomplete information. A fourth group was given paper and pencil, told what information was relevant, and told to record it. In this group, 9 of 16 met criterion. Thus, it appears that a major difficulty blocking performance when the random-presentation procedure is used in the memory requirement. When given an external memory aid, college students may eventually arrive at the correct hypothesis.

Franks (1976, Exp. 1) extended the Franks et al. study (1974), again using the random procedure but testing 10-year-olds as well as college students and allowing a maximum of 90 trials to reach a criterion of 12 consecutive correct responses. Four groups were tested, one with the standard procedure, one provided with paper and pencil, one provided with paper and pencil plus pretraining on how to record relevant information, and one provided with paper and pencil plus pretraining on transitive and intransitive conceptual relations. The results are summarized in Table 1. As indicated in the table, only 10% of the children given standard training reached criterion (1 of 10 children), and the external memory aid was not helpful. College students, in contrast, were helped by the external memory aid, without

Table 1

Transverse Patterning by Children and Adults[a]

	Percentage reaching criterion	
Group	10-year-olds	College students
Standard	10	15
Paper only	0	80
Paper plus notation training	10	80
Paper plus concept training	10	70

[a]Adapted from Franks (1976), Experiment 1.

which only 15% (3 of 20 subjects) solved the problem. However, questioning revealed that some of the college students used the recorded information to solve the problem as a matching-to-sample task. Franks did not include a control for matching to sample, and therefore the proportion of the college students who actually learned transverse patterning is indeterminate. One control, suggested by Franks, would be to remove the notes as soon as criterion is reached and continue testing to see whether performance remains at the criterion level. If it deteriorates, then presumably the subject was matching his choices against the pairings recorded in the notes. Another control would be to use verbalization of the correct solution as the learning criterion, as in the Franks *et al.* (1974) study.

Franks reported that even with the notation training, some subjects recorded incomplete or inaccurate information. He therefore ran a second study (Franks, 1976, Exp. 2), again with 10-year-olds and college students. One group was given the standard problem, and another group was given the same problem but after each response the experimenter verbalized relevant information and required the subject to repeat it (e.g., "The circle was right, while the square was wrong"). A maximum of 60 trials was allowed to reach a performance criterion of 12 consecutive correct responses. In addition, the subjects were periodically probed for verbalization of the problem solution. None of the children in the standard condition reached the performance criterion, but 30% (3 of 10 children) reached the performance criterion when task-relevant information was provided verbally. The corresponding percentages for the college students were 25% reaching criterion in the standard group and 65% in the information group (5 and 13 subjects reaching criterion, respectively).

A somewhat different picture emerged when the criterion was verbalization of the problem solution. None of the children given standard training verbalized the solution, but 60% (6 of 10) verbalized the solution in the information group. The corresponding percentages in the college groups were 40% with standard training and 75% with information provided (8 and 15 subjects, respectively). The finding that some subjects could verbalize the solution but did not attain the performance criterion of 12 consecutive correct responses can be interpreted to reflect the influence of memory on performance; that is, a subject may know the correct general hypothesis ("Which one is correct depends on what it is paired with") yet fail to remember which is correct in each specific pair. He may know the correct contextual hypothesis but not remember the details of the correct situational hypothesis (see Section II,D,3 for a discussion of contextual and situational actions). Therefore, in order to understand the performance, it is necessary to consider the competence–performance distinction, which in this case is a distinction between a generally conceptualized contextual hypothesis and a specifically realized situational hypothesis. Acquisition of both is facilitated by reducing the memory requirement, either by providing an external memory aid or by providing verbal formulations that can serve as internal memory aids. Even with a memory aid, however, subjects become confused when the pairs are presented at random, and their performance underestimates their strategic competence.

One final point to be considered is Thompson's success with chimpanzees in contrast to the poor performance of human subjects in standard training conditions. This contrast should not be taken to indicate that chimpanzees are better at hypothesis sampling and testing than are human subjects, according to the Soviet view, because the animals' performance is to be interpreted behavioristically and the human performance cognitively. Thus, it would be consistent with the Soviet view to suggest that the chimpanzees learned and performed consistently with Croll's (1967) extension of Spiker's stimulus-interaction theory, while the human subjects performed consistently with a hypothesis theory in which not perfect memory but near-zero memory is assumed.

C. Acquired Distinctiveness and Equivalence of Cues

1. The Function of Pretraining

Kendler (1972) studied the acquired distinctiveness and equivalence of cues in children and adults. In pretraining, two stimuli were assigned one "name," the word *one,* and two other stimuli were assigned another name, the word *two.* The transfer task was a successive discrimination problem involving one stimulus from each set. As soon as a subject met a criterion of 10 consecutive correct responses in the transfer task, a test phase began. The two stimuli from the transfer task continued to be presented, with correct responses reinforced, and interspersed among these stimulus presentations were presentations of the other stimulus from each set, with all responses to these stimuli reinforced. Having learned different names for the two stimulus sets should yield acquired distinctiveness between these sets, and having learned the same name for the two stimuli within a set should yield acquired equivalence within sets. In the test phase, the acquired distinctiveness and equivalence should yield the same motor response to the test stimuli as were conditioned to the same-set transfer-task stimuli.

The purpose of Kendler's study was to differentiate between production and control deficiencies as a function of age level, which was manipulated by comparing subjects from kindergarten, second grade, fourth grade, and college. Half the subjects were required to emit the stimulus names during the transfer-task and test phases, and the other subjects were not. The overt-names group provided an estimate of control deficiency, since this group produced the names and therefore had no production deficiency. Thus, by comparing the performance of this group with the performance of the group that did not use names overtly, Kendler was able to derive empirical estimates of the probabilities of production and control deficiencies (see Kendler for the estimation equations and required assumptions). Production deficiency was estimated to have a probability of about .5 in all three groups of children and about .1 in the college group, while control deficiency was estimated at about .4, .2, and .1 in the kindergarten, second grade, and fourth grade, respectively, and 0 in the college group. Thus, production deficiency was more frequent than control deficiency at all ages and was relatively common during childhood but relatively rare in adults. Further, when production occurred, control deficiency was not uncommon in kindergartners, but control usually occurred in older children and always occurred in adults.

An interpretation can be derived from learning theory or from cognitive theory. As noted earlier (Section III,A,1), learning is a basic phenomenon in learning theory and is derived from memory in cognitive theories. It follows that according to a learning-theory interpretation of the acquired-distinctiveness–acquired-equivalence task, the effect of pretraining is on learning; and according to a cognitive interpretation, the effect is on memory. A learning-theory interpretation of the function of naming is that the overt motor response that follows a name is automatically conditioned to the name. Therefore, naming will always affect performance by providing a second habit connecting a stimulus with a response. The stimulus itself is linked to the response directly through $_sH_R$ and is indirectly linked to the response through the mediating name. Given this interpretation, Kendler's estimates refer to the probability of production deficiency with respect to naming and to the probability that when produced, the names will mediate (control) overt motor responding.

A second stimulus–response interpretation is that the names are used for rehearsal. In stimulus–response associationism, rehearsal is most easily interpreted to be free-operant verbal behavior, specifically a chain of names designating the stimuli and responses. For example, in the Kendler study, rehearsal could take the form, "one, left; two, right." Presumably, this behavioral chain is occasioned by a discriminative stimulus associated with the intertrial interval and generalized from similar tasks experienced in the past. The rehearsal is ineffective, however, unless the verbal chain mediates the appropriate overt instrumental behavior during the test interval. In other words, the subject emits the verbal chain covertly during the intertrial interval, providing training trials that strengthen the association between the name of the stimulus and the name of the response. At the end of the intertrial interval, a stimulus is presented, and it must elicit (or "occasion") the name conditioned to it during pretraining; this stimulus name must then arouse the response name conditioned to it during the intertrial interval, which then must arouse the motor response.

Kendler's estimates can be interpreted within either the stimulus–response or the cognitive model, referring to production of and control by single-unit mediators—names—in the stimulus–response model and to evocation and utilization of mnemonic strategies in the cognitive model. However, if the function of the names is to aid rehearsal, then the overt-names group in Kendler's study was not necessarily prevented from production or evocation deficiency; that is, in the stimulus–response model this group had no production deficiency with respect to naming the stimuli, but could have been production deficient with respect to rehearsing the stimulus names with names of the responses. If so, then the estimate of control deficiency includes both production and control deficiency with respect to rehearsal. It follows that in the stimulus–response model Kendler's estimate of production deficiency refers to a failure to produce the stimulus names, which are required for rehearsal; and her estimate of control deficiency refers to the conditional probability, given no production deficiency in stimulus naming, of a production deficiency in rehearsal plus any control deficiency in rehearsal. In the cognitive model the overt-names group had no evocation deficiency with respect to the naming strategy, as demonstrated by their naming the stimuli in compliance with the instructions, which also, incidentally, demonstrates the absence of a deficiency in the utilization of the naming strategy. However, this group could have been evocation deficient with respect to the rehearsal strategy. Thus, the estimate of control deficiency provided by this group refers to the conditional probability, given no evocation and utilization deficiency in the naming strategy, of an evocation deficiency in the rehearsal strategy plus any utilization deficiency in this strategy; and the estimate of production deficiency therefore refers only to a failure of evocation or utilization of the naming strategy.

In both models, therefore, if names are useful only for rehearsal, then Kendler's estimates indicate that children often do not spontaneously name stimuli, hence cannot rehearse, while adults usually use the names that are available, and when they use the names, they always use them for rehearsal. Kindergarten children who name the stimuli may or may not use the names for rehearsal, and if they rehearse, the rehearsal may have no effect on performance.

In cognitive theory, rehearsal is a processing operation, but it is assumed to be a maintenance operation rather than a storage operation; that is, material that is rehearsed is not transferred from short- to long-term memory but rather is maintained in short-term memory. While the rehearsal continues, the material remains in short-term memory; but when the rehearsal stops, the material begins to fade from short-term memory and is lost after the standard duration interval (up to 30 seconds). The rehearsal would have the same form as in the stimulus–response model, consisting of a verbal chain, but it would yield improved memory only on a short-term basis.

An implication is that from the stimulus–response perspective rehearsal would normally be expected to require a number of trials to be effective, to permit habit strength to increase, while from the cognitive perspective rehearsal should be effective as soon as it begins, provided that the rehearsal is continuous or that the interval between the end of rehearsal and the time of emitting the discriminative response is shorter than the duration of short-term memory, which seems usually to be the case. Thus, if the effect of pretraining is to provide names for use in rehearsal, then the effects of pretraining should appear gradually in a transfer task according to the stimulus–response model and should appear rapidly according to the cognitive model.

2. Evidence for Cognitive Influences

Reese (1972) studied the acquired distinctiveness and equivalence of cues in children from kindergarten and first and second grades. He found that the effects of the pretraining appeared as early in the transfer task as the experimental design permitted, on Trial 3. Performance on Trial 3 of the transfer task, involving successive discrimination, was facilitated by acquired-distinctiveness pretraining and hindered by acquired-equivalence pretraining, relative to the effect of "same–different" control pretraining. In addition, although the acquired-distinctiveness effect persisted across the remaining 37 trials, the acquired-equivalence effect disappeared after Trial 3. This pattern of results fits the cognitive theory better than it fits the stimulus–response theory. The rapidity with which the effects developed can be explained within learning theory, but more gradual acquisition is generally expected. In cognitive theory, the rapid effect is expected if it reflects the effects of verbal processing on short-term memory, affecting performance and not learning.

The rapid disappearance of the acquired-equivalence effect is unexpected in learning theory, in which the disappearance would presumably be attributed to extinction of the verbal responses as a result of the frequent errors mediated by the common label. In cognitive theory, however, the rapid disappearance of the acquired-equivalence effect is expected because it reflects rejection or suppression of a maladaptive strategy—"use names learned in pretraining"—which is adaptive in the acquired-distinctiveness group. Note that in the cognitive interpretation, the strategy of using names was retained in the acquired-distinctiveness group, hence the names continued to aid short-term memory and consequently continued to facilitate performance. But the acquired-equivalence group rejected this strategy as soon as it was found to be confusing (on Trial 3) and hence exhibited no further interference with performance. In rejecting the naming strategy, the acquired-equivalence group was presumably left with the same performance mechanism as whatever was being used by the "same–different" control group, hence performed like this control group after Trial 3.

Another finding in the Reese study was that performance improved significantly across ages, but the relative effects of the conditions did not vary with age (i.e., there was a main effect of age and no age by condition interaction). Thus, between kindergarten and second grade it appears that the developmental changes in cognitive processing were quantitative and not qualitative; the processing became more efficient but remained the same in kind.

Fitzgerald (1974) replicated the Reese study, but with preschool children $4\frac{1}{2}$ to $5\frac{1}{2}$ years old, half of whom were required to emit the pretrained names during the transfer task, while the other half were not required to verbalize. The subjects were categorized as either exhibiting an effect of pretraining (correct response on Trial 3 in the acquired-distinctiveness group, error in the acquired-equivalence group) or not exhibiting an effect. Fitzgerald hypothesized that the names would function as classifiers rather than mediators, in agreement with the conclusion of Osler and Madden (1973), and therefore that the effect of the names would depend on the children's classification ability, defined (and measured) as a cognitive process consistently with the Piagetian analysis. Specifically, classifiers (children who can classify) should exhibit the effects of pretraining, especially when required to emit the names overtly; but nonclassifiers should not exhibit the effects even when required to emit the names overtly. The basic hypothesis was supported, in that 87% of the classifiers showed an effect of the pretraining, while only 41% of the nonclassifiers showed an effect. The refined hypothesis, referring to differential effects of vocalization, was not supported, in that vocalization increased the percentage of nonclassifiers who showed an effect (50% showed an effect with vocalization, 33% without vocalization) as well as increasing the percentage of classifiers who showed an effect (90% with vocalization, 83% without vocalization). As expected, vocalization enhanced performance in the acquired-distinctiveness condition (nonsignificantly, however) and hindered performance in the acquired-equivalence condition (significantly).

In a general way, Fitzgerald's results support the cognitive analysis, but with some discrepancies. The percentage of classifiers who showed an effect of pretraining was large (87%), but lower than the theoretically expected percentage (100%). Similarly, the percentage of nonclassifiers who showed an effect of pretraining (41%) was lower than that of classifiers, but also somewhat lower than the percentage theoretically expected if responding on the critical trial was random (50%). However, perhaps these discrepancies resulted from errors of assessment rather than from a deficiency in the theoretical analysis. The effect of pretraining was assessed on the basis of dichotomous performance on a single trial; hence, the assessment was probably relatively unreliable. Furthermore, the test of classification ability may have been low in reliability or validity. Either interpretation is plausible, especially the low-validity interpretation, because Fitzgerald included pass, decalage, and transitional subjects in the classifier group. According to the best definitions, pass subjects give correct judgments and explanations; decalage subjects give correct judgments and explanations on some tasks but not on others that involve the same cognitive operations; and transitional subjects give correct judgments but incorrect explanations (cf. Reese & Schach, 1974). Thus, pass subjects have the operations and use them; decalage subjects have the operations but do not always use them; and transitional subjects, like pretransitional ones, do not have the operations and therefore cannot use them. In the dialectical model, pass subjects select and use relevant actions; decalage subjects know the relevant actions but do not always recognize their relevance; transitional subjects have the relevant actions but cannot subordinate them to the goal at hand; and pretransitional subjects do not have the relevant actions.

D. Learning Set

1. Species and Age Differences

The term *learning set* has been defined in two ways, one lenient and one strict. According to the lenient definition, it refers to improvement in performance across a series of problems of the same kind; and according to the strict definition, it refers to improvement culminating in 1-trial solution of new problems of the kind used in the series (Reese, 1970b). Learning sets are differentiated on the basis of the kind of problem used in the acquisition series. The most extensively studied kind is discriminative learning set, acquired by training on a series of 2-stimulus simultaneous-discrimination problems, all with different stimulus materials.

The leniently defined kind of discriminative learning set has been demonstrated in all species and at all age levels that have been studied, but the strict kind has not been obtained in studies with species below the primate level (see Levinson & Reese, 1967; Reese, 1963, 1964, 1970b). Thus, there seems to be a phylogenetic discontinuity in the ability to acquire the discriminative learning set, presumably reflecting a qualitative difference in the mechanisms underlying performance.

Within the primate level there is a sharp discontinuity in speed of acquisition, separating the human level from other primates. Even young children can acquire a learning set considerably more rapidly than the lower primates, suggesting either a qualitative difference in the mechanisms underlying performance or a marked quantitative difference in the operating efficiency of the same mechanisms. Within the primate level, learning set has been obtained at all ages studied, but with large age differences in the speed of acquisition. For example, in the only human life-span study, Levinson and Reese (1967) trained each subject to a criterion of 93% correct in a block of new problems, with 4 trials on each problem in the series. The median problems through criterion were 20.4 for preschool children, 10.8 for fifth-graders, 6.7 for college students, and about 120 for old persons ranging from 60 to 97 years of age. By way of comparison, Levine, Levinson, and Harlow (1959) used comparable procedures and 4-trial problems with rhesus monkeys and found that after 360 problems, performance had not yet reached a mean of 90% correct. The age differences, like the differences among primate species, could reflect qualitative or quantitative differences in the underlying mechanisms. An examination of other data from the relevant studies suggests that the species and age differences are qualitative, as has been noted elsewhere (Reese, 1976a; Reese &

Porges, 1976). Specifically, the other data refer to consistent but incorrect patterns of responses, termed "error factors" by Harlow (1950, 1959), "hypotheses" by Levine (1963), and "strategies" by Bowman (1963).

2. Types of Errors in Learning-Set Acquisition

Most of the error factors, hypotheses, or strategies that appear during learning-set acquisition can be defined by performance on Trials 1 and 2 across a series of acquisition problems. These error factors are stimulus preference and alternation, position preference and alternation, "differential-cue error," and "response-shift error." (Others, such as double alternation, require examination of more than the first two trials; they are not surveyed in this chapter.) The differential-cue error is defined as a greater probability of errors on problems in which the position of the rewarded object changes from Trial 1 to Trial 2 (differential-cue problems) than on problems in which the position of the rewarded object is unchanged (multiple-cue problems). The response-shift error, according to one definition, is a greater probability of error on Trial 2 following a correct choice on Trial 1 than following an error on Trial 1.

The Levine hypotheses are defined by referring to: (a) the outcome of the Trial 1 response, *win* (rewarded response) or *lose* (error), (b) the dimension responded to on Trials 1 and 2, either *object* or *position* cues, and (c) whether the Trial 2 response is to the same object or position as on Trial 1—*stay*—or the other object or position—*shift*. The resulting eight hypotheses are:

Hypothesis 1: Win-stay-object Lose-shift-object (problem solution; choose last-rewarded object)

Hypothesis 2: Win-shift-object Lose-stay-object (opposite to problem solution; avoid last-rewarded object)

Hypothesis 3: Win-stay-position Lose-shift-position (solution to a position discrimination; choose last-rewarded position)

Hypothesis 4: Win-shift-position Lose-stay-position (avoid last-rewarded position)

Hypothesis 5: Win-stay-object Lose-stay-object (stimulus preference)

Hypothesis 6: Win-shift-object Lose-shift-object (stimulus alternation)

Hypothesis 7: Win-stay-position Lose-stay-position (position preference)

Hypothesis 8: Win-shift-position Lose-shift-position (position alternation).

The strengths of the hypotheses can be estimated by applying equations developed by Levine (1963) or equations developed by Bowman (1963) (see Levinson & Reese, 1967, for a derivation of the relationship between these sets of equations). The Levine equations provide absolute estimates, but for the difference between paired hypotheses rather than for individual hypotheses. The Bowman equations provide range estimates, but separately for the win and lose components of the Levine hypotheses rather than for any one hypothesis as a whole. The only serious problems of interpretation that arise are related to assumptions underlying the equations. For example, Levine assumed that the probability of a correct response following a win is equal to that following a loss, an assumption that application of the Bowman equations has called into question (Levinson & Reese, 1967). Further, Levine assumed that a subject responds either to positions or to objects, regardless of whether the first response was a win or a loss; but again application of the Bowman equations has called this assumption into question (Levinson & Reese, 1967). Another assumption, common to both sets of equations, is that the subject consistently uses a particular hypothesis throughout the block of problems that provides the data for the equations. This assumption may well be false but cannot be checked when the trial block is already so small that a smaller block will yield unreliable data or insufficient data for application of the equations.

The hypotheses identified by Levine have counterparts in Harlow's system of error factors, with the exception of Levine's Hypothesis 2 (Win-shift-object Lose-stay-object; avoid last-rewarded object) and Hypothesis 4 (Win-shift-position Lose-stay-position; avoid last-rewarded position). Preferences and alternations referring to objects or positions appear in both systems. Further, Levine's Hypothesis 3 (Win-stay-position Lose-shift-position) is the same as Harlow's differential-cue error (Levine, personal communication, cited in Levinson & Reese, 1967, p. 86). On differential-cue problems Win-stay-position and Lose-shift-position will both yield errors, and on multiple-cue problems Win-stay-position and Lose-shift-position will both yield correct responses, yielding the differential-cue error. Thus, the differential-cue error reflects a tendency to respond to the previously rewarded position rather than to the previously rewarded object. Levine's Hypothesis 6 (Win-shift-object Lose-shift-object) is normally identified as stimulus alternation, but is the same as Harlow's response-shift error as defined above, since stimulus alternation will yield a greater frequency of errors on Trial 2 following a correct response on Trial 1 than following an error in Trial 1.

3. Age Differences in Error Types

Levinson and Reese (1967) found that the differential-cue error (Hypothesis 3) and response-shift error (Hypothesis 6) were the most common and persistent incorrect hypotheses in preschool children, appearing in all but the fastest learning subgroup. Response shift was more persistent than the differential-cue error. The other incorrect hypotheses appearing with notable frequency were Hypothesis 7 (position preference) in one subgroup and Hypothesis 8 (position alternation) in two subgroups. In addition, the slowest learning subgroup exhibited Hypothesis 2 (avoid last-rewarded object) and Hypothesis 4 (avoid last-rewarded position). In this subgroup, furthermore, as well as in two of the subgroups learning at intermediate rates, the Bowman equations revealed that in several blocks of problems (10 problems per block) the dominant win component and the dominant lose component were inconsistent in that one referred to objects and the other to positions (see marked rows in Table 2). Either the combinations of object and position

Table 2

Dominant Components in Learning-Set Acquisition by Preschoolers[a]

Subgroup[b]	Blocks of 10 problems	Dominant components[c]		Inconsistent components
I	1	Win-stay-object	Lose-shift-object	
II	1	Win-stay-position/stay-object	Lose-shift-object	x
	2	Win-stay-object	Lose-shift-object	
III	1	Win-stay-position	Lose-shift-object/shift-position	x
	2	Win-stay-position	Lose-shift-object/shift-position	x
	3	Win-stay-object	Lose-shift-object	
IV	1	Win-shift-object	Lose-shift-object	
	2	Win-shift-position	Lose-shift-position	
	3	Win-stay-object	Lose-shift-object	
	4	Win-stay-object	Lose-shift-object	
VII	1	Win-shift-object	Lose-stay-position	x
	2	Win-shift-object	Lose-shift-object	
	3	Win-stay-position/stay-object	Lose-shift-object	x
	4	Win-stay-position/stay-object	Lose-shift-object	x
	5	Win-stay-object	Lost-shift-object	
	6	Win-stay-position	Lose-shift-object	x
	7	Win-stay-position/stay-object	Lose-shift-object	x

[a] Adapted from Levinson and Reese (1967).
[b] Subgroups are criterion-reference groups formed on the basis of problems through criterion.
[c] Slash means that two win (or lose) components were equally strong.

components reflect hypotheses that are impossible in Levine's system, or else the components were not combined at all but rather were acquired independently. In agreement with the latter alternative, the lose component of problem solution— Lose-shift-object—was acquired before the win component—Win-stay-object (but this result could reflect the strong response-shift error because in a two-trial definition of response shift the win component is Win-shift-object). This piecemeal acquisition of problem solution did not appear at the other age levels sampled, suggesting that while the older subjects used hypothesis-sampling systems, the younger subjects used simpler mechanisms than hypotheses.

Fifth-grade children exhibited position hypotheses, particularly Hypothesis 4 (avoid last-rewarded position) and Hypothesis 8 (position alternation). Hypothesis 3 (differential-cue error) appeared only in the fastest learning subgroup; and Hypothesis 6 appeared only in the slowest learning subgroup and a group that never met criterion. In the latter group, Hypothesis 6 was the dominant error throughout, and in the slowest learning subgroup it was the dominant error in the first (of three) blocks of problems. Thus, Hypothesis 6 was relatively rare, but markedly interfered with learning-set acquisition when it did appear. A problem of interpretation is that Hypothesis 6 may actually reflect stimulus alternation in fifth-graders and not response shift. Response shift is interpretable as a "playful" response, a tendency to try out all objects in the situation or to see if the experimenter is playing fair. So interpreted, it seems more likely to occur in preschoolers than in fifth-graders. Fifth-graders are considered anecdotally to be the most "docile" elementary-schoolers in the sense that they are the most willing to work hard on a learning task. They should be serious about the task, testing reasonable hypotheses rather than playful ones. On this tenuous argument, then, Hypothesis 6 is assumed to reflect stimulus alternation in fifth-graders rather than response shift.

The same trends were observed in college students as in fifth-graders in that Hypothesis 6 appeared only in the slowest learning subgroup and a subgroup that did not meet criterion. Presumably, Hypothesis 6 reflects stimulus alternation rather than response shift in college students, as in fifth-graders. The nonlearning subgroup of college students also exhibited some differential-cue error in the first and third (last) blocks of problems, and exhibited position alternation in the first block and position preference in the second and third blocks. Thus, the college students were like the fifth-graders in that Hypothesis 6 was rare but interfered markedly when it occurred, and position hypotheses also appeared and interfered with acquisition.

In a sample of old persons, the slower the acquisition, the stronger was the differential-cue error (Hypothesis 3). Hypothesis 6 appeared only in the first block of problems, and only in two subgroups, but stimulus preference (Hypothesis 5), position preference (Hypothesis 7), and position alternation (Hypothesis 8) appeared in strength in various groups. A group of seven subjects who never met criterion provided enough data for individual-subject analyses, in 50-problem blocks. One of these subjects exhibited position preference for three-blocks—150 problems—and then exhibited the differential-cue error for 300 problems. A second subject exhibited the differential-cue error throughout 450 problems, and a third alternated between the differential-cue error and position alternation for 450 problems. Three other subjects exhibited position hypotheses: One subject exhibited position preference throughout, one exhibited position alternation throughout, and one shifted from position preference to position alternation. The seventh subject shifted between stimulus preference and stimulus alternation.

To summarize: (a) Preschoolers in the Levinson and Reese study exhibited especially persistent response shift, but position hypotheses also occurred, particularly the differential-cue error. They also sometimes combined position and object components, thus forming impossible hypotheses or exhibiting piecemeal acquisition of the problem solution. (b) Fifth-graders also exhibited position hypotheses, but the differential-cue error was uncommon. Response shift—or, more likely, stimulus alternation—was rare but markedly interfered with acquisition when it occurred. (c) No incorrect hypotheses were especially prevalent in college students, although as in fifth-graders stimulus alternation was rare but markedly interfered with acquisition when it occurred. (d) Stimulus alternation was relatively rare in old persons and did not markedly interfere with acquisition, but stimulus preference, position preference, and position alternation appeared in strength in various subgroups, and the differential-cue error was stronger the slower the acquisition.

Another finding, implied but not emphasized above, was that incorrect hypotheses tended to be most persistent in the old persons, next most persistent in the preschoolers, and least persistent in the college students. Thus, the age differences in acquisition seem to reflect both the number of hypotheses sampled and the persistence of incorrect hypotheses. The greatest variety of strong hypotheses appeared in the oldest group, in which incorrect hypotheses were most persistent and acquisition was slowest. The next greatest variety of strong hypotheses appeared in the preschool group, in which incorrect hypotheses were next most persistent and acquisition was next slowest. The smallest variety of strong hypotheses appeared in the college group, in which persistence of incorrect hypotheses was least and acquisition was fastest.

Rhesus monkeys seem to exhibit a small variety of incorrect hypotheses, which tend, however, to be highly persistent (e.g., Reese, 1976a). The response-shift and differential-cue errors are strong and persistent; stimulus preference is strong but much less persistent; and stimulus alternation, position preference, and position alternation are weak. (Note: The relevant data on response shift and stimulus alternation are for sequences longer than two trials; hence, response shift is not the same as stimulus alternation.) Another difference between the learning-set acquisition of children and monkeys is that training to criterion on a single simultaneous-discrimination problem can yield the learning set in preschool children (Reese, 1965) but interferes with learning-set acquisition in monkeys (see Reese, 1964).

A strong argument can be made that learning-set acquisition by monkeys is consistent with stimulus–response learning theory (Reese, 1964). The major problem in such an analysis is the response-shift error, but it seems to be explainable. In contrast, the data for human subjects seem to be more consistent with a cognitive model, specifically hypothesis-sampling theory. These conclusions are consistent with the Soviet view, in which animal and human learning are assumed to be different, as already mentioned.

IV. Conclusions

Although behavioristic theories of discriminative performance have been notably successful, many features of this performance—especially developmental features—seem to be interpretable more readily within cognitive theory, specifically hypothesis theory merged with the Soviet dialectical model.

The information-processing theories of memory and of discriminative performance were designed to deal with performance by the adult, and although their application in developmental research has yielded rich descriptive data on age effects, they can provide no explanation of these age effects unless merged with a developmental theory (e.g., Reese, 1973, 1976d). Attempts to merge information-processing theories of memory with Piagetian theory have not been successful (Reese, 1976b), but a merger with dialectical theory seems to be highly promising and may yield an explanation of memory changes not only during childhood but throughout the life span (Reese, 1976b). Similarly, although a merger of hypothesis theory—an information-processing theory of discriminative performance—with Piagetian theory has been suggested (Gholson & Beilin, 1976; Gholson et al., 1976), a merger with dialectical theory seems more reasonable. The major reason is that the dialectical approach seems to deal more adequately with the decalages among learning tasks. Decalage can be seen as a lack of immediate transfer, a situation in which the child's reasoning is linked to specific settings, objects, and other task-specific variables, according to Piagetian theorists (R. R. Turner, personal communication, April 12, 1976). In the Soviet view, in contrast, decalages are related to the ways tasks are interpreted and, especially, to subordination of actions to goals. Thus, decalages for Piaget amount to extrinsic interaction between person and environment, and in dialectics to intrinsic interaction—analogous to error variance versus true variance (cf. Lindquist, 1956).

Elsewhere, the writer argued that a merger of dialectical theory with a depth-of-processing model of memory yields an account of memory development across the life span, attributing declines in old age to the same processes that explain increases during childhood (Reese, 1976b). Briefly, in the terminology of the present chapter, the argument is that changes in the structure of motives in old age yield changes in the extent to which actions and operations are practiced, with consequent changes in the subordination of certain operations that would be especially relevant to episodic memory requirements.

The merger of dialectical theory with hypothesis theory can also cover the life span; and again, changes in discriminative performance in old age would be attributed to the same processes that yield changes during childhood. For example, one important determinant of discriminative performance by preschoolers is their instrumental dependency upon adults. Even though instrumental and emotional dependency begin to be discouraged during the preschool age, and independence encouraged, adults typically continue to aid the preschool child before the child requests aid, and the preschool child seems often to request aid before it is needed. One consequence is that in a discriminative task the procedures designed to avoid the Clever Hans error make the task unnatural for the child, in that the Clever Hans phenomenon is the essence of the child's approach to such problem-solving tasks. A related example is the leading position of the play motive in the young child, which takes on a strong social character during the preschool period. One consequence is that a discriminative task is apt to be interpreted as a game, and, for the older preschooler, as a social game.

Similar kinds of processes are encountered in old age. Instrumental and perhaps emotional dependency are promoted, especially in old persons living in institutions, but apparently also in old persons in the extended family. In addition, the social motive seems to be predominant in old age. There are, then, ties between preschool and old age. There are also differences, however; for example, the structure of motives may be more complex in the old person, yielding differences in task interpretations and task goals. Nevertheless, it seems clear that as in the memory domain, a life-span dialectical model of discriminative performance is not only possible but also highly promising.

The analysis of discriminative performance proposed in this paper is highly theoretical, but is intended to have an empirical base. Much research is needed to provide this base. For example, we need to identify the motives that are characteristically dominant at different age levels, the situational and contextual actions and operations that become available, and the changes in society's demands that produce the changes in dominant motives and the sequence of acquiring actions and subordinating them as operations. A multidisciplinary approach is required, with coordinated efforts by empirical behavioral and social scientists.

REFERENCES

Adams, M. J., & Shepp, B. E. Selective attention and the breadth of learning: A developmental study. *Journal of Experimental Child Psychology,* 1975, **20**, 168–180.

Antrobus, J. S., Antrobus, J. S., & Singer, J. L. Eye movements accompanying daydreaming, visual imagery, and thought suppression. *Journal of Abnormal and Social Psychology,* 1964, **69**, 244–252.

Ash, M. J. The relation between discrimination-shift performance and three related tasks: Some parameters of the Kendler model of optional-shift behavior. *Child Development,* 1975, **46**, 408–415.

Baltes, M. M., & Reese, H. W. Operant research and operant paradigm: Contradictions are apparent but not real. In J. M. LeBlanc, D. M. Baer, & B. C. Etzel (Eds.), *New developments in behavioral research.* Hillsdale, N.J.: Lawrence Erlbaum Associates, 1977. Pp. 11–30.

Baltes, P. B., Reese, H. W., & Nesselroade, J. R. *Life-span developmental psychology: Introduction to research methods.* Monterey, Calif.: Brooks/Cole, 1977.

Bearison, D. J., & Isaacs, L. Production deficiency in children's moral judgments. *Developmental Psychology,* 1975, 11, 732–737.

Berch, D. B. Stimulus interaction and problem difficulty in children's discrimination learning. *Journal of Experimental Child Psychology,* 1972, 13, 115–127.

Berch, D. B., & Israel, M. Solution of the transverse patterning problem: Response to cue-cue relations. *Psychonomic Science,* 1971, 23, 383–384.

Berch, D. B., & Israel, M. The effects of setting similarity on children's learning of the transverse patterning problem. *Journal of Experimental Child Psychology,* 1974, 18, 252–258.

Bergmann, G. *Philosophy of science.* Madison: University of Wisconsin Press, 1957.

Blank, M. Eliciting verbalization from young children in experimental tasks: A methodological note. *Child Development,* 1975, 46, 254–257.

Bowman, R. E. Discrimination learning-set performance under intermittent and secondary reinforcement. *Journal of Comparative and Physiological Psychology,* 1963, 56, 429–434.

Bronfenbrenner, U. Development research, public policy, and the ecology of childhood. *Child Development,* 1974, 45, 1–5.

Brown, A. L. The development of memory: Knowing, knowing about knowing, and knowing how to know. In H. W. Reese (Ed.), *Advances in child development and behavior* (Vol. 10). New York: Academic Press, 1975. Pp. 103–152.

Brown, J. S. *The motivation of behavior.* New York: McGraw-Hill, 1961.

Bugelski, B. R. The definition of the image. In S. J. Siegel (Ed.), *Imagery: Current cognitive approaches.* New York: Academic Press, 1971. Pp. 49–68.

Buss, J. L., & Rabinowitz, F. M. The intermediate-hue transposition of children after same-different and seriation pretraining. *Journal of Experimental Child Psychology,* 1973, 15, 30–46.

Campione, J. C., & Brown, A. L. The effects of contextual changes and degree of component mastery on transfer of training. In H. W. Reese (Ed.), *Advances in child development and behavior* (Vol. 9). New York: Academic Press, 1974. Pp. 69–114.

Casey, M. B. The effect of training procedures on the overlearning reversal effect in young children. *Journal of Experimental Child Psychology,* 1975, 20, 1–12.

Cole, M. A probe trial procedure for the study of children's discrimination learning and transfer. *Journal of Experimental Child Psychology,* 1976, 22, 499–510.

Cole, M., & Medin, D. Comment on Gollin and Rosser. *Journal of Experimental Child Psychology,* 1974, 17, 545–546.

Croll, W. L. Oddity discrimination learning as a function of the number of dimensions along which the correct stimulus is odd (Doctoral dissertation, University of Iowa, 1967). *Dissertation Abstracts International,* 1968, 28, 3487B. University Microfilms No. 68-915.

Eimas, P. D. Attentional processes. (With editorial insertions.) In H. W. Reese & L. P. Lipsitt (Eds.), *Experimental child psychology.* New York: Academic Press, 1970. Pp. 279–310.

Eimas, P. D., & Doan, H. *Stimulus compounding and conditional discrimination learning in rats.* Paper presented at the meeting of the Eastern Psychological Association, Atlantic City, April 1965.

Elkonin, D. B. Development of speech. In A. V. Zaporozhets & D. B. Elkonin (Eds.), *The psychology of preschool children* (J. Shybut & S. Simon, trans.). Cambridge, Mass.: MIT Press, 1971. Pp. 111–185.

Fitzgerald, J. M. Verbalization effects in young children: When and how a label becomes a label. (Doctoral dissertation, West Virginia University, 1974.) *Dissertation Abstracts International,* 1974, 35, 1936B. University Microfilms No. 74-21, 847.

Flavell, J. H. Developmental studies of mediated memory. In H. W. Reese & L. P. Lipsitt (Eds.), *Advances in child development and behavior* (Vol. 5). New York: Academic Press, 1970. Pp. 181–211.

Flavell, J. H., Beach, D. R., & Chinsky, J. M. Spontaneous verbal rehearsal in a memory task as a function of age. *Child Development,* 1966, **37**, 283–299.

Franks, G. J. The transverse patterning problem with ten-year-olds and college students. (Doctoral dissertation, West Virginia University, 1976.) *Dissertation Abstracts International,* 1977, **37**, 4182B. University Microfilms No. 77-2563.

Franks, G. J., Reese, H. W., & Kohn, J. P. Unpublished research, West Virginia University, 1974.

Friedrichs, A. G., Hertz, T. W., Moynahan, E. D., Simpson, W. E., Arnold, M. R., Christy, M. D., Cooper, C. R., & Stevenson, H. W. Interrelations among learning and performance tasks at the preschool level. *Developmental Psychology,* 1971, **4**, 164–172.

Fry, C. L., & Hampson R. B. *Influence of task difficulty and age on speech to noise modulation in preschoolers.* Paper presented at the Fourth Biennial Southeastern Conference on Human Development, Nashville, April 1976.

Gagné, R. M. *Essentials of learning for instruction.* Hinsdale, Ill.: Dryden, 1974.

Gholson, B. *Hypothesis sampling systems and development.* Paper presented at the Fourth Biennial Southeastern Conference on Human Development, Nashville, April 1976.

Gholson, B., & Beilin, H. *A developmental model of human learning.* Unpublished manuscript, Memphis State University, 1976.

Gholson, B., & Danziger, S. Effects of two levels of stimulus complexity upon hypothesis sampling systems among second and sixth grade children. *Journal of Experimental Child Psychology,* 1975, **20**, 105–118.

Gholson, B., Levine, M., & Phillips, S. Hypotheses, strategies, and stereotypes in discrimination learning. *Journal of Experimental Child Psychology,* 1972, **13**, 423–446.

Gholson, B., O'Connor, J., & Stern, I. Hypothesis sampling systems among preoperational and concrete operational kindergarten children. *Journal of Experimental Child Psychology,* 1976, **21**, 61–76.

Gollin, E. S., & Rosser, M. On mediation. *Journal of Experimental Child Psychology,* 1974, **17**, 539–544.

Gollin, E. S., & Schadler, M. Relational learning and transfer by young children. *Journal of Experimental Child Psychology,* 1972, **14**, 219–232.

Harlow, H. F. Analysis of discrimination learning by monkeys. *Journal of Experimental Psychology,* 1950, **40**, 26–39.

Harlow, H. F. Learning set and error factor theory. In S. Koch (Ed.), *Psychology: A study of a science* (Vol. 2). New York: McGraw-Hill, 1959. Pp. 492–537.

Horowitz, F. D., & Armentrout, J. Discrimination-learning, manifest anxiety, and effects of reinforcement. *Child Development,* 1965, **36**, 731–748.

House, B. J., Brown, A. L., & Scott, M. S. Children's discrimination learning based on identity or difference. In H. W. Reese (Ed.), *Advances in child development and behavior* (Vol. 9). New York: Academic Press, 1974. Pp. 1–45.

House, B. J., & Zeaman, D. Miniature experiments in the discrimination learning of retardates. In L. P. Lipsitt & C. C. Spiker (Eds.), *Advances in child development and behavior* (Vol. 1). New York: Academic Press, 1963. Pp. 313–374.

Hurlock, E. B. *Child development* (4th ed.). New York: McGraw-Hill, 1964.

Ingison, L. J., & Levin, J. R. The effects of children's spontaneous cognitive sets on discrimination learning. *Journal of Experimental Child Psychology,* 1975, **20**, 59–65.

Jeffrey, W. E. Variables affecting reversal–shifts in young children. *American Journal of Psychology,* 1965, **78**, 589–595.

Jenkins, J. J. Remember that old theory of memory? Well, forget it! *American Psychologist,* 1974, **29**, 785–795.

Katz, D. *Animals and men: Studies in comparative psychology.* London: Longmans, Green, 1937.

Kendler, T. S. An ontogeny of mediational deficiency. *Child Development,* 1972, **43**, 1–17.

Kendler, T. S. The effect of training and stimulus variables on the reversal–shift ontogeny. *Journal of Experimental Child Psychology,* 1974, 17, 87–106.

Kendler, T. S., & Kendler, H. H. Experimental analysis of inferential behavior in children. In L. P. Lipsitt & C. C. Spiker (Eds.), *Advances in child development and behavior* (Vol. 3). New York: Academic Press, 1967. Pp. 157–190.

Kendler, T. S., Kendler, H. H., & Learnard, B. Mediated responses to size and brightness as a function of age. *American Journal of Psychology,* 1962, 75, 571–586.

Krechevsky, I. "Hypotheses" in rats. *Psychological Review,* 1932, 39, 516–532.

Kuhn, T. S. *The structure of scientific revolutions.* Chicago: University of Chicago Press, 1962.

Kvale, S. Memory and dialectics: Some reflections on Ebbinghaus and Mao Tse-tung. *Human Development,* 1975, 18, 205–222.

Lambert, K. Explanation and intention. In A. Jacobs & L. B. Sachs (Eds.), *The psychology of private events.* New York: Academic Press, 1971. Pp. 7–16.

Lawler, J. Dialectical philosophy and developmental psychology: Hegel and Piaget on contradiction. *Human Development,* 1975, 18, 1–17.

Lee, L. C. Concept utilization in preschool children. *Child Development,* 1965, 36, 221–227.

Levine, M. Mediating processes in humans at the outset of discrimination learning. *Psychological Review,* 1963, 70, 254–276.

Levine, M. (Ed.). *A cognitive theory of learning.* Hillsdale, N.J.: Lawrence Erlbaum Associates, 1975.

Levine, M., Levinson, B., & Harlow, H. F. Trials per problem as a variable in the acquisition of discrimination learning set. *Journal of Comparative and Physiological Psychology,* 1959, 52, 396–398.

Levinson, B., & Reese, H. W. Patterns of discrimination learning set in preschool children, fifth-graders, college freshmen, and the aged. *Monographs of the Society for Research in Child Development,* 1967, 32(7, Serial No. 115).

Lindquist, E. F. *Design and analysis of experiments in psychology and education.* Boston: Houghton, 1956.

Lisina, M. I., & Neverovich, Ya. Z. Development of movements and formation of motor habits. In A. V. Zaporozhets & D. B. Elkonin (Eds.), *The psychology of preschool children* (J. Shybut & S. Simon, trans.). Cambridge, Mass.: MIT Press, 1971. Pp. 278–366.

Martin, W. E., & Blum, A. Intertest generalization and learning in mentally normal and subnormal children. *Journal of Comparative and Physiological Psychology,* 1961, 54, 28–32.

McGraw, K. O., & McCullers, J. C. The distracting effect of material reward: An alternative explanation for the superior performance of reward groups in probability learning. *Journal of Experimental Child Psychology,* 1974, 18, 149–158.

Meacham, J. A. The development of memory abilities in the individual and society. *Human Development,* 1972, 15, 205–228.

Meacham, J. A. Soviet investigations of memory development. In R. V. Kail, Jr. & J. W. Hagen (Eds.), *Perspectives on the development of memory and cognition.* Hillsdale, N.J.: Lawrence Erlbaum Associates, 1977.

Miller, G. A., Galanter, E., & Pribram, K. H. *Plans and the structure of behavior.* New York: Holt, 1960.

Miller, L. B., & Estes, B. W. Monetary reward and motivation in discrimination learning. *Journal of Experimental Psychology,* 1961, 61, 501–504.

Moore, C. S. Control of the memory image. *Psychological Review Monograph Supplement (Psychological Monographs),* 1903, 4(1, Whole No. 17), 277–306.

Morello, V., Turner, R. R., & Reed, N. *An analysis of problem solving strategies as a function of socioeconomic status and cognitive level.* Paper presented at the Fourth Biennial Southeastern Conference on Human Development, Nashville, April 1976.

Osler, S. F., & Madden, J. The verbal label: Mediator or classifier? *Journal of Experimental Child Psychology,* 1973, 16, 303–317.

Osler, S. F., & Trautman, G. E. Concept attainment: II. Effect of stimulus complexity upon concept attainment at two levels of intelligence. *Journal of Experimental Psychology,* 1961, **62,** 9–13.

Overton, W. F. On the assumption base of the nature–nurture controversy: Additive versus interactive conceptions. *Human Development,* 1973, **16,** 74–89.

Overton, W. F., & Reese, H. W. Models of development: Methodological implications. In J. R. Nesselroade & H. W. Reese (Eds.), *Life-span developmental psychology: Methodological issues.* New York: Academic Press, 1973. Pp. 65–86.

Paden, L. Y., & Soto, D. H. *Transverse-pattern learning in preschool children.* Unpublished manuscript, University of Kansas, 1967.

Paivio, A. *Imagery and verbal processes.* New York: Holt, 1971.

Pepper, S. C. *World hypotheses.* Berkeley: University of California Press, 1942.

Peterson, C. C. The effect of time on mediation deficiency in children and adults. *Journal of Experimental Child Psychology,* 1973, **15,** 1–9.

Rabinowitz, F. M., & Cantor, G. N. Children's stimulus alternation, response repetition, and circular behavior as a function of age and stimulus conditions. *Child Development,* 1967, **38,** 661–672.

Rappoport, L. On praxis and quasirationality. *Human Development,* 1975, **18,** 194–204.

Reese, H. W. Verbal mediation as a function of age level. *Psychological Bulletin,* 1962, **59,** 502–509.

Reese, H. W. Discrimination learning set in children. In L. P. Lipsitt & C. C. Spiker (Eds.), *Advances in child development and behavior* (Vol. 1). New York: Academic Press, 1963. Pp. 115–145.

Reese, H. W. Discrimination learning set in rhesus monkeys. *Psychological Bulletin,* 1964, **61,** 321–340.

Reese, H. W. Discrimination learning set and perceptual set in young children. *Child Development,* 1965, **36,** 153–161.

Reese, H. W. *The perception of stimulus relations: Discrimination learning and transposition.* New York: Academic Press, 1968.

Reese, H. W. Age trend in efficiency of mediation. In H. W. Reese & L. P. Lipsitt (Eds.), *Experimental child psychology.* New York: Academic Press, 1970. Pp. 257–261. (a)

Reese, H. W. Set. In H. W. Reese & L. P. Lipsitt (Eds.), *Experimental child psychology.* New York: Academic Press, 1970. Pp. 263–278. (b)

Reese, H. W. Acquired distinctiveness and equivalence of cues in young children. *Journal of Experimental Child Psychology,* 1972, **13,** 171–182.

Reese, H. W. Models of memory and models of development. *Human Development,* 1973, **16,** 397–416.

Reese, H. W. *Basic learning processes in childhood.* New York: Holt, 1976. (a)

Reese, H. W. The development of memory: Life-span perspectives. In H. W. Reese (Ed.), *Advances in child development and behavior* (Vol. 11). New York: Academic Press, 1976. Pp. 189–212. (b)

Reese, H. W. Discussion. In H. W. Reese (Ed.), Conceptions of the "active organism." *Human Development,* 1976, **19,** 108–119. (c)

Reese, H. W. Models of memory development. *Human Development,* 1976, **19,** 291–303. (d)

Reese, H. W., & Lipsitt, L. P. (Eds.). *Experimental child psychology.* New York: Academic Press, 1970.

Reese, H. W., & Overton, W. F. Models of development and theories of development. In L. R. Goulet & P. B. Baltes (Eds.), *Life-span developmental psychology: Research and theory.* New York: Academic Press, 1970. Pp. 115–145.

Reese, H. W., & Overton, W. F. On paradigm shifts. *American Psychologist,* 1972, **27,** 1197–1199.

Reese, H. W., & Porges, S. W. The development of learning processes. In V. Hamilton & M. D. Vernon (Eds.), *The development of cognitive processes.* London: Academic Press, 1976.

Reese, H. W., & Schach, M. L. Comment on Brainerd's criteria for cognitive structures. *Psychological Bulletin*, 1974, 81, 67–69.

Repina, T. A. Development of imagination. In A. V. Zaporozhets & D. B. Elkonin (Eds.), *The psychology of preschool children* (J. Shybut & S. Simon, trans.). Cambridge, Mass.: MIT Press, 1971. Pp. 255–277.

Restle, F. The selection of strategies in cue learning. *Psychological Review*, 1961, 69, 329–343.

Rieber, M. Discrimination learning in childhood. In H. W. Reese & L. P. Lipsitt (Eds.), *Experimental child psychology*. New York: Academic Press, 1970. Pp. 183–194.

Riegel, K. F. Dialectical operations: The final period of cognitive development. *Human Development*, 1973, 16, 346–370.

Riegel, K. F. Subject-object alienation in psychological experiments and testing. *Human Development*, 1975, 18, 181–193.

Schadler, M. Development of relational learning: Effects of instruction and delay of transfer. *Journal of Experimental Child Psychology*, 1973, 16, 459–471.

Shirai, T. *Developmental variation in the visual discrimination of cube size by children 2 to 13 years of age.* Unpublished master's thesis, University of Toronto, 1951.

Slaughter, J. W. A preliminary study of the behavior of mental images. *American Journal of Psychology*, 1902, 13, 526–549.

Spence, K. W. Theoretical interpretations of learning. In C. P. Stone (Ed.), *Comparative psychology* (3rd ed.). New York: Prentice-Hall, 1951. Pp. 239–291.

Spence, K. W. The nature of the response in discrimination learning. *Psychological Review*, 1952, 59, 89–93.

Spence, K. W. *Behavior theory and conditioning.* New Haven: Yale University Press, 1956.

Spiker, C. C. The hypothesis of stimulus interaction and an explanation of stimulus compounding. In L. P. Lipsitt & C. C. Spiker (Eds.), *Advances in child development and behavior* (Vol. 1). New York: Academic Press, 1963. Pp. 233–264.

Spiker, C. C. An extension of Hull-Spence discrimination learning theory. *Psychological Review*, 1970, 77, 496–515.

Spiker, C. C. Application of Hull-Spence theory to the discrimination learning of children. In H. W. Reese (Ed.), *Advances in child development and behavior* (Vol. 6). New York: Academic Press, 1971. Pp. 99–152.

Spiker, C. C., & Cantor, J. H. Applications of Hull-Spence theory to the transfer of discrimination learning in children. In H. W. Reese (Ed.), *Advances in child development and behavior* (Vol. 8). New York: Academic Press, 1973. Pp. 223–288.

Stevenson, H. W. Learning in children. In P. H. Mussen (Ed.), *Carmichael's manual of child psychology* (3rd ed., Vol. 1). New York: Wiley, 1970. Pp. 849–938.

Stevenson, H. W., Friedrichs, A. G., & Simpson, W. E. Learning and problem solving by the mentally retarded under three testing conditions. *Developmental Psychology*, 1970, 3, 307–312.

Stevenson, H. W., Hale, G. A., Klein, R. E., & Miller, L. K. Interrelations and correlates in children's learning and problem solving. *Monographs of the Society for Research in Child Development*, 1968, 33(7, Serial No. 123).

Stevenson, H. W., Iscoe, I., & McConnell, C. A developmental study of transposition. *Journal of Experimental Psychology*, 1955, 49, 278–280.

Stevenson, H. W., & Odom, R. D. Interrelationships in children's learning. *Child Development*, 1965, 36, 7–19.

Thompson, R. Approach-avoidance in an ambivalent object discrimination problem. *Journal of Experimental Psychology*, 1953, 45, 341–344.

Tindall, R. C., & Ratliff, R. G. Interaction of reinforcement conditions and developmental level in a two-choice discrimination task with children. *Journal of Experimental Child Psychology*, 1974, 18, 183–189.

Warren, J. M. Solution of sign-differentiated object and positional discriminations by rhesus monkeys. *Journal of Genetic Psychology*, 1960, 96, 365–369.

Washburn, M. F. *Movement and mental imagery.* Boston: Houghton, 1916.

White, S. H. Evidence for a hierarchical arrangement of learning processes. In L. P. Lipsitt & C. C. Spiker (Eds.), *Advances in child development and behavior* (Vol. 2). New York: Academic Press, 1965. Pp. 187–220.

White, S. H. The active organism in theoretical behaviorism. In H. W. Reese (Ed.), Conceptions of the "active organism." *Human Development,* 1976, 19, 99–107.

Wozniak, R. H. Dialecticism and structuralism: The philosophical foundation of Soviet psychology and Piagetian cognitive developmental theory. In K. F. Riegel & G. C. Rosenwald (Eds.), *Structure and transformation.* New York: Wiley, 1975. Pp. 25–45.

Yendovitskaya, T. V. Development of attention. In A. V. Zaporozhets & D. B. Elkonin (Eds.), *The psychology of preschool children* (J. Shybut & S. Simon, trans.). Cambridge, Mass.: MIT Press, 1971. Pp. 65–88. (a)

Yendovitskaya, T. V. Development of memory. In A. V. Zaporozhets & D. B. Elkonin (Eds.), *The psychology of preschool children* (J. Shybut & S. Simon, trans.). Cambridge, Mass.: MIT Press, 1971. Pp. 89–110. (b)

Zaporozhets, A. V., & Elkonin, D. B. Foreword. In A. V. Zaporozhets & D. B. Elkonin (Eds.), *The psychology of preschool children* (J. Shybut & S. Simon, trans.). Cambridge, Mass.: MIT Press, 1971. Pp. xv–xxiii. (a)

Zaporozhets, A. V., & Elkonin, D. B. (Eds.). *The psychology of preschool children* (J. Shybut & S. Simon, trans.). Cambridge, Mass.: MIT Press, 1971. (b)

Zaporozhets, A. V., Zinchenko, V. P., & Elkonin, D. B. Development of thinking. In A. V. Zaporozhets & D. B. Elkonin (Eds.), *The psychology of preschool children* (J. Shybut & S. Simon, trans.). Cambridge, Mass.: MIT Press, 1971. Pp. 186–254.

Zeaman, D., & House, B. J. Approach and avoidance in the discrimination learning of retardates. *Child Development,* 1962, 33, 355–372.

Zeaman, D., & House, B. J. The role of attention in retardate discrimination learning. In N. R. Ellis (Ed.), *Handbook of mental deficiency.* New York: McGraw-Hill, 1963. Pp. 159–223.

Zeiler, M. D. Transposition in adults with simultaneous and successive stimulus presentation. *Journal of Experimental Psychology,* 1964, 68, 103–107.

Zeiler, M. D. Stimulus definition and choice. In L. P. Lipsitt & C. C. Spiker (Eds.), *Advances in child development and behavior* (Vol. 3). New York: Academic Press, 1967. Pp. 125–156.

CHAPTER 12

Behavioristic Perspectives on a Dialectical Model of Discriminative Learning and Transfer

JOAN H. CANTOR

UNIVERSITY OF IOWA
IOWA CITY, IOWA

I. Basic Premises

Professor Reese (Chapter 11, this volume) has provided a very interesting and provocative contribution in which he has proposed a dialectical model of discriminative learning and transfer. An attempt on my part, however, to carry out the discussant's assigned role of presenting an opposing point of view has produced what may be akin to a "dialectical dilemma." On the one hand, it is difficult for a neobehaviorist to know where to begin in commenting on a dialectical model. I find myself, at this point, in sympathy with Professor Reese when he declares that "Between-paradigm debates are fruitless." On the other hand, there is certainly a scientific obligation for that same neobehaviorist to reply to Professor Reese's major assertion that "the dialectical approach resolves major problems of the behavioristic approach, including problems of the behavioristic approach to development."

My comments regarding the specific theories in question are based on a set of premises that are at variance with those of Professor Reese. A complete statement of my methodological position with respect to definitional criteria for scientific concepts, the structure of laws and theories in psychology, and the nature of explanation and prediction in science is beyond the scope of this discussion. My views on these matters, however, are quite well represented by H. H. Kendler and Spence (1971) in their explication of the tenets of neobehaviorism. There are nevertheless several points that I wish to make explicit here.

First and foremost, I can see no need for giving up a philosophy of science (Bergmann, 1957) that has served the scientific disciplines so long and so well. Accordingly, the term *explanation* in psychology is reserved for the deduction of behavioral laws from a set of basic axioms. From this point of view, teleological explanation remains outside the realm of scientific explanation. With respect to the role of prediction in psychology, I vigorously reject any a priori arguments that there are aspects of behavior that are in principle unpredictable. Furthermore, it is difficult to understand how there could be any argument on empirical grounds for rejecting determinism in a science as young as psychology. I, for one, have not seen the slightest shred of evidence regarding human behavior that would shake my faith in a thoroughgoing principle of determinism.

I must also take issue with the commonly held view expressed by Professor Reese that stimulus–response (S–R) psychology can be characterized as "mechanistic." To take the position that there are laws to be discovered in psychology that relate behavior to characteristics of the individual, as well as to the conditions of his environment, does not imply that man is by nature a mechanical being. Predictability in nature is by no means limited to machines, and the basis for this analogy has never been clear to me. It would seem just as reasonable to conclude that, since many current cognitive theories include such terms as *coding, storage, retrieval, input,* and *output,* they represent a "computeristic" world view, which might be considered the ultimate in mechanism. Such oversimplified analogies are, in my view, a disservice to the field in that they polarize the positions taken by those holding differing theoretical points of view. A search for common ground among opposing theoretical positions would do far more in producing scientific progress.

My final point of issue regarding basic premises is concerned with the assertion by Professor Reese that within behavioristic theories "Such concepts as 'rule,' 'strategy,' and the like are not analogous to overt responses, hence are not definable as unobserved responses." I object strongly to this apparent dictum that complex verbal behavior is "out of bounds" to the behaviorist in explaining learning. On what basis has it been decided that one-word verbal responses are the limit for behavioristic theories? I would argue that not only are such concepts definable within behavioristic theories, but that they will undoubtedly be needed to provide a full explanation of the learning of older children and adults. As noted by Professor Reese, a number of behaviorists have already begun to incorporate such concepts into their theories. I disagree that such an incorporation necessarily produces "a useless confusing eclecticism." It is only confusing when the terms are not defined. Such concepts may be useful within any theory provided that the empirical operations needed to determine when a subject is using a particular rule or strategy are clearly specified.

Although I would not rule out such terms as *hypothesis* and *strategy* from the behaviorist's vocabulary, I would argue that he, like all theorists, has a responsibility to avoid producing unnecessary confusion in the field by using an old word in a new way. Failure to accept this responsibility produces widespread miscommunication of the type described by Professor Reese with respect to the term *mediation.* This term, which had a clear usage of long standing within S–R theories, was adopted by cognitive theorists to refer to far more complex processes. The result is that the current mediation literature is a mass of apparently conflicting statements about mediation and, in particular, about mediational deficiencies. Professor Reese has pointed out, for example, that the term *production deficiency* refers to the failure to name the stimulus within current S–R theories (e.g., T. S. Kendler, 1972), but includes the failure to use a strategy such as rehearsal within cognitive theories (e.g., Flavell, Beach, & Chinsky, 1966). Since failure to rehearse is expected to produce control deficiency rather than production deficiency within the S–R theories, the result is that children who do not rehearse are said to have a production deficiency within the context of cognitive theories and a control deficiency within the context of S–R theories. I can attest to the fact that the resulting confusion is great, not only among the active participants in these areas, but especially among students who are new to the area. The solution, of course, is for all theorists to find new words for new concepts, until such time that empirical findings make it clear that multiple concepts can be collapsed into a single concept.

In my remarks thus far, I have indicated some major points of disagreement with Professor Reese regarding issues pertaining either directly or indirectly to the scientist's starting point—his philosophy of science. Although it should be clear by now that I see no need for a new philosophy of science, I am nevertheless most eager to find the best possible theory of discrimination learning. I would certainly be prepared to give up the particular theory I work with if a better one came along—by "better" I mean one having greater scope and greater quantitative precision in predicting behavior. Professor Reese has proposed a dialectical model of discrimination learning that he believes is an improvement over existing behavioristic theories. I shall comment on his proposal by posing two questions and then addressing each in turn. First, "What do we stand to lose if we give up current behavioristic theories?" Second, "What do we stand to gain if we adopt the dialectical model proposed?"

II. Current Stimulus–Response Theories

To begin an answer to the first question, I would like to quote two statements by Professor Reese with which I can wholeheartedly agree: "The best articulated behavioristic theories are those formulated to deal with discriminative performance, and a vast experimental literature indicates that these are the most successful behavioristic theories." Later in the chapter he states that "Spiker's stimulus interaction theory is the best articulated and most successful stimulus–response theory of discrimination performance." Of course, I have taken these quotes out of context, and in each case, he went on to argue that these theories have run into difficulties of sufficient magnitude that a search for a new theoretical approach is warranted.

The general question of how we decide when it is time to discard a theory or set of theories is not a simple one (cf. Spiker, Chapter 4, this volume). Obviously, the decision will depend in part on how serious the difficulties are that are encountered and whether there are ways to solve the explanatory crises with changes in, or additions to, the axioms of the theory. Factors that weigh heavily in such a decision are the scope and precision of the existing theory—in other words, how broad a range of behavioral laws does it explain and with what degree of accuracy?

The reference by Reese to the vast experimental literature encompassed by existing behavioristic theories attests to their impressive scope. Spiker's modified Hull–Spence theory (1970, 1971; Spiker & Cantor, 1973), the Zeaman and House attention theory (1963, 1974), and the H. H. Kendler and T. S. Kendler developmental mediation theory (1962, 1968) successfully account for the effects of many experimental variables in the acquisition and transfer of discrimination learning. The Spiker theory and the Zeaman and House theory both have the additional advantage of being highly quantified. Prediction equations have been derived within the Spiker theory for a wide variety of discrimination problems, and quantitative fits have been made to the data of many experiments. In a series of 18 such quantitative fits reported for acquisition of various types of successive, simultaneous, and mixed simultaneous–successive problems, as well as reversal, nonreversal, and optional shifts, the average percentage of variance of the group trial-block means accounted for by the theory is well above 80%. To the best of my knowledge, such estimates of the proportion of variance accounted for by other theories are not available for comparison.

The answer to the first question, then, is that we stand to lose a great deal of explanatory power in giving up these theories, unless the new theory can do a comparable job. Have these behavioristic theories really run into difficulties that should cause us to "challenge the basic tenets of the theory," as suggested by Reese? I do not think so, but before I give my reasons for disagreeing, I shall turn to the second question I posed earlier.

III. The Proposed Dialectical Model

What do we stand to gain by adopting the dialectical model? It seems to me that Reese has pointed to the following as major advantages of the dialectical model: (1) the theory is able to explain rapid acquisition of discrimination learning under certain conditions; (2) the incorporation of developmental stages provides an explanation of developmental changes in discrimination performance; and (3) the theory is better able to explain what are referred to as competence–performance discrepancies, or decalages. Again postponing the issue of whether these really are serious problems for existing theories, let us address the question of whether the proposed theory does in fact accomplish these goals. Although this question needs to be asked, it cannot be answered, because it is impossible to judge the explanatory power of the theory in its present form. The child's motives, actions, operations, and interactions appear to be the basic subject variables that are to be used in deducing the laws of discrimination learning, yet it is not clear how these subject states are to be identified, and it is difficult to imagine how they might be quantified. For example, Reese states that lack of interrelatedness among optional shift, transposition, free recall, and paired-associate learning tasks "can easily be explained by identifying differences in goals, actions, or operations associated with the different tasks." It is not clear to me, first of all, why any theory would expect intercorrelations in such diverse tasks. I know of no theory in which it is assumed that there is one mediational process with a capital M and that a child who mediates does so in all situations. But, leaving that issue aside, it is also not clear how this outcome is predicted by the dialectical theory. How do we go about "identifying differences in goals, actions, or operations?"

Another example of the problem appears in the context of the explanation offered for "unsystematic hypothesis testing." Reese suggests that a child might "intend" to use a particular strategic hypothesis-sampling system (such as the local consistency rule) and yet not show the expected pattern of responses because of "incomplete subordination of the relevant memory operations to the problem-solving goal." How do we know when an operation is subordinated to a particular goal, and if it is, how do we know if the process is complete or incomplete? Does it depend on the child's chronological age? On his learning history? On the nature of the task? More generally, how do we know when actions are voluntary or involuntary? How do we know which motive is dominant? Under what conditions does an "action become a motive" and under what conditions does an "action become an operation?" Clearly, it is necessary to have some independent means of assessing all of these subject states if they are to be used as a basis for predicting the level of performance in specific discrimination tasks. In the absence of these independent measures of the subjects' cognitive states, concluding that the discrimination performance reflects a particular configuration of motives, actions, and operations offers nothing more than a description of the behavior in cognitive terms. Such a description may give some readers a feeling of intuitive understanding of the behavior, but it does not provide a basis for the prediction of discrimination performance.

Reese obviously did not intend to present a formal set of axioms in his contribution, and he has indicated the need for an empirical base for the theory. However, until such empirically based axioms are available, there is simply no basis for judging even the potential explanatory power of the theory. Thus, I would argue that we are being asked to give up some highly successful theories for an unknown quantity.

IV. Is a New Theoretical Approach Needed?

Finally, let us return to the issue of whether the established theories are in the kind of deep trouble that should cause us to "challenge the basic tenets of the theory."

Reese seems to view the major shortcoming of these theories as the inability to explain rapid changes in performance in learning and transfer tasks. He pointed to three shift studies for which Spiker and Cantor (1973) reported some difficulty in fitting the early-trial data of shift learning in certain subgroups. Actually, the portion of variance unaccounted for in these studies only ranged between 5% and 18%. The important point, however, is that Spiker and Cantor indicated that the problem was basically a methodological one rather than a theoretical one. The unit of theoretical analysis was an eight-trial block, and in some conditions a significant portion of learning occurred within the first block of trials. The cure suggested was not the abandonment of the theory but rather the design of future studies to permit analysis based on smaller blocks of trials.

Rapid learning per se is not a problem in these theories. Certainly the learning-rate parameters in both the Spiker theory and the Zeaman and House theory permit the derivation of rapid learning. Rather, the question that Professor Reese raises is one that must be faced on all theoretical fronts—namely, what are the conditions under which learning and transfer are rapid, rather than gradual? Once these conditions are known, the particular explanatory mechanism would vary from theory to theory. Rapid changes in performance may, for example, reflect a shift in the observing response from one dimension to another in the Zeaman and House theory, a shift in dimensional cue-producing responses in the Spiker theory, a shift in the representational mediating response in the Kendler and Kendler theory, and a shift in hypotheses in the Levine (1975) theory. Thus, I would argue that the problem that needs to be addressed is not basically theoretical; it is empirical. We must discover the laws that will permit us to predict the development of, the transfer of, and the shifts in attention, verbal mediators, hypotheses, motives, actions, operations, or whatever. The search for these laws is currently being undertaken within the context of the S–R theories of Zeaman and House, Kendler and Kendler, and Spiker, and also within the context of cognitive theories such as those of Campione and Brown (1974) and Levine (see Phillips & Levine, 1975).

Reese also claims an advantage for the dialectical theory over existing theories in accounting for developmental trends in discrimination learning, and the incorporation of the Soviet version of a stage analysis makes it clear that the explanation of age changes is considered to be of central importance in the theory. For example, it is stated that performance in discrimination tasks "reflects operations intended to satisfy the problem-solving goal, which is determined by the dominant motives of a particular stage of development." Are age changes in discrimination performance a serious problem for behavioristic learning theories? In my view, age trends do not constitute a special type of theoretical problem for any theory. Discrimination performance is obviously dependent on many variables. It is also just as obvious that the child is changing in a multitude of ways as he gets older. Why should we choose age as a basic variable in our theories? Why aren't we talking about "height trends in mediation" instead of "age trends in mediation?" After all, evidence for mediation increases as the child grows taller, too. I sometimes think that the particular nature of our educational system is the source of what I consider to be an overemphasis on age and developmental stages as explanatory concepts. When we ask the school system for subjects, we find them grouped by age. If we still had the old one-room schoolhouses, and if children came to our experiments unselected by age, we would still note that evidence for mediation varies from child to child. But instead of talking about age trends, we might have gone by a more direct route to the important question of what are the basic determinants of mediational behavior. Somewhat parenthetically, I have often thought that the gap in our available subject pools in the range from 1 to 3 years of age has also had a profound and unfortunate effect on some of our theorizing. For example, do we really believe that when a 1–2-year-old child solves a discrimination learning task, he sequentially tests hypotheses or he "considers the conditions of the problem, forms an intention, and then executes it"?

Having taken a rather extreme position regarding age in order to make the above points, I must now express my view that the study of age trends is an important aid in the development of our theories. The observation of age trends is helpful in the search for the basic determinants of learning. Clearly, the differences in performance that constitute these age trends must be explained by our theories—I think many of them are, and the rest will be eventually. However, what we need to know in order to be able to predict, for example, optional shift behavior, is not how old the child is or what stage he is in; rather, we need to know, depending upon our theory, what are his cue-producing responses, observing responses, hypotheses, or operations. At best, knowing that he is in Stage X is a shortcut way of specifying these initial subject states, and we would still have the problem of specifying how we know that he is in Stage X.

Finally, do the behavioristic theories have a special problem in explaining what Reese refers to as competence–performance discrepancies or decalages? Again, my answer is no. Furthermore, it seems very puzzling that the age-old learning–performance distinction should suddenly become a new theoretical issue. This distinction is a familiar one to every student of introductory psychology. Children know how to do a great many things that they don't perform in a given situation. Why is this fact now being viewed as a contradiction? Indeed, one of the major tasks of the learning psychologist is to find out under what conditions the child performs what he has previously learned to do. To be more specific, why should it be viewed as a contradiction that a child knows how to mediate but doesn't do so in a particular task? This is an interesting and important scientific fact, but not a contradiction. It seems to me that the contradiction lies in the theorist who expects the child to mediate and is surprised that he doesn't. The solution will not be obtained by building a theory in which it is assumed that there is a contradiction inside the child. Rather, if we go about the business of discovering the determinants of mediation, then we will no longer be surprised at the experimental outcomes.

V. Concluding Comments

In conclusion, I would like to reiterate the general theme that has run through all of my comments. Theory construction is a complex, arduous, fascinating, and often frustrating process. Building a theory with any degree of scope and precision requires time and patience, and several generations. The only way to improve such a theory is to find out where it is in trouble and then to make the necessary changes and additions. What is frequently needed at a given point in time is the discovery of new behavioral laws, not the development of new theories. Psychology has reached a stage of maturity where we have theories with considerable explanatory power. It is not necessary to start anew with each morning sun, though that may be more exciting than doing the necessary reconstruction of parts of the established theories. If it really becomes necessary to replace our established theories with a new theory, then we have a responsibility to demonstrate that we have registered a gain in overall explanatory power.

REFERENCES

Bergmann, G. *Philosophy of science.* Madison, Wis.: University of Wisconsin Press, 1957.

Campione, J. C., & Brown, A. L. The effects of contextual changes and degree of component mastery on transfer of training. In H. W. Reese (Ed.), *Advances in child development and behavior* (Vol. 9). New York: Academic Press, 1974, Pp. 69–114.

Flavell, J. H., Beach, D. R., & Chinsky, J. M. Spontaneous verbal rehearsal in a memory task as a function of age. *Child Development,* 1966, 37, 283–299.

Kendler, H. H., & Kendler, T. S. Vertical and horizontal processes in problem solving. *Psychological Review,* 1962, 69, 1–16.

Kendler, H. H., & Kendler, T. S. Mediation and conceptual behavior. In J. T. Spence (Eds.), *The psychology of learning and motivation* (Vol. 2). New York: Academic Press, 1968. Pp. 197–244.

Kendler, H. H., & Spence, J. T. Tenets of neobehaviorism. In H. H. Kendler & J. T. Spence, (Eds.), *Essays in neobehaviorism.* New York: Appleton, 1971. Pp. 11–40.

Kendler, T. S. An ontogeny of mediational deficiency. *Child Development,* 1972, 43, 1–17.

Levine, M. (Ed.). *A cognitive theory of learning.* Hillsdale, N.J.: Lawrence Erlbaum Associates, 1975.

Phillips, S., & Levine, M. Probing for hypotheses with adults and children: blank trials and introacts. *Journal of Experimental Psychology: General,* 1975, 104, 327–354.

Spiker, C. C. An extension of Hull-Spence discrimination learning theory. *Psychological Review,* 1970, 77, 496–515.

Spiker, C. C. Application of Hull-Spence theory to the discrimination learning of children. In H. W. Reese (Eds.), *Advances in child development and behavior* (Vol. 6). New York: Academic Press, 1971. Pp. 99–152.

Spiker, C. C., & Cantor, J. H. Applications of Hull-Spence theory to the transfer of discrimination learning in children. In H. W. Reese (Eds.), *Advances in child development and behavior* (Vol. 8). New York: Academic Press, 1973. Pp. 223–288.

Zeaman, D., & House, B. J. The role of attention in retardate discrimination learning. In N. R. Ellis (Ed.), *Handbook of mental deficiency.* New York: McGraw-Hill, 1963. Pp. 159–223.

Zeaman, D., & House, B. J. Interpretations of developmental trends in discriminative transfer effects. In A. D. Pick (Ed.), *Minnesota Symposium on Child Development* (Vol. 8). Minneapolis: University of Minnesota Press, 1974. Pp. 144–186.

CHAPTER 13

A Transactional Model of Remembering[1]

JOHN A. MEACHAM

STATE UNIVERSITY OF NEW YORK
BUFFALO, NEW YORK

I. Development of Remembering Abilities

A transactional model of remembering is outlined in this chapter in order to assist in understanding a specific class ·of phenomena, namely, those changes in remembering abilities that are age-related and thus developmental in nature. The major concern is with the appearance and subsequent modification of remembering operations, strategies, or abilities, rather than with the detailed functioning of those operations at a single age level, for example, the adult rememberer. A brief review of the phenomena to be explained as well as the issues that alternative models need to address is necessary before the proposed transactional model can be presented and evaluated.

Developmental changes in remembering abilities in children and adolescents have been summarized recently by Brown (1975) and by Hagen, Jongeward, and Kail (1975), and so can be mentioned here briefly. An elementary datum is the increase in the number of items that can be recalled, from approximately four by a child of 5 years to seven by a child of 12. Of more interest, however, are changes in the operations or abilities employed in order to facilitate acquisition and retrieval. Among these are rehearsing as preparation for serial recall (Belmont & Butterfield,

[1] This chapter reflects a variety of helpful and encouraging transactions with Klaus Riegel, Joseph Rychlak, H. L. Ansbacher, and with the students in a graduate seminar on memory and cognitive development, in particular Jan Elrod.

1969; Hagen, 1972; Hagen, Meacham, & Mesibov, 1970), verbal and visual elaboration in paired-associate tasks (Reese, in press; Rohwer, 1973), and the use of
organizing abilities during acquisition (Moely, Olson, Halwes, & Flavell, 1969;
Neimark, Slotnick, & Ulrich, 1971) and during retrieval (Kobasigawa, in press;
Ritter, Kaprove, Fitch, & Flavell, 1973). A further category includes changes in the
child's understanding of his own remembering abilities, with older children more
able than younger children to be planful in the choice of appropriate strategies and
to be reflective in discussing remembering abilities (Flavell, Friedrichs, & Hoyt,
1970; Flavell & Wellman, in press). Developmental changes during adulthood and
old age take place in both acquisition and retrieval processes. For example, Heron
and Craik (1964), Hulicka and Grossman (1967), and Hultsch (1971) provide
evidence of age differences in the organization of information and the use of
elaboration strategies during acquisition. Age differences are also found in the time
required for search during retrieval (Anders, Fozard, & Lillyquist, 1972).

Unfortunately, there have been relatively few attempts to integrate what is
known regarding developmental changes in remembering abilities across the entire
life span other than those that have been stimulated by the Life-Span Conferences
(Botwinick, 1970; Goulet, 1973; Kausler, 1970; see also Reese, 1973a). Among the
issues that an integrative model ought to address are, first, the relationship between
the rate and sequence of development of remembering abilities and other cognitive
changes. More specifically, the model ought to describe instances of production
deficiency, that is, points in the developmental sequence at which the individual
does not engage spontaneously, despite training, in remembering operations that
are, however, within his range of abilities (Flavell, 1970; Hagen, Hargrave, & Ross,
1973; Meacham, 1972a, pp. 213–218). Second, the model ought to consider the
relationship between remembering abilities and other developing cognitive abilities,
for, as Bartlett (1932, p. 186) warned many years ago, to attempt to understand
any higher mental process in isolation is to indulge in a subtle kind of faculty
psychology (see also Brown, 1975; p. 103; Jenkins, 1974, p. 794; Meacham, 1972a,
p. 206).

Third, the model ought to consider the relationship of the development of
remembering abilities in the individual to conditions and changes occurring both
within the cultural-historical context and within the personal life space of the
developing individual. Recently, Scribner (1974), Wagner (1974), and Meacham
(1975c) have presented evidence that remembering abilities can vary as a function
of exposure to formal education and modern living circumstances. Furthermore,
Reese (1974) has shown that preschoolers' ability to benefit from the use of
pictorial elaboration in learning paired associates has been influenced by the
broadcasting of *Sesame Street*. The hypothesis that remembering abilities mature in
a regular way independently of a specific cultural-historical context is no longer
tenable. As Cole and Scribner (in press) have noted, it is a relatively infrequent
occurrence, even in technological societies, for individuals to engage in remembering operations when the only goal is to remember, as is the case in most research
and theory on remembering. More often, remembering takes place in the service of

a variety of superordinate activities or motives, and these in turn are a reflection of the cultural-historical context. The social context is a factor not only in the development of the specific means or operations for remembering but also in a determination of the purposes to which remembering abilities can be and are applied (see Meacham, in press-b).

In the following sections, a distinction will be made between interactional and transactional models, as frameworks for conceptualizing the development of remembering activities. The transactional model will be applied to three different context areas, chosen in part for their coverage of remembering throughout the life span: (1) the onset of deliberate remembering in early childhood; (2) the use of more sophisticated operations or strategies for remembering in later childhood and adolescence; and (3) reminiscing as a special application of remembering during late adulthood and old age.

II. Interactional and Transactional Models

In keeping with the theme of this volume, a number of key aspects of dialectical approaches can be mentioned briefly. Dialectical models are constructed so as to provide an important role for the cultural and historical contexts in the development of the individual (Kvale, 1975; Reese, 1976; Riegel, 1975d). The cultural-historical context is not, however, merely a supportive context within which psychological development may take place; rather, this context itself must be viewed both as an active participant in the development of the individual and as proceeding along a developmental course in its own right (Meacham & Riegel, in press; Riegel, 1975a). In addition, the primary emphasis is upon activity and continuing changes, rather than upon stability and permanence (Riegel, 1975b, 1975d; Rychlak, 1968, p. 356). Because change is a primitive rather than a derived construct within dialectical models (Overton, 1975), such models are quite appropriate for conceptualizing developmental processes (Reese, 1973b, 1976). Implicit within the dialectical model is the view that the relationship between the individual and the cultural-historical context, and between the various subsystems of the individual, is one of reciprocal causality rather than unidirectional causality (Meacham, 1976; Overton & Reese, 1973, p. 77). In relations of reciprocal causality each element affects and is affected simultaneously by the other. It is this aspect of dialectical models that is emphasized and elaborated in the present chapter.

All these aspects of dialectical models are present in Soviet psychology, which, in contrast to non-Soviet psychology, is primarily a theory of development of the individual and society. For example, the work of Rubinstein has focused in part upon the relationship of mind to its material bases, that is, to the cultural-historical context (Payne, 1968; Riegel, 1973). A fundamental assumption of Soviet psychology is that it is not possible to develop a generalized psychology that will be descriptive of human behavior in different cultures and in different historical periods (see, e.g., McLeish, 1975, p. 179; Meacham, in press-b). Also salient is the assumption that the truth that describes reality most adequately is that the essence of reality, and of truth itself, is change (McLeish, 1975, p. 150). Although this latter assumption is at variance with mechanism, it is not inconsistent with the principles of contextualism (Jenkins, 1974; Pepper, 1942/1970; see also Reese's chapter in this volume). Within the contextualist approach, "change is categorical and not derivative in any degree at all [Pepper, 1942/1970, p. 234]." Furthermore, within contextualism "there is no final or complete analysis of anything. . . . In the extended analysis of any event we presently find ourselves in the context of that event, and so on from event to event as long as we wish to go [p. 249. Copyright © 1970 by Stephen C. Pepper; reprinted by permission of the University of California Press.]."

The purpose of the preceding paragraphs is to indicate that much of what is to follow is continuous with many of the concepts previously introduced at the Life-Span Conferences (Overton & Reese, 1973; Riegel, 1973, 1975a) as well as consistent with current emphases in non-Soviet (Jenkins, 1974) and Soviet psychology. In order to pursue these concepts in more depth, however, it will be useful to introduce a distinction between what Dewey and Bentley (1949/1960; see also Sameroff & Chandler, 1975) have termed *interaction* and *transaction*. Interaction assumes elements that can be located and described independently of one another. Inquiries are then made into the relations between such elements, that is, the manner in which each element acts causally upon the others within some organization. Transaction, however, is assumed to be an activity, and elements are derived as secondary categories within the transactional system. Examples of such elements, which depend for their definition upon a prior understanding of the transactional activity, are buyer and seller, borrower and lender, and so on. Once an activity of exchange is assumed, then buyer and seller may be defined easily as the elements derived from a reciprocal and permanent exchange. Similarly, borrower and lender are defined by a one-way, temporary exchange; and thief and victim by a one-way, permanent exchange. In transactional models

> systems of description and naming are employed to deal with aspects and phases of action, without final attribution to "elements" or other presumptively detachable or independent "entities," "essences," or "realities," and without isolation of presumptively detachable "relations" from such detachable "elements" [Dewey & Bentley, 1949/1960, p. 108].

Whereas in the interactional model the individual and the cultural-historical context are viewed as primarily static elements that act upon each other, in the transactional model these are viewed as continually changing derivatives of an ongoing activity or transaction. It may be argued that there is a similarity between the transactional model, in which the individual and the social context have a derived status, and an interactional model composed of the individual and the social context, each acting in a unidirectional manner upon the other. Nevertheless, a continuing problem with interactional models has been the tendency to focus too much on either the individual (heredity) or the context (environment) to the exclusion of the other, ignoring the fact that each depends upon the other. In addition, interactional models are unlikely to give a sufficiently substantial role, relative to the basic individual and context, to such derived elements as tools, verbal concepts, signs, and memories (cf. Soviet psychology). Within a transactional model, however, such products of the transaction have the same derived status as do the individual and the social context. The transactional model, in emphasizing change and the interdependence of elements within a system of activity, is consistent with the general dialectical approach, as well as with contextualism.[2] To summarize briefly, interactional models assume stability and seek to explain change; transactional models assume change and seek to explain momentary stabilities.

The distinction between the transactional model and alternative models may be illustrated further by borrowing and modifying somewhat a baseball analogy first introduced by Cantril (1957). Three umpires are exchanging their understandings of what they are and what they do. The first umpire reports: "Some's balls and some's strikes, and I calls 'em as they is." The epistemology revealed by this umpire's statement is less than that of an interactional position, for the umpire plays no role in the knowing activity other than to copy what is given. The second umpire states: "Some's balls and some's strikes, and I calls 'em as I sees 'em," acknowledging that he actively participates, as an independent entity, in the construction of what is known (see Reese & Overton, 1970, pp. 132–134 for a parallel discussion). The third umpire, however, indicates that "Some's balls and some's strikes, but there ain't nothin' until I calls 'em." Thus, not only the balls and the strikes but the role of the umpire, too, are dependent upon and derived from the transaction or the activity of calling. Prior to the calling, neither the balls and strikes nor the umpire have meaning.

Already transactional models have been constructed in order to give new direction to a variety of issues, especially in the areas of perception and communication. For example, the transactional approach to problems of perception, within which both the perceiver and the world-as-perceived are products of the processes of perception, has been the impetus for extensive investigations of movement, illusion, and constancies (Cantril, Ames, Hastorf, & Ittelson, 1961). Similarly, interpersonal communication may be explored in terms of what happens, rather than in terms of stable characteristics that individuals bring to the communication setting. For example, Pearce and Sharp (1973) have argued for the need to view self-disclosure as a process of communication rather than as a personality trait (for further discussions of the transactional approach in communication, see Barnlund, 1970; Toch & MacLean, 1967/1970). In moral judgments, an evaluative relationship has implications not only for the individual who is judged, but also for the self-esteem of the one who judges, and so both are changed as an outcome of the judgment process (Meacham, 1975a, p. 163). Sameroff and Chandler (1975; Samer-

---

[2] Overton and Reese (1973) have used the term *interaction* as an equivalent to *reciprocal causality*. In the present chapter, *interaction* is seen as equivalent to *unidirectional causality*, and *transaction* as equivalent to *reciprocal causality*.

off, 1975) have documented the inadequacy, in predicting the consequences of trauma in infancy, both of main effects models, in which either constitution or environment is a factor, and of interactional models, in which each unique combination of constitution and environment has a specified developmental outcome. They propose a model in which both the infant and the caretaking environment are continually altered as a result of transactions between the two. Overton (1973) has also distinguished between additive or weak interactions between organism and environment, and strong interactions, which preclude the identification of specific causes in development. Riegel (1975c) has pointed out that linguistic units, such as words and syllables, can be considered as mere abstractions from communicating and that the transaction itself merits closer study. As a final example, Gutmann (1975) and Datan (1976, p. 47) have argued recently that adult personality derives from the basic activity of caretaking and from the basic conflict or tension between the interests of the parent and those of the child. In all these examples, an ongoing activity or process is assumed to be basic, and individuals and their characteristics are derived from the basic transactions.

The discussion to follow is based upon a distinction made in Soviet psychology between various aspects of *activities,* namely, actions and operations (Leont'ev, 1972/1974; Meacham, 1972a, in press-b; see also Reese's chapter, this volume). Activities determine the nature of, and the transactions between, the individual and the social context, and it is through activities that the individual is able to understand and attribute meaning to himself and his social world. Activities motivate specific *actions* (acts), which are processes structured and directed by conscious goals (Leont'ev, 1972/1974, p. 23). A particular activity or motive can instigate attempts to reach a variety of goals, and an action can be subordinated to various motives. Actions themselves are carried out subject to the limiting conditions of each task. Because of these conditions, different *operations* or means of action are employed (Leont'ev, 1972/1974, p. 26). An action can be performed by various operations, depending on the conditions of the task, and a particular operation can facilitate numerous actions. An operation is acquired first as an independent, goal-derived action, and only in a second step can this new action become an operation by being subordinated as a means of accomplishing some other action (Meacham, 1972a, p. 216).

Understanding the development of remembering abilities requires an understanding of the origins of those operations such as rehearsing, elaborating, and organizing that are used as means to facilitate the action of remembering. A partial answer to this question concerning origins is implicit within Leont'ev's (1959/1964) statement that a "first and most general principle" of mental development is that

changes do not occur independently of one another but [are] intrinsically connected with one another. In other words, they do not represent independent lines of development of the various processes (perception, memory, thinking, etc.). . . . For example, the development of memory creates an associated series of changes, but the need for them is not determined by the relationships occurring within the development of memory itself but by relations depending on the place which memory occupies in the child's activity at the given level of its development [p. 184].

Thus, developmental psychologists may be considering too narrow a range of phenomena in their efforts to understand the development of remembering abilities. As Leont'ev suggests, (1) the origins of operations that will be used later to facilitate the action of remembering can be sought in contexts and psychological processes other than those directly related to remembering; and (2) the development of remembering as an independent, goal-directed action can be understood better by considering the various activities or motives within which remembering takes place. This need to consider the relationship of remembering to other cognitive abilities and to the context within which remembering takes place has been remarked upon previously (Bartlett, 1932; Brown, 1975; Jenkins, 1974; Meacham, 1972a; see also Chapter 11, this volume). Soviet psychology has provided a structure for the examination of these relationships.

The remainder of this chapter consists of examples chosen from across the life span to illustrate a dialectical or transactional model of remembering (earlier versions are proposed in Meacham, 1975b, in press-b). In each example, an ongoing transactional system is assumed, from which the individual rememberer, the memories, and the social context are derived. For purposes of description, the system must be entered at some point, for example, a new, independent goal-oriented action is acquired in one of the psychological domains. Subsequently, the original context of development is changed, both as a result of the acquisition of the new action and as a result of the subordination of this action as an operation in other domains. For example, when an infant becomes able to crawl, the conditions for further development are radically changed. The crawling restructures the relationship between the infant and the environment, as the range of obtainable objects and places is greatly increased. The action of crawling is soon subordinated as an operation for the purpose of carrying out other actions related to motives of competence, affiliation, and so on. These changes in turn constitute the conditions for the acquisition of additional actions, for example, standing and walking. Thus, there arise possibilities for new activities in the cultural-historical context and so for further development of the individual. Through transaction, the individual rememberer, his memories, and the social context are changed, continually creating the potential for further transaction and development.

III. Remembering and Motor Actions

The origin of the operation of verbal encoding as a means of remembering may be found in a psychological domain other than remembering, namely, in describing the outcomes of completed motor actions. The development of deliberate remembering may be understood by considering the transactions or activities within which remembering occurs. In particular, remembering develops in subordination to future-directed actions, and only later is this goal differentiated to include the recall of information from the past. These arguments have developed out of a consideration of the possible role that verbal actions may play in guiding motor actions, especially as illustrated in a series of investigations carried out by the Soviet psychologist Luria (1959/1969). Luria's research has generally been considered within the framework of verbal mediation theory. However, as Wozniak (1972, p. 26), Meacham (1972b, in press-a), Wilder (1976), and others have noted, this framework is inappropriate for interpreting many of the phenomena that Luria describes. In fact, several investigations with preschoolers have found that verbal actions characteristically follow rather than precede the motor actions that are guided theoretically by the verbal actions (Birch, 1971; S. A. Miller, Shelton, & Flavell, 1970; Zaporozhets, Zinchenko, & Elkonin, 1964/1971, p. 213). The argument to be presented here permits a guiding role for verbal actions, at least to the extent that the operation of verbal encoding assists in remembering the anticipated goals of motor actions, so that the actual outcome of a motor action may be evaluated relative to the anticipated goal and corrective action engaged in if necessary (for a more complete presentation, see Meacham, in press-a).

Do preschoolers forget the anticipated goals of their motor actions? The possibility that preschoolers have difficulty in remembering a goal long enough to consummate it in motor action may seem more reasonable if we first consider a more familiar example: It may happen that, although one has come to a restaurant with a particular dish in mind, consideration of the menu leads to the substitution of a different entree. Assuming that the meal goes well, one is likely to consider afterwards that the anticipated goal was fulfilled, although in fact the goal had changed in the course of being fulfilled. It is not that preschoolers' motor actions are not goal-oriented, but rather that engaging in a particular course of motor action may lead to the substitution of the actual outcome for the anticipated goal.

Evidence that such is the case is found in a study by Strommen (1973), who investigated the development of the ability of preschool, kindergarten, first-, and third-grade children to play "Simon Says." Of approximately 40 children at each age, 11 preschoolers, 8 kindergartners, and 4 first-graders

> proceeded to err on every inhibition trial even through they "understood" the task as presented in the instructions. These children gave no indication of recognizing any discrepancy between their performance on example trials and on test trials, whereas other children frequently reacted to errors on test trials with expressions of dismay, sheepish grins or giggling, or body motions that appeared to serve as competing responses [p. 852].

One interpretation of Strommen's observation is that in the course of engaging in the inappropriate motor action, these children forgot the initial command to inhibit and consequently substituted the actual outcome of their motor action for the anticipated goal.

Further indirect evidence of difficulty in remembering is provided by observations that young children engage in motor activity immediately upon being presented with, by means of an adult's verbal command, the goal of the motor action. In other words, the child engages immediately in action toward the goal before it is forgotten. Lisina and Neverovich (1964/1971, p. 334) report an investigation by Yendovitskaya in which children were asked to put construction materials into three boxes in a given sequence. Younger preschoolers performed the task by following only the instructions that related to the goal, while ignoring instructions that pertained to the method for achieving the goal.

What are the implications of the child's forgetting the goals of actions for the quality of motor actions? One general structure for considering this question is the Test-Operate-Test-Exit, or TOTE, schema (G. A. Miller, Galanter, & Pribram, 1960), according to which motor actions are initiated and guided by the discrepancy between the anticipated state and the current state of the organism. Within such a structure, testing of ongoing or completed motor actions requires both a memory of the anticipated goal and a perception of the current outcome of the motor activity. But how is an exit accomplished if the anticipated goal has been forgotten in the course of the motor action? One means would be to substitute the actual outcome for the anticipated goal, as did, apparently, the children in Strommen's investigation. Such a substitution would have no unfortumate consequences as long as the motor activity has been appropriate; but if the motor action is inappropriate, such a substitution would lead to an exit with no further corrective or compensatory motor action. In this manner, the quality of motor actions is dependent upon remembering what one anticipated doing, and verbal actions may play a role as operations that facilitate remembering the goals of motor actions.

Some data to illustrate this role of verbal actions in remembering the goals of motor actions are provided in an investigation by Meacham (1972b, in press-a), in which an association was found between the occurrence of verbalizing and the change to a more appropriate motor action following an initially inappropriate motor action. Children were instructed to ride a tricycle appropriately following the commands "Go," "Stop," "Up," and "Back," presented in a random sequence, and to repeat simultaneously each of the commands as it was presented. Instances during which the child engaged in an inappropriate motor action and then changed to a more appropriate motor action were contrasted with those during which the child continued to engage in the inappropriate motor action. Changing to the appropriate motor action was more likely if the child also verbalized appropriately than if the child did not verbalize. According to the argument being made presently, the verbalizing serves as an operation to facilitate the remembering of the anticipated goal, which is then available for comparison with the actual outcome of the motor action.

What is the origin of this operation of verbal encoding? According to Leont'ev (1959/1964, p. 181), any operation, such as verbal encoding, is first formed as an action. In other words, the origin of verbal encoding as an operation to facilitate remembering must be in some psychological domain in which verbal encoding itself is a goal-directed action (see also Meacham, 1972a, p. 216; in press-b). There is some evidence that verbal actions can play an important role in informing the young child more completely of the outcome of his motor actions. Kohlberg, Yaeger, and Hjertholm (1968) suggest that one function of collective monologue in private speech

is communicating information to the self, is communicating the meaning or nature of the child's activity to the other, and hence is establishing the meaning for the self. . . . From

Mead's view . . . the young child does not have an awareness of his own action prior to communicating about it to others [p. 704].

Kohlberg *et al.* suggest that private speech includes "remarks about the self's activity which communicate no information to the listener not apparent from watching him [p. 707]." In other words, such verbal actions may be important to the child in describing the continuing sequence of outcomes of his own motor actions. Lisina and Neverovich (1964/1971) express a similar view of the role of verbal actions in enriching the perception of the outcome of motor actions: "Verbal directions isolate the most essential aspects of action for children, which may be difficult for the child to isolate out of the totality of circumstances from visual observation [p. 345]." Zaporozhets *et al.* (1964/1971) describes a stage in which

speech becomes a means for reflecting the situation. The experimenting child while executing a movement . . . immediately states it in his speech, thus describing what appears to be a verbal form of the activity, a copy of his behavior and the situation [p. 213].

In this early stage, because the verbal activity describes the outcome of the motor activity, it follows the motor activity (cf. the findings of Birch, 1971; S. A. Miller *et al.,* 1970).

Once this action of verbal encoding has been practiced sufficiently and established, it may, within Leont'ev's framework, be subordinated to some other action, for example, the action of remembering the anticipated goals of motor actions. There is a continuity in the function of the verbal action in each of these two stages, that is, describing the products or outcomes of motor actions. Nevertheless, the transition from describing actual to describing anticipated outcomes or goals is a critical one in development, for by describing anticipated goals, the child is better able to remember them, and so it becomes possible to compare the remembered thought with the actual outcome. Within this later stage, motor actions are not initiated or directed by verbal actions, but verbal actions play a role in guiding the motor action by facilitating the remembering of goals and the evaluating of outcomes. The achievement of this stage is summarized nicely by Luria and Yudovich (1956/1959):

By comparison of the result obtained during the process of activity with that system of connections which underlay the project, the child ought to reach a position where he could objectively evaluate this product apart from his activity and consequently also take up a critical relation to it [p. 84].

The preceding analysis, according to which the remembering of the goals of actions is facilitated by an operation or strategy developed in another context— describing the outcomes of actions—represents a new perspective on the relationship between the development of strategies for remembering and the development of voluntary or planned behavior. Previously the development of abilities for remembering information about the past has been emphasized (e.g., Brown, 1975; Flavell, 1970; Meacham, 1972a). In this chapter, however, the emphasis has been upon the remembering of goals of *future* actions. Recently, research directed at understanding the development of remembering abilities in very young children has employed tasks that require remembering the goals of future actions, rather than remembering information about the past. For example, Wellman, Ritter, and Flavell (1975) asked 2- and 3-year-old children to remember for 40 seconds the location of a toy dog hidden under one of several cups. Delay period activities such as looking and touching the cup were found to facilitate remembering the location of the dog. What is required is to keep in mind or to continue to attend to the anticipated goal of a motor action, that is, pointing to the cup that hides the dog. It may be only later in development that operations directed specifically at the remembering of information about the past are differentiated from the preparation for future action. This developmental sequence has been described previously by de Laguna (1927/1963):

> Memory is not originally a distinct and independent function. *It occurs first as a moment in the complete act.* The distinct living over of past experience, memory proper, becomes only gradually freed from the control of the particular act and the particular occasion, and at the same time distinguished, as the *recall* of the past from the imagination of the possible future [p. 179].

In summary, remembering as traditionally investigated is likely a later development than remembering as an operation to facilitate the carrying out of planned action. The particular operation of verbal encoding, as employed to facilitate remembering, may have its origins in describing the outcomes of completed actions.

IV. Remembering and Cognition

Let us return to Leont'ev's "first and most general principle" and consider for a somewhat older child the possible relationships between remembering and the development of various other cognitive processes that might be subordinated as operations to facilitate remembering, as well as the relationships between remembering itself and the various activities, motives, or social contexts within which it may take place. The general model is that operations subordinate to the action of remembering must first be acquired as independent, goal-directed actions. Already, verbal encoding has been mentioned to illustrate this sequence. The further development of verbal means to facilitate remembering may depend on the prior acquisition of writing and role-taking skills as a means of communicating over extended durations of time with persons other than oneself; that is, the child needs to be able to view him- or herself in a future role as one who may not know or be able to remember what he or she knows or experiences now. Later, these skills may be subordinated as operations or means to ensure effective communication of information to oneself at a later time. As additional examples, the use of organizing as an acquisition or retrieval strategy is clearly dependent upon the prior development of organizational schemes of sufficient generality and stability to be successfully subordinated to the goal of remembering. Similarly, rehearsing as a memorizing strategy depends on the prior acquisition of iteration abilities, which can then be subordinated to the goal of remembering. Such iteration abilities may be acquired in the context of private speech, which often includes instances of repetition, echolalia, playing with words and sounds, and so on. Once such iteration abilities are firmly established, but before this action is subordinated as an operation to the goal of remembering, a state of production deficiency may be said to exist, that is, the subordination can be accomplished only through the intervention of an adult. The manner in which the social context facilitates such subordination clearly deserves continued attention and research.

Remembering itself may be subordinated as an operation to facilitate various other actions. For example, Inglis (1959) has provided evidence to show the role that remembering can play. Patients suffering from memory disorders did not perform as well in a test of conceptual ability as did patients of equal age and intelligence but without memory disorders. Bryant and Trabasso (1971) have shown that facilitating the remembering of premise information can lead to better performance on transitive inference tasks. McLaughlin (1963) has provided an interpretation of Piaget's theory in terms of increases in remembering abilities so that the child's ability to operate with classes is increased. Eimas (1970) has shown that the provision of memory aids can lead to improvement in children's ability to evaluate and eliminate inappropriate hypotheses. Together, these examples suggest the need for further research, both into the origins of the various actions that are later subordinated as remembering strategies or operations and also into the impact that remembering itself may have as it is subordinated as a means of carrying out other, higher-order actions.

The impact of developing remembering abilities upon other cognitive domains can be illustrated, by analogy, by citing various examples from the historical development of remembering systems (Meacham, 1975b). Of course, the transactions from which various remembering systems have been derived through the course of history will rarely be the same as those that lead to the development of remembering abilities in the individual. Nevertheless, historical examples may be a source of questions and possible answers regarding the development of memory abilities in the individual. In the history of remembering systems, a major development was the invention of writing. Writing was not developed initially as a means of communication, but rather because it was necessary, particularly in commerce, to have a system of reminding (Ong, 1971). Early writing systems, because they were merely reminding systems, assumed that the reader was already familiar with what was to be remembered. Thus, fragments of clay tablets inscribed by a trader, or hieroglyphics on a monument, remain unclear to us, because we were not present as the trading negotiations took place, nor did we fight in the wars that led to the erection of the monument. Writing, however, is quite different from the remembering system that preceded it, that is, the oral epics (Havelock, 1971). In particular, ideas that have been written can also be reflected upon as ideas, and further, writing also became a means of communication of new information, for example, Caesar has crossed the Rubicon. Thus, writing was originally subordinated as an operation in one context, the context of reminding, and then was elaborated as a system and subordinated to facilitate other actions such as reflection in thought and communication among individuals. As a result, the context for further development of technology and culture was significantly altered.

The method of places and images (Yates, 1966) was similarly developed as a remembering system appropriate to the context of rhetoric, but was later extended to a variety of other contexts. For example, in the Middle Ages, the method was used to organize and remember the extensive elaboration of Christian ethical teachings brought about from the introduction by the Arabs of many classical Greek works on moral themes. Later, the method of places and images was used widely in philosophy because the ability to remember extensive tracts of philosophy or knowledge was thought to bring one closer to God. Yates (1966) argues that it was through the elaboration of remembering systems, such as that of Ramon Lull which involve a series of concentric circles, that the way was prepared for the rapid growth of science during the last few hundred years. As the circles in Lull's remembering system were turned, new relationships were constructed between the elements on the circles, and gaps in the organization of what was known and remembered were exposed and could later be filled in.

One of the earliest remembering systems was the oral poem or epic. Although early classical scholars have viewed works such as Homer's as constructions for the purposes of entertainment, it has recently become clear that a major purpose of such oral remembering systems was to assist nonliterate societies in remembering and transmitting to new generations the memories of technical skills necessary for the maintenance of the society (Havelock, 1971). Homer's poems reminded the people of the proper way to raise children, communicate with the gods, prepare for war, conduct funerals, carry on politics, and so on. The capability of remembering such skills no doubt contributed to the view within a society that it had integrity, continuity, and purpose. What are the implications of these examples from history for the development of remembering abilities in the individual? In general terms, it becomes clear that actions, once acquired, may be subordinated as operations in a variety of contexts, as was the case with writing and with the method of places and images. The subordination of a new operation or means to an old problem may bring about a qualitative change in the range of transactions that are possible, as when writing made possible accurate communication over extended times and distances, and when the systematization of knowledge made possible an explosion of new, scientific knowledge. Finally, by extension from the historical example, remembering may provide the individual rememberer with the sense that he has integrity, continuity, purpose, and so on; this last idea will be explored in the next section.

V. Remembering and Personality

The role that remembering may play as an operation to facilitate the constructing of a personality, distinctive pattern of acting, or outlook on life characterized as having integrity, continuity, and purpose will now be considered. In particular, the focus will be upon the process by which one's own past experiences are recalled, that is, reminiscing. Although children as young as perhaps 10 years of age appear to engage in reminiscing, for example, as shown in diary records, reminiscing is more often associated with the late adult years. The salient question is whether the function of reminiscing ought to be regarded as a symptom of psychological decline, as escapism, as an occurrence out of the control of the individual, or rather as an adaptive means by which a review, evaluation, and integration of experiences over one's life span is carried out (Butler, 1963).

Evidence that reminiscing should be considered not in isolation but rather as it is subordinated to more general, adaptive transactions is provided by several investigations. For example, Havighurst and Glasser (1972) obtained self-reports on the frequency and affective quality of reminiscence by means of a questionnaire. Among the findings were correlations between pleasantness of reminiscences, the respondent's positive evaluation of himself, life satisfaction, and frequency of reminiscing. Similar data are reported by McMahon and Rhudick (1967), who found more frequent reminiscing in nondepressed individuals, and by Lewis (1971), who found individuals who reminisce often to be resistant to changes in self-esteem when tested in a situation in which their opinions were challenged. Costa and Kastenbaum (1967) analyzed interview protocols of 276 centenarians and found that successful recall and differentiation of memories was related to the presence of future ambitions.

Recently, an effort has been made to establish a connection between reminiscing and satisfactory adjustment in old age, as described by Erikson's (1950) theory. Boylin, Gordon, and Nehrke (1976) employed a modified version of Havighurst and Glasser's (1972) reminiscing questionnaire, plus a scale on which individuals indicated the extent to which various items concerning intimacy, generativity, and ego integrity applied to themselves. Frequency of reminiscing was significantly correlated with ego integrity, but not with items pertaining to the earlier stages in Erikson's theory, intimacy and generativity. These studies taken together suggest strongly that reminiscing can serve as a means to facilitate adaptive processes of life review and personality reorganization in late adulthood and old age. A similar suggestion is present in the work of Adler, for whom early recollections are not indicative of efficient causes in development, but rather should be viewed as current constructions of the individual which are related to the individual's life-style or personality. Thus, it is acknowledged readily that the products of reminiscing are not veridical with respect to past events, but rather are "tendentious and biased and in the service of the purposes and goals of the individual [Ansbacher, 1973, p. 143]."

The thrust of this section, the subordination of reminiscing to current personality functioning, is paradoxical in view of many traditional conceptions of memories as stable and permanent (Meacham, 1976); memories presumably have greater value as they are thought to be more complete, accurate, and easily remembered. However, our principal means of judging the accuracy of memories is not through an assessment of their correspondence with the past but rather through a determination of whether or not they provide information that is appropriate or useful in the context of current personality and social conditions. The role changing memories may play in the support of present personality functioning is illustrated by Woodruff and Birren's (1972) finding that although individuals may believe that they have changed in positive ways from how they remember their personalities to be 25 years previously, longitudinal data indicate little or no change in personality for these same individuals. The issue here is not whether or not these individuals' memories are permanent and accurate, but rather the fact that the memories are consistent with, and no doubt have an impact upon, how these individuals currently conceive of themselves.

The dialogue between the individual and his memories is similar to that between the historian and his work (see also Chapter 2, this volume). The historian, writing of necessity from within a contemporary cultural and historical context, is biased in his selection and interpretation of only certain events from all those that have occurred. Subsequently, the historian's recorded interpretations become the "true" historical context within which the historian himself acquires a meaningful role as an individual and within which further constructions by the historian occur. Thus, as he continues to work from his current point of view, through the products of his work he continually alters the context within which he works and within which he and his work have meaning. Similarly, the individual, through reminiscing within a present context, constructs memories that, once constructed, provide integrity and purpose for the individual within his current context. An important dimension of this process which should not be neglected is that the historian continues to exchange his interpretations with those of other historians and with the readers of his works. Similarly, as Marshall (1974) has argued, we must not neglect that reminiscing and the life-review process are not only individual actions but also take place within a social context, that is, reminiscing takes place within the presence of, and often with the active support and assistance of, other individuals. Lewis (1973) has suggested that one reason for the reminiscer's efforts to communicate with other persons is to gain social support for the validity of his own system of beliefs and values.

VI. Conclusion

To summarize, it has been argued in the preceding sections that both the rememberer, including various operations for remembering, and memories themselves may be regarded as products of transaction or activity. In the case of motor actions, the strengthening and subordination of verbal encoding permits a qualitative change in the efficiency of planned action; in the case of cognition, operations for remembering permit changes in various problem-solving actions; and in the case of personality, remembering facilitates reorganization of personality in late adulthood and old age. In each case, it is through transactions that various remembering abilities such as verbal encoding, rehearsing, and so on, which define the current developmental stage of the rememberer, become available.

In constructing a transactional model of remembering, one which permits appropriate consideration of the development of remembering abilities in the individual, it has been essential to begin by assuming a general system of activity, transaction, dialogue, communication, or exchange. The purpose or function of such a system can be expressed initially only in general terms, for example, to maintain the organized functioning of the individual, to permit appropriate adaptation of that functioning within changing environmental circumstances, and to invent and attribute psychological significance to the changing activities and products of the system. At the outset, it is not possible to make definite commitments as to the components of such a system or to the content with which the system may be concerned, for these latter aspects, continually in flux, are derived from the ongoing activity of the system. The overall activity of such a system may be facilitated if the system can make use of certain knowledge of past experience which may be relevant for functioning in the present. As a derivative of the basic activity that has been assumed, memories are constructed as a means of representing that knowledge of past experience. The construction of memories is not an end in itself, however, but merely a means toward facilitating more general systemic goals. Similarly, as a derivative of the activity or transaction, an individual rememberer is also constructed, as a means of experiencing and making use of the knowledge of past experience. Finally, through transaction, meaning is attributed to the environment, and so a social context is constructed.

Two points can be emphasized in what has just been stated: First, the system is not merely the individual rememberer, but includes also the rememberer, the memories, and the social context. Second, neither the rememberer nor the memories are stable entities, for both are dependent upon the continued functioning of the transactional system; as the system functions, the rememberer and the memories are changed. Additional emphases may be made apparent by comparing this transactional model with alternative views of the relationship between the rememberer and his memories. Several alternatives may be distinguished, according to whether the rememberer and his memories are each seen as basic and stable, on the one hand, or derived and changeable, on the other (see Figure 1). One such view (a) is that the individual consists of a *collection* of memories of events occurring in the environment. Such a view, in addition to neglecting the active role that is played by the individual in the construction of memories, does not consider that memories are constructed for a further purpose than merely to have knowledge of the past. The

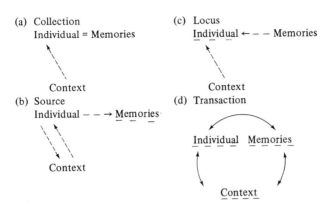

Fig. 1. Relationships between the individual rememberer and his memories. Dashed lines indicate derived actions or elements.

memories should be viewed as a means to the end of continuing functioning and adaptation, but not as an end in themselves.

A more popular view (b) is that memories are changeable, as they are constructed by the individual rememberer, who, although a *source* of memories, nevertheless remains unchanged. Of course, it is widely acknowledged that we alter and distort the accuracy of our memories in order to suit our present motivations and knowledge schemes, but such a view assumes an abstract, isolated rememberer and neglects the impact that such memories, once constructed, have upon the individual rememberer. It is this latter aspect that has been emphasized in the present chapter, that is, many current theories have emphasized the active role of the rememberer in constructing memories (Bartlett, 1932; Liben, in press; Paris & Lindauer in press; Piaget & Inhelder, 1973), but the transactional model also gives recognition to the active role of memories, as products, in constructing the individual rememberer and his remembering abilities.

For the sake of completeness, a third view (c) can be mentioned, in which the individual changes but is a *locus* of memories that remain stable. The case of Luria's (1968) mnemonist, however, illustrates the disadvantages of better-than-average remembering abilities. Luria's patient, for example, found it difficult to read poetry, for the imagery of the opening lines persisted, refusing to be forgotten or to be integrated within the context of the later lines. As another example, functioning in the present can be made difficult for persons who continue to recall spontaneously the memories of earlier traumatic experiences, and therapy, the purpose of which is to bring about a change and a reinterpretation of the persisting memory, may be indicated. To summarize, each model is appropriate in a limited context.

The most comprehensive is (d) the transactional model, which regards both memories and the individual rememberer as changeable events, derived from a more basic process of *transaction,* communication, or exchange. Not only are the memories constructed, but the individual in turn depends upon the memories. The social context is interpreted through the individual's memories, and the memories are always constructed within a current social context (see also Chapter 9, this volume).

How is the transactional model presented in this chapter dialectical? First, the model emphasizes change rather than permanence. The individual rememberer and the memories may be apprehended only as temporary stabilities in the flux of activity from which they are derived. Second, not only the individual, but also the memories and the cultural-historical context are derived as products of the transaction; they acquire meaning as a result of the activity of the system. Third, the relationship between the individual, the memories, and the social context is one of reciprocal causality. The memories, as products of the transaction, act upon the individual and change the nature of the individual's motor actions, cognitions, and personality. Through transaction, a continuing opposition is created between the individual, the memories, and the social context, and thus the conditions for further development in the system are continually being presented. Whenever a new remembering ability is presented, the relationship of the individual to the social context is changed, and the potential for further change in the individual exists.

It is important to note that the development of the individual rememberer is not a matter of the individual changing or constructing himself, nor of the program for remembering reprogramming itself with newer and more efficient operations. On the contrary, the system, through its activity, produces memory abilities and memories that in turn act upon the individual rememberer. Thus, it is through the basic activity or functioning, and through no more specific process, that individual development occurs. In this context, it is appropriate to refer to the Soviet psychologist Rubinstein: "By his labour man changes and so creates a new environment and new conditions for development. It is in this sense that man can be said to create himself by his own labour—by transforming nature to transform himself [Payne, 1968, p. 90]."

REFERENCES

Anders, T. R., Fozard, J. L., & Lillyquist, T. D. The effects of age upon retrieval from short-term memory. *Developmental Psychology,* 1972, **6,** 214–217.

Ansbacher, H. L. Adler's interpretation of eary recollections: Historical account. *Journal of Individual Psychology,* 1973, **29,** 135–145.

Barnlund, D. C. A transactional model of communication. In K. K. Sereno & C. D. Mortenson (Eds.), *Foundations of communication theory.* New York: Harper, 1970.

Bartlett, F. C. *Remembering: A study in experimental and social psychology.* Cambridge, Eng.: University Press, 1932.

Belmont, J. M., & Butterfield, E. C. The relations of short-term memory to development and intelligence. In L. Lipsitt & H. Reese (Eds.), *Advances in child development and behavior* (Vol. 4). New York: Academic Press, 1969.

Birch, D. Evidence for competition and coordination between vocal and manual responses in preschool children. *Journal of Experimental Child Psychology,* 1971, **12,** 10–26.

Botwinick, J. Learning in children and older adults. In L. R. Goulet & P. B. Baltes (Eds.), *Life-span developmental psychology: Research and theory.* New York: Academic Press, 1970.

Boylin, W., Gordon, S. K., & Nehrke, M. F. Reminiscing and ego integrity in institutionalized elderly males. *Gerontologist,* 1976, **16**, 118–124.

Brown, A. L. The development of memory: Knowing, knowing about knowing, and knowing how to know. In H. W. Reese (Eds.), *Advances in child development and behavior* (Vol. 10). New York: Academic Press, 1975.

Bryant, P. E., & Trabasso, T. Transitive inferences and memory in young children. *Nature (London),* 1971, **232**, 456–458.

Butler, R. The life review: An interpretation of reminiscence in the aged. *Psychiatry,* 1963, **26**, 65–76.

Cantril, H. Perception and interpersonal relations. *American Journal of Psychiatry,* 1957, **114**, 119–126.

Cantril, H., Ames, A., Jr., Hastorf, A. H., & Ittelson, W. H. Psychology and scientific research. In F. P. Kilpatrick (Ed.), *Explorations in transactional psychology.* New York: New York University Press, 1961.

Cole, M., & Scribner, S. Cross-cultural studies of memory and cognition. In R. V. Kail, Jr. & J. W. Hagen (Eds.), *Perspectives on the development of memory and cognition.* Hillsdale, N.J.: Lawrence Erlbaum Associates, in press.

Costa, P., & Kastenbaum, R. Some aspects of memories and ambitions in centenarians. *Journal of Genetic Psychology,* 1967, **110**, 3–16.

Datan, N. Male and female: The search for synthesis. In J. F. Rychlak (Ed.), *Dialectic: Humanistic rationale for behavior and development.* Basel: Karger, 1976.

de Laguna, G. A. *Speech: Its function and development.* Bloomington: Indiana University Press, 1963. (Originally published, 1927).

Dewey, J., & Bentley, A. F. *Knowing and the known.* Boston: Beacon Press, 1960. (Originally published, 1949.)

Eimas, P. D. Effects of memory aids on hypothesis behavior and focusing in young children and adults. *Journal of Experimental Child Psychology,* 1970, **10**, 319–336.

Erikson, E. H. *Childhood and society.* New York: Norton, 1950.

Flavell, J. H. Developmental studies of mediated memory. In H. W. Reese & L. P. Lipsitt (Eds.), *Advances in child development and behavior* (Vol. 5). New York: Academic Press, 1970.

Flavell, J. H., Friedrichs, A. G., & Hoyt, J. D. Developmental changes in memorization processes. *Cognitive Psychology,* 1970, **1**, 324–340.

Flavell, J. H., & Wellman, H. M. Metamemory. In R. V. Kail, Jr. & J. W. Hagen (Eds.), *Perspectives on the development of memory and cognition.* Hillsdale, N.J.: Lawrence Erlbaum Associates, in press.

Goulet, L. R. The interfaces of acquisition: Models and methods for studying the active, developing organism. In J. R. Nesselroade & H. W. Reese (Eds.), *Life-span developmental psychology: Methodological issues.* New York: Academic Press, 1973.

Gutmann, D. Parenthood: A key to the comparative study of the life cycle. In N. Datan & L. H. Ginsberg (Eds.), *Life-span developmental psychology: Normative life crises.* New York: Academic Press, 1975.

Hagen, J. W. Strategies for remembering. In S. Farnham-Diggory (Ed.), *Information processing in children.* New York: Academic Press, 1972.

Hagen, J. W., Hargrave, S., & Ross, W. Prompting and rehearsal in short-term memory. *Child Development,* 1973, **44**, 201–204.

Hagen, J. W., Jongeward, R. H., Jr., & Kail, R. V., Jr. Cognitive perspectives on the development of memory. In H. W. Reese (Eds.), *Advances in child development and behavior* (Vol. 10). New York: Academic Press, 1975.

Hagen, J. W., Meacham, J. A., & Mesibov, G. Verbal labeling, rehearsal, and short-term memory. *Cognitive Psychology,* 1970, **1**, 47–58.

Havelock, E. A. *Prologue to Greek literacy.* Cincinnati: University of Cincinnati, 1971.

Havighurst, R. J., & Glasser, R. An exploratory study of reminiscence. *Journal of Gerontology,* 1972, **27,** 245–253.

Heron, A., & Craik, F. I. M. Age differences in cumulative learning of meaningful and meaningless material. *Scandinavian Journal of Psychology,* 1964, **5,** 209–217.

Hulicka, I. M., & Grossman, J. L. Age-group comparisons for the use of mediators in paired-associate learning. *Journal of Gerontology,* 1967, **22,** 46–51.

Hultsch, D. Adult age differences in free classification and free recall. *Developmental Psychology,* 1971, **4,** 338–342.

Inglis, J. Learning, retention, and conceptual usage in elderly patients with memory disorder. *Journal of Abnormal and Social Psychology,* 1959, **59,** 210–215.

Jenkins, J. Remember that old theory? Well, forget it! *American Psychologist,* 1974, **29,** 785–795.

Kausler, D. H. Retention–forgetting as a nomological network for developmental research. In L. R. Goulet & P. B. Baltes (Eds.), *Life-span developmental psychology: Research and theory.* New York: Academic Press, 1970.

Kobasigawa, A. Retrieval strategies in the development of memory. In R. V. Kail, Jr. & J. W. Hagen (Eds.), *Perspectives on the development of memory and cognition.* Hillsdale, N.J.: Lawrence Erlbaum Associates, in press.

Kohlberg, L., Yaeger, J., & Hjertholm, E. Private speech: Four studies and a review of theories. *Child Development,* 1968, **39,** 691–736.

Kvale, S. Memory and dialectics: Some reflections on Ebbinghaus and Mao Tse-tung. *Human Development,* 1975, **18,** 205–222.

Leont'ev, A. N. *Problems of mental development.* Washington, D.C.: Joint Publications Research Service, 1964. (Originally published, 1959.)

Leont'ev, A. N. The problem of activity in Soviet psychology. *Soviet Psychology,* 1974, **13,** 4–33. (*Voprosy Filosofii,* 1972, **9,** 95–108.)

Lewis, C. N. Reminiscing and self-concept in old age. *Journal of Gerontology,* 1971, **26,** 240–243.

Lewis, C. N. The adaptive value of reminiscing in old age. *Journal of Geriatric Psychiatry,* 1973, **6,** 117–121.

Liben, L. S. Memory in the context of cognitive development: The Piagetian approach. In R. V. Kail, Jr. & J. W. Hagen (Eds.), *Perspectives on the development of memory and cognition.* Hillsdale, N.J.: Lawrence Erlbaum Associates, in press.

Lisina, M. I., & Neverovich, Y. Z. Development of movements and formation of motor habits. In A. V. Zaporozhets & D. B. Elkonin (Eds.), *The psychology of preschool children* (J. Shybut & S. Simon, trans.). Cambridge, Mass.: MIT Press, 1971. (Originally published, 1964).

Luria, A. R. *The mind of a mnemonist.* New York: Basic Books, 1968.

Luria, A. R. Speech development and the formation of mental processes. In M. Cole & I. Maltzman (Eds.), *A handbook of contemporary Soviet psychology.* New York: Basic Books, 1969. (Originally published, 1959.)

Luria, A. R., & Yudovich, F. I. *Speech and the development of mental processes in the child.* London: Staples Press, 1959. (Originally published, 1956.)

Marshall, V. S. *The life review as a social process.* Paper presented at the meeting of the Gerontological Society, Portland, October 1974.

McLaughlin, G. H. Psycho-logic: A possible alternative to Piaget's formulation. *British Journal of Educational Psychology,* 1963, **33,** 61–67.

McLeish, J. *Soviet psychology: History, theory, content.* London: Methuen, 1975.

McMahon, A. W., & Rhudick, P. J. Reminiscing in the aged: An adaptational response. In S. Levine & R. J. Kahana (Eds.), *Psychodynamic studies on aging: Creativity, reminiscing, and dying.* New York: International Universities Press, 1967.

Meacham, J. A. The development of memory abilities in the individual and society. *Human Development,* 1972, **15,** 205–228. (a)

Meacham, J. A. Verbal-motor interactions during sequences of motor activity (Doctoral dissertation, University of Michigan, 1972). *Dissertation Abstracts International,* 1973, **33**, 5545B. (University Microfilms No. 73-11, 205) (b)

Meacham, J. A. A dialectical approach to moral judgment and self-esteem. *Human Development,* 1975, **18**, 159–170. Also in K. F. Riegel (Ed.), *The development of dialectical operations.* Basel: Karger, 1975. (a)

Meacham, J. A. *Dialectics, cognitive development, and history.* Paper presented at an interdisciplinary conference on Dialectics: Paradigm for the Social Sciences, Toronto, August 1975; also presented at the meeting of the American Psychological Association, Chicago, September 1975. (b) [Also in A. E. Harris (Ed.), *Dialectics: A paradigm for the social sciences.* Book in preparation]

Meacham, J. A. Patterns of memory abilities in two cultures. *Developmental Psychology,* 1975, **11**, 50–53. (c)

Meacham, J. A. Continuing the dialogue: Dialectics and remembering. *Human Development,* 1976, **19**, 304–309.

Meacham, J. A. The role of verbal activity in remembering the goals of actions. In G. Zivin (Ed.), *Development of self-regulation through speech.* New York: Wiley, in press. (a)

Meacham, J. A. Soviet investigations of memory development. In R. V. Kail, Jr. & J. W. Hagen (Eds.), *Perspectives on the development of memory and cognition.* Hillsdale, N.J.: Lawrence Erlbaum Associates, in press. (b)

Meacham, J. A., & Riegel, K. F. Dialectical perspectives on Piaget's theory. In G. Steiner (Ed.), *Piaget's developmental and cognitive theory within an extended context* (Vol. 7), *The psychology of the 20th century.* Zurich: Kindler, in press.

Miller, G. A., Galanter, E., & Pribram, K. H. *Plans and the structure of behavior.* New York: Holt, 1960.

Miller, S. A., Shelton, J., & Flavell, J. H. A test of Luria's hypotheses concerning the development of verbal self-regulation. *Child Development,* 1970, **41**, 651–665.

Moely, B. E., Olson, F. A., Halwes, T. G., & Flavell, J. H. Production deficiency in young children's clustered recall. *Developmental Psychology,* 1969, **1**, 26–34.

Neimark, E., Slotnick, N. S., & Ulrich, T. Development of memorization strategies. *Developmental Psychology,* 1971, **5**, 427–432.

Ong, W. J. *Rhetoric, romance, and technology: Studies in the interaction of expression and culture.* Ithaca: Cornell University Press, 1971.

Overton, W. F. On the assumptive base of the nature–nurture controversy: Additive versus interactive conceptions. *Human Development,* 1973, **16**, 74–89.

Overton, W. F. General systems, structure, and development. In K. F. Riegel & G. C. Rosenwald (Eds.), *Structure and transformation: Developmental aspects.* New York: Wiley, 1975.

Overton, W. F., & Reese, H. W. Models of development: Methodological implications. In J. R. Nesselroade & H. W. Reese (Eds.), *Life-span developmental psychology: Methodological issues.* New York: Academic Press, 1973.

Paris, S. G., & Lindauer, B. K. Constructive aspects of children's comprehension and memory. In R. V. Kail, Jr. & J. W. Hagen (Eds.), *Perspectives on the development of memory and cognition.* Hillsdale, N.J.: Lawrence Erlbaum Associates, in press.

Payne, T. R. *S. L. Rubinstein and the philosophical foundations of Soviet psychology.* New York: Humanities Press, 1968.

Pearce, W. B., & Sharp, S. M. Self-disclosing communication. *Journal of Communication,* 1973, **23**, 409–425.

Pepper, S. C. *World hypotheses.* Berkeley: University of California Press, 1970. (Originally published, 1942.)

Piaget, J., & Inhelder, B. *Memory and intelligence* (A. J. Pomerans, trans.). New York: Basic Books, 1973.

Reese, H. W. Life-span models of memory. *Gerontologist,* 1973, **13**, 472–478. (a)

Reese, H. W. Models of memory and models of development. *Human Development,* 1973, **16**, 397–417. (b)

Reese, H. W. Cohort, age, and imagery in children's paired-associate learning. *Child Development,* 1975, 45, 1176–1180.

Reese, H. W. Models of memory development. *Human Development,* 1976, 19, 291–303.

Reese, H. W. Imagery and associative memory. In R. V. Kail, Jr. & J. W. Hagen (Eds.), *Perspectives on the development of memory and cognition.* Hillsdale, N.J.: Lawrence Erlbaum Associates, in press.

Reese, H. W., & Overton, W. F. Models of development and theories of development. In L. R. Goulet & P. B. Baltes (Eds.), *Life-span developmental psychology: Research and theory.* New York: Academic Press, 1970.

Riegel, K. F. Developmental psychology and society: Some historical and ethical considerations. In J. R. Nesselroade & H. W. Reese (Eds.), *Life-span developmental psychology: Methodological issues.* New York: Academic Press, 1973.

Riegel, K. F. Adult life crises: A dialectic interpretation of development. In N. Datan & L. H. Ginsberg (Eds.), *Life-span developmental psychology: Normative life crises.* New York: Academic Press, 1975. (a)

Riegel, K. F. From traits and equilibrium toward developmental dialectics. In W. J. Arnold & J. K. Cole (Eds.), *1974-75 Nebraska Symposium on Motivation.* Lincoln: University of Nebraska Press, 1975. (b)

Riegel, K. F. Semantic basis of language: Language as labor. In K. F. Riegel & G. C. Rosenwald (Eds.), *Structure and transformation: Developmental and historical aspects.* New York: Wiley, 1975. (c)

Riegel, K. F. Toward a dialectical theory of development. *Human Development,* 1975, 18, 50–64. (d)

Ritter, K., Kaprove, B. H., Fitch, J. P., & Flavell, J. H. The development of retrieval strategies in young children. *Cognitive Psychology,* 1973, 5, 310–321.

Rohwer, W. D., Jr. Elaboration and learning in childhood and adolescence. In H. W. Reese (Ed.), *Advances in child development and behavior* (Vol. 8). New York: Academic Press, 1973.

Rychlak, J. F. *A philosophy of science for personality theory.* Boston: Houghton, 1968.

Sameroff, A. Transactional models in early social relations. *Human Development,* 1975, 18, 65–79. Also in K. F. Riegel (Ed.), *The development of dialectical operations.* Basel: Karger, 1975.

Sameroff, A. J., & Chandler, M. J. Reproductive risk and the continuum of caretaking casualty. In F. D. Horowitz (Ed.), *Review of child development research* (Vol. 4). Chicago: University of Chicago Press, 1975.

Scribner, S. Developmental aspects of categorized recall in a West African society. *Cognitive Psychology,* 1974, 6, 475–494.

Strommen, E. A. Verbal self-regulation in a children's game: Impulsive errors on "Simon Says." *Child Development,* 1973, 44, 849–853.

Toch, H., & MacLean, M. S., Jr. Perception and communication: A transactional view. *Audio Visual Communication Review,* 1967, 10, 55–77. Also in K. K. Sereno & C. D. Mortenson (Eds.), *Foundations of communication theory.* New York: Harper, 1970.

Wagner, D. A. The development of short-term and incidental memory: A cross-cultural study. *Child Development,* 1974, 45, 389–396.

Wellman, H. M., Ritter, K., & Flavell, J. H. Deliberate memory behavior in the delayed reactions of very young children. *Developmental Psychology,* 1975, 780–787.

Wilder, L. Recent developments in Soviet research on the verbal control of voluntary motor behavior. In K. F. Riegel & J. A. Meacham (Eds.), *The developing individual in a changing world* (Vol. 1), *Historical and cultural issues.* The Hague: Mouton, 1976.

Woodruff, D. S. & Birren, J. E. Age changes and cohort differences in personality. *Developmental Psychology,* 1972, 6, 252–259.

Wozniak, B. H. Verbal regulation of motor behavior—Soviet research and non-Soviet replications. *Human Development,* 1972, 15, 13–47.

Yates, F. A. *The art of memory.* Chicago: University of Chicago Press, 1966.

Zaporozhets, A. V., Zinchenko, V. P., & Elkonin, D. B. Development of thinking, in A. V. Zaporozhets & D. B. Elkonin (Eds.), *The psychology of preschool children* (J. Shybut & S. Simon, trans.). Cambridge, Mass.: MIT Press, 1971. (Originally published, 1964).

CHAPTER 14

Some Thoughts on Memory
or Some Revised Memories of Some Old Thoughts[1]

JOHN W. HAGEN

UNIVERSITY OF MICHIGAN
ANN ARBOR, MICHIGAN

For some time now I have thought of myself as a part of a new wave—developmental cognitive psychology. Numerous paper sessions, symposia, and collaborative articles with which I have been involved have been devoted to spreading the new word and criticizing the old. The constructs of stimulus–response chains, mediating links, and secondary reinforcers have given way to encoding, short-term stores, and feedback loops. The old notions of memory as espoused by the developmental as well as the differential psychologists—the "memory span" or "memory ability"— have been replaced by "strategies for remembering" and "mnemonic devices." Today, however, I suddenly find myself somewhat on the defensive. Dialectical perspectives seem to be everywhere and applicable to just about everything. The merging of developmental and cognitive theory may not be what it is purported to be. A challenge to one's position often provides the best reason for critical examination, articulate counterarguments, and, perhaps most important, reconsideration of the position. Let's see if I am able to meet the challenge.

Jack Meacham (Chapter 13, this volume) has made a good case for the applicability of the dialectical approach to experimental work on the development of memories. Earlier, Hayne Reese (1973) presented a provocative argument for the necessary components that are to be included in an adequate model of memory development. Today I shall address myself to some of the issues raised. In the process, some empirical work with which the reader may already be familiar will be cited, and some very recent studies that have direct bearing on the arguments will be considered as well.

One of my first responses to Meacham's position, as presented here and elsewhere (Meacham, 1977), is, Yes, I agree! It is important to consider all aspects of development that may bear on the focus of one's research, whether it be learning, memory, or some other process. What one ought to do and what one is able to do are often not the same thing. Further, the dialectical position is not always specific in pointing to what are likely to be the most important "other" aspects to consider. For practical as well as theoretical reasons, there are limitations on the number of variables that can be studied and on the complexity of the design used. Moreover, much of our work proceeds through induction rather than deduction. We may be fairly certain what our next study should be, but the one after that is much less predictable. While the guidelines of a particular perspective may serve the investigator in his overall conceptualizing and in his generation of empirical studies, there is so much more that enters the picture before the particular project reaches fruition. Many of us deal with models rather than theories these days, and one is often as happy to see the model destroyed as to find evidence consistent with it.

Another point raised by Meacham, and stated in somewhat different form by Reese (1973) is that, "the development of memory abilities depends upon developments in various cognitive domains . . . . (Meacham, 1977)." It should be noted here that a recent chapter authored by myself, Robert Jongeward, and Robert Kail (Hagen, Jongeward, & Kail, 1975) is titled "Cognitive Perspectives on the Development of Memory." A volume edited by Robert Kail and me is being called *Perspectives on the Development of Memory and Cognition* (Kail & Hagen, 1977). While Meacham will argue that the important point from the dialectical perspective is that the relationship between the memory abilities and other aspects of cognitive functioning must be reciprocal, I shall reply for my coauthors as well as myself that we agree! To the extent that the research thus far does not reflect enough of this reciprocal relationship, it is more a problem of the infant state of the research rather than a bias against it. When we undertook our initial review of the literature, Jongeward, Kail, and I were impressed with the great breadth shown by the current research. Not only has the definition of memory been broadened and refined drastically in the past 10 to 15 years, but the role that memory is seen as playing in other psychological processes is so pervasive that it is difficult to organize the literature in any straightforward way.

When we realized how superficial a one-chapter review would be, we decided to undertake organizing a volume on the development of memory abilities. A look at its table of contents illustrates my point. There are two sections. The first deals with basic memory processes from a cognitive perspective. The chapters deal with the following: encoding, constructive processes, acquisition strategies, organizational and retrieval factors, metamemorial processes, the role of imagery, and Soviet research on memory development. The second section is concerned with the role of memory in other aspects of cognitive development. The chapters cover: cross-cultural studies of thought, the development of logical thought, memory abilities of the mentally retarded, the role of memory in Piagetian research, and memory as related to the educational process. These 14 chapters do, indeed, cover a lot of territory. While one might be impressed with both the quality and breadth of research covered, one can of course be discouraged at the limitations. One could take any two of these chapters at random and try to integrate and synthesize the material and probably find the task difficult if not impossible. That there is no comprehensive theory of memory development is obvious. Being an optimist, this state of affairs emphasizes the challenge to me. If our knowledge is expanded as much in the next decade as it has been in the past one, we may be on the verge of a real theory in 1986.

Another limitation, of special relevance to many of the contributors to the present volume, is the limited developmental age range that is dealt with in our book. However, again the optimist can point out that it is considerably more comprehensive than dealing only with such subjects as rodents or college sophomores. I should make my point again here concerning the inductiveness of much of the research in this area. Neither I nor others interested in the acquisition of strategies in memory had a particular interest in studying children from 5 through 12 years of age. Our work pointed to fascinating and demonstrable changes occurring in this age period; hence, we have become "expert" in getting children of this age range to reveal to us their ways of solving various memory problems. As we proceed and the sophistication of our approach improves, the complexity and "ecological validity" of the tasks increase.

In order to make concrete just how some of this progress (as I see it) comes about, I shall refer to some recent research by my students and myself at the University of Michigan. A series of cross-cultural studies by Daniel Wagner has proved to be invaluable in helping us understand some of the contributions of setting, that is, location and certain environmental factors. However, the basic memory task we have used will be reviewed briefly for those not familiar with it.

The serial recall task was first used with children by Atkinson, Hansen, and Bernbach (1964). Picture cards in a horizontal display are shown one at a time to the individual. The first card is shown briefly, then placed facedown and the second card is shown next and then placed facedown beside the first. The procedure continues until all cards are lying facedown in a row. A series may include from four to eight cards for a given trial. The order of the cards is varied on subsequent trials; thus, locations for particular pictures cannot be learned. A cue card, a replica of one of the cards in the series, is shown after the last (or recency) card is seen, and the individual's task is to point to the card lying facedown in the row that matches this cue card. Tests are made at all positions over trials. The performance is measured in two ways. First, total number of pictures recalled correctly over trials is recorded. Second, the correct responses are recorded by serial location or position. The initial positions in the series occupy the primacy positions, and the most recently seen pictures occupy the recency positions. The remaining positions may be termed intermediate positions.

In our initial study (Hagen & Kingsley, 1968), children from 4 through 10 years of age were included. Simple naming or labeling of the pictures to be remembered was required of half the children at each age level. An overall increase in total recall with increasing age level was found, regardless of the labeling condition, as expected. Labeling affected recall, but only at certain ages. Facilitation was found due to naming at the intermediate age levels but not at the youngest or oldest age levels. The data were then examined for serial position effects. At the left-hand, or primacy portions, of the serial position recall curves, labeling did not facilitate performance and in fact resulted in a decrement in recall at the oldest age level. In the no-label condition, recall increased at the primacy positions. For the recency positions, performance was high at all ages and did not show developmental trends. Furthermore, labeling facilitated recall at the recency positions for all ages studied.

The effects on recall of this simple manipulation were found to be complex and dependent on the developmental level of the individuals involved. Rehearsal of the to-be-remembered items, of the sort described by Flavell and his colleagues (Flavell, Beach, & Chinsky, 1966), appeared to be a possible explanation for the "strategy" being used by older children in the serial recall task. This rehearsal apparently facilitates recall at the primacy positions. Numerous other studies have been published that lend support to our argument for the development of "rehearsal strategies," and will not be summarized here (see Hagen, 1971, for a review of these studies).

An interesting study, however, is that of Dan Wagner, who has done cross-cultural work. Wagner had been a volunteer with the Peace Corps before coming to graduate school at the University of Michigan. He was very eager to combine his interest in cognitive development with his newly acquired skills in surviving in relatively undeveloped foreign countries. Thus, we arranged for him to travel to the Yucatán Peninsula, Mexico, to pursue research on memory (Wagner, 1974). We were interested in learning whether the development of memory abilities in other cultures showed characteristics similar to the ones found in ours. The serial-position recall task was adapted for use in Yucatán. Many adaptations, of course, are needed when a paradigm is transported to a culture such as this one. New pictures were needed. The game of "Lotto" was known and played almost universally in Yucatán, among literates and illiterates alike. Hence, the pictures from this game were substituted for ours. Even though Dan spoke Spanish fluently, he did not speak Mayan, the first language of many of these people. A shoemaker was hired as the experimenter; he was fluent in both languages and displayed excellent testing skills. It was decided to increase the age span upward, so that the oldest group of individuals tested was 27 years of age. Considering that the mean life span is about 40 in this culture, we might argue that this was a life-span study.

Individuals from both urban and rural environments were tested. Those in the urban environment at older age levels also had more years of formal education than those in the rural environment. A modified version of the task was used so that a measure of incidental recall was available on each individual as well as total and serial recall (for a description of this task and relevant research, see Hagen & Hale, 1973). The results obtained in this task for the urban population were remarkably similar to those found in the studies with Americans, except that the performance was delayed among Yucantanese by 2 to 3 years. Total memory increased across the age span tested, while incidental memory decreased after 16 years of age. The findings for the rural population were very different, however, and provided some challenges to our thinking. Recall on the total (or central) task was low and relatively invariant across the 20-year age range. Incidental recall showed some increase up to about 21 years of age, and then declined. It seemed to Wagner that these individuals were not intellectually inferior but that they did not approach the tasks in the same way as the urban dwellers. He speculated that formal education might be a crucial difference in their settings.

In a second study, Wagner (1975) used the verbal labeling condition described earlier with the urban Yucantanese subjects. The results were remarkably similar to those found by Hagen and Kingsley (1968), both for total recall and for serial-position recall. It appears that rehearsal strategies were being invoked by these individuals in order to maintain performance on the task at hand.

In Wagner's dissertation (1976) he reports on massive amounts of data gathered over a 2-year period in Morocco. I shall just mention a small portion of his data, that which is most comparable to the data of Yucatán.

Once again the stimuli were modified to meet the needs of the new culture. Pictures of animals and simple objects easily recognized by Moroccans of many backgrounds and ages were used. Native testers were employed. The major advantage of this study over the previous one is that amount of schooling and urban versus rural environment were not confounded. Thus, four major groups of individuals were included: schooled and nonschooled, urban and rural. In all other ways, the research was identical to the research in Yucatán. Since Wagner had spent his Peace Corps days in Morocco, he had many advantages in pursuing this work.

Across the age range of 7 through 20 years, total recall improved for all groups except for the rural, nonschooled group. The group with the greatest increase with age and reaching the highest level was, not surprisingly, the urban, schooled group. The two other groups fell between these. It is apparent that chronological age does not account for the developmental trends found so frequently in short-term memory. From these findings, it appears that both schooling and an urban environment contribute to higher performance in these recall tasks. At the younger ages, there were no differences in recall due to schooling within an urban setting, and the schooled children in the rural setting also performed at a comparable level. At the older ages, however, the importance of schooling became more apparent. The age-related increase in total memory was sharpest for schooled individuals.

The recall for various portions of the serial-position curves proved interesting. Recency recall was least affected by these variables. In all cases, recency was quite high, supporting the notion that recency recall is present regardless of age or environmental considerations. Recall at middle positions was qualitatively similar for all groups of subjects, although each main effect was significant. For the primacy recall, the interactions that were found for total recall again appeared. There were increases in primacy recall with age among schooled individuals only, and this increase was enhanced by the urban setting. Our theory, that verbal rehearsal becomes, with development, a dominant cognitive strategy in performing tasks such as this one, is strengthened. We would like to check into just what factors might be important in the school and urban environments that foster the development of such strategies.

Cross-cultural research is difficult to do in many respects and, of course, there are limitations in the findings just discussed. However, we have gained from this work a new confidence in the replicability and generalizability of our earlier findings. Further, I believe we now have some better ideas concerning at least some global environmental and setting variables that relate to the development of certain aspects of the ability to remember.

One can well imagine that what is remembered, as well as how one goes about remembering, are changed as a people change from a rural to an urban setting and as the availability and usage of formal education increases. Meacham's argument concerning reciprocal causality within the dialectical model seems critically relevant here, and investigators ought to be able to draw on our current knowledge to come up with new ways to test empirically for bidirectional causality. Some factors to consider are obvious—changes in ability or willingness to follow directions or to comprehend instructions, and changes in the acquisition of ideas, concepts, motivations, and incentives, among others. Reflecting further on Meacham's comments, one can see that a host of less obvious factors should also be considered. Perhaps the games that children play are also modified by changes in the setting. New objects may become available to be used in play, and revised or new rules may be suggested either by these objects or by new persons who enter the environment for the first time. Social interactions among family members, among peers, and with new individuals in the society are almost certain to be modified. The demands on the child as he or she passes from one developmental phase to another no doubt are quite different when he or she must interact with many more adults as well as a wider range of peers. If more must be learned and remembered, new ways of going about these tasks are also needed. Strategies for performing that were seldom needed or even useless in the original environment may now be crucial for certain kinds of success. Those individuals who are adept at developing these skills are the ones who will emerge with the needed competencies in the new society.

I am not necessarily referring here to only those groups of people who undergo a sudden or radical change in their environment, although such changes occur. These comments are appropriate as well to those people who experience gradual changes over years or even generations. Of course, in these cases it will be much more difficult for the social scientist to uncover and study the particulars of the environment that might be leading to changes in cognitive growth and to look for reciprocal changes that might, in turn, be occurring in the environment.

What are some of the possible influences of formal education on memory abilities? Meacham has pointed to the active role of memories in constructing the remember as well as his or her remembering abilities (and vice-versa, which is the more popular position). Somewhere the child learns that it is neither possible nor desirable to try to acquire and retain all information available. This learning process no doubt emerges from basic, unlearned mechanisms that appear in infancy (Hagen, 1971). Throughout the toddler and preschool years, the child becomes able to select and control, to some extent at least, what it is he learns and retains from the multitude of settings he encounters in daily life. These selected memories in turn no doubt serve to influence the selection of new information.

When the child begins to spend significant portions of his life in formal school settings, he is faced daily with the requirements to learn and retain all kinds of things that are not intuitively or obviously important or interesting. Even though the motivation to do so may be extrinsic and negative sanctions may be as influential as rewards, most children still do make genuine attempts, throughout this long period of their lives in the role of student, to master as much of this "stuff" as possible. Here, our focus as investigators should be on the process, that is, the acquisition of remembering abilities, not on the content. However, features of the content may be needed to be incorporated into our research in order to get an accurate look at the processes, a point to be discussed later. One set of abilities that merits investigation concerns those activities we call studying. The importance of studying increases with grade level. An important goal of studying is to remember information at some future time. Plans, attention, verbalization, mnemonics, and metamemory are just some of the phenomena that no doubt come to play here.

Two recent graduates of our doctoral program have pursued some interesting work on memory in classroom settings, using material chosen for its school-like qualities, yet having some interest to the children. However, before this work is described, two findings on memory will be discussed. It has been well documented in studies of adults' memory ability that when a stimulus is repeated in a list presented for free recall, as the spacing between the initial presentation and the repetition is increased, the probability of recall also increases. In paired-associate paradigms, the optimal spacing has been found to be eight intervening pairs. The other finding concerns the effects of immediate testing on later recall for serial-ordered items. Immediate recall, of course, yields serial-position curves as described earlier. For individuals who have both an immediate test and a later test, recall is higher at all positions except recency, as compared to individuals who receive the later test only (Craik, Gardiner, & Watkins, 1970)

Robert Jongeward and Barbara Hayes-Roth constructed stories, composed of 10 sentences each from information obtained in a children's encyclopedia. There were two major experimental conditions. The first concerned whether the children were tested for recall immediately following a presentation of information via the sentences. Here one-half of the children, all sixth-graders, were tested for recall at the time of initial testing, while the remaining children instead had a *repetition* of the sentences but were not required to make a response. Two weeks later children in both groups were administered the set of questions on each story they had heard. There was an additional condition, however, to look at the effects of intervening sentences on final recall. Within each group of subjects, there were three levels of intervening sentences, an immediate, a massed, and a spaced condition. In the immediate condition, as soon as a sentence was given, the child was either asked to repeat it aloud or it was given to him again (depending on whether he was in the "question" or the "repetition" condition). In the massed condition, the entire 10 sentences for a given story were presented, followed by either the 10 questions or a repeating of the entire story. In the spaced condition, the 10 sentences were given, followed by 10 sentences from another story, and then either the appropriate 10 sentences or a repetition of the initial story was given. Twelve different stories were used and randomly assigned across conditions. Topics ranged from Carole King, American Car Races, and Indian Pipes, to Hairy Spiders and Woodpeckers. But each story was the same length and contained 10 grammatically comparable sentences.

The results were as follows. The group of children who answered questions during the initial testing did considerably better on the 2-week recall than did the children who heard repetitions of the stories, regardless of the number of intervening sentences. So, for sixth-grade children at least, the advantage of immediate recall for later recall was evident. The findings for the number of intervening sentences between presentation and immediate test for recall are more complex. First, the findings for those children tested on recall during initial presentation are considered. Their recall was best when immediate testing was given, as compared to massed or spaced testing for recall. However, after 2 weeks, the recall data were just reversed. The condition that was tested immediately after a sentence was read resulted in poorest recall, while for both massed and spaced initial testing, recall was definitely better 2 weeks later. The results were similar but less pronounced for those children who heard repetitions only during the initial presentation of the stories. In a second study, the design of the first was replicated, except that several degrees of spacing were employed. The results of the first were essentially replicated, and the evidence is now even clearer that 2-week recall is facilitated by increasing the number of intervening stories (or sentences) up to three stories (or 19 sentences).

These studies are valuable in that they indicate ways in which laboratory studies can be extended to provide information concerning memory in real-life settings. Recall of material that is both meaningful and similar to that which is learned in school has been shown to be dependent both on the opportunity to engage actively in the learning process at the time of presentation (via answering questions during presentations) and on the duration of time between presentation and subsequent recall. The findings call into question some of the conclusions advocated by those who employ behavior modification and programmed learning in the classroom. One would urge that long-term as well as short-term retention be considered whenever the effects of variables such as practice and testing are under study. In addition, the type of research just discussed could be extended to examine how information acquired and retained via the story format influences acquisition and retention of information in future situations, a paradigm that would be of relevance to Meacham's major argument.

In conclusion, I want to stress how valuable it has been for me to be able to study and respond to Jack Meacham's contribution here. I realize that the empirical studies cited do not meet many of the objections posed by the dialectical viewpoint concerning developmental research on memory and cognition. However, I do not believe it possible at this point in time to meet all the possible objections. We must still wait for the adequate theory. One limitation of the dialectical perspective is that it does not give specific enough guidelines for the form new research should take. Thus, many of us will continue to pursue our interests in ways not unlike the ways we have used in the past. No doubt, though, familiarity with the views expressed in this volume will help us in seeing directions we should take and in avoiding pitfalls that are not now obvious.

REFERENCES

Atkinson, R. C., Hansen, D. N., & Bernbach, H. A. Short-term memory with young children. *Psychonomic Science*, 1964, **1**, 255–256.

Craik, F. I. M., Gardiner, J. M., & Watkins, M. J. Further evidence for a negative recency effect on free recall. *Journal of Verbal Learning and Verbal Behavior*, 1970, **9**, 554–560.

Flavell, J. H., Beach, D. R., & Chinsky, J. M. Spontaneous verbal rehearsal in a memory task as a function of age. *Child Development*, 1966, **37**, 283–299.

Hagen, J. W. Some thoughts on how children learn to remember. *Human Development*, 1971, **14**, 262–271.

Hagen, J. W., & Hale, G. A. The development of attention in children. In A. Pick (Ed.), *Minnesota Symposia on Child Psychology* (Vol. 7). Minneapolis: University of Minnesota Press, 1973.

Hagen, J. W., Jongeward, R. H., Jr., & Kail, R. V., Jr. Cognitive perspectives on the development of memory. In H. W. Reese (Ed.), *Advances in child development and behavior* (Vol. 10). New York: Academic Press, 1975.

Hagen, J. W., & Kingsley, P. R. Labeling effects in short-term memory. *Child Development*, 1968, **39**, 113–121.

Jongeward, R. H., Jr., & Hayes-Roth, B. Unpublished research, Human Performance Center, University of Michigan, 1975.

Kail, R. V., Jr., & Hagen, J. W. (Eds.). *Perspectives on the development of memory and cognition.* Hillsdale, N.J.: Lawrence Erlbaum Associates, 1977.

Meacham, J. A. Soviet investigations of memory development. In R. V. Kail, Jr. & J. W. Hagen (Eds.), *Perspectives on the development of memory and cognition.* Hillsdale, N.J.: Lawrence Erlbaum Associates, 1977.

Reese, H. W. Models of memory and models of development. *Human Development*, 1973, **16**, 397–417.

Wagner, D. A. The development of short-term and incidental memory: A cross-cultural study. *Child Development*, 1974, **45**, 389–396.

Wagner, D. A. The effects of verbal labeling on short-term and incidental memory: A cross-cultural and developmental study. *Memory and Cognition*, 1975, **3**, 595–598.

Wagner, D. A. *Memories of Morocco: A cross-cultural study of the influence of age, schooling and environment on memory.* Unpublished doctoral dissertation, University of Michigan, 1976.

CHAPTER 15

Dialectics and Operant Conditioning

JON E. KRAPFL

WEST VIRGINIA UNIVERSITY
MORGANTOWN, WEST VIRGINIA

I. Introduction

What follows is my view of operant conditioning and a dialectical perspective on it. Before presenting that view, I feel that it is important for me to identify environmental events that have come to control my behavior, as evidenced in this chapter. We are disposed to see an individual as speaking or writing as he does because of a particular philosophical perspective. To say that I am dialectical or operant is, perhaps, to assume too much about what accounts for my behavior. It would be better to say that my behavior has been affected in certain ways by the literature of operant conditioning and dialectical psychology. The environmental events that compose the former have been frequent, of long standing, often complex, and pervasive, whereas the contingencies reflected in the latter are more recent in my history and not so prevalent. My dialectical views have therefore been markedly affected by an environmental history that has been predominantly operant. However, I have recently come to see certain common features of the dialectical and operant perspectives and that both stand in contrast to what I consider to be a suffocating perspective dominating contemporary psychology, namely, methodological behaviorism, with its associated roots in positivism and operationism. Dialectical and operant perspectives are alike in their rejection of this methodological behavioral position as too narrow and restrictive.

In this chapter, therefore, I shall explore some of the similarities of dialectical and operant perspectives, and describe several major operant activities within a dialectical framework. The objective in doing so is not to convert either dialectician or behavior analyst, but to describe commonalities in the two positions and to identify differences more sharply.

II. Methodological and Radical Behaviorism

The use of the term *dialectical* should be herein specified. Even a limited view of the literature reveals differences, perhaps controversy, over the definition of the term. It shall be used here to imply the study of movement and interaction as opposed to the study of objects in a static state and in isolation from other objects. Contradiction, too, fits within my use of the term, even radical self-contradiction, though I must admit to being confused by this concept.

When I read Lawler's (1975) discussion of the concept, I found myself nodding in agreement when he states that cause and connections between species no longer need be supplied from outside nature and that connection between organisms and their environment, involving a dialectical unity of opposites, provides the basis of understanding biological nature from its own inner laws.

However, when concepts of interaction and contradiction are discussed as outgrowths of empirical knowledge that, at a certain point in their development, require the understanding of things within their own "inner connection," I wonder whether our empirical knowledge has reached that point of development or whether we have here another instance of empty abstraction which the dialecticians presumably wish to abolish.

Insofar as we can agree that utility in practice is the key to knowing or understanding our subject matter, I believe I have no disagreement with the dialectical perspective.

Similarities in the Skinnerian behavioral and dialectical perspectives have been addressed by others, most notably James Holland (Chapter 16). For my part, I intend to restrict my analysis to the practices of the operant conditioner–scientist, principally in the laboratory.

Let us now discuss the term *operant conditioning.* Operant conditioning is the process of altering the probability (frequency) of behavior as a function of manipulation in the environment. While technically that is all I will be discussing, I prefer a broader definition, first because operant conditioning has come to be identified with methodological behaviorism, and second because the term *behavior analysis* generally describes a much broader range of intellectual activity than is usually conveyed by operant conditioning.

It is important to distinguish between the various behavioral positions currently espoused. The failure of the contemporary academic community in psychology to draw any distinction between the extreme behavioral position as represented by Hull (1952) or Spence (1944), for example, and the radical behavioral position as developed by Skinner (1953b, 1957) has been a source of exasperation and amazement to behavior analysts.

It would appear to be the case that whatever it is that controls the intellectual behavior of academic psychologists, it is something other than primary sources. Secondary sources (e.g., the critique by Chomsky, 1959) in psychology have been largely misinterpretations of Skinner's work. One must go outside psychology to find serious criticism (e.g., Wheeler, 1972). Furthermore, after Skinner developed a paradigmatic orientation, as he did in *Behavior of Organisms* (1938), research was implemented throughout the world, but the continued major developments, such as *Science and Human Behavior* (Skinner, 1953b) or *Verbal Behavior* (Skinner, 1957), were so different they were ignored within the field.

The problem is that the scientific community has, by and large, ignored these developments that Skinner would undoubtedly regard as among his highest achievements.

In his more popular works, such as *Beyond Freedom and Dignity* (Skinner, 1971), Skinner continues his sustained lifelong attack on mentalism. This attack is often taken as prime facie evidence of Skinner's position as a methodological behaviorist, when, in fact, the inherent mentalism of the methodological behaviorists is seen by Skinner as extremely unfortunate because of its subtlety, its vociferous antimentalistic claim to the contrary notwithstanding.

Basically, Skinner's analysis of behavior is an attempt to control behavior (the dependent variable) by identifying and manipulating the environmental events (independent variables) of which behavior is a function. Specifying the relations between behavior and environment is an activity identified as the functional analysis of behavior. Skinner insists that the independent and dependent variables be described in physical terms and claims that it is unnecessary to refer to inner states or outer forces if we deal with directly observable data (Skinner, 1953b, p. 36). There are a number of features of the Skinnerian or radical behaviorial position that distinguish it from the methodological behavioral system. Among the more important are an insistence that behavioral analyses need not and usually should not be reductionistic, a reliance on response probability (usually frequency) as the basic datum, a reliance on direct observation of contingencies in action as a major tool of the scientist, a thorough and detailed analysis of individual organisms over time rather than an interpretation of averaged performances of many organisms, and finally a reliance on the development of effective techniques for controlling the actions of others and for controlling ourselves.

Each of these features of the analysis of behavior can be accounted for through a behavioral analysis of the variables that control the behavior of the behavior analyst. A detailed explanation will not be offered here, but one can be found in texts such as Sidman's *Tactics of Scientific Research* (1960).

Of course, many of the characteristics of the analysis of behavior have been adopted by the methodological behaviorists, but in doing so, they were unimpressed with the fact that these procedures had evolved from the laboratories of Skinnerians and not from their own, thus suggesting different contingency arrangements affecting the experimenter. One area in which clear distinctions in position can be seen is in the radical and methodological positions on private events.

The traditional behaviorist's position has actually taken one of two forms. One position, and an early one in behaviorism, was that, ultimately, there are only public events. There are no events which, by their nature, must remain private. Events that currently remain inaccessible will ultimately become public with the development of technologies. An alternate approach in behaviorism has been to admit to the existence of private events but to rule them out as a legitimate subject matter of scientific inquiry. The former has been described as *metaphysical behaviorism,* in which mental events are metaphysically denied, and the latter as *methodological behaviorism,* in which mental events are admitted but discarded as a concern of scientists. Contemporary behaviorists of a nonradical sort generally subscribe to one of these two positions.

The radical behavioral position on the issue is somewhat different. Skinner subscribes to the utility of private event analyses, but claims that private events are not the same thing as mental events because private events have physical status. In an early paper, Skinner (1959; originally written in 1945) points up four difficulties raised by the public–private distinction. A quick review of two of them may make the methodological and radical positions more discriminable.

Skinner (1959) says:

> The public–private distinction emphasizes the arid philosophy of truth by agreement. The public, in fact, turn out to be simply that which can be agreed upon because it is common to two or more agreers. . . . the solitary inhabitant of a desert isle could arrive at operational definitions. . . . The ultimate criteria for the goodness of a concept is not whether two people are brought into agreement, but whether the scientist who uses the concept can operate successfully upon his material. . . . What matters to Robinson Crusoe is not whether he is agreeing with himself, but whether he is getting anywhere with his control over nature [pp. 284–285].

Thus, it is clear that Skinner has no objection to private events and does consider them legitimate subject matter for scientific inquiry. Skinner claims that workability is the key to agreement, and not, as others claim that agreement is the key to workability; that is, if we examine and describe events that are successful in controlling nature, we will, at least eventually, come to agree on them. We need not agree on them in advance and only then assess their workability.

Skinner (1959) goes on to describe further problems in the public and private distinction:

> The distinction between public and private is, by no means, the same as that between physical and mental. That is why methodological behaviorism (which adopts the first) is very different from radical behaviorism (which lops off the latter term in the second). The result is that while the radical behaviorist may, in some cases, consider private events (inferentially, perhaps, but nonetheless meaningfully), the methodological operationist has manuevered himself into a position where he cannot. "Science does not consider private data" says Boring. . . . But I contend that my toothache is just as physical as my typewriter, though not public, and I see no reason why an objective and operational science cannot consider the process through which a vocabulary descriptive of a tooth-

ache is acquired and maintained. The irony of it is that while Boring must confine himself to an account of my external behavior, I am still interested in what might be called Boring-from-within [p. 285].

Skinner's continuing objections, then, are to mentalisms, but not to private events. Failure to discriminate between the two had led to serious misinterpretations of his work and to a general failure (in the psychological community) to discriminate between radical and methodological behaviorism. Distinctions between mentalism and private events are subtle if you lack the appropriate repertoire. I would refer the listener to basic sources, such as the chapter on private events in *Science and Human Behavior* (Skinner, 1953b).

It is hoped that this short explanation of the distinction between methodological behaviorism and the analysis of behavior will suffice.

III. Experimental, Applied, and Conceptual Analysis of Behavior

We return now to an examination of three major areas of investigation in the analysis of behavior, each of which, together with behavior analysis as a general approach to the study of behavior, can be cast within a dialectical framework. Each of these three areas of behavior analysis has its own journal, and each engages in activities that, while lacking topographical similarity to the others, shares a common conceptual base. The first area is that known as the experimental analysis; its journal is the *Journal of the Experimental Analysis of Behavior*. The second area is that portion of behavior modification known as applied behavior analysis. Its journal is the *Journal of Applied Behavior Analysis*. The third area is that of the conceptual analysis, with its journal *Behaviorism*.

Many activities characteristic of the first area, the experimental analysis, have been adopted by nonbehavior analysts. Yet, there are a number of activities and their consequences that, in concert, uniquely characterize this area of behavior-analytic study.

The experimental analysis of behavior is that branch of biology concerned with the relationship between an organism and its lifetime environment. Lifetime environment is used here in contrast to the evolutionary environment of the species, which is the focal concern of ethology (Schnaitter, in press). The basic datum for the experimental analysis of behavior is probability of response, measured as rate or frequency (Skinner, 1966). Such measures are typically taken under controlled laboratory conditions, where stimuli are presented and behavior is recorded with electromechanical or other automated equipment. Typically many responses are recorded over a protracted period of time, and from only a few subjects. This stands in contrast to common experimental procedures requiring a relatively small amount of behavior from a large number of subjects, relatively little time, and a small behavior sample of each subject. A major feature of the experimental analysis is the fact that the data are not summarized or averaged. A cumulative recorder keeps a record of each behavior when it occurs, the consequence of the occurrence, and the environmental conditions under which the occurrence was observed.

The independent variables consist of all features of the environment that come to affect the probability of response. These stimuli are described by their physical properties or in terms of manipulations carried out by the experimenter (Skinner, 1966). Data are analyzed and discussed in terms of a three-term contingency consisting of the observed behavior and its associated reinforcing and discriminative stimuli. The procedures to be employed in the experimental analysis of behavior are very flexible. There are very few rules about the conduct of this kind of research since the evaluation of the practices of an experimental analyst are seen as empirically based rather than philosophically or rule-based (Sidman, 1960). Where there are rules or maxims, they generally relate to ways of regulating the environmental influences on the experimenter. But this brings us to a major dialectical feature of the experimental analysis of behavior, to be discussed shortly.

The experimental analysis is an analysis of behavior–environment relations in microcosm. Its products are statements about predictable relations between behavior and environment. Occasionally these predictions are of sufficient importance and predictability that they are said to acquire the status of laws or principles, though both concepts are, to some extent, misleading from a radical behavioral perspective.

When these principles or laws are used to deal with problems of social concern such as mental health, education, rehabilitation, or developmental disabilities, we call it applied behavior analysis, or behavior modification, the second area of behavior analysis. Experimental and applied analysts of behavior share an interest in the lifetime environment of the organism and in the control involved in behavior–environment interactions. For applied behavior analysts, response frequency is typically the basic datum, and many responses of individual subjects for protracted periods are, again, the data of interest. Independent variables are sought in the environment, and explanations generally take the form of the three-term contingency.

There are some characteristics of the applied analysis of behavior that are unlike the experimental analysis. The contingencies that control the experimenter's selection of responses in experimental analysis can be summarized as contingencies of convenience. The bar press or key peck is a response of potentially high frequency and short duration, easily adapted to mechanical manipulation and data recording. There are no other unique features of these responses that recommend them for analysis. In the applied analysis, however, there is considerable response variation. Some responses are of long duration and occur only infrequently. The contingencies that govern response selection are social and generally relate to client, third-party, or cultural dissatisfaction, or to demand for improvement.

In applied behavior analysis environmental arrangements are usually not nearly as tightly controlled as in experimental analysis in that controlling stimuli in social situations are typically multiple, complex, and only partially subject to experimenter management. Since social contingencies and not convenience control response selection, many behaviors investigated in the applied analysis of behavior cannot be subjected to the momentary rate analysis possible with the cumulative recorder. Consequently, the intricate analyses found in experimental studies are often not possible in the applied analysis of behavior. It is unlikely, therefore, that very much in the way of laws or principles will emerge from applied behavior analysis.

An additional set of contingencies control the behavior of applied behavior analysts. Both experimental and applied analysts are influenced by the pressure of scientific peers to provide a convincing demonstration of their claims that certain events control the occurrence of behavior (Baer, Wolf, & Risley, 1968). But, in addition, applied behavior analysts must demonstrate the utility of their manipulation. In other words, it must be demonstrated that whatever costs (such as risk or dollar expenditures) are required to carry out their manipulations, there is, in the long run, a potential for sufficient societal or individual gain to justify the taking of the risk. From society's perspective the costs and risks must not outweigh the benefit. Applied behavior analysts, then, must show not only that they have isolated independent-variable effects, but also that dependent-variable changes are socially significant and worthwhile.

The third major component of behavior analysis is the conceptual analysis. This entire area finds no support from methodological behaviorists. The major activity of the conceptual analyst of behavior might be termed *behavioral extension.*

Behavioral extension consists of the use of "principles" demonstrated to hold in the laboratory to account for events not (yet) investigated under laboratory conditions. The best example of behavioral extension is probably Skinner's *Verbal Behavior* (1957). In this book, which almost no psychologists have read, but strangely, few psychologists approve, Skinner uses laboratory-derived principles to account for verbal behavior, an area of behavioral investigation not yet subjected to an experimental analysis.

These exercises in interpretation that we call behavioral extension are not designed to meet the typical criteria used to judge theories, nor are they designed to fit the requirements of the traditional constraints of psychological science. The value of such extensions, as of all radical behavioral work, is ultimately to be determined by the adequacy and the utility of the accounts provided. The assumption here is that if you are correct (also read *useful*), your scientific statements or activities will ultimately be reinforced by the scientific community and/or by the community at large. A further point here is that these behavioral extensions are, by no means, end products of our science. They will never result in the rejection of empirical or experimental data.

In addition to *Verbal Behavior,* a second major focus for the conceptual analysis of behavior has been that of the philosophy of the science of human behavior. Radical behavioral philosophy of science is a result of behavioral extension. Principles derived from the experimental analysis of behavior are used to account for the behavior of the scientist himself (Skinner, 1956; Wood, 1973).

IV. Dialectical Characteristics of Behavioral Analysis

Having now proceeded through a cursory review of the major features of behavior analysis and having distinguished between behavior analysis and methodological behaviorism, we can now identify the principal dialectical features of the former. The distinction between radical and methodological behaviorism is important for a dialectical analysis, since, although both can be cast in a dialectical framework, radical behavioral analysis is far more compatible with the dialectical position because of its emphasis on reciprocal controller–controllee or controllee–environment relations, whereas methodological behaviorism retains its emphasis on the scientist as objective observer watching a world that obeys natural laws, from which the observer, in his observations, is presumably exempt.

In radical behaviorism, of course, there are only two events—behavior and environment. Behavior is controlled by environment and controls the environment. Stimuli occurring prior to behavior occasion or heighten the probability of its occurrence, and stimuli following behavior affect the future probability of its occurrence. The only additional requirement is that we take into account the organism's history of interaction with the environment, which has also altered the probability of behaving in certain ways. We can thus say that the environment controls behavior, and we have a rather simple dialectical model in which organism and environment produce behavior through interaction.

But there is considerably more to the analysis. Skinner (1938) has labeled behavior that produces reinforcement as operant behavior. The word *operant* was selected because Skinner wished to emphasize that behavior of this sort operates on the environment to produce some effect. When behavior operates on the environment, it alters that environment in some way. It is critical to note that the reinforcer is an altered environment. It is not something such as food, a smile, or water. It is the presentation of the event after its absence, or the removal of the event after its presence. Grain does not reinforce a pigeon's peck; it is the presentation of grain when it has been absent that functions as a reinforcer. Furthermore, the degree of environmental change produced by the operant behavior has a great deal to do with the strength or future probability of occurrence of that behavior. This notion of reinforcement as a relation between behavioral and environmental events is described in detail by Premack (1965).

In this context, then, we see strong evidence of both interaction and contradiction. The environment controls behavior and alters its future probability of occurrence. Behavior operates on the environment and changes it in some very fundamental way. We have, then, a fundamental dialectical relation between behavior and environment. Each controls and is controlled by the other. Each is fundamentally changed by the other as a function of their interaction, and each stands in contradiction to the other as it both controls and is controlled by the same event. Questions of the organism as active or reactive therefore become difficult. In the Skinnerian analysis, both or either are true.

But the dialectical arrangement is even more complicated. Behavior and environment cannot be assumed to be dichotomous classes of events, separate structural entities that exist independent of each other. The analysis of behavior is a functional and not a structural analysis. There is no objection to structuralism, but the emphasis is on functional relations. Behaviors are looked at in terms of the consequences they produce, and the environment is looked at in terms of the behavior it generates. The topographical features of a child crying or a pigeon pecking a key are not nearly so interesting as the fact that the former is found to be attention-producing behavior and the latter grain-producing behavior. This distinction is important because it is possible for the same event to function as both behavior and environment. There is clear empirical evidence for this apparent contradiction (Premack, 1965). Obviously, in everyday life we can see clear instances of this in social interactions in which the behavior of A serves as a controlling stimulus for the behavior of B, but these are common and uninteresting cases. The more interesting case is that demonstrated by Premack (1965) in which the relation between a particular behavior under the control of a particular environmental consequence can be shown, under altered conditions, to function as an effective consequence for the behavior referred to as the effective consequence in the first instance. An example is required: An experimenter can place a rat in a chamber and establish a certain probability for the rat running in a wheel and for the rat eating grain. When placed in a contingency arrangement such that the occurrence of one (let us say eating) is contingent upon the occurrence of the other (the running), one can increase the probability of the running responses. Thus, we have two behaviors emitted by the same organism, one serving as a controlling environment for the other. By changing the deprivation condition, one can show the reversibility of the reinforcement relation such that the rat that previously ran in order to eat will now eat in order to run. Precisely the same events, then, can be shown to control the occurrence of each other, with the controlling relation working in opposite directions.

The synthesis of these apparent contradictions lies in the recognition of the functional and dialectical approach of the behavior analyst. Behavior and environment have no interesting independent reality status to the behavior analyst. One can only be accounted for in its relation or interaction with the other, and in interaction with the scientist-observer. When we place the experimenter in the analysis and see the further, more complicated interactions produced by his manipulations (and their reciprocal effects on him), we see that an event is defined as behavior or as environment by the observer, and that we have nothing more than a way for the observer to develop his control over his subject matter. The definitions are functional—or, if you prefer, purposeful—though I find the introduction of mentalism into the account unnecessary. It would be possible to show the dialectical arrangements that led to the selections of pigeons and rats as experimental organisms and to the use of a bar press or key peck as the experimental response. It would also be possible to show how the behavior of the experimental organism led to the development of the experimental chamber and apparatus used by operant conditioners. A very detailed account of the interlocking or reciprocal controls that led to these developments has been provided by Skinner (1959).

In establishing the basic model for experimental investigation, Skinner was highly influenced by a simple but important statement from Pavlov stating essentially that if you control your conditions, you will see order. Skinner (1959) applied this concept to the study of the individual case: "We are within reach of a science of the individual. This will be achieved not by resorting to some special theory of knowledge in which intuition takes the place of observation and analysis, but through an increasing grasp of relevant conditions to produce order in the individual case [p. 95]."

For the experimental analyst of behavior, the important thing is to get his behavior under the control of the experimental organism. He does this by observing behavior directly, not by using statistical and theoretical techniques. The basic method, then, is to emphasize the interaction between organism and experimenter. This requires prolonged contact since the behavior of an organism is continuous, as is the behavior of the observer. It is not the case, as in traditional scientific methodology, that one holds the behavior still for inspection (Skinner, 1953a). One looks at the behavior as it continues to occur, a process that is often very disorderly. One does not design experiments with well-defined beginnings and ends. The experimenter and organism are placed in prolonged dialectical interaction, the product of which it is hoped will be a recognition of orderliness in behavior–environment relationships. The control is bidirectional.

In describing the scientific method Skinner (1959) says:

> the organism whose behavior is most extensively modified and most completely controlled in research of the sort I have described is the experimenter himself. . . . The subjects we study reinforce us much more effectively than we reinforce them. In describing the experimental analysis of behavior I have been telling you simply how I have been conditioned to behave [p. 98].

The Skinner paper that has been extensively quoted in this discussion of dialectical features of the experimental analysis of behavior is Skinner's "A Case History in Scientific Method" (1959). In this paper Skinner gets immediately to the interlocking accounts of the behavior of the scientist-observer and the experimental subject, rejecting any formal account. He rather facetiously offers five principles for the analysis of behavior, but they are to be taken seriously in that each describes the experimenter's sensitivity to and the alternation of his behavior as a function of his subject's behavior. The five principles are as follows:

Principle 1: When you encounter something interesting, drop everything else and study it.

Principle 2: Some ways of doing research are easier than (efficiency) others.

Principle 3: Some people are lucky (discovery of cumulative recorder).

Principle 4: Apparatuses sometimes break down.

Principle 5: In looking for one thing, one often finds something else (serendipity).

If there is a common theme running through these principles and my descriptions of radical behavioral science, that theme is the interaction of scientist and subject, a focus on reciprocal controlling relations. This focus and sensitivity to behavior rather than its by-products or correlates, the focus on individual organisms, the long period of observation—all fit within a dialectical model in that they allow for reciprocal controlling relations through interaction, though it should be pointed out that this approach was not developed because it was dialectical, but rather because it worked, and this important distinction highlights a difference between dialectical and radical behavioral psychology that must be dealt with later.

Since behavior is the subject matter of behaviorists' investigations, there may be value in looking at the dialectical features of the behaviorist as he experiments. The setting is one with which most investigators are at least vaguely familiar. We have a convenient experimental organism—the pigeon—inexpensive to purchase and maintain, requiring little space, and easily managed. We have an experimental space, usually called a Skinner Box, lodged in a soundproof chamber. One wall has a manipulandum, a small key on which the animal responds and lights, and/or a tone generator with which to signal the experimental subject. Below and to the right of the manipulandum is a hopper in which food is occasionally available. The light and sound stimuli are presented to the organism by means of an electromechanical apparatus programmed by the experimenter. Responses, too, are recorded automatically on a cumulative recorder which allows a momentary analysis of responses and the conditions under which they occur. There is a second organism in the environment—the experimenter. As we observe that the manipulation of contingencies by the experimenter affect the behavior of the pigeon, we also see that change or the lack of change affects the way in which the experimenter manipulates experimental conditions. As the animal begins to respond, the experimenter checks his apparatus and makes certain that his programming and recording apparatus are working properly. As the interaction continues, the scientist's history (expectation) leads him to seek the orderly evidence of performance that begins to emerge on the cumulative recorder. If such order does not emerge, the scientist's behavior is affected in the sense that he now begins to search for apparatus failure or improper programming of the equipment.

It is interesting to observe the behavior of new students when order fails to emerge from this same experimental situation. Typically they begin to describe their pigeon as retarded, psychotic, or somehow incapable of grasping or understanding what is required. They have not yet been brought under the control of their subject matter and do not see that the organism's unpredicted or undesirable responding is a controlling stimulus for their own behavior. In behavior analysis we are likely to refer to scientists as skilled or seasoned when they begin to interact with their subject matter, controlling and coming under the control of it. As the organism continues to respond and we observe the frequency of his responding over time, we are engaged in a dialectical interaction with that organism in an ever-changing, ever-developing relationship. When an orderly relation has developed, the experimenter begins to push or move the environment around. He changes something in the environment and watches its effect on his subject's responding. As the subject alters his response or does not, the experimenter may repeat the alteration or change it slightly to assess its parameters. It is at this point that we are at the cutting edge of science and can see the most interesting dialectical features of the experimental analysis of behavior. The scientist's attempts at discovery are best described as attempts to be controlled by the subject matter. The point at which there is a change from a condition in which reciprocal controlling relations are established is the point at which discovery occurs. Each scientist goes through his own personal discovery of his control over and by nature. When many individuals have already experienced this control, one is talking about training. When new reciprocal controlling relations occur, one calls it scientific advancement.

Many levels of analysis are possible since multiple sources of reciprocal control are possible. For the sake of brevity, I have chosen a very simple level of analysis. It is important to note that an experienced organism and experienced experimenter behave very differently with respect to each other.

In addition to this interaction of experimenter and subject, there is an interesting contradiction in the experimental situation as well. In the short term—that is, through the experimental session—as the experimenter establishes control, he loses it. Reinforcement only works when an organism is deprived, but as the experimenter establishes that control through reinforcement, he loses it through satiation. This condition does not distinguish methodological and radical behaviorists, however.

Many will find that the examples of dialectical relations in operant conditioning that have been cited are essentially uninteresting cases in that, as described, they do not specify a sufficiently strong dialectical relation. I am aware that many will find that no true dialectical model is possible in operant conditioning because the control is bidirectional rather than totally interactive and that in the Skinnerian analysis one direction is held constant, at least momentarily, in order to study the effects on the other. Thus the radical behaviorist does not take the total episode into account as a unified whole.

This belief is basically correct. Behavior analysis does not precisely fit this stronger dialectical model, and no behaviorist would attempt to make his work fit the model. It appears unnecessary. The question must be asked: What do we miss in the dissection that is not missing in the total account? It appears that behaviorist and dialectician agree significantly that experience is the best test of the value of scientific activity. It has to be acknowledged that the analysis of behavior at the weaker dialectical level works, and behavior analysis, as a field, has had a history of remarkable success and rapid development at the basic experimental as well as at the applied level. It is up to the dialectician to demonstrate that there is utility in a stronger model. To me it appears not helpful, but incapacitating to urge the field beyond bidirectional analysis until adequate interactive methods are developed. Though my familiarity with the area is admittedly limited, I find no consistent interactive methodology emerging. Global verbal analyses are available, but no one seems able to promote a sufficiently careful account that can be put to a serious empirical, much less controlled, experimental test. Bidirectional analysis seems sufficient to get on with our study, and until such time as someone can show why such analyses are insufficient, there seems to be no advantage in supporting the stronger account.

A more comprehensive analysis of the epistemological bases of dialectics and radical behaviorism is required to get at the significant distinctions between a dialectical and a radical behavioral approach to our subject matter.

Both Skinner (1959) and Lenin (1929) have criticized the positivistic view for its insistence upon the existence of a world independent of a knower. Both Skinner (1959) and Hegel (1968) reject a concept of essential difference in favor of an analysis of things as they relate to something other, and possibly to themselves. Lawler (1975), after he distinguishes between intuitive and scientific dialectics, claims that dialectical theory provides a general framework to be validated by its utility in promoting scientific growth.

Mao (1962) says, "In judging the trueness of one's knowledge or theory, one cannot depend upon one's subjective feelings about it, but only upon its objective result in social practice. Only social practice can be the criterion of truth [p. 201]."

Engels (1968) claims that "the success of our actions proves the correspondence of our perception with the objective nature of the object perceived," and finally, Lenin (1909) recognizes the relativity of all our knowledge, not in the sense of the denial of objective truth, but in the sense of the historical conditions that determine the degrees of our knowledge as it approaches this truth.

Such statements suggest an empirical epistemological basis for dialectical approaches. They suggest that knowing is a dynamic process, ever changing through interaction with reality. Lenin (1929) says that "practice ought to be the first and fundamental criterion of the theory of knowledge [p. 127]."

But for the behaviorists there remain disturbing elements in some dialectical accounts. Wozniak (1975) specifies, as a critical feature of dialectical concepts of knowing, the concept of reflection. Are dialecticians still caught in copy theories of knowledge? Wozniak (1975) talks about consciousness as the reflection of an objective reality and Lenin talks of the correspondence of our perception with the objective nature of the object perceived.

Such mentalistic accounts are truly surprising to me in that they again bring back the old dichotomies of mental–physical, subjective–objective, and so on. They speak of a world of essences that would have dialecticians seek to avoid. Obviously some do, as demonstrated by Kvale (Chapter 9, this volume). However, through his beautiful dialectical analysis, Kvale has forced me to seriously qualify the last section of this contribution.

In regard to his description of knowing, Skinner does not acknowledge any representation or conscious content in the mind or brain; we have an organism behaving. Knowing is behaving. Skinner (1969) says: "At some point the organism must do more than create duplicates. It must see, hear, smell, and so on as forms of action rather than reproduction. It must do some of the things it is differentially reinforced for doing when it learns to respond discriminatively [p. 231–232]."

Whereas some who have supported the dialectical position describe a copy of reality theory of consciousness, the behavioristic position on conscious experience is that

> seeing does not imply something seen. We acquire the behavior of seeing under stimulation from actual objects, but it may occur in the absence of these objects under the control of other variables. We also acquire the behavior of seeing, that-we-are-seeing when we are seeing actual objects, but it may also occur in their absence. It took man a long time to understand that when he dreamed of a wolf, no wolf was actually there. It has taken him even longer to understand that not even a representation of a wolf is there [Skinner, 1969, p. 234].

Knowing, to a behaviorist, is behaving. It is action. It is not a reproduction. It lacks any quality of thingness. We do not call up some thing to consciousness when we recall. We simply come under the control of certain features of the environment and behave accordingly.

For the radical behaviorist, there is no thought, but only thinking, no dream, but only dreaming, no copy, no reflection, no reproduction, but only behaving.

When we think of knowing, not as a thing or as a product of action, but as an event, as behavior itself, we have not only a radically behavioral but, I would think, also a radically dialectical description of knowing. Whether or not this statement is true will be left to the reader to decide.

By way of summary, I should like to point to some major commonalities and distinctions in the dialectical and radical behavioral positions on behavior and development.

Both positions are metatheoretical. Each describes not only a way of studying psychology, but human affairs in general. Each has, implicitly if not explicitly, its own unique philosophy of science, its own ethics, its own epistemological concepts. Both positions are optimistic about man's future, in contrast, for example, to Freud, and both agree that the methodological behaviorism based on positivism that currently grips psychology restricts the advancement of science and the development of good scientists. Both are fundamentally interested in the interaction of scientist and subject matter, though the descriptions of interaction may not be the same.

Both positions stress the importance of focusing on the importance of change over time and the interdependence of short-term and long-term effects of change over time. Both positions stress the importance of historical and cultural influences on the scientist. Neither framework supports the reductionistic position, though for the dialectician, nonreductionism seems a point of principle, for the behaviorist, a functional point, and dialecticians probably see behaviorists as reductionistic.

Neither position supports the comparative methods of contemporary scientific practice, but for the behaviorist such practices are inherently wrong because they do not bring and have no potential of bringing the scientist into effective contact with his subject matter. For the dialectician, comparative analyses are seen as early or preliminary steps in scientific development. Neither position supports concepts of static states such as Freudian or Piagetian stages. Both see the organism and its environment as continually active, acting upon, and being acted upon by the environment.

There is a major difference in the two dialectical perspectives represented in this volume, and I believe that difference can properly be labeled as mentalism. In Kvale's contribution (Chapter 9), I can't discriminate between radical behaviorist and dialectician. In the work of cognitive dialecticians, there is no reliance upon operationism and logical positivism, but there still seems as much structural as functional emphasis, and in this way, I feel, this work remains open to the criticisms that Lawler (1975) has lodged against empiricism, namely, that it places too much emphasis on the thing and not enough on the process.

But I am convinced that radical behavioral science is closer to dialectical perspectives than to methodological behavioral perspectives, and I support an expanded influence of the sort described by Kvale and Riegel for its broadening effect on the science and the training of scientists.

REFERENCES

Baer, D. M., Wolf, M. M., & Risley, T. R. Some current dimensions of applied behavior analysis. *Journal of Applied Behavior Analysis* 1968, **1**, 91–97.

Chomsky, N. A review of Skinner's *Verbal behavior. Language,* 1959, **35**, 26–58.

Engels, F., *Dialectics of nature.* Moscow: Progress Publishers, 1968.

Hegel, G. W. F. *The logic of Hegel.* London: Oxford University Press, 1968.

Hull, C. L. *A behavior system.* New Haven: Yale University Press, 1952.

Lawler, J. Dialectical philosophy and developmental psychology: Hegel and Piaget on contradiction. *Human Development,* 1975, **18**(1 & 2), 1–17.

Lenin, V. I. *Philosphical notebook;* in *Collected works.* Vol. 29. New York: International Publishers, 1929.

Mao Tse Tung. On practice. In A. Fremotte (Ed.), *Mao Tse Tung, An anthology of his writings.* New York: New American Library Mentor Books, 1962. Pp. 200–213.

Premack, D. Reinforcement theory. In D. Levine (Ed.), *Nebraska Symposium on Motivation.* Lincoln: University of Nebraska Press, 1965. Pp. 123–180.

Schnaitter, R. A review of Skinner's *About behaviorism. Journal of the Experimental Analysis of Behavior,* in press.

Sidman, M. *Tactics of scientific research.* New York: Basic Books, 1960.

Skinner, B. F. *The behavior of organisms: An experimental analysis.* New York: Appleton, 1938.

Skinner, B. F. The analysis of behavior. *American Psychologist,* 1953, **8**, 69–79. (a)

Skinner, B. F. *Science and human behavior.* New York: Macmillan, 1953. (b)

Skinner, B. F. A case history in scientific method. In B. F. Skinner (Ed.), *Cumulative Record.* New York: Appleton, 1959. Pp. 76–100.

Skinner, B. F. *Verbal behavior.* New York: Appleton, 1957.

Skinner, B. F. The operational analysis of psychological terms. In B. F. Skinner (Ed.), *Cumulative record,* New York, Appleton, 1959. Pp. 272–285.

Skinner, B. F. What is the experimental analysis of behavior? *Journal of the Experimental Analysis of Behavior,* 1966,

Skinner, B. F. Behaviorism at fifty. In B. F. Skinner (Ed.), *Contingencies of reinforcement.* New York: Appleton, 1969. Pp. 221–268.

Skinner, B. F. *Beyond freedom and dignity.* New York: Knopf, 1971.

Spence, K. W. The nature of theory construction in contemporary psychology. *Psychological Review,* 1944, 51, 47–68.

Wheeler, H. *Beyond the punitive society.* Stanford: Stanford University Press, 1972.

Wood, W. S. *A note on the behavior of behaviorists.* Unpublished manuscript, Drake University, 1973.

Wozniak, R. H. A dialectical paradigm for psychological research: Implications drawn from the history of psychology in the Soviet Union. *Human Development,* 1975, 18(1 & 2), 18–34.

CHAPTER 16

Behaviorism and the Social System

JAMES G. HOLLAND

UNIVERSITY OF PITTSBURGH
PITTSBURGH, PENNSYLVANIA

In demonstrating the common features of radical behaviorism and dialectical materialism, Jon Krapfl corrects the gross misunderstandings of radical behaviorism shared by too many psychologists with an interest in cognitive development. I am in complete agreement with Jon's excellent account. Rather than provide a summary of a redundant endorsement of his analysis, I will present the direction suggested by the political or social implications of his analysis. As interesting as the parallel is between dialectical and behavioral perspectives, radical behaviorism has progressed without any deliberate use of the dialectical perspective, and the Marxian theory of economics and history has done well without the help of radical behaviorism. However, it is exactly in the area that Krapfl avoids, the area of political and social change, that the science of behavior change and the theory of social revolution can join together to provide workable solutions for the problems of humanity.

Skinner's book *Verbal Behavior* (1957) opens by stating that people

> act upon the world, and change it, and are changed in turn by the consequences of their action. Certain processes . . . alter behavior so that it achieves a safer and more successful interchange with a particular environment. When appropriate behavior has been established, its consequences work through similar processes to keep it in force. If by chance the environment changes, old forms of behavior disappear, while new consequences build new forms [p. 1].

Compare this with Karl Marx's (1800/1961), view of the relation of man to work. Work is seen as the special product of humans, and, most interestingly, humans themselves are a special product of their labor. "By thus acting on the external world and changing it, he [or she] at the same time changes his [or her] own nature [p. 173]." Skinner and Marx both view behavior as highly adaptable— highly malleable by circumstance—and both view people as the creators of *future* circumstances. There is a basis for optimism in the perfectibility of people and in the perfectibility of their culture. Both Skinner and Marx see a natural evolution of culture to a more humanitarian form. This is not to say that Skinner is a Marxist, nor Marx a Skinnerian; but, rather, to suggest that one can comfortably be both a radical behaviorist and a political radical in looking toward a future, "more perfect" society—of the people, by the people, and for the people.

Either perspective is likely to see our current circumstances in class terms. There are controllers and controllees in the token economies designed by behavior modifiers or in the already existing forms of control that the planned system emulates. The form of behavior control in our society is seen as manipulative, dominated by profit-oriented corporate interests, and aimed at maintaining our current stratification of wealth and power. Managers define criteria and arrange contingencies to control their subordinates. This stratified form for behavior control is found in the workplace, in the schools, even in the form of our own behavior modification schemes (Holland, 1975).

To see the effects of such stratification, behaviorists might look at the phenomenon called scientific management, which swept the business world of the early 20th century and found its ultimate expression in the assembly line (Braverman, 1974). In the workplace, scientific management separated people's work from its direct products. By contrast, in early industrialization, techniques of production were almost literally in the *hands* of skilled craftsmen. In the intimate interplay between the craftsman's activity and the product of that activity, sophisticated skills developed. The craftsman was the proud producer, the individual craftsman being indispensable to the company. Scientific management, or "Taylorism," was introduced to distribute the various small components of each craft across unskilled and consequently easily replaceable workers. Taylorism alienates workers from the creative products of their work. The worker becomes an insignificant cog in the machine, lacking in the experience of intrinsic reinforcement from work. No longer are there suitable products of work for shaping sophisticated skills in the worker. The scientifically managed workplace produces great quantities of products, driving down the price of individual products and driving out the work of individual craftsmen.

This "Tayloring" process took place before behavioral psychology and certainly continues without leadership from behaviorists, despite the view of many activist groups that see behaviorists as the prime villains. Nevertheless, as I have stated elsewhere (Holland, 1975), we have stepped into positions where we act on behalf of those in power to control persons on subservient levels for the goals of those who hire us, though, in dispensing with aversive control, we can often claim to have established a more humanitarian orientation in these institutions.

The behavior modifier, whether working in corporations, mental hospitals, prisons, or schools, has most often attempted to fix the troublesome behavior of subordinates to fit the aims of managers (troublesome behavior, that is, as defined by the managers). Hence, in the workplace the cycle is broken between the behavior (work), the product of the behavior, and the change in future behavior. The natural processes of growth in human potential made possible as workers "act upon the world, change it, and are changed in turn by the consequences" are confined to trivial, sequential tasks with rigid limits placed on the behaviors. The worker alienated from the product of work cannot develop in skill.

A similar alienation of action from product of action goes on in the expert management of the social sphere. Most interesting for my purposes are the several different plans generated by concern over the great population increase as compared to the future availability of resources. The need for direct intervention to control population growth has considerable support from intellectuals in our society. Here, too, we may see how control by a select strata in the open society parallels the control and resulting alienation in the workplace. In both instances, control is effected through arbitrary reinforcers instead of an arrangement of natural reinforcers—reinforcers inherent in the activity. In both, the narrow, sequential definition of contingency imposes limits on human potential, removes responsibility, and makes the person less able. One familiar population control plan is that of family planning with education, contraception, and abortion. This is most often met with disappointing results in those underdeveloped countries that we view as in greatest need of population control.

A second plan has been proposed by Kingsley Davis (1973), a demographer working for the Environmental Fund. His plan involves a coercive limit to family size.

> If people want to control population it can be done with knowledge already available
> .... For instance, a nation seeking to stabilize its population could shut off immigration and permit each couple a maximum of two children, with possible license for a third. Accidental pregnancies beyond the limit would be interrupted by abortion. If a third child were born without a license, or a fourth, the mother would be sterilized [p. 28].

The reader may recognize this plan as almost identical with one that the Indian government is attempting to implement. Note that it was not first suggested by some distant tyrannical government, but by an American technocrat supported by foundation funds.

A third plan is called the "lifeboat theory," proposed by Garrett Hardin (1971). He calls for the starving of people in underdeveloped countries; that is, starving the unworthy. He stated:

> A lifeboat can hold only so many people. There are more than 2 billion wretched people in the world—10 times as many as in the United States. It is literally beyond our ability to save them all. ... Both international graineries and lax immigration policies must be rejected if we are to save something for our grandchildren [p. 1297].

A fourth plan, based on behavior modification, by contrast, will certainly appear humanitarian. An experiment begun in Taiwan begins a bank account for a newly married couple, and deposits are made periodically so long as the couple has no more than two children. If a third child is born, the bank account is cut in half. And if there is a fourth child, the bank account is abolished. Withdrawals can only be made for purposes of education for the children (Fennigant & Sun, 1972).

A fifth solution to the population problem, although one would hesitate to call it a plan, is the natural stabilization of population that Barry Commoner (1976) has documented. Commoner has shown data from a number of sources—England before the Industrial Revolution, India prior to English rule—that in a premodern society both birth rate and death rate are high, with population stable. In the next stage, as agricultural and industrial output grows and living conditions improve, death rate begins to fall. Birth rate stays high for a time, and as a result, population size rapidly increases. With increasing numbers of people there is an increased demand on natural resources, increased economic activity that in turn causes an increased average age at marriage. As the quality of life continues to improve, there is a higher standard of living and a decrease in birth rate. After development, the size of the population is greater than in the premodern period. However, both premodern and modern societies reach a stable population size. This last solution no less reflects behavioral processes than the other four plans. The individual decisions of members of society in arriving at their family size reflect the intrinsic adaptability of behavior.

The same forces behind the first four population control plans are behind the public campaigns in this society which make us so certain that professional intervention is needed to control family size. We learn that overpopulated and underdeveloped countries are starving, and we conclude that they are underfed because of insufficient resources for their great numbers of people. Yet Commoner demonstrates that the world produces twice as much food as that which is needed for our current 2 billion people. The problem of hungry people is not an overpopulation/insufficient resource problem. It is a political problem, of which unequal distribution of resources is the source.

Just as scientific management in the company alienates the product from the worker and hence eliminates intrinsic reinforcement and the potential shaping function of productive labor, so would the "successful" population plans alienate the people from the natural consequences of daily living. A different direction must be taken if we are to avoid the manipulative control of arbitrary reinforcers arranged by a higher stratum. People must come before profit and public good before individual gain. For science and technology to be a part of this it must be a technology for the people and of the people (Holland, in press).

Ultimately, we need a new social order, an egalitarian society with full participation by all, all motivated to work toward the public good, and all sharing equally in the wealth produced, a community of equality with service to others and responsibility for others as the guiding principles—as the criteria by which a collection of equals would reinforce each other. When all the day-to-day acts of each individual are evaluated communally in terms of the criterion for public service, small beginnings of elitism or personal gain at the expense of others can be immediately assessed and criticized.

Decisions regarding work would be made collectively by the workers. The role of the work in meeting the needs of society would be discussed, and individual responsibilities in meeting work goals decided collectively. Therefore, the work itself would provide intrinsic reinforcement, from the value of the work and from the awareness of its social importance. When people can contribute fully to creative work, they can contribute to the developing technology of that work, and their human potential will be increased. Remember the basic tenet of behaviorism with which this chapter began: People act on the world, change the world, and in turn, are changed by the consequences of their actions. Similarly, when people act as full participants in social decision making, their potential social fulfillment increases.

A whole social order doesn't change overnight. Some speak of a grand seizure of power and of revolution. But the problem of creating the new social order would remain. A close look at revolutionary development shows that even with such seizure of power, true social change involves a steady, gradual progression, which the behaviorist is already so familiar with when extensive behavioral changes are necessary.

Let us consider an analogy from China. When the Red Army and the Kuomintang were locked in battle in the province of Yenan, the peasants were experimenting with a series of farming arrangements. The Swedish sociologist Jan Myrdal (1972) documented these farming arrangements in extensive interviews he held with many citizens of this rural community. The peasants first divided the land into small farms and worked the plots individually. After some discussion some of the peasants formed work teams to share in the work on one another's farms. Later, they entered into cooperatives while maintaining their separate plots, but shared work and pooled produce cooperatively. At first not all participated, believing for whatever reason that their own best interests were served in individual farming. As the cooperatives proved successful, the holdouts began to join in. Subsequently, several cooperatives joined together to form communes, with private plots no longer being maintained. Hence, there was experimentation, and with the proven success, a new system emerged. The Communist Party found these communes functioning successfully and became technological disseminators of the new system. China's strategy for technical and social change continues to start with the practicing people, learn from them, synthesize what is learned into theory and principles, and return these principles and methods to the people for improved solutions to their problems. This farming development was a technological one, beginning of the people and ending for the people. It is true that these experiments emerged from bleak necessity, and it is not suggested that a direct translation from the Chinese experience would serve our purpose.

Today's reader may not see the American agrarian peasant as a source of desperation so bleak as to require the initiation of a new social order. But there are other groups, indeed, manifesting such bleak despair, caused by the impact of our massive corporations on the environment and the life of the individual in the workplace. Many have dropped out, taken to the woods, and joined very inward-looking communal groups. But for our purpose the more interesting ones are those who are developing a new soft technology, toward which our present society could naturally evolve. They are evolving systems that regard people, and the long-term survival of people, as central, and that seek to meet people's needs without damage to the environment. One example is the new Alchemist Institute (Green, 1976). It is experimenting with sources of energy, such as solar and windmill-generated energy, that do not use nonrenewable resources, and with a technology of small-scale fish farming in tanks barely larger than a dining room. All members of the Institute make the same income, and all participate in decision making.

Along a similar vein is the work of E. F. Schumacher, author of *Small Is Beautiful* (1973) and founder of the Intermediate Technology Development Group. This group specializes in developing tools that fit the needs of poor people in underdeveloped countries. Schumacher's ideal is to assist small-scale, village-level industry that serves the needs of the people for work. Here, too, he suggests not only full participation in the work, but also full participation in decision making.

There are many other reactions to corporate exploitation. Consumer coops are increasing, usually with some form of sharing in the work load and sharing in the decisions. Also in America's own underdeveloped areas, as in the rural South, producers' coops and associations of producers' coops are forming.

All of these various activities depend on people's participation. They are more or less designed to encourage imitation and further experimentation. They all involve, at their base, the behavior of people, but people behaving in different social arrangements. The behaviorists prepared to take seriously their belief in the adaptability of behavior can be a part of this movement. We, above all, should be able to learn from the actions of the people to formulate principles based on successful practices and to arrange ideal teaching situations. We should also disseminate educational materials evolving from these activities in order to further their development.

REFERENCES

Braverman, H. *Labor and monopoly capital*. New York: Monthly Review Press, 1974.

Commoner, B. *The poverty of power*. New York: Random House, 1976.

Davis, K. Zero population growth: The goal and the means. *Daedalus*, Fall 1973, pp. 15–30.

Fennigant, O. D., & Sun, T. A. Planning, starting, and operating an educational incentive project. *Population Council*, 1972, **3**, 1–7.

Greene, W. The new alchemists. *New York Times*, August 8, 1976, p. 12.

Hardin, G. The survival of nation and civilization. *Science*, 1971, **172**, 1297.

Holland, J. G. Behavior modification for prisoners, patients, and other people as a prescription for the planned society. *Mexican Journal Analysis of Behavior*, 1975, **1**(1), 81–95.

Holland, J. G. Behaviorism: Part of the problem or part of the solution? *Journal of Applied Behavior Analysis*, in press.

Marx, K. *Capital* (Vol. 1). Moscow: Foreign Language Publishing House, 1961.

Myrdal, J. *Report from a Chinese village*. New York: Vintage Books, 1972.

Schumacher, E. F. *Small is beautiful*. New York: Harper, 1973.

Skinner, B. F. *Verbal behavior*. New York: Appleton, 1957.

CHAPTER 17

Psychology, Thomian Topologies, Deviant Logics, and Human Development[1]

ROY FREEDLE

EDUCATIONAL TESTING SERVICE
PRINCETON, NEW JERSEY

I. Overview

Discussions of development typically make hidden assumptions. These assumptions pervade our methods for data collection, data interpretation, and theory construction. If these assumptions are wrong, all the data collection in the world will not alter the adequacy of our theories resting upon these assumptions.

My purpose in this chapter is to raise the possibility that not every theory of human development must rest upon two very ubiquitous assumptions made by most theorists—smooth functions relating stimuli to responses and classical logic, which insists that both p and not p cannot be true simultaneously. The possibility that discontinuities may relate many stimuli to many responses is evident in Thom's (1975) theory of topological surfaces. The possibility of sensibly modeling behavior such that both p and not p may be true simultaneously—the law of dialectical contradiction—is made possible by recent developments in mathematical logic (Freedle, 1976; Wolf, 1975). We shall see further that some aspects of these deviant logics can be modeled on the Thomian topological surfaces.

In order to discuss intelligently the implications of these two recent breakthroughs in human understanding for human development, we must build up our

---

[1] This chapter is a greatly condensed version of a fuller statement, of book length, that is in preparation; to be published by Lawrence Erlbaum Associates, Hillsdale, N.J., 1978.

demonstrations in several steps. First, a nontechnical example of how we psychologists study and model sensory thresholds—both absolute as well as difference thresholds—is introduced in order to show that Thomian topologies provide a more accurate description of the known facts than previous discussions of thresholds have made possible. This example serves to familiarize us with some of Thom's ideas without an extensive mathematical preparation. Furthermore, while of interest in itself, this example of intraindividual behavior provides us with our first example of how the "law" of the excluded middle, from Aristotelian logic, is readily violated when we deal with Thom's ideas as models of behavior; that is, the law of the excluded middle says that either p or not p must be true (while the "law" of contradiction says that both cannot be true simultaneously). We shall see that neither p nor not p is true for some regions of Thomian surfaces. Hence, this demonstration, while not of direct relevance to human developmental issues, provides us with a clear example of how to merge the recent discoveries of algebraic deviant logics with the recent discoveries of algebraic Thomian surfaces, which allow for discontinuous functional relations between stimuli and responses. A topological *Fold* will suffice here.

Second, the interaction of a mother and her infant is explored by showing that the conditional probability of vocalizing over successive 10-second intervals can be interpreted geometrically as a topological Fold. Thus, we see that the same topological form can have a variety of interpretations when applied to psychological data. In addition we are led to see that different mathematical methods (conditional probability on the one hand, deviant logic on the other) can be applied to the same topological form, depending upon the phenomenon we are studying.

Third, we then outline the next more complex topological form, called the *Cusp*, which actually consists of a smooth series of Folds placed "end" to "end" such that the smaller Folds are near the "rear" of our three-dimensional surface, while the larger Folds are nearer the "front." A more complex statement about thresholds is then made using the Cusp.

Fourth, using the Cusp, we introduce a new topic: Kohlberg's moral development model. The conditional probability argument advanced earlier for the Fold is here extended to the probability of a transition from one moral stage to the next higher one. Data fitted by a Markovian transitional probability model reveals that the conditional probability of moving to the next higher moral stage becomes increasingly more difficult the higher one's current moral stage. These numerical facts are argued to be well fitted by the Cusp; the possibility is left open, however, that a series of Cusps (one is called the *Butterfly*) may eventually be required to fully model the complexity of moral development.

Fifth, we introduce a number of topics that seem to require a more complex Thomian surface: the Butterfly. We return to the early topic of sensoriperceptual psychology so as to model visual illusions that change their "state" as a function of time; one of these is the "staircase" illusion. Another interesting sensory phenomenon is binocular rivalry, which changes its perceptual state over time. At the interindividual level of societal changes that induce generational differences, we briefly consider a topological model of some cohort differences. One part of this model uses the Butterfly surface. We then point out that such forms as the Butterfly allow us to model the logic of contradiction, thereby completing our mapping of some aspects of deviant logic within the Thomian perspective. Some developmental consequences of nonstandard logics are then explored.

Sixth, we outline sequences of topological transformations to show the long-term consequences of development from the perspective of topological modeling. All our previous examples (except the cohort one) dealt with changes over a narrow time or, as in the case of Kohlberg's moral development model, seemed simple enough to be captured by a single topological surface. While not every developmental transformation need be topological in the Thomian sense, for those that are, we need a broad classification scheme by which to explore their patternings over time.

II. Sensory Thresholds and the Fold Curve

The last 2000 years of scientific thinking and modeling have been dominated by Aristotelian logic and, more recently, by Newtonian calculus. While I maintain that both these movements are interrelated, our more immediate concern is to outline Thom's ideas on how to overcome the limitations of Newtonian model building. Thom's concern (1975) was with transcending the limitations on theory construction due to Newton's insistence upon functions that were smooth and continuous. The phenomena that could be well modeled by Newtonian differential calculus were also of the smooth and continuous type. Of course, phenomena that involve *breaks,* or discontinuities, in the functions relating, say, a stimulus scale to a response scale can still be approximated by Newtonian functions—but they necessarily ignore fine points of the phenomena that a careful inspection of the data should reveal. For the topological surface called the Cusp, and for a cross section of the Cusp that we shall call the Fold (an S-shaped curve), there are five characteristics that signal the presence of a Thomian model over a Newtonian one. They are as follows: (a) a sudden transition or *discontinuity* in the behavior, (b) *hysteresis* (a shift in where the sudden transition occurs), (c) a region of *inaccessibility,* (d) the property of *divergence,* wherein a slight change in the stimulus *can* but need not produce a catastrophic change in the behavior, and (e) the behavior should be *bimodal.*

Although the sensory threshold has been studied since the beginnings of experimental psychology 100 years ago, an adequate model of the threshold is still not at hand. I say this in spite of the brilliant work on signal detection, which follows essentially in the Newtonian spirit (Luce, 1963; Swets, 1964). I maintain that an equally plausible model of the threshold can be constructed from the Thomian perspective and that such a perspective may eventually replace the Newtonian ones (see Kuhn, 1970, for scientific paradigm shifts). The main reason for this claim is that the earliest studies of the absolute threshold (as well as difference limens) showed the existence of hysteresis (to be described later). Yet very little is made of this property in the Newtonian models; even Luce and Galanter (1963) deal with hysteresis as an external-response *bias* property and do not consider the phenomenon as intrinsic to the threshold itself. In addition to hysteresis, all remaining properties of the Cusp (and its cross section, called the Fold) can be found for sensory thresholds. Because of this, a topological model is here favored over Newtonian ones.

The five topological properties of the threshold are illustrated in Figure 1.

In Figure 1 the *x*-axis represents a stimulus-intensity dimension, while the *y*-axis represents a behavioral response dimension. The curve relating stimulus to response is here represented by an S-shaped curve (cross section of the Cusp). The middle part of the S shape is shaded to illustrate a region of inaccessibility (to be described more fully later). Along the *x*-axis are located stimulus-intensity points *a* and *b;* corresponding points *a′* and *b′*, representing the *same* stimulus intensities, have been transposed upward so as to lie on the top part of the S-shaped curve. The significance of this will be described in a moment.

One of the earliest methods for locating the threshold with respect to the intensity on the *x*-axis that evokes a shift from saying that no signal is present to saying that a signal is present is the method of limits. An ascending series of

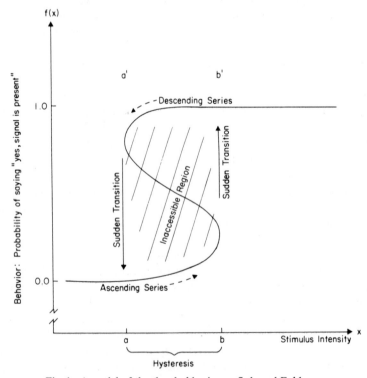

Fig. 1. A model of the threshold using an S-shaped Fold curve.

increasing intensity is used to locate the first estimate of where the threshold is; and a corresponding descending series of intensities is used to again estimate this location. The next procedure, after many such ascending and descending measures are obtained, is usually to average the x values so as to locate the "true" position of "the" threshold. Such a procedure clearly has made prior assumptions (stemming from the Newtonian and Aristotelian schools). The assumptions are that the same x value must evoke only one corresponding response value on the y-axis. The other assumption is that the order of ascending and descending values should not really make a difference in isolating the threshold since there is only a simple functional relationship assumed to hold between stimulus values and response values. Hence, one has no compunction about averaging the two series.

The difficulty here is that the ascending series usually gives a threshold estimate consistently different from the descending series. This has become known as hysteresis.

In Figure 1, for an ascending series the intensities are begun some distance to the left of point a and then increased by some regular interval until one passes point b. The response evoked by the increasing intensities is usually "no, no signal is present" for all the values to the left of b, but as soon as values of b and greater are reached, the subject suddenly jumps to the top part of the Fold and responds "yes, a signal is present." For the ascending series, then, the threshold is located at b. For the descending series, the experimenter presents signals well above this threshold value, b, and continues to decrease the intensity by some regular interval. The response is typically "yes, a signal is present" as one moves past point b' (on the top part of the S curve). The subject continues to say "yes" until reaching point a'; at this point the subject suddenly jumps to the bottom part of the Fold and begins to say "No, no signal is present." (The sudden transition in behavior is called a discontinuity, or catastrophe.) The descending series yields point a' (which is equivalent to point a) as the location of the threshold. But clearly, points a and b do not coincide. If they did (as illustrated in Figure 2), we would have no reason to doubt the adequacy of a Newtonian model, which postulates a simple function relating stimulus to response. But since the values consistently differ, we need another model to describe the data—averaging them will simply not do justice to the facts. Obviously we have a model of the desired type in the Thomian surfaces. The five properties described earlier as requiring demonstration for postulating the existence of a Cusp model (or a cross-sectional S curve) are here argued to exist for the sensory threshold (and for difference limens; see Stevens, 1957, for hysteresis effects using his magnitude estimation scale). The five properties are as follows.

Hysteresis is exhibited by the fact that points a and b do not coincide; in other words, two thresholds exist, not one. *Inaccessibility* is exhibited by the shaded region of Figure 1. What this means is that it is not possible to hold the behavioral response in some intermediate level of saying "yes and no, the signal is and is not present" for values lying between a and b. *Discontinuity* exists, as we have already pointed out, because behavior shifts suddenly from "yes" to "no" (and vice versa) for different regions of the x-axis. *Divergence* exists because there exist regions on

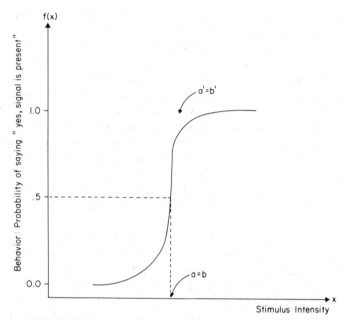

Fig. 2. A model of the threshold using a Newtonian function, which requires a unique value of $f(x)$ for every value of x.

the x-axis where a *slight* change in the stimulus magnitude *can* yield catastrophic change in behavior. Such regions exist in the ascending series around point b, and for the descending series, around region a'. Finally, the curve is essentially *bimodal*, as is obvious from the fact that two threshold curves—one from the ascending and another from the descending series—are placed together to yield the S-shaped Thomian curve. For those requiring further mathematical reasons for why the inner part of the S curve is inaccessible, see Zeeman's (1973) mathematical treatment of the cyclic heartbeat.

Before we move on to new sets of data, we should reexamine Figure 1 because it contains an important violation of Aristotelian logic. Let us agree to call the lower part of the S curve simply p. Since there is only one other behavior allowed by the S-shaped curve (the top part), let us call this top part *not p*. The shaded part of Figure 1 is the inaccessible region. In this region neither p nor *not p* is true. This violates one of Aristotle's logical postulates. By itself this is of little significance; however, when we consider more complex Thomian surfaces later in the chapter, we shall also argue that a second violation of Aristotle's axioms occurs. At that point we shall consider Thomian surfaces as potential models of the so-called deviant logics discussed by Wolf (1975) and Haack (1974). Then we shall consider their possible significance for developmental models viewed from the Thomian perspective.

III. Mother–Infant Vocalization Interaction Modeled
by Pairs of Fold Curves

A number of recent papers have studied the sequential interaction of mother and infant (3 months old) vocalizing to each other over successive time intervals (Freedle & Lewis, 1971, 1976; Lewis & Freedle, 1973). In this section I shall propose a Thomian model of these social interactions.

Six states of the vocalization were defined and fitted by a Markov chain (Freedle & Lewis, 1971). In order to avoid needless complexity I shall simply define two states for the infant: either the infant vocalizes in a particular 10-second interval or he does not vocalize. Similarly, for the mother two states are considered: either she vocalizes or not. Our concern will be to define conditional probabilities with respect to the two states of the infant's behaviors (and separate conditional probabilities for the two states of the mother's vocalizations). Once we have defined these, we will show a correspondence between the conditional probabilities and the Thomian Fold.

Let an infant vocalization be designated by the symbol i, and no infant vocalization by 0. Now consider the following string of symbols: $iiii000i0iii000000$. The first four i's mean that the infant vocalized during the first four 10-second observation periods, during the next three he did not vocalize, and so on. For this particular illustrative string we want to count the number of times i follows an i, and then we will count how many times a 0 follows an i. For five times out of eight an i follows an i, and the remainder of the time a 0 follows an i (three times of eight). The conditional probability of an i following an i is therefore $5/8 = .625$, and the conditional probability of 0 following i is $3/8 = .375$. Now we calculate the conditional probability of a 0 following a 0, and the number of times an i follows a 0. We find that seven of nine times a 0 follows a 0 (and two of nine times an i follows 0). So the conditional probability of 0 given 0 is $7/9 = .778$. And the corresponding result for i following 0 is $.222$. Notice that the probability of *remaining in the same state* is usually larger than that of moving to another state of the vocalization system; that is, $.625$ is larger than its matched entry, $.375$; also $.778$ is larger than $.222$. Another way of saying this is that the organism tends to persist in the same activity over successive time intervals. Actual data confirm this persistence of state over hundreds of individuals.

For the same data string we can examine whether or not the mother vocalized, and we can construct a set of four conditional probabilities that are by and large very similar in patterning to those found for the infant vocalizations illustrated above, wherein the tendency to persist in the same state is larger than the tendency to shift to another vocalization state over successive time intervals. Let m symbolize a mother's vocalization in a 10-second interval and let $\emptyset$ symbolize no vocalization. Then for the string $\emptyset\emptyset mmmmmmmmm\emptyset\emptyset\emptyset\emptyset\emptyset\emptyset\emptyset\emptyset$ we have the conditional probability of m following a $\emptyset$ [designated by $p(m/\emptyset)$] equal to $1/9$; and so $p(\emptyset/\emptyset) = 8/9 = .889$. Also we have $p(\emptyset/m) = 1/8$; and so $p(m/m) = 7/8 = .875$. We can represent

Table 1

Transitional Probability Matrices for
Mother–Infant Vocalization States

A. Two infant vocalization states

		Trial $n + 1$	
		i	0
Trial n	i	.625	.375
	0	.222	.778

B. Two maternal vocalization states

		Trial $n + 1$	
		m	$\emptyset$
Trial n	m	.875	.125
	$\emptyset$	.111	.889

both sets of results—for the infant and for the mother—by a pair of 2 X 2 matrices. These are given in Table 1.

In Table 1 the diagonal entries of .625 and .778 are called entries along the *main diagonal* (the reader should pay special attention to this concept because it will be used again for more complex ideas in a later section). In the same way, the entries of .875 and .889 are main diagonal entries for the mother's transitional probability matrix.

Now we can begin to map these numerical results onto the Thomian Fold—the S-shaped cross section of a Cusp. Figure 3 shows how this is done.

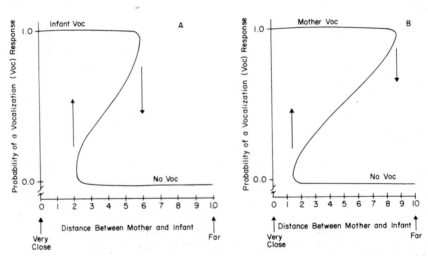

Fig. 3. Hypothesized relationship between distance separating mother and infant and its effect on a vocalization response. (A) The effect on the infant's two vocalization states. (B) A corresponding effect on the mother's vocalization states.

In Figure 3A we have a Fold model to account for the conditional probability matrix of the infant. The x-axis is here interpreted as representing the stimulus property of a situation which governs the elicitation of a vocalization. We see that the Fold curve is here the mirror image of the earlier curves we saw; to be more accurate, then, we should say we are dealing with a *mirror image* of an S-shaped curve. But for convenience we shall just say it is another S-shaped curve.

Notice that the top part of the curve represents the occurrence of a vocalization state. Notice too that it spans a little more than six units of the x-axis. We shall let this represent the quantity .625 that occurs in the infant's transitional probability matrix of an i following an i. Because the x-axis covers a total of 10 units, we see that a little less than 4 units are left over; this shall represent the competing probability of switching to another state—the 0 state. Again the value is meant to reflect the entry in Table 3A of .375. On the lower part of the S curve in Figure 3A we attempt to model the conditional probabilities for maintaining a large value of persistence in the state of 0, given that one is already in state 0 (this being $p(0/0)$ for the infant's data). Almost 8 units are spanned by the lower part of the "no vocalization" state, which is intended to match the value of .778 observed in the infant's transitional probability matrix. The rest of the x-axis interval represents the competing state of $p(i/0)$, which is equal to .222.

A similar but slightly different S-shaped curve is generated for the mother's data, as can be seen in Figure 3B. Her curve is more nearly symmetric in the sense that the two main diagonal entries in her transitional probability matrix are nearly equal (i.e., .875 and .889 are almost equal).

The careful reader will note that it is possible to draw some S-shaped curves on a 10-unit scale which do not always yield the largest entries for the main diagonal. (The same reader will no doubt note that it is possible to prove that *if* the curve is S-shaped, then *at least one* of the two diagonal probabilities will be the largest in its row.) It is interesting that occasionally data of mother–infant vocalization interactions are obtained that fit such a pattern—it seems to vary with the situational setting they are in (see Freedle and Lewis, 1976, for data on the effects of situational setting on transitional probabilities of vocalizations).

What we have done in Figure 2 is to argue that it is quite natural to map some of Thom's ideas onto the mathematics for conditional probabilities. In this way we have attempted to model some developmental data, but in the process we have introduced many simplifications. To do fuller justice to the complexity of vocal interaction we must consider fitting Thomian surfaces involving not just a simple Fold, but *many* such Folds on an n-dimensional surface; the exact number will be a function of the number of vocalization states actually required to fit a given set of data. The reader is referred to a larger monograph (from which the current chapter is excerpted), which relates Thomian models to psychology (Freedle, 1977).

Before we leave this topic of using Fold curves to model psychological data, we should point out that the vocalization Folds for mother and infant represent an *interpersonal* behavior, while the sensory threshold represents an *intrapersonal* behavior. It should be clear that both x-axes of the mother and infant Fold curves are not independent of each other, because if the mother is 5 feet away from the infant, then it necessarily follows that the infant is 5 feet away from the mother. Hence, the momentary value taken on by the x-axis for one member of the dyad is also the value taken on by the other member. That is why we classify the *pair* of S-shaped curves as a model of interpersonal behavior.

IV. The Cusp Model of Moral Development

We have mentioned several times before that the Fold curve in the sense in which we are using it is a cross section of the more complex Cusp surface. The Cusp requires three dimensions to represent it: typically this means two stimulus dimensions and one behavioral response dimension. A whole series of S-shaped curves together form the Cusp. Near the rear of the Cusp, the S-shaped curves are small and the depth of the fold is also fairly shallow. But as one moves "forward" in the Cusp, the S-shaped curves become larger and the depth of the Fold also increases. The top part of Figure 4 illustrates these aspects of the Cusp.

Without dwelling on a description of Figure 4, we shall sketch a rationale for how moral development becomes implicated with a Cusp model. Once we accomplish this, we shall describe Figure 4 in more detail and then shall give one further example of the Cusp from the perspective of sensory thresholds.

With regard to developmental issues, we can represent aspects of Kohlberg's moral development theory as a Cusp model. The reasons for this assertion come from some data of Kohlberg (1964) that I fitted by means of a Markovian model to a Cusp model several years ago. The data show the proportion of individuals of a given age (and a given country and socioeconomic class) who are in each of Kohlberg's six moral stages. The younger the population of subjects, the greater the tendency for the earlier stages to be representative of the population. With older groups one can see the proportion of the earlier stages dropping systematically to lower values, while the later stages begin to reveal a heavier contribution. It is the systematic movement of these population curves that suggests that a much simpler mathematical model can be used to account for the data. I will next describe a two-parameter Markovian model; then, after one additional parameter is introduced, I will show why these results implicate a Cusp model.

In order to fit a two-parameter Markovian model to the data, I postulated that for each moral stage that one is in, there is a fixed probability, p, that one will move to the next higher stage, given that some "critical moral event" has occurred. By a procedure that is too involved to discuss here, I was able to estimate the value p for each population of subjects. Furthermore, the Markovian model simultaneously gave me an estimate of how many, on the average, critical moral events were experienced by that population—the *power* of the transition matrix provided this estimate; this assertion will become clearer in a moment. The other assumptions that we made were as follows. All young subjects started in Stage 1. This was used to yield values for what is called "the initial probability vector." Next one

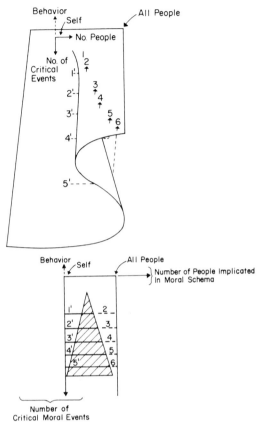

Fig. 4. A Cusp model of Kohlberg's moral development stages. The shaded triangular part of the lower diagram can be regarded as a projection of the top folded curve onto a flat two-dimensional surface. The solid horizontal lines passing through the triangular part of the lower figure represent the amount of space taken up by the primed states as they pass under the folded part of the Cusp, while the dashed horizontal lines continuing to the right of the solid lines represent the amount of space taken up by the *remainder* of the top sheet of the Cusp.

needed a transitional probability matrix. This was obtained from the assumption that no matter what stage one is in, there is a fixed probability of moving to the next higher stage. Table 2 shows what this assumption looks like when translated into a conditional probability matrix.

The initial fit of the model to the data indicated that a third parameter was needed. This third parameter attenuates the probability of moving to the next higher stage as a function of what stage one is in currently. What this meant was that for early moral development stages there was still a fairly large probability of moving to the next higher stage, but as one got more and more advanced, it became increasingly difficult to move out of one's current stage into the next higher one.

Table 2

Transitional Probability Matrix for
Kohlberg's Moral Development Theory

Current moral stage	Moral stage following a critical event					
	1	2	3	4	5	6
1	$1-p$	p				
2		$1-p$	p			
3			$1-p$	p		
4				$1-p$	p	
5					$1-p$	p
6						1.0

Finally, the "last" stage appears to so fully capture the person that it is almost impossible to move out of it into some presumably undefined "higher" stage.

As I said, this third parameter of attenuation appeared to be required in order to fit the data. It affects only the transitional probability matrix. This is shown in Table 3A. In Table 3B we see a numerical example of what the transitional probability matrix looks like for a particular value of p (here $p = .30$) and for a particular value of a (here $a = .80$). We see that along the main diagonal in Table 3B the probability of remaining in the same state is the largest entry in each row, and furthermore, these values of maintaining the same state *increase* as we move into the higher moral development stages.

We shall use these two findings of the Markov chain in order to construct a Cusp model of moral development; that is, we shall reintroduce our conception of conditional probability that applied to the S-shaped Fold curve in order to interpret why the probability of remaining in the same state is the *largest* entry in each row, and furthermore, we shall use the systematic increase in this holding state to rationalize the ever-increasing depth of overlap readily seen as a prominent aspect of the Cusp. Therefore, as one moves into higher and higher moral stages, this moves one forward along the folded part of the Cusp into the regions where the depth of overlap increases systematically. The increase in depth of folded overlap is here made analogous to the increase in the conditional probability of remaining in the same moral stage as one progresses forward in Kohlberg's theory. This is evident by examining Figure 4.

In order to further rationalize the choice of a Cusp representation of the quantitative results, we must also be prepared to label the three dimensions that are used to construct the Cusp, two of these typically being stimulus dimensions and the third a response dimension. One stimulus axis that propels the individual forward with the passage of time and experience is tentatively identified as the number of individuals who get implicated in each successively higher moral stage.

Table 3

Modified Matrix for Kohlberg's Moral Development
Theory and a Numerical Example

A. Kohlberg's moral development theory

Current moral stage	Moral stage following a critical event					
	1	2	3	4	5	6
1	$1-a^0 p$	$a^0 p$				
2		$1-a^1 p$	$a^1 p$			
3			$1-a^2 p$	$a^2 p$		
4				$1-a^3 p$	$a^3 p$	
5					$1-a^4 p$	$a^4 p$
6						1.0

B. Numerical example: $p = .30, a = .80$

Current moral stage	Moral stage following a critical event					
	1	2	3	4	5	6
1	.70	.30				
2		.76	.24			
3			.81	.19		
4				.85	.15	
5					.89	.11
6						1.00

For example, in the first stage the self is implicated, which amounts to one individual. In the next stage the mother and father (or perhaps the whole immediate family) get implicated in the moral framework (including oneself); this implicates at least three individuals. Next the individual must include not only the family but also larger social units, such as the immediate community or neighborhood. Then one implicates the whole class or society, the nation, and finally, all individuals of all nations into one's single code of morality. This sequence comprises one stimulus dimension.

Another stimulus dimension comes from the Markov chain that was fitted to the Kohlberg data. Each time that a hypothetical critical moral event occurs, on the average, for the population of subjects of a given age, the proportion of people that will be in each of the stages as a consequence of experiencing this moral event gets shifted upward into the higher moral stages. This distribution is calculated by multiplying the conditional probability matrix by the initial probability vector. One counts the number of times the matrix has to be multiplied by the vector in order to achieve a good fit to the observed data. This number provides an estimate of the average number of critical moral events that a particular distribution of individuals experienced to yield their current distribution of moral development stages. For the age range from 7 years to 11 years the number of estimated critical moral events ranged from 9 for the 7-year-olds to 20 for the 11-year-olds—these figures varied depending upon country and socioeconomic status of the populations, however. Therefore, if our Markovian model is correct, the younger population experienced on the average 9 critical events, while the older children experienced an average of 20. Hence, the second stimulus dimension of our Cusp model is hypothesized to be the number of critical moral events experienced. While the density per unit time of these critical events may vary somewhat from country to country, with the passage of "sufficient" time every group seems to converge upon a similar distribution, judging from Kohlberg's data.

In Figure 4 we can summarize our discussion of moral development by mapping and labeling the Cusp surface contained in a three-dimensional space. Several aspects of how the Cusp has been placed with respect to the axes deserve comment. Notice that Stage 6 of moral development begins to "touch" the axis labeled "Number of critical moral events" at some unspecified point; perhaps the exact place varies from individual to individual. In terms of our conditional probability argument made earlier in this chapter, this indicates that no other stage higher than Stage 6 can compete for attention; therefore, there is no way to leave Stage 6. In other words, the conditional probability of remaining in Stage 6, given that one is already in that stage, is equal to 1.00, as Table 3B indicates. Another unusual feature of Figure 4 is that we represent each moral stage twice: once *without* a prime, and then again *with* a prime. The significance of this is as follows. One's initial stage is assumed to start on the top part of the Cusp, the unprimed Stage 1. When a critical moral event is experienced, the individual slips precipitously over the leftmost edge of the top surface onto the lower surface. At this point the individual is in the primed stage (Stage 1′). The individual struggles with the import of this critical event and attempts to resolve the tension by either jumping up to the next higher stage (here, Stage 2), which implicates a larger number of individuals in the moral system, or by remaining in his or her current stage (Stage 1′) on the lower sheet of the Cusp. Notice that the only permissable path to jumping to the higher stage is by moving to the rightmost edge of the lower sheet and then jumping precipitously (catastrophically) upward onto the top sheet (an action somewhat hard to visualize given the way the figure is drawn). The proportion of individuals who successfully jump to the higher sheet—which is an index of the difficulty of resolving the moral dilemma—gets smaller and smaller as one moves forward in the Cusp figure. This occurs in our representation of the Cusp because the amount of surface along which one can move once one is on the lower sheet *increases* as one moves into the higher primed stages. Because this surface increases while the competing surface of the top sheet decreases, one generates larger and larger conditional probabilities of remaining in the current moral stage as one moves higher and higher up the moral "ladder." Finally, when one reaches Stage 6, one's further progression is "blocked," even with the experience of additional critical moral events, because the top surface of the Cusp in the region of Stage 6 does not allow one to slip over the leftmost edge onto the lower sheet. The blockage occurs because the top sheet touches the axis (and the dimensional space is not defined beyond that point).

Obviously many fine points should be worked out in exploring other ways to represent Kohlberg's theory; the current theory is meant to provide heuristic stimulation for using topological theory in advancing our ideas about human development. Before we leave this topic, though, we should point out that the concept of hysteresis is here represented by the different patterns of conditional probabilities of advancing to higher stages—as such, moral development is less obviously a Thomian model than was the case for the simple threshold. Precipitous change in moral development (the movement to a primed stage for struggling with moral dilemmas and the further sudden synthesis of higher moral principles) is here more in the nature of hypothesis in need of demonstration. Divergence in the model is presumably related to the following: The experiencing of a simple story that contains a moral dilemma—certainly a small enough event—can turn the person precipitously into an emotionally aroused person grappling with issues that one had falsely believed had been fully thought out. Biomodality and inaccessibility are also easily found in our model. But at this point one begins to suspect that a much more complex topological model will have to be considered in order to account for the cognitive issues that lie behind the moral principles. The present topological model is perhaps too restrictive in allowing only two stimuli parameters to "explain" moral development. It appears that what it does explain are *some* aspects of the quantitative and qualitative movement of populations through neatly labeled moral categories. Possibly Thomian models involving higher dimensional Cusps—the Cuspoids—or the class of topological models called *Umbilics* may have to be studied and pursued before an adequate information-processing account of moral development can be obtained. This possibility remains to be realized.

V. The Cusp Model of the Threshold

We return to the sensory threshold in order to convey how one might go about embellishing the simpler model as soon as additional stimulus dimensions are known to contribute to the effect. First we consider how varying the intertrial interval of a graded series of ascending (or descending) intensities of fixed size may affect the location of points of sudden transition in response probability.

When the intertrial interval for an ascending (or descending) series is quite long, we anticipate that this will generate an S-shaped curve near the rear of the Cusp. When this intertrial interval is systematically shortened, we begin to move forward in the Cusp, so that the magnitude of the hysteresis effect gets larger and larger.

We can also anticipate that for auditory thresholds as the pitch is systematically varied, a number of slightly different Cusp forms will be generated. Similarly for visual thresholds, as the wavelength is varied over experiments, a number of interrelated Cusps are likely to be generated. Combining all these Cusps together may lead to a higher-dimensional Cuspoid to represent all the results on a single topological surface. However, such a possibility remains to be seen.

For visual-intensity effects we can rationalize the Cusp model as follows: Just as Zeeman (1973) attempted to analyze the stimulus dimensions of the Cusp model of the heartbeat into a more detailed treatment of the neurochemical events that underlie these dimensions, so too might we inquire what biochemical events underlie our particular Cusp model interrelating intensity and intertrial interval with signal-detection probabilities. One possibility, which stems from early theoretical work of Hecht (cited in Stevens, 1951), is that the rate of the formation of decay of visual rhodopsin is systematically tied to the graded series of ascending and descending stimulus intensities and the intertrial interval. We still need the Cusp model to summarize the hypothetical findings, but if Hecht's ideas are relevant, we have reduced the complexity of the topological model to more analytic terms. A further possibility involving stimulus traces over trials was outlined in an earlier paper (Freedle, 1971).

Stevens (1957) speculated, on the basis of several experimental results, that prothetic continua (such as visual brightness, auditory loudness, and other intensive continua) may all show evidence of hysteresis effects, using the method of bisection. Metathetic continua (such as judging visual position and possibly auditory pitch changes) may not reveal hysteresis effects. As already mentioned, we can use these findings to speculate that a Cusp model may be required to summarize the hysteresis effects for ascending and descending series as a function of visual wavelength. A particular experiment selects a particular wavelength and generates an S-shaped curve from the ascending and descending method of limits. Another group of experiments varies the wavelength but carries out basically the same procedure. Collecting the S-shaped curves together from each of these experiments should generate the Cusp surface as a more general model. Other Cusp models for each of the prothetic continua could easily be suggested here.

VI. The Butterfly Cuspoid as a Model
for Some Psychological Phenomena

The next most frequently employed Cusp model involves four stimulus dimensions and one behavior dimension; it is called the Butterfly. Actually our representation of it will be with respect to the control space—one dimension less than the full model. Just as in Figure 4 we saw that the two-dimensional triangular control space was a projection from the three-dimensional Cusp onto a flat two-dimensional surface below it, so too we should remember that the three-dimensional control space for the Butterfly is actually a projection from a four-dimensional surface. Since we cannot visualize such a space, we will have to make do with the control space to guide our creative intuitions.

In Figure 5 we see that we still have part of the control space which forms S-shaped curves that gather together into the form of Cusps; but now there are three such Cusps on the same surface. Three distinct levels of the surface can be visualized: the lower surface and the upper surface (just like in the single Cusp model) and an intermediate surface, which links the lower to the upper surface by another route. We can still have a precipitous behavioral catastrophe by following Route 1 from the bottom sheet to the top sheet or by following Route 2, which takes us quickly from the top to the bottom sheet. In addition we can have a slow, smoother transition from the bottom to the top by following Route 3, and from the top to the bottom by following Route 4.

I shall now very quickly cover several sensoriperceptual phenomena at the level of intrapersonal behaviors in order to show the usefulness of this intermediate stage; then later I shall cover one example of interpersonal behavior at the level of societal change over generations.

A. Visual Illusion

For illusions that change as a function of time (as opposed to those that are static, such as the Muller–Lyer illusion), we have interesting prospects for modeling the changes of perceptual state. For the so-called staircase illusion, if we stare at a line drawing of a staircase (two-dimensional and without shading), we will typically see the staircase from several perspectives: from above looking down on the staircase, from below the staircase looking upward, and as some unclear intermediate phase that is either some mixture of the two other states or simply the perception of the drawing as a flat surface (which is what it is). Sometimes the time it takes to switch from seeing the staircase from below to seeing it from above (or vice versa) can be quite rapid, and sometimes it appears to be a slower progression that involves the intermediate state. We can suggest that, with respect to the general surface represented by Figure 5, if we let the lower sheet represent seeing the staircase from below, there are two pathways leading to the top sheet, which shall represent seeing the staircase from above. The two paths are designated by Routes 1 and 3. Route 1 is a fast transition, while Route 3 is a slow progression that involves the intermediate transition stage. Since the illusion is reversible, we see that two other routes are also possible in moving from seeing the staircase from above to seeing it from below. Routes 2 and 4 show the two most likely pathways, with Route 2 being a fast, precipitous route, while Route 4 is a slow one. We can also represent the tendency, if any, to persist more in one state than in another (the conditional probability argument) by varying the relative surface areas of the three states. This may vary from individual to individual.

B. Binocular Rivalry

A second interesting phenomenon, which I have tested on myself, is binocular rivalry. Place a transparent red cellophane over the left eyepiece of a stereoscope and a green cellophane over the right eyepiece. Look into the stereoscope. You will find three states occurring: You will see either just green or just red, or you will see

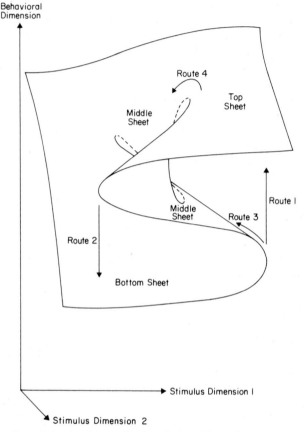

Fig. 5. The three-dimensional control space of a four-dimensional Butterfly Cuspoid.

some vague mixture of the two. These comprise the three states of the system. Sometimes the transitions are rapid and sometimes slow. The mapping of this phenomenon proceeds much as it did for the visual illusion; I leave the details to the reader.

C. Logical Contradiction on the Butterfly Surface

This section provides a bridge with a more general comment about the import of standard versus nonstandard logics in developmental theory. Here we point out that on the surface of the Butterfly control space we can violate a second Aristotelian axiom: the law of contradiction. Aristotle did not allow the following statements to be true at the same time: "A is true"; "Not A is true." On the Cusp surface we previously noted that the law of the excluded middle is violated. Here on the Butterfly surface we note that the law of contradiction is violated. This can be seen by letting the top sheet be "A is true" and the bottom sheet represent "Not A is true." The middle sheet then represents some mixture of these two states: "Both A and not A are true." If our interpretation is correct, this constitutes a violation of Aristotle's law. This raises the potentiality of modeling some of the deviant logics that have been recently discovered (Haack, 1974; Wolf, 1975) onto Thomian surfaces. The virtue of finding such a mapping is that it is hard to grasp the significance of algebraic statements but relatively easy to gain insight if these statements are easily visualized on some geometric surface. This was the motivation behind the attempted mapping of deviant logical laws onto Thomian surfaces.

VII. Deviant Algebraic Logic and Its Import for Developmental Theory

Apart from whether our mapping of logical violations of Aristotle's axioms is or is not correct, we can still legitimately pursue the concept of algebraic models of deviant logic as an important clarification of developmental issues. In this section I consider why development must concern itself with issues such as logical contradiction. I then suggest a few nonstandard logical models such as Relevant Logics and Meinongian logic as important foundations for studying commonly occurring behaviors in development—such behaviors as conservation of volume and verbal fantasy (see Freedle, 1977, for detailed examples).

Propositional and predicate logic as well as group theory have figured prominently in Piaget's theorizing about development (e.g., Flavell, 1963; Inhelder & Piaget, 1958; Parsons, 1960). In this way a model of the structural changes in thought has been constructed to show how the child's increasingly complex thought processes reflect the external contingencies of the physical world, such as the laws of the conservation of matter. Yet, fundamental advances in metamathematical theory concerning mathematics (including logic and group theory) raise the following difficulty for such theories: Assuming that behavior, beliefs, and knowledge can be axiomatized into a set of logical propositions with laws of composition (operations), *the more complex and complete* we make our developmental theory in terms of adding more operations and more interpretive axioms for each area of cognitive competence, the more likely it is that we increase the occurrence of internal inconsistencies (logical contradictions) in the theory. This is true for theories based on *classical logic*. In such theories, when a single contradiction is found, the whole system collapses, since any proposition can be proven to be true; hence, contradictions abound. This observation should motivate our search for non-Aristotelian logics as a way out of this difficulty.

Using classical logic as a base, as the child moves from concrete operational thinking to formal operations, so as to reveal the lawfulness of operating upon the world that goes beyond the particularized situations for which earlier stages were adequate representations, he runs the risk of moving from logical consistency to logical inconsistency. This is certainly a true dilemma for models based on classical logic, since the person has enlarged and generalized his theory of the world so as to increase his power of prediction and problem solving. Yet, this gain in generality is often at the cost of logical inconsistency. (An example of logical inconsistency would be to choose proposition Q by one route of reasoning in the more complex system and then to choose the opposite of Q, that is, −Q, by another route of reasoning but with the *same* theory.) Of course, if one chooses not to increase the complexity and scope of one's model of the world, one runs the risk of describing and explaining too little of the world, and hence the risk of remaining trivial and superficial.

Thus, if only classical logic is used as the base model plus additional axioms that semantically interpret this logic for different experimental settings and different behavioral domains, then we as individuals must be faced with fundamental contradictions in our reasoning as we move higher and higher toward a more complete and abstract systematization of knowledge. Similarly, we as scientists who develop more and more complex theories (using classical logic) run the risk of violating what appears to be a "sacred" principle of theory construction, namely, logical consistency.

If one insists that classical logic is appropriate for theory construction in development, there is a possibility that suggests itself as a way of minimizing the occurrence of logical inconsistency. Consistency may be retained by developing a separate system of principles for each situation or area in which one uses logical structures. What this amounts to is an assumption of parallel development of somewhat similar reasoning principles, wherein each system is restricted to the area of experience to which it applies. This might work in development when the individual has not yet concerned himself with whether logical consistency or the same principles hold across various domains of experience. The fact that some subsystems may share similar principles may not automatically initiate a search for total consistency using a single overall system of thought. The existence of a decalage effect across different conservation tasks, for example, suggests that a parallel development hypothesis may not be too farfetched, yet as theorists, we tend to avoid such hypotheses because they contravene the concept of parsimonious theory construction.

The foregoing picture is bleak in its implications for general theory construction, but there is a way out.

Human language has been the source of many mathematical systems, including classical logic. In its variety, human language also has suggested the existence of logical systems such as modal logic ("John *can* walk vs. "John *is* walking"), temporal logics ("John walked" vs "John is walking"), and other logics, to be sketched momentarily. Classical logic deals with *present-tense declarative statements* and so is a very special subset of the richness that language allows. Because classical logic is so restrictive in its range, it seems implausible and unfortunate that it alone should be used to model the complexities of thought and the changes in thought operations over the course of human development.

A little thought will indicate that the other logical structures are prevalent in early development. For example, when a child first entertains a mapping of some fictional world onto the real world, he is acting like a proponent of what is called Meinongian logic (Wolf, 1975). Why is this? When a child says, "Let's *pretend* that this box is a castle," he is violating classical logic because, since the time of Bertrand Russell's work, classical logic is intended to refer to existent real-world items and to specifically exclude nonexistent or impossible items. But to the child it is meaningful and significant to exercise his imaginative powers. He will push forward, ignoring the classical logicians, and imagine that box to be a castle, a car, a fearful tunnel, or whatever. So what? This example should alert developmentalists to the possibility that there is more richness allowable in theory construction than is made evident by the restrictive propositional- or predicate-logic formats. This does not mean that classical logic never applies; instead, it suggests that different situations are sometimes well modeled (in a scientific sense) by nonclassical logics (and there are many), while at other times, and for other situations, classical logic may very well be adequate.

The idea that logical consistency (noncontradictory propositions) is a necessary aspect of any logical system is false. Recent axiomatization of different types of logic (Wolf, 1975) indicates that systems can be categorized as either *locally* or *globally* inconsistent. When they are global, we get the dilemmas presented in the early part of this section for theories built on classical logic, such as Piaget's. When they are of the type that produces only local inconsistencies, the dilemma does not threaten to disrupt the foundations of our thought processes. In like manner, the local-inconsistency systems appear to be more realistic models of how scientists themselves construct their formal theories when they are working in the so-called "normal" paradigm mode (see Kuhn, 1970, for a discussion of the rational behaviors associated with the normal paradigm mode as contrasted with the nonanalytic behaviors associated with the challenge of innovative paradigms). In the normal paradigm mode, if the data do not fit the predictions of theory, the theory is not totally discarded because of a single inconsistency. Rather, it is slightly modified to try to accommodate the new data. Such a conception leads to a somewhat different emphasis than Piaget's analysis would allow. The reason is that Piaget's model employs a classical logic, and if strictly applied, *any* inconsistency between data and theory should yield total system breakdown. True, Piaget may not have claimed such a rigid adherence to classical logic, but the fact remains that he has not provided us with an alternative foundation that *can* accommodate to internal contradictions.

Some of the new logics that are capable of dealing with local inconsistency are called *Relevant Logics* or *R-logics*. They are meant to formalize our intuition that we should worry about inconsistency only when comparing propositions M and N that share variables or are semantically related to each other. If a contradiction occurs elsewhere in the system of propositions (say, S and −S occurs, where S is not related to M or N), it will not disrupt our thinking about M and N because contradictions are localized to just those propositions that share a similar meaning.

The foregoing would appear to be an appropriate foundation for theorizing about the laws of conservation that lead to variable (contradictory) results when new materials are introduced into the experimental task (as in substituting clay for water in testing for the conservation of volume). When different substances give different results, one might inquire whether separate learning configurations have occurred in constructing a cognitive rule representation for each substance. This does not exclude the possibility that with further development the child may discover that a more inclusive system applies to many or all substances that can evenly fill the volume of some container. If the child discovers this, he may *seem* to move toward an abandonment of a Relevant Logics foundation, but not necessarily. He may have generalized only *some* features that define his criterion of what proposition is semantically relevant to another proposition. Totally to abandon a semantic-relevance criterion (as in classical logic) in his reasoning about the world will place him again at the mercy of total breakdown with the occurrence of a single contradiction. To avoid this, the suggestion is here made that as the individual develops and reasons about such restricted phenomena as conservation, he alters the *scope* of his base relevance features. In so doing, he still is assumed to operate within the foundations of a Relevant Logic but has slightly altered the semantic components of his logical system.

It is not my intention in this section to review all new logical systems since there are many: Meinongian Logic, 15 or more Temporal Logics, Modal Logics, Relevant Logics, Dialectical Logics, and so on. Furthermore, for each such logic there is a syntactic, semantic, and pragmatic elaboration needed to adapt the theory for scientific-modeling purposes. Establishment of such elaborations would clearly be a monumental task. My real purpose in the foregoing has been to sound a note of pessimism about theories that rest on a classical foundation, such as Piaget's, and to point out the reasonableness of using other logics for modeling problems in human development. That such a new orientation should also be related to the new theoretical breakthrough of Thomian topological surfaces, as suggested earlier, is a stroke of good fortune, since we scientists can use all the iconic aids that we can lay our hands on in order to select from and work within the difficult framework of pure algebraic logic.

VIII. Development as a Sequence of Topological Surfaces

To motivate our search for a classification of sequences of topological surfaces over developmental stages, consider the following example.

Given cohort differences, one postulates that different generations (the time period may vary from 10 to 20 years or so) may have experienced such different developmental environments that they each end up with very different cognitive orientations to the external world. The political radicalism of the 1960s seems to have allowed only two cognitive states—political involvement or indifference. With the onset of the 1970s three cognitive states seem to be emerging—we still find those who are either politically involved or indifferent, but now we also find a group that expresses a profound political cynicism. This last group seems to represent stimultaneously an attitude of cognitive awareness plus emotional indifference to political issues. For the sake of illustration, suppose we imagine that the individuals growing up in the 1960s could be represented using the Cusp as a model for sudden transitions in behavior from being politically neutral to being suddenly politically radicalized (and vice versa). However, let us suppose that the new developments of the 1970s require a Butterfly surface to represent the third new group of individuals who grow up expressing an attitude of political cynicism, this being represented by the so-called middle sheet of the Butterfly control surface. If so, then cohort differences have been modeled as a *transition sequence from a simple Cusp to a more complex Butterfly.* What I propose in Table 4 is a classification of a number of such sequences of the Cuspoids to represent a wide variety of sequential patternings of developmental stages. The table illustrates only transitions among the Cuspoids so as to keep the number of patterns manageable, but a fuller table could easily be drawn up not only using the Umbilics at various places in the sequencings but also including *n*-dimensional Euclidean space as alternative elements in the sequences.

Table 4

A Representation of Development from the Perspective of Sequences of Topological Surfaces

Symbol designating the topological sequence	Earliest topological form	Subsequent topological form(s)	Comment
U	Fold	Cusp, then Butterfly	Increasing complexity of Cuspoid
V	Butterfly	Cusp, then Fold	Decreasing complexity of Cuspoid
W	Cusp	Fold or Butterfly	Development is viewed as a choice point either to a surface of decreased complexity (e.g., Cusp to Fold) or to increased complexity (e.g., Cusp to Butterfly)
X	Fold or Butterfly	Cusp	Development is viewed as a convergence to a surface of intermediate complexity
Y	Cusp	Fold, then Butterfly	A U-shaped transition of complexity is suggested over time
Z	Fold	Butterfly, then Cusp	An inverted U-shaped transition is suggested over stages

The entries in Table 4 are self-evident. We have suggested patterns that increase systematically in complexity over time or decrease systematically. We have convergent and divergent sequences and we have sequences that are U-shaped or inverted U-shaped in complexity over time. Cyclically reoccurring patterns might also have been included, but they would be difficult to represent within the format of Table 4. For each of these sequences it would be a stimulating exercise in creative discovery to find developmental examples that may be interpreted from within the framework not only of a topological perspective but also from the viewpoint of what conditions in development lead to the changes in topological complexity. Furthermore, one would like many examples that would follow out in detail the nature of logical violations occurring for each topological surface and to examine the consequences for gross behavior as well as the manifestations at the level of cognitive awareness.

To carry out this enterprise and to exploit the new intellectual tools of theory construction made possible by topology and nonstandard logic must involve a creative group effort among developmentalists. A new paradigm is now available; let us work cooperatively to make it a reality.

REFERENCES

Flavell, J. *The developmental psychology of Jean Piaget.* Princeton: Van Nostrand, 1963.

Freedle, R. Review of Coombs-Dawes-Tversky and Restle-Greeno mathematical psychology texts. *Psychometrika,* 1971, **36,** 322–328.

Freedle, R. Dialogue and inquiring systems: Towards the development of a social logic. *Human Development,* 1975, **18,** 97–118.

Freedle, R. Human development, the new logical systems, and general systems theory: preliminaries to the development of a psychosocial linguistics. In G. Steiner (Ed.), *Piaget, and beyond.* Zurich: Kindler, 1976.

Freedle, R. *Thomian topologies for doubting psychologists: Non-Newtonian and non-Aristotelian perspectives.* Hillsdale, N.J.: Lawrence Erlbaum Associates, 1978.

Freedle, R., & Lewis, M. Application of Markov processes to the concept of state. (ETS RB 71-34.) Princeton, N.J.: Educational Testing Service, 1971.

Freedle, R., & Lewis, M. Prelinguistic conversations. In M. Lewis & L. Rosenblum (Eds.), *Communication and language development.* New York: Wiley, 1976.

Haack, S. *Deviant logics.* London & New York: Cambridge University Press, 1974.

Inhelder, B., & Piaget, J. *The growth of logical thinking from childhood to adolescence.* New York: Basic Books, 1958.

Kohlberg, L. Development of moral character and moral ideology. In M. L. Hoffman & L. W. Hoffman (Eds.), *Review of child development research* (Vol. 1). New York: Russell Sage Foundation, 1964.

Kuhn, T. *The structure of scientific revolutions* (2nd ed.). Chicago: University of Chicago Press, 1970.

Lewis, M., & Freedle, R. Mother-infant dyad: The cradle of meaning. In P. Pliner, L. Krames, & T. Alloway (Eds.), *Communication and affect: Language and thought.* New York: Academic Press, 1973.

Luce, R. D. Detection and recognition. In R. D. Luce, R. Bush, & E. Galanter (Eds.), *Handbook of mathematical psychology* (Vol. 1). New York: Wiley, 1963.

Luce, R. D., & Galanter, E. Psychophysical scaling. In R. D. Luce, R. Bush, & E. Galanter (Eds.), *Handbook of mathematical psychology* (Vol. 1). New York: Wiley, 1963.

Parsons, C. Inhelder and Piaget's growth of logical thinking. Review article. *British Journal of Psychology,* 1960, **51,** 75–84.

Stevens, S. S. (Ed.). *Handbook of experimental psychology.* New York: Wiley, 1951.

Stevens, S. S. On the psychophysical law. *Psychological Review,* 1957, **64,** 153–181.

Swets, J. A. (Ed.). *Signal detection and recognition by human observers.* New York: Wiley, 1964.

Thom, R. *Structural stability and morphogenesis.* Reading, Mass.: Benjamin, 1975.

Wolf, R. *Contradictions and logical systems.* Paper presented at the conference Dialectics: Paradigm for the social sciences, York University, Toronto, 1975.

Zeeman, E. C. Differential equations for the heartbeat and nerve impulse. In M. M. Peixoto (Ed.), *Dynamical systems.* New York: Academic Press, 1973.

CHAPTER 18

Early Experience as the Basis for Unity and Cooperation of "Differences"[1]

HERBERT KAYE

STATE UNIVERSITY OF NEW YORK
STONY BROOK, NEW YORK

I. The Preamble Ramble

This chapter is presumptuous in its attempt to integrate the philosophy of science and developmental psychology—although it is not without precedent. The current attempt is undoubtedly highly speculative and logically flawed. However, the author's attempt is prompted by his feeling that the field of developmental psychology is suffocating under the pile of its own meaningless research. The research suffers in part from methodological inadequacies, which are only secondarily a focus of this chapter. More seriously, the field of developmental psychology suffers from an overabundance of models and quasi-theories, and few guidelines for relating research to these systems. This has prompted researchers to plug their results willy-nilly into whatever theoretical framework relates to their personal bias, regardless of the relationship of their empirical work to their specific theories' implicit constraints. Because of the impossibility of a smooth interface between this heuristically organized empirical work and any one theoretical framework, it becomes necessary to bridge the data gap with hypothetical constructs; these often generate a whole new research area whose relationship to a theoretical "reality" is one further step removed from the theory's methodological requirements. And so, paper is piled on paper, intervening constructs lose their primary evaluation in independent verification, and the field slowly suffocates.

[1] This paper was prepared, in part, with assistance from NICHD Grant No. R01-HD09867.

These problems are multiplied manyfold by the continuous failure to replicate major empirical findings. However, even if we were to assume the impossible dream that all published research was replicable, the problem would not be solved. For as the field of developmental psychology has grown, two strategies have emerged that have increased the thanatotic syndrome. The first is the assumption that leveling or control variables such as age, sex, social class, and ethnicity are *atheoretical*. The second is that *all* developmental phenomena must be explainable within the structure of a given developmental theory for that theory to be useful. We will not focus on the first problem in this chapter other than to suggest strongly that these control variables are neither atheoretical, nor is their use in most experiments without its destructive consequences. However, the second problem is more widely critical, and in discussing its consequences, there may emerge the solution to how one should handle the first problem.

In particular, the second problem relates to the question of whether all developmental phenomena can be explained within the limited set of presuppositions that make up the features of any given developmental theory. (By way of example, the attempt to describe, in the context of a behavioristic approach to development, the "learning" of conservation of volume, in which "conservation of volume" is derived from cognitive theory, is not meaningful.)

These presuppositions to which I have referred above form the implicit dimensions of those constructs explicitly employed in a given theory. Constructs, when integrated into theory-related empirical studies, carry implicit constraints on how relationships to other constructs may be interpreted. Constructs whose presuppositional characteristics or features are antagonistic should not be correlated. The attempt to correlate any two phenomena without regard to their presuppositional features provides no more than an exercise in mathematics. Interpretation of these correlations is impossible unless the potential weighting of the similarities and differences in presuppositional features can be decided on, and for this the presuppositions must be understood. In developmental psychology there are at least four major approaches to the sequential organization of behavior over time. These are the biobehavioral, the behavioristic, the cognitive, and the psychoanalytic approaches. Of the four, the feature differences could probably be arrayed in an 18-dimensional space using the dichotomous prescriptive terms proposed by Watson (1967).

However, since 18 dichotomies taken two or more at a time yield a very large number of possible presuppositional sets, it is obvious that some a priori weighting system has to be employed to derive hierarchical theory families. None of this sort of theory evaluation has been more than primitively carried out in any of the sciences, and for developmental psychology, the features of the four approaches are only vaguely understood (Langer, 1969) and often disagreed upon. In lieu of a theory of family hierarchy, overgeneralized models seem to have served as a theoretical sorting agent.

Several years ago Reese and Overton (1970) and Overton and Reese (1973) suggested that two different models typified the major approaches employed by developmental psychologists. Taking a page from Pepper's (1942/1961) thesis on world hypotheses, they indicated that the mechanistic and organismic models allowed one to dichotomize certain prescriptive elements in ways that provided a shopper's guide to fulfillment in theory buying. They described the mechanistic model as one that views humans as reactive, atomistically constructed of parts whose characteristics are quantifiable and whose interaction with other phenomena is, in principle, predictable. The parts assemble into wholes according to the properties of the parts, and thus, also in principle, there are no new laws needed to describe emergent forms.

The organismic approach, in contrast, was described as a view of the organism as active, holistic, not strictly quantifiable, qualitatively novel in emergent characteristics, and, in principle, not predictable in its interactions with other phenomena.

Furthermore, they suggested that different world views, as metaphors, could not be mixed. "If two theorists adopt different basic models, there can be no fruitful debate between them; their views are irreconcilable. Between theories in the same family [we assume they mean models], however, there may be debate or disagreement; but even so, there can be no issues of theory construction—no metatheoretical issues [Reese & Overton, 1970, p. 129]."

At first, this comforted me since it made it no longer necessary for me to debate with the nonbehaviorists who made up the opposing camp. But then, this began to disturb me. Was I, as a developmental psychologist, doomed to study all phenomena in terms of unidirectional, deterministic, push–pull, atomistic notions simply because this approach best fit a set of studies I devoted myself to in one area of my work? Could I not study different phenomena using different world views? After all, in analyzing my everyday life, I would be hardpressed to fit my approach to different phenomena within a single set of presuppositions; that is, I feel that I bring different notions of time, space, causality, reality, and so on, to bear on the problems, issues, and cognized goals of my experiential world. However, this coexistence does not obviously refer to the same classes of events (job, family life, political orientation, economic organization, etc.) in my universe, and thus, the contradiction and eclecticism of which I might be accused is not (overly) apparent. But if I can dwell in several world views with respect to my everyday life, why shouldn't this possibility exist within my general field of study, where the structures of experience often seem quite independent and minimally related? It would seem that many of the phenomena in psychology, as is true of the phenomena in my everyday life, do not yield easily to a single system of organization, but seem most efficiently explained by theories with different presuppositions.

In essence, this chapter is designed as an attempt to reconcile the cognitive basis of my scholarly pursuits with my everyday mode of operating. There will be some personal satisfaction and momentary peace of mind in arriving at a coherence between these two aspects of my existence. It may be the case that this satisfaction will be mine alone. However, in the context of this volume, that sort of motivation cannot be faulted. It seems that the theoretical and often speculative presentations in this book have often satisfied most of the individual predilections of their authors'. I hope, nevertheless, that the general problem of merging and separating the many issues and relationships we consider to exist in psychology may be aided; and, in this process, perhaps some of the issues that have generated excessive quantities of paper may be placed in an orderly perspective. This chapter can be considered to be an outline, rather than a complete thesis. A great deal of exemplification could be added, but the limits of writing space and preparation time prohibit full support for a proposal such as this. In addition, aside from Pepper (1942/1961), whose argument for world hypotheses forms the basic point of departure for this chapter, few of the other scholars whose thoughts have contributed to the author's thinking have been cited. They may well apreciate that fact.

And so, I offer the following intuitive constructions for the reader's consideration.

II. Introduction

The point of departure for these considerations is the author's evaluation of the field of psychology as a nonunified and ultimately nonunifiable discipline. Rather than there being one psychology, there are many psychologies, not only with respect to academic topics and theories, but also from the more fundamental perspective of the phenomenal organization of everyday experience. Although it would seem that a multidimensional perspective should dictate families of holistic unities, in my vision of reality things are nested within things, relate as things to things (within limits), defy total absorption, and moreover, exist in several contexts simultaneously.

There is, in the course of writing these lines (as an example of a phenomenon), a multileveled, autonomous set of events that are separable (sentences divided into words), mergeable (letters organized as words), analyzable as parts-to-wholes (phoneme-to-phoneme clusters), wholes-to-wholes (semantics), and wholes dictating parts (syntax). These relationships are not easily fitted within a single topic in psychology, since the total event exists, ultimately, in the context of all events in the current cultural epoch. Furthermore, the various components do not fit within a single theory since the structural components of the event each fit into separately developed, relatively autonomous frameworks. The event of the above sentence, in addition, consists of placing ink on paper, forming motor patterns in complex sequences, coordinating intersensory signals, sequencing symbolic units, ignoring extraneous events, planning means toward ends, self-correcting, taking readership and page limits into account, and so on. Each of these dimensions calls out cognitive evaluations that represent very different categories. In terms of space and time, these various events exist (more or less) in the phenomenal present, and each can be focused on separately or in the context of the others. Explaining these various components in all these relationships is the goal of psychology; understanding the theories of explanation is the goal of the philosophy of science.

With respect to this latter goal, Pepper (1942/1961) published a creative philosophical thesis that has had a growing influence on theoretical considerations for structuring scientific systems. It is the basis for some of the suggestions made by Reese and Overton (1970).

Pepper's thesis is simple in conceptualization and complex in implication for psychology, and, in particular, developmental psychology. In brief, he suggests that approaches to the structure of theory, which he calls "world hypotheses," are based on *root metaphors*. A root metaphor (as I interpret it) is a concept arising from the experience of a relationship or set of events that is so powerful or salient that it provides the organizational basis for cognitive presuppositions; that is, these root metaphors provide certain ontological implications for the critical cognizing of theoretical structures. The abstraction of the constructs of reality from the root metaphor provides the basic categories or presuppositions of a particular world hypothesis. Each of the world hypotheses provides a different means for establishing the truth that corroborates the structure of its particular theories. A world hypothesis is all-encompassing. Pepper admits to the potential availability of several root metaphors on which theory could be built but provides a critical analysis of only four that he feels are currently adequate to the task of organizing the various areas of philosophy, science, history, and so on. Because the current author feels that some of Pepper's argument has been misconstrued or "selectively" generalized, and because the structure of Pepper's argument is necessary to the argument in this essay, a brief outline of the features of his theory will be presented. After reviewing his theory, some suggestions will be made concerning how the notions of world hypotheses can be more meaningfully fitted to current topics in psychology in general, and specifically to developmental psychology. The title of this chapter will be "folded into" the conclusions.

III. Pepper's Schema

Following a section in which Pepper (1942/1961) argues against the philosophical stance of dogmatism and skepticism, he suggests that all knowledge starts from the "prerefined, preanalytic cognitive material" called "common sense (p. 39)." This mass of material related to our cognizing of everyday experience is secure because it is the ubiquitous uncritical accompaniment of our ongoing activity, but this material is also highly questionable and inexact since it is not, in this initial state, the subject of critical evaluation.

The development of the less refined levels of common sense into more refined levels of knowledge takes place, according to Pepper (1942/1961), in two ways: through multiplicative corroboration and through structural corroboration:

We noted two main types of corroboration, which we called multiplicative and structural.

Multiplicative corroboration consists in attesting to the repetition of the "identical" item of evidence in many different instances. . . .

Structural corroboration requires a theory or hypothesis for the connection of the various items of evidence, and what is said to be corroborated here by the convergence of evidence is not so much the evidence itself as the theory which connects it together [pp. 47, 48].

He then critically separates data from danda; the former being associated with multiplicative corroboration, the later with structural corroboration. Data he associated with the atheoretical position of the positivists; danda being facts whose specifics are controlled by the theories to which they apply as evidence. (The attempt to set off positivism as opposed to the structural attributes of world hypotheses he himself criticizes, but this cannot be gone into in any detail. Suffice it to say that positivists, when forced to admit to their presuppositions, appear to fit most easily into one of the four world hypotheses to be discussed.)

As mentioned, Pepper suggests that there are four basic world hypotheses which represent the primary characteristics of thinking in a number of scholarly areas: these labeled *formism, mechanism, contextualism,* and *organicism.* Each has its intuited root metaphor in commonsense experience, and each provides a set of presuppositions (categories) that constrain both the ways in which the world may be organized and the ways in which "truth" may be evaluated. He points to two general criteria for the evaluation of the adequacy of a world hypothesis: precision and scope. Precision has to do with the specifiability of the facts of evidence, be they in the context of description or prediction. Scope, on the other hand, tends inevitably toward an inclusion of all evidence in its structure. (Further on, we will focus in detail on this requirement of world hypotheses. There is a potentially important contradiction in the notion of all-inclusiveness that relates to the current chapter.)

The root metaphor not only serves as an entree to the critical cognitive appraisal of knowledge but, in addition, helps reduce the number of potential world hypotheses from a huge number to a manageable few. Although Pepper suggests that there are only eight or ten root metaphors, he only names three in addition to the four above: these are animism, mysticism, and mythology. The first two are discredited in detail; animism for lack of precision, mysticism for lack of scope. Mythology is merely mentioned.

The four adequate world hypotheses will now be described in brief detail. This will provide little more than a feeling for the complexity and potential elegance of Pepper's proposal.

A. Formism

The root metaphor for formism is *similarity.* However, there are two sources of the commonsense notion of similarity. The first is the simple comparison of object with object, called imanent formism. The second is the similarity of object with plan, called transcendent formism. Although closely allied, they have some different basic categories. "Formism is often called 'realism' or 'Platonic idealism' and is associated with Plato, Aristotle, the scholastics, neoscholastics, neorealists, and modern Cambridge realists [Pepper, 1942/1961, p. 141]." Formism is *analytic*, facts being basically in the form of elements, and *dispersive*, in that facts are fitted to structure as they arise. Formism, in general, is considered to be weaker in precision than in scope.

1. Immanent Formism

Two basic categories of immanent formism are *particularity* and *quality*. These are distinct, although always integrated. However, "[any] number of particulars may have a single quality, and any number of qualities may characterize a single particular [Pepper, 1942/1961, p. 153]."

There are several other categories. Each describes critical properties of the formistic system. For example, from the analytic perspective, a *relationship* is the pairing of particulars that have a given quality. The term for the merging of relations and qualities is *character*, and the particularization of a character is called *participation, attribution,* or *predication.* Other categories of the system that are relationlike, such as "otherness" or "difference," are called *ties. Classes* are collections of particulars that participate in one or more characters.

2. Transcendent Formism

The basic categories of transcendent formism are (a) norms; (b) matter for the exemplification of norms; and (c) a principle of exemplification which materializes the norms. Again, each of these characterizes the basic presuppositions of this general approach. Norms characterize the notion of the plan. Norms and classes differ in that classes include within their purview a group of particulars, whereas norms relate in a vaguer way to exemplifications that radiate in degrees of less and less similarity out from the norms' description. The suggested amalgamation of these two types of formism is based on the notion that characters may be able to participate in norms, and norms can be considered as particulars of a second order. In this scheme, transcendent categories can be superimposed on immanent categories.

Causality, in both types of formism, "is the result of the participation of patterns, norms, or laws in basic particulars through the forms of time and space [Pepper, 1942/1961, p. 175]. "Laws are "bridges from one set of basic particulars to another set, determining the character of one set of basic particulars to another set, determining the character of one set by those of the other [Pepper, 1942/1961, p. 177]." "A law is a form... 'but' ... is not to be identified with a concrete existence." This is one of the major differences between formism and mechanism. "The theory of truth which grows out of formistic categories is the correspondence theory. Truth consists in a similarity or correspondence between two or more things, one of which is said to be true of the others [Pepper, 1942/1961, p. 180]."

In its refined form, truth becomes the formal relationship of description to referent (i.e., equation, sentence, or map, or image to object.) Further, "[There] are two kinds of truth in formism, depending upon the categorical status of the objects of reference: historical truth, and scientific truth [Pepper, 1942/1961, p. 182]." The first is related to immanent formism, the second to transcendent formism.

For the formist, statements of empirical uniformity provide only half truths, whereas full "truths are descriptions which accurately correspond with facts that have occurred or with laws that necessarily hold [Pepper, 1942/1961, p. 183]."

B. Mechanism

The distributive characteristic of formism gives way to the more integrative characteristic of mechanism under the experiential persuasion that the world is a highly organized machinelike entity. Pepper takes as the example of the root metaphor for mechanism the simplest machine, the lever. Mechanism is often called naturalism or materialism and is associated with philosophers such as Democritus, Lucretius, Galileo, Descartes, the British empiricists and, more recently, Reichenbach. Mechanism is analytic and integrative, accepting elemental facts in complexes of integrated relationships. As with formism, mechanism is considered to be weaker in precision than in scope.

The basic categories for mechanism are (a) location, (b) quantification (also known as primary qualities), (c) laws that hold among the elements (functional equations), (d) secondary qualities that although present, are not critical to the functioning of the machine, (e) adherence of secondary qualities to primary qualities, and (f) laws relating secondary qualities one to another.

Together these extend the scope of the mechanistic world hypothesis, although some (i.e., materialists) may be said to ignore the secondary qualities and others (i.e., idealists) to ignore the primary qualities.

An important addendum to the current mechanist–organicist debate is the often ignored suggestion by Pepper that there are two types of mechanists: discrete and consolidated. The discrete mechanist (usually focused on by the organismic proponents) may be represented as the prerelativistic Newtonian theorist. Reality for the discrete mechanist requires a discrete location of elements in absolute space and time. In contrast to immanent formism, discrete mechanism states that only particulars exist. In discrete mechanism, laws define the deterministic relationship among elements. Determinism is basically antagonistic to statistical laws. Given that time and mass (the most salient primary qualities) are separated, then the configurations of reality are static, requiring laws of transfiguration to produce change. However, without this more dynamic agent, the separation of discrete mechanism from formism narrows, and the mechanistic world hypothesis approaches a state wherein it may be absorbed into immanent formism. The potential contradiction is partially resolved in the spatiotemporal context of relativistic theory. From this perspective, the absolute notion of space and time are replaced by a configuration of interrelated elements in a spatiotemporal field, one in which all parts are critical to the understanding of the configuration. This, Pepper calls *consolidated mechanism. For this type of mechanistic theory, statistical laws are acceptable as convenient instruments for prediction. However, determinism still exists in principle.*

Adhering to the primary qualities of the spatiotemporal-gravitational-electromagnetic field are the secondary qualities, which include all of the categories of perception. The connection of secondary and primary qualities is through correlations that emerge as a function of human physiological-neural configurations. In fact, for the mechanist, the primary qualities are only cognizable in terms of their correlated secondary qualities. In part, the test of the adequacy of mechanistic theory lies in this correlation of secondary qualities and neural configurations; that is, mechanistic theory implies a reductionism.

Truth for the mechanist is embodied in the principle of causal adjustment. This is the relationship of structure as represented in the physiological configuration and the events in a spatiotemporal (etc.) world. There is, in this, an aspect of both correspondence theory (seen in formism) and prediction (as will be seen in operational contextualism). However, in mechanism, an adequate theory of truth remains according to Pepper, problematic.

C. Contextualism

The root metaphor for contextualism is the historic event, not as a past occurrence, but as current act within its total setting or context. Contextualism is commonly called pragmatism, and is associated with philosophers such as Pierce, James, Bergson, Dewey, and Mead. Contextualism is synthetic, focusing on wholes as opposed to elements, but it is distributive in that the wholes may exist without necessary relationships one to the other. Contextualism is said to be relatively stronger in precision than in scope.

Two basic presuppositions of this world hypothesis are embodied in the terms *change* and *novelty*. Change is continuous and often disorderly, although order is not denied. Events have stability but only within a limited epoch, giving way to novelty and, by definition, the advent of a new epoch. Within an epoch, consistent structure may be described in terms of *qualities* and *textures*. Within quality is included *spread* of the event to all related phenomena, the *change* in the character of the event as one shifts aspects of the context, and the *fusion* of the related parts of the event into new organizational totalities. Fusion is an active principle in contextualism and is related to the structures of texture. Textures are the dimensions of qualities, made up of details called textural *strands* (which exist in their own contexts), and *referential* dimensions, such as *linear means–ends* relationships, *means–ends blocking*, and *instrumental processes* for achieving an end when it is blocked. Thus, contextualism accepts purpose as an implicit agent for creating structural wholes. The structure of the whole determines the instrumental action in terms of means–ends relationships. Causality is formalistic.

Truth theory for contextualism is primarily a form of operationalism. This is expressed in two ways. The first describes the manner for verifying hypotheses through prediction of means–ends relationships. The second stresses the relationship of symbol to quality and the relationship of quality to structure.

D. Organicism

The root metaphor for organicism is the expansive notion of the integrated organism, including some aspects of an integrative history. For this world hypothesis, the notion of integration is dynamic and synthetic. Organicism is often called absolute idealism and is associated with philosophers such as Schelling, Hegel, and Royce. Organicism, like contextualism, is said to be relatively stronger in precision than in scope. The categories are divided by Pepper (1942/1961) into progressive and ideal sets. To quote him once again:

> These are: (1) fragments of experience which appear with (2) *nexuses* or connections or implications, which spontaneously lead as a result of the aggravation of (3) *contradictions,* gaps, oppositions, or counteractions to resolution in (4) an *organic whole,* which is found to have been (5) *implicit* in the fragments, and to (6) *transcend* the previous contradictions by means of a coherent totality, which (7) *economizes,* saves, preserves all the original fragments of experience without any loss. The fourth category is the pivotal point of the system and should be included in both the progressive and the ideal sets. It is the goal and final stage of the progressive categories and it is the field for the specification of the ideal categories. So, categories 1 to 4 inclusive constitute the progressive set, and categories 4 to 7 the ideal set [p. 283].

In opposition to some philosophers of science (such as von Bertalanfly), the categories of organicism, imply to Pepper (1961) a determinateness:

> Precise and determinate predictions which become verified are for the organicist, the best evidence of the truth of the organization of the data that produced the predictions. For verified prediction is the very action of organic implication [p. 297].

As with mechanism, the notion of determinateness is all-inclusive. However, for the organicist, this determinateness is structured in terms of the notion of the *absolute,* the final resolution of all hierarchical syntheses; that is, a determinism in terms of final cause.

The theory of truth for the organicist is called by Pepper *coherence* theory. Coherence theory is built on the criteria of inclusiveness, determinateness, and organicity—the notion of truth ideally merging with the notion of the absolute. In approaching the notion of the absolute, truth exists in degrees determined by the relative level of the structure with respect to its approximation to the absolute.

E. Summary

If one tabulates this material, the following comparisons emerge:

Table 1

Summary of the Attributes of Pepper's World Hypotheses System

	Formism		Mechanism		Contextualism	Organicism
Root Metaphor:	Immanent	Transcendent	Discrete Machine (absolute)	Consolidated Machine (relativistic)	History	Organicism and integration
	Similarity	Plan				
Classical name:	Realism, Platonic idealism		Naturalism	Materialism	Pragmatism	Absolute idealism
Fact type:	Analytic		Analytic		Synthetic	Synthetic
Organization:	Dispersive		Integrative		Dispersive	Integrative
Relative corroborative strength:	Scope		Precision		Scope	Precision
Type of causality:	Material		Efficient		Formal	Final
Ultimate structure status:	Indeterminate		Determined		Indeterminate	Determined

Basic categories:	1. Particularity
	2. Quality
	3. Character
	4. Participation
	5. Ties
	6. Classes
		1. Norms
		2. Norm exemplification
		3. Principles for materializing forms
			1. Absolute space and time
			2. Primary qualities
			3. Primary laws
			4. Secondary qualities
			5. Relations of 2 and 4
			6. Secondary laws
				1. Relativistic space and time
				(remainder same as absolute)
					1. Change
					2. Novelty
					3. Quality
					  a. Spread
					  b. Transition
					  c. Fusion
					4. Texture
					  a. Strand
					  b. Strand Context
					  c. Reference
					    i. Means—ends
					    ii. Blocking
					    iii. Instrumentalization
						Fragment
						Nexus
						Contradiction } Progressive set
						Organic Whole
						Implicit structure
						Transcending } Ideal set
						Economy

Truth theory:	Correspondence		Causal adjustment		Operationalism	Coherence

It should be kept in mind that Pepper was writing in 1942, before computers and systems theory were developed. Had he had the advantage of foresight, he might have expanded his mechanistic model to include the computer as a metaphor, and his organic model to include systems theory. In this expanded version, the mechanistic model would have gained some flexibility, and the organic model's characteristic of determinism would have merged more with the flexible indeterminism of contextualism (Overton, 1975; see von Bertalanfly, 1967).

IV. Criticism of Pepper's Schema

Prior to an attempt to extend Pepper's notion of world hypotheses to developmental psychology, three interrelated criticisms seem necessary. The first revolves around the issue of the all-inclusive nature of any given world hypothesis; the second concerns the nonindependence of evidence and the theories to which they relate; and the third concerns the salience of root metaphors and their relation to structural corroboration.

1. *All-inclusiveness:* The notion that a world hypothesis is all-inclusive suggests that all events in the world of experience can, in principle, be related. This implies a unity of events that must be reducible to a common root language, such as symbolic logic or mathematics. In philosophy, one approach, positivism, has focused on the unity of all science, regardless of topic, etiology, and context. In the sense developed by Pepper, positivism "devolves" to the lowest definitional agreement of human with human as to what comprises an event. Although presuppositions must be assumed to be implicit in the process of agreement, the dogmatic antihypothetical stance taken by the positivist merges in spirit with the stance taken by the adherents of a single world hypothesis when the latter accept the notion that there is a single, all-inclusive, factual world that can be corroborated within the structure of their general theory. Furthermore, if, as Pepper proposes, several world hypotheses can be articulated, and each is said to carry near equivalent strength from the dual perspective of scope and precision, this poly-world-hypothesis notion must be based on the presupposition that the questions that each seeks to answer are common. If the questions are orthogonal, then scope and precision cannot be compared, since the scales for evaluating scope and precision are question bound. The resolution to this problem would be to replace the notion that world hypotheses are relevant to all questions with the notion that world hypotheses are relevant to sets of autonomous questions. These questions are all-inclusive in their scope, but their scope is bound by the phenomena relevant to each of their structures. Since each structure emerges from the critical cognizing of commonsense knowledge based on some metaphoric abstraction from experience, *questions* can be construed as related to the experiential root metaphor. *The root metaphor, therefore, is not only the etiological basis for a specific world hypothesis, but also the basis of the questions posed to that world hypothesis.* This brings us to the second criticism.

2. *Autonomy of evidence:* If the questions that are posed for world hypotheses to answer are based on the constraints implicit in the root metaphor, then the evidence used for structural corroboration must also be considered similarly constrained. Facts are, therefore, only facts within a given structure and have no status within other structures. This is so even when the operational description in the positivist sense is isomorphic across theories. In terms of the previously mentioned world hypotheses, formism shares no evidence with mechanism, contextualism, or organicism since even the agreed upon interpretation of sensory phenomena, such as, say, "yellowness," would contain different dimensions in each of the four. Thus, *evidence related to a specific world hypothesis may be considered autonomous of the evidence of any other world hypothesis.* This brings us into the context of the third criticism.

3. *Salience of root metaphors:* Although the root metaphor may represent no more than a device for generating a finite number of world hypotheses, its implied emergence as a function of everyday experience suggests that its etiology is based on the special salience of some critical events. The path from common sense to corroborated structure is a function of cognizing fact–fact relationships under the rules demanded by the structure. However, the path is best represented by a continuum that approaches by degrees both adequate structure and adequate techniques for providing meaningful evidence. In a sense, the structure is always in the process of becoming, while one may say that the root metaphor is always in a state of being. At the point where the structure explains all the evidence relevant to its questions, it becomes "one" with its metaphor, and structural *becoming* passes into structural *being.* This sort of completion is, at best, far off; but the process may itself serve as a metaphor for behavioral ontogeny and, as such, may help us understand a potentially strong relationship between human developmental psychology and world hypotheses.

V. The Relation of World Hypotheses to Ontogenetic Development

There are still four other intuitions that must be pursued in describing the relationship of the revisions in the metastructure suggested above to developmental psychology. These concern, first, the relationship of the "questions of psychology" to experience; second, the relationship among levels of questions in psychology; third, the relationship of "modes of study" to the structure of psychological processes; and, fourth, the relationship of root metaphors to ontogeny.

1. The relationship of the "questions" in psychology to the phenomena of experience: Regardless of the definition one accepts for the term psychology, and there are many, a phenomenal boundary for this term would seem to be describable. This boundary, although not sharp, encompasses a number of general questions related to human attributes. The domain that encircles these questions represent a *discipline.* The questions in psychology arise from human interactions

with events in the world, and always relate to facts that include the organism as one aspect of the relationship sought. The general form of the questions posed by psychology may be articulated as: "How do humans x in the presence of y?" The x may represent seeing, walking, imaging, saying, crying, eating, and so on. The y may include school, other people, previous experience, the color red, tigers, catastrophe, thoughts, and so on. Questions that belong to the other disciplines may include some psychological questions plus a predominant number of questions whose forms could be viewed as: "How do humans construe the relationship of x and y?" Each of these other disciplines have an appended descriptive clause that follows, such as: "in the domain related to the production, distribution, and consumption of wealth and the various related problems of labor, finance, taxation, and so on" (economics); or, "in the domain related to human physical and cultural characteristics, distribution, customs, social relationships, and so on" (anthropology); or, "in the domain related to the composition and properties of substances and the reactions by which substances are produced from or converted into other substances, and so on" (chemistry).

The relationship of questions to topics is, at its root, "common sense." Experience is cognized in terms of those salient dimensions relevant to operating within the commonsense categories called out by a specific experience. For example, ambulation is cognized in terms of constructs related to bodily adjustments, movement, patterns, goals, surfaces, gravity, and so on. Verbal communication patterns are cognized in terms of linguistic attributes, articulatory mechanisms, situational variables, other personedness, and so on. These various constructs are the obvious, commonsense features of the experience, and it is these seemingly salient features in the context of psychological questions that produce the topics of psychology. A topic is an imaginary circle that contains all of the questions related to a given experiential domain. Topical boundaries represent social agreement on what is salient in generally accepted divisions of experience. Topics are in some sense universal, in that they encompass all aspects of the experience to which they relate. However, the number of question sets in any topic may vary. In addition, a question set may exist at many levels, and this takes us to the next intuitive suggestion.

2. Levels of questions in psychology: Not all the questions in a topical domain can be related meaningfully to one another, although they are all, by definition, related to the experience which generated them. Questions within a domain "clump" in terms of their structural interdependence. These clumps are autonomous with respect to each other, in that their specific explanations are not interactive. Let us take, for example, language. The questions in the topic of "language" may be considered potentially to spread out to or touch on all other topics to one degree or another. The questions having some degree of salience in the topic would relate to issues such as the character of the sensory events in referential relationships, the likelihood of speech units occurring in specifiable relations one to the other, the sociocultural determinants of certain speech in different contexts, and so on. A clump of questions would occur where the structural characteristics of such questions are dependent to some degree on the structure of each of the other

questions in the clump; that is, a clump defines a *covarying question subset*. Question sets would thus be made up of subsets with degrees of autonomy. In the topic of language, for example, phonemic characteristics would make up a question subset that would include issues related to the physical structure and role of articulators, the number of phonemic types, the possibility of phonemic combinations, the description of changes in phonemic events in different phonemic contexts, and so on. However, the structural rules that explained this subset of questions would be quite independent of the rules that organized another subset, say, the relation of any phonemic event to its objective referent (semantics). In this latter subset, sound combinations existing in any language could, in principle, refer to any objective referent. Moreover, in studying semantics, the sound combination is the "given," and its level of organization is basically of trivial importance. Taking this one step further, it would not matter one whit what the rules for word–object or word–word relationships are when explaining the relationship of words to situations. The social constraints of speech take as the given the other dimensions of language. Thus, it is suggested that although an experiential event defines the questions whose phenomenal aspects suggest a topical domain, the questions themselves group within that topic into autonomous levels, each of which has a structural organization predicated on covarying characteristics. The structural organizations that explain a subset of questions is a *topical process*. But if there are levels of questions within a topic, how do these units merge in phenomenal experience? The only reasonable guess on the author's part seems to be that this is an epiphenomenal event that reflects a spatiotemporal integrative inevitability. Events occurring in spatiotemporal proximity merge. However, the structural organization underlying the components of these events, that is, their processes, remain coherent and autonomous. (The characteristics of humans that make these features salient cannot be explored at this point. Suffice it to say, the unity of commonsense experience would require some sort of innate processing constraints.)

The unifying hypothesis that ties aspects of topics together is the second-order commonality in the structure of topical processes. These I will call *psychological processes*. This last point becomes obvious in summarizing the structure of the argument to this point.

(a) Experience is the prerequisite for all constructions of reality.
(b) Experience produces commonsense wholes.
(c) These wholes, represented as a nonarbitrary consensus about salient features in experience, describe topics.
(d) Topics contain questions related to topical structures.
(e) Questions group in terms of covarying characteristics.
(f) Covarying sets of questions within topics are called topical processes.
(g) Topical processes are autonomous with respect to each other.
(h) The merging of topical processes into topically related experiences is the epiphenomenal outcome of spatiotemporal integration.
(i) Second-order structures derived from the commonalities across topical boundaries are represented as psychological processes.

3. The relation of modes of study to psychological process structure: As pointed out, topical structures are derived from the relations among topical question subsets. It is suggested that these subsets bring with them intuitive constraints on how the questions may be integrated into topical process structures. In essence, a question carries within it intuitions of what types of answers will be acceptable. These characteristics of a subset of questions define a methodology. The second-order structures (i.e., psychological processes) thus include methodological commonalities. The abstracted methodological commonalities are inseparable from the structural relationships in psychological processes, and together these define empirical or evidential validity. This latter construct limits acceptable evidence for structuring psychological processes to that which is acquired through certain methods. Methods are not, in other words, independent of psychological structures. However, the understanding of what methods—what modes of empirical challenge— adhere to a specific psychological process is not immediately evident. A method's usefulness (degree of adequacy) interpenetrates with the degree of completeness of the explanation of psychological processes it serves. Methods or modes for creating empirical relationships between questions and structures are more at the whim of historical antecedents than they are the salient descriptive features of a phenomenon. Methods may change radically through the intuition of new dimensions to the structures. These shifts in both methods and structural wholes are what I interpret Kuhn (1962) to mean by the term *scientific revolutions*.

4. The relationship of root metaphors to ontogeny: As has been noted, the root metaphor has its etiology in the common sense explanation of everyday experience. The salient features that make up the metaphors proposed by Pepper are similarity, machine, history, and integration (the latter of which may also be thought of as going-togetherness). All of these metaphors are easily exemplified in the everyday experience of the child. The most esoteric one is probably the contextualistic metaphor of history, but even this, in Pepper's sense (and in Dewey's sense of the "act"), may be available to the extremely young. But if all of these modes of experience are available and if each carries with it an *equivalent* salience, it seems more likely that they may all exist simultaneously within certain limits. These limits, as suggested above, are set by the restriction that the same set of events or question set may not be explained using the categories of more than one world hypothesis. The possibility of this limit being theoretically feasible is predicated on the autonomy of salient features of experience from which the root metaphor is drawn. Let us pursue this line of thought from the perspective of human ontogeny.

The experientially (relatively) naive infant comes into the world open to the type of experiences that will lead to each of these metaphorical extractions. It must be assumed that humans have available at birth salient feature extractors. With these, the undifferentiated attributes of the experienced world give way in all structural systems to some form of progressive differentiation. The nature of these salient feature extractors can only be constructed from the orderliness in the infant's behavior. The critical question, then, becomes, "What is the experiential etiology of each of these metaphors in terms of these stabile organizations?" Let the following serve as some mundane possibilities. For the very young child, similarity is first based on sensory correspondence. This would be denoted systemically by the physiological commonality across experiences. The constraints for similarity would be present in the organic maturity and the sensory history of the system. Thus, for example, if the system did not yet have a physiology sufficient to provide a different "signal" for two shades of red or to respond as a "whole" to edges in juxtaposition, then its responses might be similar to a triangle and a square when the one is light pink and the other a nonsaturated pink of equal brightness. Similarly, if the organism's history did not have sufficient experience with the potential of varying brightness and its primary response to novelty was a "startle," the intensity of which blocked sensory processing of specific stimulus qualities, then again, the cortical organization embodied in the sensing of these adult-differentiated events would be functionally similar. Extracting the construct "similarity" from these sets of events would only occur in the context of events whose sensory characteristics were differentiable by the organism. At some point, the higher-order construct of similarity as a descriptor of classes of events in the world would be assumed to be written into the organizing characteristics of the organism, and the salience of this descriptor would emerge as a potential tool for organizing a variety of relevant, everyday experiences.

The operational metaphorical notion of mechanism, in a similar fashion, could emerge from the everyday experience of instrumental manipulation of the environment by the infant. Its etiology may be as primitive as the relationship of tongue and lip movements to the grasping and squeezing of the nipple in the earliest feeding situations.

Contextualism could have its etiology in the varied actions related to the scheduling of the infant's activities, and organic integration could find its roots in the dyadic interaction of the infant with its caretaker. Similarly, even those inadequate world hypotheses such as animism and mysticism could be considered to represent aspects of early experience, although the metaphor of "human" (for animism) and "emotion" (for mysticism) might arise later than those described for what Pepper considers are the four adequate world hypotheses.

It is thus suggested that the different root metaphors may arise from different aspects of everyday experience and, as a function of their autonomous characteristics, could be considered to develop simultaneously but along different lines. Each would represent a primitive structure to which certain questions would adhere and for which certain methods of generating evidence would be appropriate.

One other hypothesis provides the critical relationship of root metaphors to ontogeny. If one considers the possibility that these structures not only explain the organization of events *but also generate the means and rationales for developing domains of information,* then what emerges is a coherent relationship between the ontogeny of these domains and the systems adequate to explain their structure. In short, it is hypothesized that topics in psychology reflect the experiential contexts that generate the salient root metaphors and that these contain the appropriate or relevant techniques for developing, in fact, as well as in theory, the evidence for their ultimately full determination. This shifts the focus of the etiology of world hypotheses from the root-metaphor method to the richer phenomenal experience of ontogenetic development, which contains implicit metaphor, method, and cognized structure.

VI. The Relationship of Developmental Psychology to the Proposed Scheme

Developmental psychology is here considered to be the study of organismic change in the domain of psychology as represented by shifts in psychological processes over the life span. This field, from the broadest perspective, is considered to represent a higher order abstraction of structure from the configuration of psychological processes within a topic and across topics during the total life span. However, psychological processes are assumed to have no single metric that defines their structure in the context of time, and so it is convenient to divide each psychological process into epochs that appear to have a greater continuity or efficiency of explanation than those encompassing the whole span. This strategy would seem particularly useful at this point in the development of these subdisciplinary structures, since both theory and empirical evidence within theory are still so primitive in developmental psychology. Let us, then, expand the suggested relationship of root metaphors and ontogeny into developmental psychology.

If the experiences we have during the earliest part of the life span generate the primitive structures (root metaphors) through the abstraction of salient features from that experience; and if these salient features can be considered to be the questions implicit to the explanation of process structures at each point in time; and if we assume that process structure is always in equilibrium until, in Piagetian terms, it assimilates "information" to which it cannot accommodate; and if the attempt to accommodate is carried out "methodologically" in a manner consonant with the topical process to which the equilibration attempt relates, then (is it not reasonable to suggest that . . .) the ontogenetic development of the child uses the same program of structural development as is found in the analysis that best explains topical process changes. In other words, it is suggested that there is an isomorphic relationship between the explanation of the ontogeny of psychological processes (developmental psychology) and the method the growing organism employs to secure these changes. If this is so, then what one has *in* the psychologically developing organism is a configuration of orthogonal processes representing the covarying questions emerging from experience, second-order abstractions representing the psychological processes, and the growing phenomenal sense of development representing the configuration of these psychological processes as they change with respect to each other.

The topical processes develop within their own experiential domains at a pace related to the application of challenges to the questions raised by experience. The set of questions across epochs (developmental stages), as was already suggested, is not fixed, but rather grows as more salient features are extracted from additional experience.

VII. Conclusions

What, it may be asked, is gained by this scheme? The "points" that are gained by accepting this scheme for theory in general are:

1. Several different world views may coexist as guides for different theories, although each will relate to its unique set of experiential events. This decreases the need to try to fit every phenomenon into the same framework. This stance allows theory to emerge from the salient features of experience rather than from forcing the framework of the theory "over" the ill-defined and often antagonistic dimensions of experience.

2. The scheme provides some intuitive means for identifying domains of information both within and among topics within a discipline, and probably among topics across disciplines. The commonsense features of material that can be merged represent a common set of structural imperatives, including question types and question-structure methodologies.

3. The scheme creates a hierarchy of structures wherein the topical boundary loses its sacrosanct perspective, since it is only a convenience. Process characteristics become the primary structures of theory. The suggested scheme is thus both dynamic and relativistic.

4. This approach allows the "real world" to exist in our theory as well as in our experience. It suggests a rapproachement between the world as it is and the world as we experience it.

The points that are gained by accepting this scheme for psychological theory are:

1. Each of the current schools of thought may be considered to provide some insight into some of the processes psychologists wish to explain.

2. Data (as they emerge from empirical challenges) may be sorted in terms of both the theoretical and the methodological characteristics that generated them without requiring that all data in a topical area require a common theoretical integration. This should allow the quantitative aspects of some topics in psychology to exist side by side with qualitative topics, without creating unproductive controversy.

3. Theory–evidence relationships are raised to a level that requires a coherence between the relationships of each to the other. Mixed metaphors, such as "the reinforcement of cognitive plans," become unacceptable in this scheme, since the mechanistic notion of reinforcement and the organic presupposition underlying the

construct cognitive plan are more than, simply, events, but rather are events in the context of theory. In other words, theory–evidence relationships contain both structural and methodological constraints.

4. The contributions of physiology and comparative zoology become limited and more focused on those phenomena that lend themselves to certain sorts of process comparison. For example, although the limulus eye is of value in understanding retinal fields, Mach bands, and sensory inhibition, this only covers one question subset in the topic "vision." In order to understand how humans see things, second-order constructions are necessary that integrate the "givens" from several *basically* unrelated question subsets into higher order structures. This suggests a relatively high requirement of determinism at the level of topical processes and relative indeterminism at the level of topical structures. This may help to rationalize the seemingly implicit hierarchical organization of psychological topics with those metaphors that seem most appropriate for a given topic's explanation.

Finally, the points that are gained by accepting this scheme for developmental psychology are (in addition to those for general psychology):

1. Continuity in development is potentially preserved through the limitation of acceptable evidence for its evaluation. Elsewhere (Kaye, 1976) I have argued for the notion that continuity can only exist within or across epochs in a theoretically coherent system. Given that there are several coherent systems but that each is relevant to only a limited set of phenomena, continuity may only be analyzed within a given process framework.

2. On the other hand, the latter point suggests that fractures or discontinuities may exist, but that these most likely represent the outcome or performance characteristics of the spatiotemporal merging of many autonomous topical processes. The indeterminateness of these outcomes is in part a function of ongoing transactional forces, and their relationship to the state of development of the topical processes. Developmental theory in this scheme aims to describe the contextual relationship of all these parameters. It accepts implicitly the likelihood of discontinuity in performance but should start from the assumption that processes have continuity at least within topics. *Competence* in this scheme seems best described as continuity in psychological processes within an epoch. Catastrophe theory can thus play a major role in explaining performance shifts, but acquires its greatest level of parametric specificity when the structure of topical processes is relatively complete.

3. Furthermore, in this scheme, *standardized tests* can be sorted in terms of their topical location and their question level. Test–test correlations become meaningless outside the structure of theory, except as a heuristic for exploring the initial boundaries of covarying characteristics of an unknown question set. Lack of correlation between different question subsets cannot be taken as support of the null hypothesis where this suggests that the constructs these tests represent exist in the same theoretical space. The theoretical space must first be defined and then the correlation may be interpretable; never vice versa.

4. The issue of developmental psychology as either an experimental or a differential science (see Wohlwill, 1973) is partially resolved. The field of development, in the foregoing scheme, represents a higher order differential perspective predicated on experimentally determined process structures. At the experimental level, age is not meaningful, since time operates differently within each topical process. However, at the differential level, age becomes a convenient metric for the merging of processes within epochs, since it is the primary construct for representing the phenomenal "now" for an individual.

5. Similarity of performance across epochs (behavioral relativity), in this scheme, relates to performances that represent a common configuration of processes. The expression of these processes may be markedly different as a function of the transactional context for their occurrence. The same operationally describable behaviors may have a different meaning in different multivaried spaces.

6. Abnormal behavioral development, in this scheme, represents departures from the normal sequence or statistically normative performance attributes. Such deviations may be a function of atypical merging patterns, atypical processes, or a combination of the two. Atypical merging patterns would occur as a function of the cognized higher order structures imposed by the individual on his or her psychological process. The atypical processes, on the other hand, would be more related to topical process differences. These would be a function of such factors as organic damage or markedly altered experience. Since the psychological processes represent the intermediate and somewhat stable second-order structures underlying development, these may represent the best level of explanation for pathology. For example, the blind child lacks the whole category of vision, with all its question subsets, but does not lack the experience of, say, "contingency" from which a learning model may be developed. The question of *learning* as it contributes to atypical development becomes the level of focus, rather than the absent topical visual process related to contingency extraction. Among the higher order psychological processes, one would find such constructs as laterality, short-term memory, hand–eye coordination, egocentric behavior, and so on.

And so to the title of this chapter. Very simply, the title is meant to speak to the fact that the early experiences of the child call out the basic nature of what will be required in the way of structural adaptation in order to survive and prosper in the real world; that is, it provides the features of an organism in interpenetration with the world and develops the question subsets that define topical processes. These merge as a function of spatiotemporal proximity in ways that reflect a cooperation of topical processes in the pursuit of higher order, more generally efficient structures. With respect to the issue of the dialectical nature of this interpenetration, it is suggested that the merging be considered a cooperative effort rather than an antagonism or conflict of opposites. Although the tension that produces change is conceived from the viewpoint of the dialectic, as the antithesis in contrast to the thesis, the process of change would seem to me to be variously under the control of many different types of processes simultaneously. Attempting to place the emergent performance characteristics into a format that expresses those categories of operation and those dimensions of antagonism that will produce hierarchical synthesis seems an unnecessary restriction on developmental theory. Development is much more complex and multivaried than dialectical theory would allow, and the organism's progressive completion of structures is a much more positive process than dialectical theory suggests.

REFERENCES

Kaye, H. *Individual behavioral continuity during development: Issues and strategies.* Unpublished manuscript, State University of New York, 1976.

Kuhn, T. S. *Foundations of the unity of science* (Vol. 11, No. 2), *The structure of scientific revolution.* Chicago: University of Chicago Press, 1962.

Langer, J. (Ed.) *Theories of development.* New York: Holt, Rinehart, & Winston, 1969.

Overton, W. F. General systems, structure and development. In M. Lewis & L. A. Rosenblum (Eds.), *The origins of behavior* (Vol. 3), *Structure and transformation: Developmental and historical aspects* (K. F. Riegel & G. C. Rosenwald, Eds.). New York: Wiley, 1975.

Overton, W. F., & Reese, H. W. Models of development: Methodological implications. In J. R. Nesselroade & H. W. Reese (Eds.), *Life-Span Developmental Psychology: Methodological Issues.* New York: Academic Press, 1973.

Pepper, S. C. *World hypotheses: A study in evidence.* Berkeley: University of California Press, 1961. (Originally published, 1942.)

Reese, H. W., & Overton, W. F. Models of development and theories of development. In L. R. Goulet & P. B. Baltes (Eds.), *Life-Span Developmental Psychology: Research and Theory.* New York: Academic Press, 1970.

von Bertalanffy, L. *Robot men & minds: Psychology in the modern world.* New York: Braziller, 1967.

Watson, R. I. Psychology: A prescriptive science. *American Psychologist,* 1967, **22**, 435–443.

Wohlwill, J. F. *The study of behavioral development in children.* New York: Academic Press, 1975.

Subject Index

A 7
B 8
C 9
D 0
E 1
F 2
G 3
H 4
I 5
J 6

DATE DUE